Strong Winds and
Widow Makers

THE WORKING CLASS IN AMERICAN HISTORY

Editorial Advisors
James R. Barrett, Julie Greene, William P. Jones,
Nelson Lichtenstein, and Thavolia Glymph

A list of books in the series appears at the end of this book.

Strong Winds and Widow Makers

Workers, Nature, and Environmental Conflict in Pacific Northwest Timber Country

STEVEN C. BEDA

UNIVERSITY OF
ILLINOIS PRESS
Urbana, Chicago, and Springfield

Library of Congress Cataloging-in-Publication Data
Names: Beda, Steven C., 1980– author.
Title: Strong winds and widow makers: workers, nature, and
    environmental conflict in Pacific Northwest timber country /
    Steven C. Beda.
Description: Urbana: University of Illinois Press, [2023] |
    Series: The working class in American history | Includes
    bibliographical references and index.
Identifiers: LCCN 2022013692 (print) | LCCN 2022013693 (ebook)
    | ISBN 9780252044724 (hardback) | ISBN 9780252086823
    (paperback) | ISBN 9780252053771 (ebook)
Subjects: LCSH: Lumber trade—Environmental aspects—
    Northwest, Pacific. | Lumbermen—Northwest, Pacific—
    Attitudes. | Environmental economics—Northwest, Pacific.
Classification: LCC HD9757.N95 B43 2023 (print) | LCC HD9757.N95
    (ebook) | DDC 333.75/1309795—dc23/eng/20220324
LC record available at https://lccn.loc.gov/2022013692
LC ebook record available at https://lccn.loc.gov/2022013693

To Jess,
whose love brightens even the rainiest
of Northwest days

Businessmen, they drink my wine,
Plowmen dig my earth
None of them along the line
Know what any of it is worth.

—Bob Dylan

Contents

Introduction: A Place in the Forest   1

Part I: Place

1   "The New Empire"   21

2   "The Prodigal Yield of the Surrounding Hills"   47

3   "A Goodly Degree of Risk"   75

Part II: Power

4   "Conservation . . . from the Guys Down Below"   103

5   "The Many Uses and Values of Forests"   127

Part III: Problems

6   "Strong Winds and Widow Makers"   155

7   "Tie a Yellow Ribbon for the Working Man"   184

8   "We Keep Carbon-Eating Machines Healthy"   215

Acknowledgments   243

Notes   247

Index   277

Strong Winds and
Widow Makers

Introduction

A Place in the Forest

Dave Luoma, Don Zapp, and Dave Morrison had never seen anything like it. It was just past noon on May 29, 1990, and the three British Columbian loggers had wandered into a twenty-five-acre grove of inconceivably large trees hidden on the northern bank of Vancouver Island's White River. Every major species of Northwest conifer was here—western red cedar, spruce, and Douglas fir—and most were so tall that their tops disappeared into the hanging mists above, making this entire place feel as if it belonged as much to the heavens as it did the Earth. The tallest trees gave off a sweet scent and were covered in thick, almost ironlike bark speckled with the bluish-green hues of forest lichens, which Luoma, Zapp, and Morrison knew were all signs of exceptional age. The grove astounded in other ways, as well. Broad-leafed ferns sprung from buckled red clumps of dirt, and bright-green sheets of moss hung from the twisted branches of understory growth. A handful of much-older trees that'd fallen decades, if not centuries ago, slowly disintegrated into the soil, and younger trees sprouted from their decaying carcasses, each one a small reminder that in the forest, the lines demarcating life and death are not starkly drawn. Luoma, Zapp, and Morrison were used to dramatic land-scapes. Together, they had more than seventy-five years' experience working in the woods. They'd spent their lives among some of the tallest trees and densest forests found anywhere in the Northern Hemisphere. Still, nothing quite compared to what they were looking at now. The largest conifers on the northern coast of Vancouver Island typically grow to a height of about 150 feet, with an occasional specimen reaching 200 feet. Many trees in this grove stretched more than 250 feet into the air, and the largest would later be measured at more than 285 feet tall.[1]

The only thing more remarkable than the size of the timber was that until Luoma, Zapp, and Morrison discovered it, no one knew this grove existed. Or, at the very least, it wasn't identified on any maps or catalogued in any land surveys, despite the fact that all the surrounding woods had been intensely logged over the course of the preceding century. Foresters and wildlife biologists would later hypothesize that the grove's secrecy was a product of the same topographic and geographic conditions that allowed its trees to grow so tall. Generally speaking, a Northwest conifer's height is directly related to its age. As a tree grows taller and older, its inner core slowly begins to rot. Eventually, the rot spreads, and the tree loses its structural integrity and is then toppled by the high winds that whip in from the Pacific Ocean. The grove Luoma, Zapp, and Morrison found sits in a small depression carved out by the nearby river that shielded its trees from winds—and human eyes—for centuries.

The grove was so well hidden that it wasn't even visible from the nearest ridgeline to the west, which is where Luoma, Zapp, and Morrison had started their workday. Theirs wasn't a job for the faint-hearted. From the moment they tightened the laces on their caulks (pronounced "corks")—metal-studded boots that give loggers traction as they scurry over slippery logs—workers like Luoma, Zapp, and Morrison were surrounded by danger. It takes a certain sort of person to work in the Northwest woods, one with a daredevil disposition or one with few other economic opportunities, and like most who've made their living in the timber, the trio was probably equal parts both. The chief tools of their trade were massive chainsaws powered by howling two-stroke engines that could and sometimes did rip through a man's flesh as effortlessly as the densest lumber. Most of the trees they felled weighed several hundred tons and crashed to earth with the power of a wrecking ball hitting a concrete slab, sending detritus flying at high speeds in all directions. Death also came from above. Fellers' saws sent vibrations rippling up trees that loosened dead branches and sent them plummeting earthward. The full-brimmed, aluminum helmets timber workers wore protected them from all but the largest falling branches—tellingly called "widow makers" in the loggers' lexicon—even if those same helmets trapped the scream of their saws and led to premature hearing loss. Over the years, state occupational-safety agencies tried to encourage timber workers to adopt more-protective clothing. But workers often resisted. Every new piece of gear hindered movement, making it difficult to nimbly dip, dive, and duck out of danger's way. In the industrial woods of the Pacific Northwest, life and death were often a matter of rapid movements made in the most fleeting of seconds. There were the quick, and there were the dead.

The work was downright violent. Many environmentalists of this era also saw violence when they looked at logging, but they envisioned an entirely different sort of violence, one directed less at workers' bodies and more at the forests. Most of the trees that loggers like Luoma, Zapp, and Morrison fell had been growing for centuries. They'd been saplings when Coast Salish and Kwakwaka'wakw peoples, the original inhabitants of this part of the island, traded furs with British merchants in the Hudson's Bay Company outpost of Fort Victoria in the early nineteenth century. As the saplings aged, they bore witness to the history that unfolded: the displacement of those Indigenous peoples by White settlers who carved farms and homesteads into the land in the later nineteenth century, and then the displacement of those settlers by industrial lumbermen who built logging camps and mills atop the farms in the early twentieth century. For many environmentalists, the age of these trees meant they deserved special protections. Activists likened old-growth timber to antiquities and saw them as part of the region's, if not world's, shared history. They argued that old-growth was more valuable if left standing, rather than felled, milled, and transformed into construction lumber.

For men like Luoma, Zapp, and Morrison, things were more complicated. Many environmentalists of the late twentieth century came from the urban middle class, and the homes where they lived and buildings where they worked were made from the very lumber that men like the three fellers cut. Environmentalists may have scorned the labor of timber workers but reaped its rewards all the same. Environmentalists often failed to appreciate the economics of the rural towns where timber workers lived, as well. Luoma, Zapp, and Morrison came from Sayward, a small community tucked into a coastal inlet, right where the Salmon River spills into the churning tides of Johnstone Strait. Like nearly every logging town from southern Oregon to upcoast British Columbia, just about everyone in Sayward worked in the timber industry, and those who didn't ran stores or shops or worked in a service sector that relied on the spending of timber workers. If someone in a town like Sayward couldn't make peace with harvesting old-growth timber, then they didn't eat, and neither did their family. Preservation was for people bestowed with the privileges of geography and class.

These were the realities of life and labor in the late twentieth-century Northwest woods. And yet, when Luoma, Zapp, and Morrison discovered the grove roughly halfway through their workday, they didn't even have to talk amongst themselves before they knew what they were going to do. "As soon as we walked back in there and saw that stand," Zapp later said, "we just couldn't do it. That was it, right then and there." After spending an hour wandering the elk trails that wound through the stand, the men hoisted their saws on their shoulders, checked that the laces on their boots were still tight, and began ascending the muddy slope to their pickup waiting on the ridgeline above. They intended to return to town, tell their employer about the grove, and then say in no uncertain terms that they refused to cut it.[2]

By the time the men made it back to the top of the ridgeline and stowed their gear, the sun had fallen from its highpoint in the sky and dipped behind the perpetual rainclouds that cover the coast, casting an inky black shadow that made the otherwise expansive landscape feel confining. The men sat shoulder-to-shoulder in the cab of their pickup, quietly contemplating the possible repercussions of their actions as they headed back to town, the eerie quietness of dusk broken only by the rattle of their truck as it bounced over the deep ruts etched into the course-gravel logging road. Years later, Zapp would remember the tension in the moment, saying, "It was kind of a big risk," which is an understatement if there ever was one. Their employer, the Kelsey Bay Division of the Bloedel Donovan Lumber Company, was in the business of harvesting lumber, not preserving it. If Luoma, Zapp, and Morrison refused to cut the stand, then they'd likely be discharged and replaced by fellers less plagued by sentimentality. The three men were risking pensions and seniority they'd earned through years of hard labor, and most of all, they were risking good jobs in a social and economic climate where good jobs were hard to come by. Across the Northwest, logging operations were shutting down, and sawmills were closing. The sounds of industrial labor and economic stability that had once filled the air of the rural Northwest—the shriek of mill whistles calling people to work, the rumble of trucks ferrying freshly cut timber out of the woods—evaporated into the ether and were replaced by the far more somber tones of rural economic decline: shop owners boarding up their failed businesses, the desperate sighs of workers being handed pink slips, and the cold hum of neon signs in the windows of payday lenders. No one could say what was causing all this, exactly. Fluctuations in the global marketplace, tariffs and trade disputes, capital flight, and new environmental regulations—these and dozens more causes were cited as the source of the rural Northwest's economic woes. Whatever the exact reasons for the crisis, the fact remained that this was simply no time for the men to be risking their jobs—not when it'd be difficult if not impossible to find another, not when the company would find different fellers to do the job, and certainly not for a small, twenty-five-acre grove that, until a few hours ago, no one knew existed.[3]

But Luoma, Zapp, and Morrison also knew something about their community that perhaps gave them some cause for at least guarded optimism on their return to town. A fierce independence runs through the culture of the rural Northwest. People here have long voiced a distrust of government, environmentalists, tourists, and big companies and corporations most of all. It's a culture born of their relationship to the forest. It's where many of them worked, yes, but also where they hunted, fished, and found an escape from the challenges of that work. They'd long cared for and stewarded these woods, and they often didn't take well to outsiders—any outsiders—telling them how to manage what they rightfully saw as their own. True, the provincial government owned the land, and companies owned the rights to the lumber. But, really, these forests belonged to the people in ways not so easily documented on land deeds. And, indeed, no sooner had Luoma, Zapp, and Morrison returned to town than the community of loggers and millworkers in Sayward rallied to their side. Their union, Local 363 of the International Woodworkers of America—Canada, promptly issued a statement saying that no union timber worker would cut the stand, either, and that any disciplinary action taken against Luoma, Zapp, or Morrison would be promptly challenged. A few days later, several people from Sayward packed up tents and sleeping bags and set up a small camp in the grove, vowing to stay there until they knew the stand was safe.

In the end, Bloedel Donovan acquiesced and relinquished its harvest rights to the grove. Six years later, the British Columbia Parks Department made the stand a protected wilderness area. Today, it's known as White River Provincial Park, and a sign at the head of a trail that winds through the grove tells the story of the three fellers who "recognized the intrinsic values of the impressive stand of old growth and refused to fall any of the trees."[4]

It's a modest sign, one that's likely missed by the majority of visitors to the park, many of whom come from the region's more affluent and urban cores. For those who do take the time to stop and read it, it's worth wondering just how much the sign resonates. That's because the sign competes with a much-larger, more pervasive narrative, one that asserts the Northwest's rural working class is fundamentally opposed to wilderness, harvest restrictions, or anything else that might threaten their jobs. The origins of this narrative are many, but they were most certainly engrained into the broader public consciousness because of events that, ironically enough, were ongoing at the very moment Luoma, Zapp, and Morrison wandered into the grove. On the other side of the forty-ninth parallel, the line of latitude separating the American and Canadian Northwests, environmentalists were calling on state and federal land managers to significantly restrict logging to preserve the old-growth habitat of the winsome northern spotted owl. Timber workers responded that their towns and communities could not economically survive harvest reductions. They called on the same land managers to increase the allowable cut and spend less time worrying about a diminutive bird and more time worrying about struggling rural people. The spotted owl's native range only extends northward to the very tip of southern British Columbia, so the bird never became a real point of contention in the province. Even so, in places like Clayoquot Sound and Haida Gwaii (then known as the Queen Charlotte Islands), loggers and environmentalists clashed over the fate and future of old-growth forests and whether they should be preserved, even if that preservation came at the expense of rural working-class economic security.

The press called it the timber wars. It's a hyperbolic name, to be certain, but one that accurately captured the anger and intensity of the moment: the shouting in public hearings; the dozens, if not hundreds, of lawsuits and countersuits filed by environmental organizations and timber-industry representatives; the spikes driven into trees by radical environmentalists; and the disruptive rallies organized by timber workers. Every war needs heroes and villains, and because most journalists covering the story came from the urban middle class, they ascribed these roles in ways that reflected the implicit biases of their geographic and socioeconomic station. Environmentalists were cast as the protagonists, valiantly fighting to preserve what remained of the beauty and biodiversity of the Northwest's forests. Rural timber workers were cast as the antagonists, too narrowly focused on protecting their own jobs and too invested in an outmoded frontier mentality to realize that their world of resource extraction was disappearing, and no amount of shouting at public hearings could change that. The story journalists told became a popular narrative because it was an easy narrative, one of convenient moral certitude and simple dichotomies that glossed over the complexities of forest ecologies and the realities of work and life in the rural Northwest. The narrative remained pervasive, even as the timber wars came to an end in the mid-1990s, and has continued to echo through contemporary popular culture, land-use policy, journalism, and a good deal of academic literature. No simple sign at the head of a small trail in an out-of-the-way wilderness area is up to the task of taking on all that.

Yet, Luoma, Zapp, and Morrison's story reveals that this popular narrative, for all its ubiquity, obscures the more complex relationship rural working people have long had with the Northwest's forests. Work is certainly part of that relationship, and the politics of the rural Northwest have often pivoted around work. But it's a relationship that can't solely be understood through work. Hunting, fishing, foraging, and recreation have done as much as industrial wage labor to shape how working people from the Northwest woods have known, used, and valued the forests. The forest has also had less-tangible but no less-important meanings in their lives. It's been central to their understandings of home and community and directed the course of their labor activism. Across history, people from timber-working communities have worried about forest flora and fauna as often as they've worried about their own economic security, and they've defended wilderness as vociferously as they've fought for their jobs. When Luoma, Zapp, and Morrison decided to leave that grove standing, they described it as a spur of the moment decision—as Zapp later explained, it "just seemed like the right thing to do." But the three fellers' actions were also connected to an ethic of forest stewardship that has long been central to the identity, culture, and politics of the people who've lived and worked in the Northwest woods. Understanding that culture may help us better manage the forests and avoid the sorts of bitter land-use conflicts that beset the region in Luoma, Zapp, and Morrison's era and continue to do so today. This book tells that story.[5]

Similar stories could be told about other workers in other places. Wherever we find people working in nature, we are almost certain to find people who take seriously their obligation to nature. But the story I tell here is about the people who've lived and worked in Northwest timber country, the name for the verdant band of forests stretching from southern Oregon to northern British Columbia, bound by the sagebrush plains of the high desert to the east and the Pacific Ocean to the west. This is a landscape that demands humility. In the Klamath and Siskiyou Mountains of southern Oregon, trees seem to defy gravity as they cling to steep mountain faces and the rocky ledges of narrow canyons cut by emerald-green rivers that crash over massive boulders. Closer to the ocean, the land turns to rolling hills that stretch out for as far as the eye can see in all directions, and broad rivers carrying the glacial silt from the mountains high above flow out into the sea. The drama of this landscape and its history are inscribed in its place names: Mount Terror, Danger Shoal, Deception Pass, Foulweather Bluff, and Rogue River, to name just a few. Thick forests are the one constant across the landscape, though, and more than any other single factor have tied the varied topographies and geographies of this place together. In the thick, briny air of the coast to the crest of the Cascades, hemlock, cedar, spruce, and Douglas fir are the dominant tree species, though pockets of deciduous growth spring up here and there and disrupt what would otherwise be a sea of indistinct coniferous green. Past the rocky spine of the Cascades, it's pine that fills the forests and the high-mountain air with its sweet scent.[6]

The Pacific Slope has a well-deserved reputation for rain, and timber country could just as reasonably be called the gray-sky country. Other than a few places in Alaska and Hawaii, the rainiest locales in North America are all found in the Northwest. Near-constant precipitation and perpetually gray skies are the scourge of many transplants to the region, particularly recent arrivals from southern California accustomed to far-sunnier skies. But it's the rain that's directly responsible for creating the spectacular landscapes that have long drawn people to this place. The environmental historian William Cronon once argued that the sun is responsible for creating all the world's natural wealth. The same might be said of rain in the Northwest. It fills the region's rivers and brings salmon and steelhead inland, makes farmland fertile, pushes trees to incredible heights, and fills the forests with mosses, lichens, ferns, and several other species that thrive in cool, wet weather. Indeed, much like the grove that Luoma, Zapp, and Morrison found, the Northwest's forests often appear mysterious and magical, which may explain why the region has been the setting for or inspired its fair share of science fiction and fantasy.[7]

The Northwest has drawn the attention of plenty of nonfiction and academic writers, too, though the stories they've told have been more sobering and far more somber. Historian Donald Worster describes the North American West as "a culture and society built on, and absolutely dependent on, a sharply alienating, intensely managerial relationship with nature." Worster found the most-potent evidence for this in the history of western rivers, but his words apply equally to the history of the Northwest's forests—or, at least, the way most authors have seen it. The general arc of that history is that decades of White westward settlement followed by the rise of industrial capitalism and land-management bureaucracies turned the once fecund and vibrant forests of the Northwest into a malignant snarl of clearcuts and overly rational tree farms that bore little resemblance to the wild woodlands that once existed. As it's often told, the history of the Northwest's forests is a history of decline, despoilment, and, most of all, regret—regret for what was lost and what might've been, if only people in the past had possessed a little more foresight.[8]

Workers have always fit awkwardly into this story because it's not clear how they fit into the story. Several scholars have documented the difficulties and dangers of working in the woods, suggesting that the exploitation of the forest was part and parcel to the exploitation of labor. Others have documented the history of labor activism in timber country—activism that, at times, challenged the power of large timber companies and the influence they exerted over both workers and nature. In these stories, working-class history is a story of what could have been, of how the regret that permeates much of the literature about the region's forests might've been avoided, if only the power of workers had not been circumvented by states and corporations. This story, though, has been hard to square with the actions and politics of late twentieth-century timber workers, who often sided with the very companies that their fathers and grandfathers protested, and who demanded fewer environmental restrictions and more harvests, regardless of the ecological consequence. In these stories, workers are a major source of regret. Historians of the Northwest woods have tended to reconcile these two narratives in ways that reflect the story labor historians have told about the working class more broadly: sometime in the late twentieth century, as workers across the industrialized world abandoned the solidarity and progressivism of organized labor for a decidedly more conservative and reactionary politics, Northwest timber workers abandoned conservation for anti-environmentalism. Erik Loomis's relatively recent history of Northwest timber workers most clearly articulates this narrative. Loomis identifies a brief moment in the mid-twentieth century when unionized timber workers fought to restrict harvests and expand wilderness but argues they quickly abandoned that stance when layoffs and job losses began to mount in the late twentieth century. "Workers have concrete interests in environmental protection," Loomis concludes, "but their own economic security largely predicates how much support they can give those measures." Loomis's overall point is a good one, and one I certainly agree with: that land-use policy needs to take the well-being of humans as seriously as it does the well-being of flora and fauna. Still, it's a narrative that fails to account for the actions of workers like Luoma, Zapp, and Morrison, obscures the varied and complex ways they've known the forest, and glosses over their more nuanced understandings of what, exactly, it means to protect the forest.[9]

What most histories of timber workers have in common is that they treat the forest primarily as a space of work for loggers and their communities and, therefore, assume that timber country's environmental politics have hinged on protecting work. This book charts a different course and treats work as just one of a broad constellation of activities that shaped the way people from timber-working communities understood the forests. To make complete sense of their history, we have to follow them into the woods as they hunted, fished, foraged, and played as often as we follow them into the forest to analyze the patterns and cultures of industrial wage labor. All these activities impacted the ways they thought about nature, and all shaped the course of their labor activism.

In fairness, the emphasis scholars have placed on work in timber country's history is understandable. Work is and has long been an important analytical point of departure for labor and environmental historians alike. Moreover, journalists covering the timber wars focused so heavily on the politics of work that it's been easy for historians to fall into the habit of doing the same. At the very least, when I began this book, I, too, was prepared to tell a story primarily about work, one that hewed closely to the story other historians have told, one tinged with regret for the declining environmental consciousness of timber country's working class. I attribute this, at least in part, to the place and time in which I grew up. I come from suburban Chicago, a place geographically and socioeconomically distant from timber country. The timber wars were coming to an end around the time I was in high school and just starting to pay attention to the news. While I had no early ambitions to become a historian, let alone a historian of the Northwest woods, the images of angry timber workers bitterly struggling to hold on to their jobs, even if that came at the expense of spotted-owl habitat, must've burrowed itself into my subconscious. And, by the time I had decided to become a historian, and a historian of the Northwest woods specifically, that idea crawled out from the dormant place it'd been hiding and initially guided the story I intended to tell.

I'd like to report that my thinking changed as the result of intense reading and archival research, but the truth is my ideas shifted under somewhat less academically rigorous circumstances. I had the good fortune to go to graduate school in the Northwest. I chose my program because it had accomplished faculty and access to important research materials. At least that's what I told people. The real reason I chose a program in the Northwest was because it put me close to some of the best salmon and steelhead fishing in the world, and in my early days of graduate school, I, perhaps, spent a bit too much time on the region's rivers. Many of those rivers happened to flow through or near logging towns. Spend enough time on the Northwest's waters, especially during periods of strong fish runs, and you'll run into your fair share of timber workers. I found this to be quite convenient. Because I studied the timber industry, I could speak with these workers and then pass off fishing trips as "research." (For the record, few of my faculty advisers were fooled, even if they were too polite to say so.)

Yet, in important ways I didn't realize at first, research was occurring. Many of the workers I spoke with streamside explained how they'd been fishing these same rivers their entire lives and how they'd learned to fish from their fathers and grandfathers who also worked in the mills and woods. They described logging the forests during the workweek, then returning to those same forests to hunt on the weekends. Many talked about nature with a respect and reverence I thought was unique to more middle-class outdoor enthusiasts like myself. I recall one encounter, in particular, with crystal clarity. I was on Washington's Hoh River in late March, and I met a sawmill worker who, like me, was looking for steelhead. He complained about a local company's decision to harvest a forest tract near a tributary that, in his opinion, threatened spawning habitat. The shirt he was wearing was presumably one he'd also worn to work, and he brushed some sawdust from his collar as he told me this. It was an interesting juxtaposition, I thought to myself at the time, and after enough conversations like this, I finally did turn to archives to chart the origins of these ways of thinking. I stumbled across the story of Luoma, Zapp, and Morrison relatively early on and continued finding similar stories, further back in time, until I found myself looking at records from the early twentieth century.

This book is as much a result of that formal research as it is those streamside conversations. What both revealed, and what I argue here, is that more than a space of work or even a space of subsistence and recreation, the forests have been a place for working people in timber country. "Place" sounds like a fairly ordinary word, but I don't necessarily use it here in an ordinary way. "Place" refers to the meanings and values people attach to landscapes. There's a physical world that exists independent of human thought—what scholars typically call "space"—but it's the experiences people have within spaces that transforms them into places. Spaces can be located on maps. Places are more intangible, demarcated by perception, culture, and relationships. The concept of place figures heavily into a good deal of cultural geography and environmental history, but it has just as much to offer labor historians. Treating forests as a place for timber country's working class challenges the tropes of alienation and regret that characterize so much writing about workers and nature. Rather than distancing working-class communities from the environment, life in the industrial woodlands created deep connections among timber workers, their families, and the forests; made them conscious of the environmental effects of their work; and made them intensely aware of their obligation to the forest.[10]

Focusing on place encourages us to think of the forest as a site of family, home, and community, which encourages us to reassess the social history of timber country. Those familiar with the history of the Northwest timber industry, particularly, the early twentieth-century history, may well have just paused after reading those words: family, home, and community. That's because most studies about Northwest logging portray the industry's early twentieth-century workforce as overwhelmingly young, single, and itinerant—that is, their lives were defined by the absence of stable families, homes, and communities, not inclusion in them. The pages that follow, though, show that this characterization has less to do with the demographic realities of timber country and much more to do with the biases imbedded in the sources historians have used, mostly the records of social investigators and labor radicals, which, for political reasons, overemphasized labor itinerancy in the woods. Setting those sources aside and turning instead to memoirs authored by workers, recorded oral histories, and census data, reveals a more diverse social world, one populated by married workers who only rarely moved. This was a world where women and children figured in just as heavily as men, where stories of female domestic labor in hardscrabble company towns and children's experiences playing in the woods stand alongside the more common stories told about the hard and dangerous work of men, all of which paints a new and more complete portrait of how people from the Northwest woods interacted with the forests.[11]

Attending to place also allows us to tell a new story about labor activism in the woods, one filled with as many continuities as there are disconti-nuities, and one in which the political differences between early and late twentieth-century timber workers no longer appear so stark. That's not to say there weren't differences. There were. The major union at the center of this story is the International Woodworkers of America (IWA), an affili-ate of the Congress of Industrial Organizations (CIO), founded largely by American and British Columbian Communist Party members in 1937. Like many industrial unions that grew out of the tumult of the Great Depression, the IWA promised its members better hours, wages, and working conditions at the same time it posited a broad progressive vision for the future of the entire working class. A key component of the IWA's social vision was what I call "labor environmentalism," a conservationist ethic that linked strong unions and economically healthy rural communities to sustainable forest management. To achieve those ends, the IWA often worked alongside and in close partnership with activists in the mid-twentieth century's nascent wilderness movement. This stands in stark contrast to the movements that emerged in late twentieth and early twenty-first centuries. By the late 1980s workers had all but abandoned organized labor and, instead, entered into employer-employee coalitions that were far less likely to work alongside environmentalists and much more likely to hang them in effigy. Even so, these two otherwise distinct eras of working-class politics are connected in some important ways. Because people in timber-working communities have long used the forest for a variety of purposes, they've long believed that forests have to be managed for multiple uses. Maintaining working forests has been just as important as maintaining wilderness, and timber workers' labor activism has hinged on what people in timber country see as the principal threat to the maintenance of that balance. When industrial malfeasance appeared as the greatest threat, workers turned to industrial unions, and when the greatest threat was environmentalist overreach, workers looked to employer-employee coalitions. Timber-working communities of the late twentieth century were no more opposed to wilderness than timber-working communities of the earlier twentieth century were opposed to working forests. The consistent goal of timber country across history has been to ensure that the myriad uses and values of the forests are protected and reflected in land-use policy.

Finally, focusing on working-class understandings of place allows us to tell a more complicated history of the region's forests, one far less tinged by the theme of regret. A good deal of writing about the Northwest's forests relies on dichotomous ways of thinking: we can have wildlife habitat or a timber industry, ecologically healthy forests or economically healthy rural communities. It's yet another vestige of the timber wars and the way the story was told. Journalists, politicians, and environmentalists said the Northwest was at a crossroads and had to choose between its resource-extraction past or a more ecologically conscious future. But the roots of this way of thinking run even deeper, to the ways people have long understood the history of forests. Forests are often imagined as static spaces, where, if natural processes are allowed to play out of their own accord, trees grow stout and tall over millennia, and change comes slowly, if at all. Words adopted by the environmental movement in the late twentieth century, which have since become common in both scholarly and popular writing, further entrenched these ideas into public consciousness. Environmentalists and environmental writers talk about "ancient forests" and "primeval forests," suggesting that the Northwest's old-growth timberlands look much the same as they did millions of years ago and would've remained unchanged, had workers wielding saws not changed them. But forests are not now, nor have they ever been, static spaces. Forests in the Northwest, as elsewhere, are always changing, always in motion. Long before there was an industrial timber industry, naturally occurring landslides, fires, and weather events combined with Indigenous harvests and burns continually shaped and reshaped timberlands. Forest ecosystems evolved in tandem with this dynamism, and several species of flora and fauna came to depend on it. Because they've spent their entire lives in the woods and seen them change, timber workers have appreciated the fluidity of forests more than most. Timber workers understood (and understand) logging as a means of encouraging the very landscape changes that forest ecosystems need to survive and thrive. Felling a tree or harvesting a forest isn't always a somber act, one that must be met with sadness and regret. It's also an act of rebirth and regeneration, a way to encourage the very dynamism that forests depend on. Of course, when done incorrectly, logging can have devastating environmental consequences. But the same is true of preservation. As this book shows, environmentalists' efforts to limit or prohibit logging in the wake of the spotted-owl conflict have done significant harm to the region's forests. Seeing the history of the forest through the eyes of working people reveals that rarely do we have to choose between healthy rural communities and healthy forests. Both are possible and, in fact, may be mutually necessary.[12]

Of course, a big part of the story that this book tells is why the environmental attitudes of people from the rural Northwest were ignored, why many from outside timber country convinced themselves in the late twentieth century that it was a choice between forests and workers, and why, having determined this was an either-or proposition, they chose the former over the latter. Environmentalists hadn't always thought this way. The wilderness advocates who worked alongside the IWA in the mid-twentieth century had a view of forest management that hewed closely to that of timber workers. Both believed that wilderness necessarily had to exist alongside working forests. But things changed, for a variety of reasons. The demographics and political orientation of the environmental movement shifted dramatically in the late twentieth century, as did the politics and economics of timber country. My analysis here also focuses a great deal on popular culture as a means of understanding the rift that opened between environmentalists and workers, a rift that ultimately led to timber country's exclusion from the region's environmental politics. By the 1970s popular culture had convinced activists and politicians alike that the Northwest's rural working class was deeply opposed to change and would never accept new environmental regulations. In many ways, the story of timber country in the late twentieth century mirrors the cultural fate of the broader White working class in the late twentieth century. As historian Jefferson Cowie has shown, the economic upheavals of the 1970s were accompanied by equally consequential cultural upheavals that saw New Left thinkers and activists increasingly characterize White workers as bitter and resistant to progressive change. The same process Cowie describes occurred in the Northwest woods, where countercultural authors increasingly portrayed timber workers as too backwards to ever fit into an ecological future and further convinced activists and policy makers that rural workers were among the greatest barriers to protecting forests and wildlife. In the cultural reshuffling that occurred in the 1970s and beyond, timber country's long history of conservation and forest stewardship dissipated in the collective public consciousness.[13]

Countercultural writers, New Left thinkers, and environmental activists can't solely be blamed for the new cultural consensus that emerged in the late twentieth-century Northwest. People in timber country often leaned—and perhaps leaned a bit too heavily—into the new identity popular culture prescribed to them. That new identity could most clearly be heard in a regional variant of country music spilling from the jukeboxes in timber country's bars. Like a good deal of the "outlaw country" of the 1970s, timber country's music scene articulated a new, rural populism and encouraged people in the Northwest woods to be distrustful of urbanites, the middle class, and environmentalists most of all. The most popular singer to emerge from the late twentieth-century woods was Lloyd Earl "Buzz" Martin, an Oregon logger who swapped his chainsaw and caulks for a six-string and achieved some level of regional notoriety performing in timber country's dance halls and honky-tonks. The title of this book takes its name from one of Martin's songs. Martin's music could be confrontational, and "Strong Winds and Widow Makers" is, perhaps, his most confrontational track, disparaging of anyone and everyone who doesn't appreciate the dignity of good, honest, hard-working loggers. Yet, beneath Martin's quarrelsome lyrics is a certain sentimentality. His music is about the quiet dignity of rural life, the verity of work, and, above all, the connection people in timber country felt to the forest and each other. And, in the end, all that is what this book's about, too.

The story that follows unfolds over three parts. Part I, "Place," examines the Northwest timber industry's origins in the early twentieth century and how workers and their families adapted to life in the region's newly industrialized woodlands. I pay special attention to the patterns and textures of day-to-day life in the logging camps and company towns where timber workers and their families lived, showing how the migrants and immigrants who came to the Northwest woods relied on the forest for work and, just as critically, for subsistence and recreation. Those early experiences laid the foundation for the understandings of place and the ethic of forest stewardship that would be central to timber country's history for the remainder of the twentieth century and more immediately shape the labor movement in the Northwest woods during the Great Depression and mid-twentieth century. Part II, "Power," focuses in on that history of labor activism, paying special attention to the IWA and its efforts to reshape state forestry policy, expand wilderness, and protect both rural communities and the forests they relied on. The IWA's vision never fully materialized, and by the end of the twentieth century, many timber-working communities would be fighting to survive. Part III, "Problems," explores the reasons why the social, economic, and cultural status of timber country shifted so dramatically in the late twentieth century. The industry restructured in ways that made it difficult for organized labor to retain its power in logging operations and mills. A new cultural consensus emerged throughout the region, if not the industrialized world, that the rural working class couldn't be counted on to steward the forests. And, perhaps most significant of all, efforts by environmentalists to protect old-growth forests and ostensibly endangered species—chief among them the spotted owl—significantly curtailed harvests and led to the significant decline of the timber industry. Yet, even as timber country was dramatically reshaped by economic forces and environmental conflict—and as new environmental conflicts have emerged in more recent years—the ideas of stewardship articulated nearly a century ago remain potent and visible parts of timber country's culture. Understanding that culture may help us all better manage the forests in ways that benefit forests and rural communities equally.

I was reminded of that a few years ago, on an October morning while picking mushrooms on a forested ridgeline that overlooks my adopted hometown of Eugene, Oregon. The previous week had been exceptionally rainy, and now hundreds, if not thousands, of golden chanterelles had pushed their way up through the soggy soil and were ripe for the picking. It took me less than an hour to fill a five-gallon bucket, and returning to my truck to unload my haul, I saw an older man pop out of the woods opposite the gravel logging road where I'd parked. He, too, was carrying a pail full of mushrooms. As we exchanged pleasantries, he revealed he was a retired logger who'd worked these very woods, decades ago. He told me about a few close calls he'd had, what the woods looked like back when he was younger, and how he'd seen them change in the years since. If nothing else, I think his presence there that day says something significant about what the forest has meant to working people. How many of us, in retirement, would spend our time in the very spaces we spent our entire lives working? But then again, the forest has never been just a space of work to people like him. When he eventually asked why I was so interested in "the ramblings of a worn-out logger," to use his words, I explained that I was writing a book about Northwest logging that argued timber workers are environmentalists—a shorthand I'd developed over the years, for when I needed a quick and easy way to communicate the central point of my work. He shot me a knowing smile, then offered a slight correction.

"Timber workers are the *best* environmentalists," he said. "Everyone knows that."

I've thought about his statement a lot as I've worked on this book. The ridge we were on separates two valleys. He came from a logging town nestled in the small valley to the west, where boarded-up storefronts attest to the vast economic changes timber country has experienced over the last several decades. There's a deep sense of loss in many of these towns, yet also an undeniable pride—the pride of working in and stewarding the forests. Certainly, fewer today make their living working in the woods than did two or three decades ago. But enough logging trucks filled with freshly cut timber still speed through the valley's narrow rural highways to remind outsiders that logging remains central to the identity of the people in these places. In these towns, I have no doubt that there's a widespread consensus that timber workers are and have long been the best environmentalists. But the consensus is quite different in my valley, the much-larger, much more urbanized, and far more affluent valley to the east. Timber workers exist in my valley, too, though they're far outnumbered by middle-class professionals who make their livings sitting in front of computer screens. Many of those middle-class professionals don't think much about logging. To them the Northwest is a high-tech global region, and the timber industry and the rural communities it created are vestiges of a distant and little-considered past. Those who do think about logging and loggers, though, often think about them in the most disparaging of ways, as the primary political roadblock preventing the Northwest's full realization as a high-tech, global, *and* ecologically-oriented region. In my valley, far fewer people regard timber workers as environmentalists.

It's a microcosm of the geography of the Northwest, if not the North American West more broadly: urban and rural communities that sit in physical proximity are, nevertheless, separated by deep social, economic, political, and cultural divides that have, at least here in the Northwest, expressed themselves most potently in debates over forest use. Indeed, the spotted owl may no longer be fought over—or at least not fought over as vociferously as it once was—but environmental conflict remains as regular a part of the region as rain. I don't expect my book here can fully bridge this divide. Its causes are too complex and too deeply rooted in history for a single book to solve. My more modest goal, though, is to encourage people in places like my valley to take seriously the environmental attitudes and ideas of people in places like the retired timber worker's valley. The environmentalism of timber country is, to be certain, categorically different from the environmentalism often articulated in the region's urban and affluent corners. Timber country's environmentalism is rooted more in wage labor, hunting, and fishing and less in sentimentality and aesthetics. It's far more pragmatic than it is romantic. But that pragmatism holds important ways of thinking about nature that we'd all benefit from and that, perhaps, would make land-use debates less divisive.

Stop reading for a moment, look up, and take stock of just how much lumber surrounds you. If you're indoors, then behind the plaster or sheetrock of your walls likely sits a frame made of lumber. You may be sitting at a desk or in a chair made of lumber. Outside your window may sit rows of houses or apartments, and each one quite likely has lumber in it, as well. If you're reading this as a traditional book, then the pages in your hands were once trees growing in a forest, and if you're reading this book digitally, then the power lines delivering electricity to your computer are held aloft by poles that were once standing timber. Forest products appear in other, unlikely places—places most never think about. The cellulous fibers of trees are used in cosmetics, toothpaste, medications, and paints. Nearly every building you spend time in and every sheet of paper you use connects you to a forest. During the spotted-owl conflict, a popular sticker in timber country read, "Environmentalists can wipe their ass with a spotted owl," a potent, if not so subtle, reminder that even in our most personal moments, we depend on forests and the people who work in them. That dependence has only grown throughout history. One of the great ironies of late twentieth-century environmental history is that at the very moment people started demanding more protections for forests, people started consuming more forest products than ever. And consumer demand is only going to increase as the global population grows. We've yet to find an industrial commodity that can replace timber in our lives. Alternatives do exist. But many of those alternatives are far too costly, or they are produced in ways that threaten to do more environmental harm than the timber industry ever did. Given the demands we all place on forests, saying we have to preserve them is far too easy a position to take. The trickier, though far more important question we must ask is this: how do we balance global consumer demand for lumber with our desire for biodiversity, wildlife habitat, and outdoor recreational space? People in timber country have long asked this question. They don't have all the answers. No one does. But listening to them and taking seriously their history and experience may lead us in more politically and ecologically constructive directions. Who better to guide our forest-use decisions than people who've spent their entire lives in the woods?

PART I

Place

1

"The New Empire"

Roscoe Murrow likely caught his first glimpse of the Cascades somewhere in eastern Washington. It was the late summer of 1914, and Murrow was aboard a train racing westward across the sun-cracked earth of the Northwest's high-desert country. The land here is open and expansive, and on the right sort of day it's possible to see the Cascades from afar, when they appear as just a jagged edge on the distant horizon. But distance belies the range's presence, and as soon as his train left the water-starved sagebrush of the plains and began lumbering up the forested foothills of the eastern slope, the mountains would've revealed their true size. Perhaps, Murrow thought to himself, the Cascades resembled an imposing fortress wall, much too tall to be rising from the flat desert, or that they made the Blue Ridge Mountains of his native North Carolina look inconsequential by comparison. Maybe he even lifted his head to an open window and let the pine-scented breeze rush over his face, which until that moment had only known the stagnate air of the Piedmont. The journey had been long, and surely the cool mountain air brought some measure of relief, even if it couldn't entirely wash away the sense of loss that Murrow carried with him.

Like many people who came to timber country in the opening decades of the twentieth century, Murrow had been unmoored by circumstances far beyond his control. Except for a short stint in the US Army during the Spanish-American War, he'd spent most of his thirty-three years on a 120-acre farm in North Carolina's Polecat Creek, a small town named for a nearby trickling stream where everyone struggled to eke a living from hard, clay soils. Though no one prospered in Polecat Creek, no one starved, either. Neighbors helped each other with chores, shared vegetables from their gardens, and lent their labor and equipment before they were even asked. It was the sort of tightly knit rural community where most were content and few desired to leave. But economic forces are often blind to desire, especially the desires of the poor. Increasing competition from Western farms had driven wheat prices so low that by 1910 most of Polecat Creek's farmers were struggling to stay afloat, and Murrow, like many of his neighbors, was falling behind on loan payments. Many in Polecat Creek began planting tobacco to make ends meet, but Murrow, a devout Quaker who abstained from many vices, refused to do so. And so it was that, after the 1914 harvest, he auctioned off his mule team and plow, paid back some of the money he owed to the bank, and used what little remained to book passage to Washington state.[1]

Murrow was hardly the only person on that train set adrift by impersonal market forces. Next to him likely sat unemployed sawmill workers from the Upper Great Lakes, dusty farmhands looking for the next harvest, and itinerant laborers who rolled their own cigarettes and wiped loose tobacco from their fingertips onto stained Levi's. Some of the men on the train would've been recent immigrants from Scandinavia, the Mediterranean, or Eastern Europe, with the deeply calloused hands proving they'd spent most of their lives working. And it was work, or at least the hope of finding it, that was bringing these men westward. Some would look for jobs in the fishing towns of the coast, the canneries along the Columbia River, the coalfields of Washington's Kittitas County, or the orchards of Oregon's Willamette Valley. Others would seek opportunity in the regions' few urban factories. But, like Murrow, most of these men's journeys would end in one of the Northwest's logging camps or sawmills.

It would've been easy to guess that logging lay in their future simply looking out the window as the train crested the Cascades and began rapidly descending the Pacific Slope. Here, on the west side of the mountains, the timber industry dominated the landscape. Huge clearcuts, devoid of anything but gnarled stumps, spread for miles, interrupted only by logging camps strung along creek beds and sawmill complexes so large they looked like cities. On the horizon, faint wisps of smoke from burning piles of logging waste twisted skyward, blending into the low-lying rainclouds overhead. This was a landscape painted in grays and browns, the melancholy colors of early twentieth-century resource extraction. And now, if Murrow raised his face to an open window, he wouldn't have been met with the cool scent of pine but, rather, the sharp smell of creosote, the sour odor of pulp mills, and the acerbic scent of burnt machine oil.

The landscape Murrow could see from his train's window was relatively new, the product of economic changes that had occurred in just the previous two decades. In 1888 the Northwest's economy was so moribund that local boosters—a group prone to exaggerating economic opportunities—published a pamphlet bemoaning the region's sad financial state. The boosters offered several explanations for why the Northwest had failed to develop: lack of market connections, small cities, and not much of an industrial workforce. But the real cause of the region's economic troubles, the boosters claimed, was the underutilization of its forests. Millions of acres of timberland containing millions of dollars of value just sat there, unused. The boosters believed that industrial logging could unlock the value of the Northwest's forests and lift the region from its economic doldrums. "The lumber industry is the wheel which sets all other wheels in motion," they wrote, painting a vivid picture of how the growth of the timber industry would bring the Northwest to life and transform the region into "a new Empire." The empire the boosters envisioned was one of industrial benevolence, in which logging would create prosperity and spread it throughout the region, benefiting everyone.[2]

In the roughly two decades that followed the pamphlet's publication, the timber industry did, indeed, transform the Northwest. But as Murrow could see from his train's window, the boosters had been naively optimistic about logging's benevolent potential. The economic landscape that emerged in early twentieth-century timber country did not equitably spread wealth across the region but, rather, had been designed to control workers, mollify labor radicalism, and concentrate economic and political power into the hands of a relatively small number of lumbermen, as Murrow was about to discover.

"Only Speculators Make Good Profits"

The reasons why the new empire created by Northwest lumbermen failed to meet the boosters' expectations had nearly everything to do with the regional timber industry's peculiar development and why industrial capital came to the forests of the Pacific Coast in the first place. The common story about the rise of the Northwest timber trade is that after lumbermen cut through the forests of the Atlantic and Midwest, they turned their saws loose on the dense and untouched stands of the far West. While it's certainly true that the forests of the Pacific Slope are some of the richest and densest on Earth, the region's rise to a major timber-producing region was not ordained by nature. Rather, the Northwest timber industry's origins and the social and ecological problems that it would eventually create lie in the complex workings of late nineteenth and early twentieth centuries' forms of profit-seeking. Indeed, when the first midwestern lumbermen ventured to the Northwest in the late nineteenth and early twentieth centuries, the forests of the Upper Great Lakes and American South were still capable of supporting intensive harvests for decades to come. The lumbermen who looked to the Northwest's forests were not seeking uncut stands, nor did they have much desire to establish new logging operations in a region so far removed from national marketplaces. Rather, they were guided westward by what, in their time, had become the guiding maxim of the North American lumber trade: "Only speculators make good profits."[3]

If anything, the tightly packed forests of the Northwest functioned as a deterrent to established logging firms. Many trees growing in the region's alluvial plains weighed several hundred tons and were nearly impossible to harvest, at least profitably. The high-country timber in the mountains was smaller but difficult to reach. Moreover, there was little demand for lumber in the region's sparsely populated cities, and the freight rates charged by the region's steamship monopolies and early transcontinental railroads made shipping to larger markets cost prohibitive. Since the 1860s a handful of poorly capitalized companies had been running small and mostly seasonal logging camps in places with easily accessible timber. And even then, those small companies routinely failed, which only further discouraged larger investors.[4]

While environment and geography made logging the Northwest's forests appear risky, national and international lumber markets made land speculation attractive. The price of timberland has always mirrored the market price of lumber, and timber prices boomed for much of the late nineteenth century. Urban growth and state-sponsored infrastructure projects created intense demand for lumber that sent commodity prices soaring, leading to an equally steep increase in land prices. By the 1880s most lumbermen had concluded that buying timberland and then selling it off at a profit once lumber prices had increased—as they'd steadily done for the last two decades—was more lucrative and far easier than establishing logging camps and building sawmills. While lumbermen speculated in timberland across Canada and the United States, purchasing agents focused their efforts in the Northwest, where uncut stands promised the greatest return on investments and transcontinental railroads were selling off their federal land grants cheaply. State and federal laws intended to prohibit land monopolization were the only real barriers to forestland accumulation, and these were easily sidestepped with, in the words of one historian, "fraudulent claims and political machinations."[5]

Like many soon-to-be Northwest timber magnates, Frederick Weyerhaeuser owed his rapid financial rise to the availability of railroad land grants.
A stout man with a thin white beard, Weyerhaeuser initially dreamed of a
career as a brewer when he came to America from Germany in 1853. It was
only after realizing "how often brewers became confirmed drunkards" that he
began to chart a different course. In the 1860s Weyerhaeuser accepted a sales
position in a small Illinois sawmill and over the next two decades shrewdly
invested his sales commissions until he eventually controlled a sizeable timber operation that stretched across much of Minnesota and Wisconsin. The
success of his company allowed Weyerhaeuser to afford a posh estate in the
exclusive Summit Avenue neighborhood of St. Paul, Minnesota, just a few
doors down from railroad magnate James J. Hill, who in 1899 offered to sell
Weyerhaeuser 140,000 acres of Washington timberland from his Northern
Pacific Railroad land grant. The story of the negotiations, perhaps apocry-
phal, is that Hill opened at $7 an acre, Weyerhaeuser countered at $5 an acre,
and the pair shook hands at $6 an acre. Whatever the exact details, when the
transaction was finalized a year later, it became one of the largest transfers of
private land in American history and made Weyerhaeuser the single-largest
private landholder in the Northwest. When the press asked just how much
timberland he owned, Weyerhaeuser answered simply: "A great lot of it in
every single direction."[6]

Weyerhaeuser's purchase created a more intense speculative mania in the
Northwest. Fearful that the sale would attract new competition and inflate
the cost of land, scores of purchasing agents and, in the words of one observer, "scalawag timber brokers" descended upon the Northwest, buying
any and all the land they could. Oswald West watched this land rush unfold
from his small farm in Oregon's Willamette Valley: "Like buzzards," West
remembered, "[purchasing agents] swoop[ed] down upon our federal and
state owned timber lands [and] through rascality and fraud, gained title to
thousands of acres of valuable publicly-owned timber lands, at minimum
prices." The land rush was equally manic north of the forty-ninth parallel.
In 1903 the British Columbia provincial government opened Crown lands
to foreign purchasers, creating, in the memory of one observer, "a fierce
rush to stake timber." Within the span of a decade, land purchasers had
effectively privatized the Northwest's forests. A 1909 report by the Federal
Bureau of Corporations (not published until 1914) found that 50 percent
of Washington's forestland and 70 percent of Oregon's forestland were now
held in private hands.[7]

Lumbermen believed that speculation was a sure path to profits but not a quick path. It was understood as a patient waiting game between investors and markets. This game, though, had one major flaw, as Washington state forester Edward Griggs famously pointed out: "Fire and taxes wait for no man." In 1902 and again in 1910, a series of conflagrations erupted throughout the Northwest, burning hundreds of thousands of acres of forestland. It wasn't so much fire that threatened speculators' profits as it was insurance carriers who began aggressively raising their rates after the fires. At the same time, muckrakers and reformers gradually began to uncover the graft and corruption at the center of so many land sales. Progressive politicians responded by raising land taxes in an effort to recoup some of what had been looted from the public domain. In Washington, the state increased the assessed taxable value of Weyerhaeuser's holdings by 25 percent in 1906, 33 percent in 1907, and 50 percent in 1908.[8]

With insurance carriers, taxes, and Progressive reform cutting into potential future profits, many Northwest forestland owners came to believe that speculation wasn't as sure a thing as they'd initially thought. Several firms attempted to sell off their holdings, only to find that doing so would leave them at a financial loss. A market panic in 1907 had sent lumber prices tumbling for the first time in decades, leading to a precipitous decline in timberland prices. Speculators had trapped themselves in something of a financial vice, being squeezed on one side by deflating land prices and on the other by increasing carrying costs. Surveying the economic landscape before him, George S. Long, Weyerhaeuser's director of Northwest operations, wrote back to the company offices in Minnesota and counseled his firm's board that they could no longer afford to wait out the market. If they still hoped to realize a profit, "we have to commence out here sooner or later to manufacture."[9]

Long was not alone in reaching this conclusion. Many landholders quickly turned to production in the hope of salvaging their investments and, in the process, rapidly transformed the Northwest's forests from a speculative to an industrialized landscape. Necessity is the mother of invention, and the massive trees and mountain-locked timber that just a few years ago seemed out of reach were now harvested by aid of new steam-powered machines and complex cabling systems. Data documenting the total power output of logging machinery provides some sense of the scope of technological change in the woods. In 1899 all the logging and milling machinery in Washington and Oregon collectively produced 69 million watts of power; by 1909 that figure had climbed to 168 million watts. In that same ten-year span, lumbermen built more than seven hundred mills throughout the region, unmatched in size and capacity. In 1889 the Inman-Poulsen mill in Portland, then the largest in the Northwest, boasted an annual production capacity of two hundred thousand board feet (f.b.m.); in 1912 the St. Paul and Tacoma Lumber Company's mill complex could turn out that much in a single day. In 1899 the industry in Washington and Oregon collectively harvested two billion f.b.m. of lumber; in 1909 production in both states together topped six billion f.b.m.[10]

By 1910 the new empire envisioned by Northwest boosters had started to take shape, though this empire's origins in a failed speculative market would cast a long shadow across the twentieth century and, in the more immediate future, ensure this empire was more malignant than benign. Land speculators had no long-term interest in the Northwest. Their goal from the outset had been to reap financial benefits from afar and then disinvest from the region with all possible speed. The transition to production may have changed lumbermen's strategy, but their ultimate goal remained unchanged. They would harvest the lumber as quickly as possible and then sell or simply abandon the lands, what the industry's earliest critics called "cut-out-and-get-out" logging or "cut and run" logging. And, indeed, few lumbermen dwelled on the social and environmental ramifications of treating the region's woodlands as a giant resource colony, and even if they had, those thoughts would've been drowned out by the deafening whine of the steam turbines now powering their mills and the engines ripping ten-ton timbers from the forest floor.

Machines alone, however, could not get lumbermen to their goal of cutting out and getting out. They would need workers. They would need men like Roscoe Murrow.

The Peopling of Timber Country

Murrow's journey ended in Blanchard, a small logging town in the coastal lowlands of Washington's Skagit County, so close to Samish Bay that when the wind was right, you could smell brine in the air and hear gulls bickering above the oyster beds. Forested hills sloped upward to the west, and on clear nights it was just possible to see the gentle glow of the cone-shaped burners incinerating waste in Bellingham's sawmills, just a few miles to the south. The Samish Bay Logging Company owned much of the forestland surrounding Blanchard, and Murrow quickly found a job working on the company's logging railroad. On some level, the timber workers who lived in Blanchard would've felt familiar to Murrow. Just like in Polecat Creek, the people here had been made strong and sinewy by a lifetime of hard labor. But Murrow would've noticed differences, as well. Polecat Creek was a place where the same families had lived for generations. Most of the people in Blanchard were newcomers. Some, like Murrow, came from the South, many more from the Midwest, and just as many from Mediterranean and Scandinavian countries, and each one of them could likely tell a story of economic displacement similar to Murrow's.[11]

While it's true that these hard-luck migrants desperately needed the work the timber industry provided, it's equally true that employers in the industry desperately needed them. Although Northwest logging quickly became one of the most mechanized resource-extraction industries in early twentieth-century North America, lumbermen still required massive work crews. An average-sized mill employed more than two hundred men to keep the saws fed with lumber. Larger mills required upward of a thousand workers. Logging crews varied in size from a half dozen to about two dozen men. A single logging camp might run up to ten crews, and an individual logging company might operate four or five camps, though industry giants like Weyerhaeuser, Simpson, and Long-Bell ran upward of twenty camps. Companies also needed workers to fill other odd jobs: blacksmiths, saw filers, camp cooks, construction crews, railroad crews, graders, scalers, and cruisers.[12]

Lumbermen could not rely on the regional labor market to meet their intense demand for workers. In 1900 Oregon and Washington were among the least-populated states in the union, and British Columbia was among Canada's least-populated provinces. Moreover, most people who lived in the region were farmers, not industrial workers. In Oregon, for instance, more than half of the state's population of 413,000 in 1900 lived on farms. The Northwest's paucity of industrial workers hadn't been an issue throughout the late nineteenth century, when small and mostly seasonal mills and logging camps got by employing farmhands and homesteaders looking for wage work between harvests. But now that the industry required large crews working year-round, lumbermen concluded that if the Northwest wasn't populated enough to maintain the industry, then it would have to be made so.[13]

Turning the Northwest's forests into an industrial landscape, therefore, depended as much on creating new productive geographies within the region as it did on creating a new labor-market geography outside the region. At the same time lumbermen built new mills and developed logging technologies, they developed an expansive network of employment agencies, ranging from San Francisco to New York, designed to funnel recently arrived immigrants or the urban unemployed into timber country. While these employment agents functioned as the direct gateway to Northwestern labor markets, timber country's demographic growth had just as much to do with new immigrant and migrant pathways created by developing national and international markets for Northwest lumber. By the early twentieth century, railroads had become more reliable and started to offer timber companies significant freight discounts, facilitating the flow of timber out of the region and people in. Washington provided much of the lumber San Franciscans used to rebuild their city after the 1906 earthquake and fire, and in return, the city sent many displaced and unemployed workers northward to the state's logging camps and mills. Northwestern lumber supplemented steel in Chicago skyscrapers, and when those construction projects were complete, some construction workers came to the Northwest. The opening of the Panama Canal in 1914 offered lumbermen the ability to access European markets and seriously compete with the German and Scandinavian timber industry. As steamships carrying Northwest timber inched their way through the Panama Canal and then set out across the Atlantic Ocean, they passed ships sailing in the opposite direction, carrying immigrants, some of whom would find their way to the Northwest woods.

Census data show the extent of these new market and demographic connections. By 1920 more than 80 percent of the Northwest timber industry's workforce had been born outside the region. Some, like Murrow, had come from the US South, others from the Northeast, and others still from Europe. While the rise of Northwest lumbering created many new pathways into the region, census data reveal that two were dominant. In 1920 about 30 percent of all Northwest timber workers hailed from the Midwest and 14 percent from Scandinavian countries. The significant number of Midwestern migrants and Scandinavian immigrants who came to work in the Northwest woods was a result of the Pacific Coast's emergence as the world's leading timber-producing region and evidence that, in histories of working-class migration, people and capital often flow along the same channels.[14]

The migration story of John Roberts shows just how closely linked those flows could be. Roberts was born in Cumberland, Wisconsin, in 1882 and by 1900 was working as a laborer, probably in the local sawmill. Cumberland was the seat of operations for a furniture salesman–turned-lumberman named Edward Griggs. Throughout the late nineteenth century, Griggs had assembled a patchwork of timberland throughout Minnesota and Wisconsin, though he struggled to expand due to competition from larger firms like Weyerhaeuser. The desire to grow his company led Griggs to invest in Northwest logging operations earlier than most of his competitors. In 1888 Griggs incorporated the St. Paul & Tacoma Lumber Company and a year later began construction on a massive mill on Tacoma's Commencement Bay. As Griggs developed his logging operations in the Northwest, he disinvested from his Midwest operations, leaving workers like Roberts jobless. Sometime between 1900 and 1910, Roberts moved to Washington, where he found employment in a logging camp just outside of Gig Harbor, just north of Tacoma. The location was likely not incidental. The forests surrounding Gig Harbor were controlled by St. Paul & Tacoma, meaning that although Roberts had traveled more than two thousand miles across the continent, his employer likely remained the same.[15]

New Scandinavian immigrant pathways were also created as the lumber cut in Northwest's forests came to dominate the global timber market, shaping the migrations of workers like Charles Anderson. In 1890 Anderson was working as a logger in the pine forests of Norrland, an expansive region of rolling hills covering much of northern Sweden and the epicenter of the Scandinavian lumber industry. Although the early twentieth-century decline of Swedish lumbering was not as dramatic as the decline of midwestern logging, the fates of Norrland loggers like Anderson were shaped by the emergence of Northwest logging all the same. Declining shipping rates and lower labor costs allowed American and British Columbian lumbermen to sell Northwest timber in European markets and, in the words of one economist, emerge as "one of the most serious competitors of Sweden in the lumber trade." By 1920 North American Douglas fir sold in Europe at just around $30 per 1,000 f.b.m. compared to $59 per 1,000 f.b.m. for Swedish lumber. Faced with international competition, declining forest reserves, and a new conservationist impulse in Scandinavian governments, Swedish operators started restricting harvests throughout the early twentieth century and, in the process, displaced workers like Anderson. If Anderson's skills were no longer valued in his native Sweden, then they were in high demand in the Northwest. Sometime between 1901 and 1910, Anderson left for the United States, and by 1910 he was working as a timber feller in a Puget Sound logging camp.[16]

The sheer number of people drawn to the Northwest by logging had no less an impact on the region's social landscape than the rise of lumber production had on the region's economic and environmental landscapes. Washington's and Oregon's combined populations expanded from 931,639 in 1900 to 1,814,755 in 1910, a more than 94 percent increase. British Columbia's population went from 178,657 in 1901 to 392,480 in 1911, a nearly 120 percent increase. Not everyone who came to the Northwest in the early twentieth century went to work in the woods. The region's mining and commercial fishing industries were also growing. Both Seattle, Washington, and Vancouver, British Columbia, were emerging as crucial nodes in a transpacific trade network, creating new pathways for Asian immigrants and attracting dockworkers and shipbuilders. The major force reshaping the demography of the region, though, was lumber. By 1920 more than of 85 percent of all nonagricultural workers in the Northwest were employed in logging or saw milling.[17]

Experienced timber workers like Roberts and Anderson were especially valued by employers. Though early twentieth-century economists classified logging and millwork as "unskilled labor," most jobs in the timber industry required complex understandings of forest ecologies and industrial processes. Workers who possessed the knowledge to facilitate efficient and profitable operations were often in short supply. Roberts, Anderson, and men like them were already acculturated to the pace and process of industrial logging. They could fell trees without shattering them, mill out knots to produce the highest-grade construction timber, and run mainlines and set haulback lines as naturally as anyone else tied their shoes. Their experience working in industrialized woodlands elsewhere made them valuable. And it also made them a threat.

Controlling Radicalism

Employers in the Northwest woods encountered something of a paradox when it came to recruiting workers. Men like Roberts and Anderson may have possessed work experience that facilitated efficient operations, and yet, they often carried radical beliefs that if allowed to fester would most certainly disrupt production. Besides harboring the same anti-union sentiments of most early twentieth-century industrial magnates, Northwest lumbermen's opposition to organized labor was rooted in their desire for industrial speed. The shorter hours and safety precautions so often demanded by unionized workers threatened to slow down the steady flow of logs from forest to mill to market. Organized labor was anathema to cutting out and getting out. And herein lay lumbermen's problem. Both organized labor and working-class radical political movements had grown significantly in the late nineteenth and early twentieth centuries, and many of the workers now streaming into the Northwest, especially the ones with timber-industry experience, had contributed to that growth. Many midwesterners had been members of Wisconsin and Michigan sawmill-worker unions organized in the 1880s. Employers were particularly concerned with Scandinavian immigrants who, one employer cautioned, are known for their "socialistic and anarchistic tendencies." And indeed, many Swedes and Norwegians who'd previously worked in their home countries' logging and commercial fishing industries had belonged to the Landsorganisatonen (national organization), a Scandinavia-wide, socialist trade union league. Swedish and Norwegian socialists found company among the Northwest's relatively sizeable population of Finnish radicals who'd established enclaves and meeting halls in Astoria, Oregon, and Aberdeen, Washington. While immigrants from Mediterranean and Baltic countries tended to come from more conservative agricultural communities, enough Greek and Italian anarchists flowed into the Northwest to give employers pause about European immigrants, as well.[18]

Lumbermen's fears of radicals were further fueled by the increasing number of workers throughout the early twentieth-century West carrying the distinctive red membership card of the Industrial Workers of the World (IWW). Since its founding in 1905, train-hopping itinerant workers had spread the IWW throughout Western resource-extraction industries, from the oil fields of Oklahoma to the hard rock mines of Arizona and Colorado, up to Montana copper country. And, by 1910 Wobblies, as the union's members were more popularly known, had established meeting halls in timber-producing towns throughout the Northwest. What made the IWW particularly concerning to lumbermen was that it openly recruited the sorts of workers they were now employing: immigrants and the so-called unskilled. The IWW's politics were equally troubling. In song and literally standing on soapboxes, Wobblies prophesized about a time in the near future when all workers would join the IWW and undertake a massive general strike that would bring an end to capitalism.[19]

Frequent claims by Wobblies that they'd successfully organized thousands of timber workers gave lumbermen even more to worry about. What employers never quite grasped, though, was that while Wobblies claimed to speak for the working class of the Northwest woods, they rarely ever did. Most of the IWW's ostensible successes were reported in its newspaper, and the editors of the Wobbly press were prone to embellishment, never ones to let the truth get in the way of a good story of class struggle. The IWW likely had far fewer members in the woods than its paper claimed, though we can't know for certain since the union didn't actually keep membership records. One study estimates that between 1907 and 1917, the IWW attracted fewer than a thousand members in the timber industry of California, Oregon, and Washington. When many firsthand accounts of life and labor in the Northwest woods that were *not* authored by Wobblies mention the IWW, it's only to say that the union didn't have much of a presence. Several of the strikes the IWW press claimed to have led were complete fabrications or were spontaneous walkouts that Wobblies then tried to take charge of or credit for. The IWW did garner significant attention during its many free-speech fights, when Wobblies purposefully got arrested in protest of laws prohibiting political oratory, but by the union's own admission, most of the Wobblies who joined in the free-speech fights were from outside the region. The IWW elicited a strong and sometimes violent response from vigilantes and local law enforcement, which Wobblies offered as evidence of their efficacy in the woods, but an ability to provoke violence doesn't necessarily equate to effective labor organizing. On the whole, Wobbly activity in the Northwest woods amounted to a lot of smoke but precious little fire.[20]

Ironically, the IWW's ineffectiveness in the Northwest woods was the direct result of Wobblies exaggerating their union's effectiveness. Though few employers found actual evidence that IWW organizers had infiltrated their operations, most believed a Wobbly-led assault on the lumber industry was imminent and, thus, adopted prophylactic policies "aimed at eliminating IWWism," as one lumberman put it, that effectively contained radicalism before it ever materialized. Chief among these was a tool commonly used by anti-union employers in the early twentieth century: blacklists. Since at least 1910 lumbermen had been instructing employment agents to maintain lists of known unionists and require applicants to sign oaths saying they would not join a union. By World War I the timber industry's blacklisting process had become larger and more refined, and in 1923 the Western Operators' Association established the Clearing House, an office responsible for, according to social-investigator Charlotte Todes, "locating active radicals and discouraging them from working in the camps." In the course of her research, Todes found that the Clearing House maintained more than 110,000 records of men who were either actively working in the industry or had applied for work in the industry, each record carefully documenting whether a worker belonged to a union or even if he'd complained about hours or working conditions in a camp.[21]

Not all plans for weeding out radicalism were so well refined. In an effort to combat the spread of radical and foreign-language literature in camps, employers distributed free and what they described as "wholesome constructive reading material" to their workers. Lumberman Dwight Merrill was partial to the *Saturday Evening Post*, which he said contained "the best reading for a working man which has ever been printed." Other employers favored publications authored by trade groups, like the *Camp and Mill News*, a monthly newsletter that contained articles refuting socialism and referred to bosses and workers as "partners in industry." Lumberman John Anderson became a particularly fervent advocate of using the power of persuasion to combat radicalism. In 1918 Anderson began appealing to Seattle's wealthy elite for books and magazines. After dutifully removing anything that might cause "unrest and discontent," Anderson then distributed the donated reading material to workers in camps. In 1920 Anderson expanded his efforts and began hiring speakers to visit loggers and "talk Americanism." After receiving reports that most workers responded to the talks with a combination of indifference and boredom, Anderson hired a singing troupe to accompany the speakers and liven up presentations. Whether or not workers responded better to the singers than speakers is lost to history.[22]

World War I provided new opportunities for lumbermen to stamp out radicalism and increase their profits. When the United States entered the war in 1917, lumbermen intentionally limited production to drive up the price of lumber they were supplying the US military. It was a classic case of war profiteering, but radicals provided a convenient scapegoat that lumbermen used to mask their market manipulation. "Among the men of the woods there is to be found a certain percentage who have developed an outright antagonism to this country and its institutions," read an article in a lumber trade journal, explaining the reason why lumber output fell when the United States entered the war. "They are bitter. They have no interest in the nation's affairs at home and are not concerned with its successes on the battlefields." Even before employers in the Northwest began to openly call for state assistance in tamping down labor militancy, both the Canadian and US governments had passed wartime laws that effectively criminalized radicalism. But now, facing a wartime lumber shortage, the American government responded even more decisively to the threat posed by radicals in timber country, as manufactured as it might have been.[23]

In 1917 the US military dispatched Brice Disque to the Northwest woods. A recently retired army officer, Disque had made a name for himself violently suppressing the insurrection in the Philippines during the Spanish-American War. After surveying the state of labor relations in the timber industry, Disque spearheaded two plans. First, to boost lumber production, Disque recommended and the US military ultimately agreed to the creation of the Spruce Division, an army unit that sent several thousand soldiers to work in the Northwest woods. Second, hoping to provide a way for workers with legitimate grievances to find redress without turning to organizations like the IWW, Disque oversaw the creation of a new company union, the Loyal Legion of Loggers and Lumbermen (4L). Like most company unions, the 4L was a union in name only. It made little effort to represent workers and even less effort to improve wages and working conditions. Rather, what it aimed to do was, as the 4L's constitution stated, "promote a closer relationship between the employer and employee," "infuse a spirit of patriotism in the lumber workers," and "stamp out sedition and sabotage." Workers arriving in a 4L camp were immediately required to join and then sign a pledge that read, in part, "I, the undersigned, [am] firmly convinced that the best interests of both employer and employee in the lumber industry are conserved" by the Loyal Legion of Loggers and Lumbermen.[24]

Blacklists, reading literature, and company unions—to say nothing of Anderson's singers—were, however, blunt instruments that produced incomplete results, at best. Radicals dodged blacklists by using fake names. Workers joined the 4L because they were compelled to, not because they actually believed in a harmonious relationship between employer and employee. And it's hard to imagine any worker taking seriously the patronizing and infantilizing tone of most employer-authored publications. What employers in timber country needed was a more reliable solution to contain radicalism.

"More Settled, More Loyal, and More Conservative"

That more reliable solution could be found sitting next to Roscoe Murrow as his train sped westward toward timber country. Her name was Ethel Lamb Murrow, and like her husband, she'd been born into poverty in a North Carolina farming community. Though she came from a deeply Methodist family, Ethel adopted Quakerism when she and Roscoe wed in 1900 (in a decidedly modest ceremony befitting Quaker beliefs). Most who knew Ethel described her as a "wheelhouse of work," rarely content to sit still. Even when she grew older and her friends and family implored her to slow down, she never did, always claiming, "It's better to wear out than rust out." Ethel's aversion to idleness would make her well suited to life in the Northwest woods, where a working-class woman's daily chores involved chopping wood for the morning fire and fetching water from the nearby stream for coffee, all before rousing her husband out of bed before the first whistle. And if such chores didn't keep her busy enough, then raising her and Roscoe's three children certainly would. Ethel had given birth to the couple's first son, Lacey, in 1905, and then Dewey in 1907. The couple's youngest son was born in 1908, six years before they left for Washington, and was named Egbert, though everyone in the family called him Egg.[25]

Murrow was just one of thousands of workers who came to timber country with a family in tow. In 1910 roughly 27 percent of all wage workers employed in the Northwest timber industry were married, by 1920 more than half were married, and by 1930 just over 59 percent were married. Marriage rates are just one variable by which we can ascertain the prevalence of family-oriented workers in the Northwest woods and, perhaps, not even the best variable. Many of the men who worked in the woods were single, yet still lived with a family. Boys often started working in the woods at twelve or thirteen, when they were too young to marry and were still living with their parents. Older widowers worked in the woods and lived with their grown children. Families also took in unmarried brothers, uncles, and nephews. Focusing on household-type variables, rather than marriage rates, accounts for such workers and shows that for much of the early twentieth century, family men did the bulk of the work in timber country. In 1910, 52 percent of all workers lived in a family household, and by 1920 that figure had climbed to 66 percent, by 1930 to 74 percent, and by 1940 to 87 percent.[26]

With few exceptions, historians have had little to say about the preponderance of married workers in early twentieth-century timber country. Instead, most scholars have portrayed the industry's early workforce as overwhelmingly young, single, and itinerant. The defining social feature of the Northwest woods, according to most of these studies, was the near absence of families and communities. This analysis, though, has less to do with the demographic realities of the Northwest woods and far more to do with the sources historians have used. For the most part, historians have relied on the records of Progressive Era social investigators and the Wobblies to reconstruct the social life of early twentieth-century timber workers, and neither were reliable narrators on this front. For Progressives, young men detached from families wandering the road in search of work served as a powerful morality tale about the ways industrial capitalism was upending, if not destroying, traditional notions of community. For Wobblies, young, single men were the ideal revolutionary subjects, unencumbered by children and families, able to go wherever—and strike jobsites whenever—the class war demanded. Progressives and Wobblies often ignored married, stable workers like Roscoe Murrow because it was politically expedient for them to do so, and historians leaning too heavily on these archives have, likewise, ignored the married and stable workers in the industry.[27]

Timber workers tended to be married or attached to a family precisely because this is what employers wanted. If blacklists and company unions were blunt instruments in employers' efforts to contain radicalism, then recruiting workers with families was a more refined and, according to many employers, far more reliable method of shaping the politics of their employees.

"The best cure for the IWW plague," wrote the secretary of one lumber-trade group in 1912, "is the cultivation of the homing instinct in men." What lumbermen believed was that the obligations of family life would compel men with wives and children to look askance of activities that might cost them their jobs and, thus, threaten their families' financial security, like joining a union or participating in a strike. Moreover, lumbermen, like many men in the early twentieth century, regarded women as naturally conservative. Employers hoped that having women in their camps would moderate men's radical tendencies and that any worker joining a union would have to do so over the objections of his boss and, perhaps, the more strenuous objections of his wife. Lumberman Frank Lamb was not alone among employers in the Northwest woods when in 1917 he argued that encouraging families in camps was among the highest "principles of labor maintenance. . . . The married worker [is] necessarily more settled, more loyal, and more conservative."[28]

Lumbermen didn't just want families living in their camps. They wanted stable communities. Itinerancy, like singleness, was believed to encourage radicalism. Workers wandering the road in search of work might easily come under the sway of Wobblies or be introduced to radical literature in immigrant communities. Far better, employers reasoned, to keep workers tied to camp where their actions and politics could be closely monitored and potentially shaped. Discouraging itinerancy also promised to boost production. Logging technologies of the early twentieth century required crews to work together and coordinate their actions. Logging, said one employer, "calls for a high order of teamwork," and constantly shifting work crews created "disorder and loss of efficiency." Events at a Weyerhaeuser logging camp in 1918 bore this out. That summer the lumber company was forced to lay off several of its workers due to a small post–World War I depression in the lumber market. The company consolidated many of its crews, and though these men were all experienced loggers, they were unable to meet production quotas for two months. Afterwards, Weyerhaeuser's foremen recognized that there was value in having "men in the crew that are accustomed to working together."[29]

Employers used a variety of strategies and incentives to recruit and retain workers with families. Lumbermen instructed employment agencies to waive hiring fees for married men. Married workers were then extended special benefits once in camps, like first choice of work shifts and time off to participate in company-sponsored activities, like picnics and baseball games. In 1912 the Pacific Coast Loggers Association, the major trade group representing Northwest lumber operators, recommended that its member companies discourage "traveling" by offering bonuses to workers who remained in the same logging camp for more than a year. Reporting on the value of bonus systems, lumberman J. P. Van Orsdel proclaimed, "The IWW and socialists have no place in the camp where the bonus is in effect." Company-sponsored accident insurance plans also helped employers maintain a family-oriented workforce and convince their employees that they had their best interests at heart. In 1920 the Bloedel Donovan Lumber Company operating in northern Washington became one of the first timber operators to purchase insurance for its workers. When Edward Griggs of the St. Paul & Tacoma Lumber Company wrote to Bloedel Donovan to inquire about the effectiveness of the program, he was told that insurance plans "make for continuity of service, a little greater loyalty, and a general feeling . . . that something is being done for the family of the unfortunate employee."[30]

But if lumbermen were serious about maintaining a stable, family-oriented workforce, they'd need to offer workers more than just economic incentives. By the start of World War I, the lumber industry was operating at the distant fringes of the Northwest's hinterland. Many camps were more than a day's train ride from the nearest towns and cities. At the very least, this meant that employers would have to provide housing for the families they hoped to recruit. Idle workers might direct some of their excess time and energy toward labor activism, so lumbermen would have to keep their employees occupied with recreational activities in their off hours, too. They'd need schools for the children and teachers for those schools. And they would need to make sure that their camps had religion, if for no other reason than to remind workers that God was always watching and that labor activism was an affront to Him, as well. Like employers in many other industries of the early twentieth century, lumbermen built an extensive network of company towns to promote family life among their workers, discourage itinerancy, and contain radicalism. But company towns in the Northwest woods looked and functioned very differently from company towns in most other industries, and other than the work itself, nothing did more to shape working-class life in timber country.

"We Want No Extravagance"

The paternalistic company town looms large in labor history. It's been the focus of much labor activism, the topic of proletarian novels, and the subject of folk songs. But by the early twentieth century, the sort of paternalistic company town memorialized in many a country-music ballad had ceased to exist in most North American industries. Company towns experienced something of a revolution in the 1890s, after massive strikes in the company towns of Homestead, Pennsylvania (1892), and Pullman, Illinois (1894), convinced employers that paternalism was doing more to encourage radicalism than contain it. Afterwards, many industrial magnates adopted a new approach to company towns that was less paternalistic, if not in function then at least in form. Hoping to demonstrate their largesse and convince workers that company loyalty came with material benefits, employers began constructing what historian Margaret Crawford has called "working men's paradises," lavish communities with movie theaters, bowling alleys, and hospitals, where workers could rent multiroom houses furnished with modern appliances and even, in a few cases, a white picket fence surrounding a spacious lawn. The names of some of these towns are familiar (largely because the names of the companies that built them are familiar): Hershey, Pennsylvania; Kohler, Wisconsin; DuPont, Washington. While most common in manufacturing industries, some operators in resource-extraction industries, like the coal fields of southern Colorado, the timber industry of the American South, and sugarcane fields of Hawaii, also built working men's paradises. Even a handful of company towns in Appalachian coal country, places long associated with difficult living, received lavish makeovers.[31]

Yet, only two working-men's paradises were ever built in Northwest timber country: Weyerhaeuser's Vail, Washington, and Long-Bell Lumber's Longview, Washington. Most lumber-company towns of the early twentieth century were less paradise and more purgatory. Unlike the spacious, multiroom houses employers built in places like Hershey, Kohler, and DuPont, most houses in the Northwest logging's company towns were single-room shacks thrown together from fir batting and spare lumber that was too twisted or damaged to be sold on the market. Julia Bertram, who lived in a sawmill town outside Portland, remembered that her home was "made of No. 4 common, with knotholes so big you could look through into the next apartment and see your neighbors quarreling over which bills to pay." Moreover, few logging-company towns were laid out on a neat Cartesian grid or, for that matter, planned out at all. Companies simply constructed houses wherever they'd fit, tucking them in between stumps and rocks and often placing them so close to railroad tracks that the batting and boards they were built from rattled loose every time a logging train rumbled by. Sometimes companies powered workers' homes with electricity generated by their mill, but more often families lived by gaslight lamp and the dim glow coming from their woodburning stove. Shallow pits served as toilets, and the only running water in most towns could be found in nearby creeks. At a time when employers in many industries were trying to give their workforces a taste of the modern, the only thing modern about most timber towns was the mill at their center and the logging machinery at work in the hills above. Most everything else looked like it belonged to some preindustrial era.[32]

Timber country's austere company-town system was a product of cut-out-and-get-out logging. Since most firms hoped to abandon their interest in their lands once the timber had been harvested, few saw any reason to sink capital into permanent towns. The unique productive geography of the early twentieth-century logging also shaped the towns. In resource-extraction industries like mining, a single productive site could potentially sustain an individual operation for decades. A forest tract, however, could only sustain an early twentieth-century Northwest logging operation for a few years, as the large work crews and steam-powered machines employed by industrial logging operations tore through forests at a stunning pace. Most logging-company towns, therefore, looked impermanent because that's what they were designed to be.

The names of these towns often spoke to their reasons for being. Some, like McCleary, Washington, and Brookings, Oregon, had been named for the lumberman who founded them. Others, like Woodfibre, British Columbia, the work that sustained them. In places like Snoqualmie Falls, Washington; Pine Ridge, Oregon; and Lake Cowichan, British Columbia, lumbermen turned to prominent physical features for inspiration, evoking the pastoral to mask the harsher realities of life. Some, like British Columbia's Blubber Bay, recalled the industries that lumber was increasingly replacing, while others, like Port Gamble, Washington, reflected the financial instability of the logging industry. Yet, for every company town given the dignity of a proper name, there were probably twenty simply called "camp" and designated with a number, like Camp 1, Camp 2, and so on, as if lumbermen saw these towns as military outposts that could be quickly abandoned once their war had ended.[33]

Because logging company towns moved so frequently, trying to find them on a map can be an exercise in frustration. Maps represent geography as static. Company-town geography was always in motion. The network of camps and towns run by Vancouver Island's Comox Logging and Railway Company provides an example. Like many companies, Comox ran its milling operation out of a centrally located town, aptly named Headquarters, and logged out of a network of satellite camps. Camp 1 was first built in 1910, adjacent to a dairy farm south of Headquarters. In 1915 the camp moved to a new tract south of Merville and in 1918 to Miracle Beach. Camp 2 was established around the same time as Camp 1 and first built to harvest the island's coastal lowland stands. In 1918 Camp 2 moved a mile up the Comox mainline on the southern bank of the Oyster River. The camp was destroyed by fire a year later and rebuilt on the opposite side of the river. Camp 3 was built on the western bank of Dove Creek in 1914, moved to Black Creek in 1917, burned in a fire in 1922, rebuilt, burned again in 1923, rebuilt again, and burned again in 1925, after which it was abandoned.[34]

Camps in the pine country of the interior Northwest tended to be even more mobile. Starved of water and subjected to cold winters, the forests east of the Cascade crest are thinner and populated by trees much smaller than those that grow nearer the coast. Eastside logging companies, therefore, tended to cut through forests even quicker than westside companies, and their profitability demanded even greater mobility. The Shevlin-Hixon Logging Company, headquartered in Bend, Oregon, was one of several companies that responded to the mobility requirements of eastern Cascades logging by building all of its town's structures, from workers' homes to company offices, out of boxcars that could be loaded onto railroad flats and moved wherever track had been laid. The town moved so often throughout the 1920s that residents became quite efficient at packing up their belongings and could move their camp in a single afternoon. Workers would be given the day off from logging and along with their wives and children would lay dressers flat, tie down any other furniture, wrap dishes in towels, and board up windows. Once everything was secured, a logging crane would lift their home onto a railcar. In the new town site, their home would be unloaded and their front porch unfolded, and they'd settle in before the men went to work logging a new stand the next day.[35]

Everything in an early twentieth-century logging town was a negotiation between lumbermen's desire for mobility and frugality, on the one hand, and their desire to provide a livable community for families, on the other. This tension was visible in the recreational activities employers offered families in their camps. Company-sponsored recreational activities were common in nearly every industry that relied on a company-town system. Alongside accident insurance and bonus payments, employers believed that providing amusements would engender company loyalty and keep workers occupied when they might otherwise be agitating for better wages and working conditions. Employers in the Northwest woods also sought to provide recreation for their employees but, unlike industrial magnates operating more-modern company towns, sought to do so, as one lumberman said, "at the lowest possible cost." He recommended movie screenings as a fitting company-sponsored activity because they entertained and, more importantly, were cheap. A simple movie screen could be fashioned by coating a canvas "with several coats of white calcimine with just a trifle of blue in it." Company-organized baseball games were another common recreational activity in the Northwest woods. Employers liked the game because they believed it fostered teamwork and helped "Americanize" recent immigrants and because it required minimal equipment. The same tension between frugality and livability shaped other social and civic services in Northwest logging-company towns. Many companies had schools but rarely offered an education past the fifth grade. Employers wanted to encourage a sense of Christian duty among their workforces, but many towns didn't have churches. Instead, itinerant preachers called "sky pilots" crisscrossed timber country, traveling from town to town, performing weddings and funerals, and administering religious rites. When they weren't repairing logging equipment, company blacksmiths often saw to minor medical matters. More-serious health issues had to wait for a visit from a traveling doctor. Workers involved in catastrophic accidents were often put on the next train leaving camp, and it could sometimes be days before they received proper medical care.[36]

When the tensions between mobility and community comfort couldn't be easily reconciled, employers almost always chose the former over the latter. James Couack, the president of British Columbia's Western Lumber Company, in a letter to a subordinate in 1912, hints at the ways production always took precedence. The previous winter had been particularly hard on the people living in Western Lumber's Vancouver Island camps. The blizzards that began in late December did not relent until sometime in February, snowing-in every camp from Nanaimo to Campbell River. In the Western logging town known only as Camp No. 1, families had burned nearly every piece of scrap lumber they could pry from the frozen earth in a desperate attempt to stay warm. The following fall, when the days again started to grow cooler, A. H. Hilton, the camp's foreman, ordered coal-burning stoves for the company houses so that residents might be a bit warmer should they again be hit by a difficult winter. When Couack learned of the requisition, he immediately questioned Hilton on his managerial prowess: "We are up there to facilitate logging," Couack wrote, adding "while we want things to be comfortable, we do not want any extravagance."[37]

Across many early twentieth-century industries, employers sought to mollify radicalism and mask the harsh realities of work life by providing their workforces with extravagances. How, then, did lumbermen hope to contain radicalism when many, like Couack, considered something as basic as a coal-burning stove an "extravagance"? Ruth Manary's memory of life in a coastal Oregon logging camp provides some answers. Like many people in early twentieth-century logging towns, Manary was awed by the size and scope of industrial logging, the "remarkable speed" of "the work of cutting and hauling." Yet, she seemed most impressed by the railroads. By the 1920s the company that ran her town had laid hundreds of miles of track "to get into this vast Lincoln County tract of spruce," Manary explained. "[This] was a huge undertaking. Great cuts were made in hillsides covered with wild rhododendrons of all colors, as high as two-story houses. Canyons were bridged, and a trestle was driven in most of the width of Alsea Bay." Manary's description provides some sense of the rugged terrain that surrounded most logging camps and the difficulty of building tracks across that terrain and, perhaps, most important of all, speaks to the isolation of most towns. The aggressive pace of logging had pushed most companies deep into the woods, into the broad canyons and steep hillsides Manary described, far from small towns and farther still from larger cities. That alone was often enough to isolate workers from the labor movement. But as Manary's description further reveals, it was the logging companies that built, maintained, and operated the railroads that served as the only connections most towns had to the outside world, and this gave employers a significant advantage in their war on radicalism. Known labor organizers were easily barred entry into towns and radical literature easily plucked from mailbags. Nor did employers have to worry much about radical messages disseminated through the airwaves. Few people in camp owned radios, Manary recalled, because radios were new, out of financial reach of most families, and more than that, relatively useless in isolated camps. The only radio in Manary's camp was owned by the company's timekeeper, and though he "spent most every evening with his head in the horn," Manary said, "he seemed to get mostly static."[38]

Lumbermen, therefore, didn't have to provide extravagances to their workers because they controlled timber country's geography. Radicalism was mollified more through distance and space than the extravagances of welfare capitalism. And, indeed, Manary took note of the political effects of her town's isolation. She could only recall one time when the IWW attempted to reach workers in her camp, and it was a clumsy attempt at that. "The IWW ('Wobblies') pushed their propaganda," she wrote, "once sending a flimsy airplane dropping leaflets over camp. Not much attention was ever paid to these agitators."[39]

A Rough Sort of Eden

By the 1920s lumbermen could look out across the Northwest with some amount of satisfaction. The collapse of the speculative market roughly a decade earlier had disrupted their plans for easily garnered profits, but they'd responded decidedly, in ways now visible across the landscape. Among their greatest accomplishments was the transformation of the region's economic landscape. The timber industry now dominated the economy of the Northwest, and Northwest timber now dominated the national lumber market. By 1919 Washington state alone produced nearly twice as much timber as any other state in the nation. Lumbermen's ledgers also reflected the speed and scope of the Northwest's economic transformation. In 1900 the total value of all timber produced in Oregon and Washington amounted to $13.5 million; by 1919 the total value of lumber produced in both states amounted to more than $330 million. The transformative power of lumbermen was also visible in the Northwest's demographic landscape and the stunning number of people who came to timber country from across the country and world. The physical landscape bore marks of change, as well, most notably in the clearcuts that now spread out across the region's forests. But lumbermen's greatest success of all may have been in shaping the Northwest's political landscape. Alongside policies designed to root out radicals from the streams of workers flowing into their logging camps and mills, the company towns dotting the forests had effectively contained the threat posed by radicals. It's easy to imagine lumbermen taking some pleasure in Manary's story and in the fact that Wobblies had been so frustrated by their inability to reach the camps that they resorted to leaflet drops. In the early twentieth century, lumbermen had created a new empire in the Northwest woods, and like many empires throughout history, this one concentrated wealth and power into the hands of a few.[40]

Stories workers came to tell of life in these places often spoke to the hardships they endured. Themes of poverty, death, and industrial danger figure heavily into their descriptions of life in the lumbermen's new empire. But workers and their families wouldn't solely describe timber country as a landscape of exploitation. At least, Egbert, the youngest Murrow boy, wouldn't. Like many young men who came of age in the Northwest woods, Egbert started working alongside his father and older brothers as soon as he could, when he was just fourteen. The work changed Egbert, as it changed most men. His tall, lanky frame filled out, and he quickly developed a muscular chest and strong, sinewy arms. He developed stamina, skill, and an appreciation

Figure 1.1. Edward R. Murrow with his parents, Ethel and Roscoe Murrow, northern Washington. Courtesy of Lynn Lennox.

for seemingly contradictory attributes of brute force and grace required to effectively work in the woods. He learned to drink and picked up smoking, which would ultimately lead to his early death from lung cancer at age fifty-seven. His lexicon expanded along with his body. He'd later explain that he acquired an "extensive vocabulary of profanity" in the woods, what he called the "exquisite expressiveness" of timber workers, and later in life his wife would constantly have to implore him not to use "logger talk" in front of polite company. And, his name changed. The youngest Murrow boy believed that older, more experienced loggers would never accept someone with the name Egbert. He'd later say that he changed his name to avoid having to fight every logger up and down the coast. He decided on Ed, a name that bespoke masculinity with its simplicity.[41]

Edward R. Murrow eventually saved up enough money working in the woods to attend Washington State University. The details of his life thereafter are familiar to many: a job at the CBS news desk, European war correspondent during the opening years of World War II, and a life of crusading journalism, including, but certainly not limited to his public clash with US Senator Joseph McCarthy during the Red Scare of the 1950s. Yet, throughout his life, timber country remained something of a refuge for Murrow, a place he often returned to in order to find some of the stability, simplicity, and community rarely afforded by his professional life. Several times through-out his career, he quietly slipped away from his hectic New York life to find comfort in the family and friends he'd left behind in Washington. And even when the demands of his job prevented him from leaving the East Coast, he would return to the Northwest woods in his mind, daydreaming about his boyhood in Blanchard. "The woods," wrote one of Murrow's biographers, "became a symbol, the memory of a rough sort of Eden."[42]

How was it that Murrow could see timber country as an Eden when the entirety of this landscape seemed to serve only the ends of employers? The answer is that many of the families who came to call the Northwest woods home never acquiesced to lumbermen's view of land nor submitted to the control they attempted to exert. They found community in hardscrabble towns, pride in the work, and beauty in the industrial forests. They developed their own sense of place.

2

"The Prodigal Yield
of the Surrounding Hills"

It was sometime in the fall of 1913 when Angelo Pellegrini arrived in McCleary, a small company town hidden in the forested hills that roll across the southern edge of Washington's Olympic Peninsula, a lonesome place that, even today, many Northwesterners simply call "out there." Though located just sixty miles from the state capital of Olympia and one hundred miles from Seattle, getting to the town was an arduous undertaking, involving a day's-long train ride over a precipitously built railroad spur often obstructed by windfallen timbers, landslides, and the occasional elk herd. Weather could make the town feel even more isolated. Most months of the year, the peninsula is covered in thick mists that render the landscape smaller and more confining than it actually is. In the fall, when Pellegrini arrived, the rains are even heavier, and the days short and cold, which makes this place feel even lonelier.

But those very same rains create rich forests that hold the potential to redeem the dreariness of the landscape. On average, the peninsula receives 120 inches of rainfall per year, and fed by near-constant precipitation, trees here grow to incredible heights. Their crowns interconnect in thick canopies that block out most light from above, save for thin crepuscular rays that light up the forest floor much like sunbeams streaming through stained-glass windows illuminate the darkest Gothic cathedrals.

That, at least, is the forest as it exists in some parts today. The forest Pellegrini encountered was much different, a product of the lumbermen's new empire. In the decade prior to his arrival, capitalism had blazed a clearcut across much of the peninsula's southern edge and funneled its natural wealth off to distant markets in Seattle, Chicago, New York, and even as far away as

London and Hong Kong. Looking out the window as his train pulled into McCleary, Pellegrini would have seen a landscape defined less by its fecundity and more by its emptiness, as naked and uninspiring as the driest desert. Only the stumps rising from black mud and giant piles of branches sheared from trees as they were wrenched from the earth would've given him any hint at all that bareness was not the natural state of this place. Even the delicate scent of fir would've been replaced by the sharp smell of axle grease used to lubricate the giant machines partly responsible for shaping the scene that unfolded before him.

McCleary's forests may have been a product of industrial capitalism, but the town itself paradoxically looked like it belonged in some premodern era. To even call early twentieth-century McCleary a town is to stretch the very meaning of the word. It was more a collection of poorly built shacks sitting alongside muddy ditches and the main railroad line. The church on the south end of town had been built more as a matter of routine than act of devotion, and the peeling paint on the adjacent one-room schoolhouse suggested that education wasn't afforded much more consideration. Even the town's founder and namesake, Henry McCleary, was more feudal lord than twentieth-century industrialist. "A good kingdom is better than a poor democracy," he was fond of saying, and the loggers and sawyers he employed were among the poorest-paid workers in an industry known for poor wages. The only real sign of modernity in McCleary was the sour smell in the air that came from the smoke that billowed out of the two sawmills on the north end of town.[1]

Though just ten years old when he came to the Northwest, Pellegrini was still perceptive enough to understand that he'd lived, in his words, "a marginal existence." He'd been born on a tenant farm in Italy's Tuscan countryside where decades of overtilling had pulled the life from the earth, making it impossible for his family to meet their obligation to their landlord. Food was just as difficult to find as economic security. Every evening, Pellegrini's mother would gather her family around the dinner table, dutifully make the sign of the cross, hand each child a piece of stale bread with a thin sliver of Parmesan tucked inside, and say, "*Bisogna fare a miccino col formaggio perché ce n'è poco*" [We must take the cheese in tiny bites because we have so little of it]. What little hope Pellegrini had for the future rested entirely with his father, who two years earlier had left for America and found a job working on McCleary's railroad gangs. The letters he wrote back home described the Northwest as a bountiful landscape, teeming with natural wealth and tall trees, and promised that soon, once he'd saved enough money and could afford passage for his family, they'd be able to join him in what he called this "terrestrial paradise."[2]

Given the cold realities of McCleary, it's easy to imagine that Pellegrini was deeply disappointed when he finally laid eyes on timber country. Here was a place that was the opposite of the terrestrial paradise his father had promised in nearly every way, where nature had been replaced with the malignant realities of the early twentieth-century resource-extraction economy, where clearcuts had replaced dense forests, and where ugly machines made of steel and iron dominated the visible landscape.

At least that's how many of us in the twenty-first century might see it. But landscapes are as much products of perception as material realities, and to understand what Pellegrini saw, we have to try and think like an early twentieth-century working-class immigrant.

For Pellegrini, who'd known only poverty and Tuscany's infertile soils, McCleary's forests "awed and bewildered." Thick vines of blackberries and bushes full of salmonberries and huckleberries exploded to life on the edges of clearcuts, and Pellegrini "went to the forest every day and returned home laden with its precious fruit." Game roused from piles of logging waste "provided much of the meat for the dinner table." And his family's cellar was "always well stocked with jams, jellies, nuts, and fruit gathered in the woods." The wages Pellegrini's father earned on McCleary's railroad gang were only nominally better than what he'd earned as a Tuscan tenant farmer, and in pure economic terms, the family was still poor. But in another sense, they were wealthier than they'd ever been. In McCleary, Pellegrini wrote, "It seemed possible to live on the prodigal yield of the surrounding hills for no more effort than was required in gathering it. . . . In less than a year after our arrival we were rich."[3]

What Pellegrini and his family discovered in timber country was something that had long eluded them in the sun-cracked and lifeless fields of Italy: "*abbondanza*" [abundance].[4]

Like the Pellegrinis, many of the families who came to live and work in timber country in the early twentieth century encountered ramshackle towns, shabby housing, and poor wages. But they also discovered abundance in the surrounding forests—forests dense with berries and game that made it possible to survive, if not thrive in the lumbermen's new empire. Subsistence wasn't the only thing they found in the woods. They discovered opportunities for additional market activities they used to supplement poor wages and opportunities for recreation that lumbermen rarely provided. With the exception of wage labor, nothing did more to shape the way people in early

twentieth-century Northwest woods understood the forest and their relationship to it more than day-to-day life in these hardscrabble towns. The forests
became central to their survival, part of their identities, and the foundation
of their communities.

What's particularly remarkable is that the very forests that early twentieth-
century timber workers and their families described as teeming with life and
opportunity had been significantly altered by industrial activity. Because of
the influence of the late twentieth-century environmental movement, many
of us in the twenty-first century think of industrial forests as dead, lifeless
spaces. The experiences of people in early twentieth-century timber country
suggest a need to question that assumption. Like Pellegrini, workers and their
families were able to survive off nature, not in spite of the forests' industrial
transformation but because of it, and the abundance they discovered owed
a lot to the ways logging had reshaped the woods. Like a blackberry vine
twisting through a piece of logging equipment long abandoned on the forest
floor, the human, natural, and industrial worlds grew together in the company towns and logging camps of the early twentieth-century Northwest.

Company-Town Geography

As Pellegrini had discovered on his train ride to McCleary, isolation was one
of the defining features of the Northwest logging industry's company-town
system. That isolation was something Clark and Mary Kinsey also understood
well. Between 1914 and 1945, the Kinseys routinely traveled to the farthest
edges of timber country to photograph logging operations for lumbermen
who wanted pictures for trade journals and company posterity. The Kinseys
were often the first choice for this work because they offered instantaneous
photographic development—at least by the standards of the early twentieth century. While this gave them an edge in the strangely hypercompeti-
tive world of for-commission early twentieth-century photographers, it also
meant they had to haul hundreds of pounds of developing chemicals, metal
plates, cameras, tripods, and photographic paper into hard-to-reach camps.
Sometimes, the Kinseys made it to an assignment by way of a speeder, the
colloquial name workers gave the small railroad cars that traveled into camps
and towns. But logging railroads were primarily intended to ferry workers
into the woods and siphon lumber out, and rarely was there extra room for
two photographers and their equipment. So much of the time the Kinseys
hiked dozens of miles to camps, following game trails up steep hillsides,
walking rail lines down into valleys and across the rickety trestles spanning

rivers, the entire time weighed down like two pack animals carrying rucksacks bursting at the seams with equipment.[5]

The Kinseys were not crusaders, even if they were contemporaries of some of the great social-documentary photographers of the early twentieth century, like Lewis Hine and Dorothea Lange. Most of the ten thousand pictures they took over the course of their careers were impersonal portraits of equipment and logging layouts. Still, the Kinseys seem to have had at least some interest in documenting the remoteness of the places they visited, perhaps, as a means of understanding the challenges of life in timber country or maybe simply as a way to record their own challenges in reaching their assignments. Regardless of the reasons, the Kinseys frequently went out of their way to snap pictures that captured the isolation of camps, struggling up many more miles of hillsides to find a small opening that would allow them to capture the vastness of the landscape.[6]

Many of the Kinsey photographs (figures 2.1 and 2.2) reveal something of the way timber country's geography shaped understandings of nature and

Figure 2.1. Pacific National Lumber Company, town of National, southeast Pierce County, Washington, n.d., possibly 1920s. Clark Kinsey Photographs, Special Collections, CKK0483, University of Washington Libraries, Seattle.

Figure 2.2. Clemons Logging Company camp, Washington, ca. 1930. Clark Kinsey Photographs, Special Collections, CKK01998, University of Washington Libraries, Seattle.

community for the people who lived and worked in the Northwest woods: quite simply, people here had to rely on the forest and one another because there was nothing else for them to rely on. Perhaps, more than any other historical source, these pictures convey the insignificance of humans in this landscape. When seen from the distant hillsides where the Kinseys set up their cameras, the towns are barely visible but for the thin columns of steam rising from the mills at the towns' centers. The rail lines in the hills are just as imperceptible. Often the only way in or out of a camp, these lines were hastily built, frequently rendered inoperable by inclement weather, mudslides, and avalanches and, at best, offered only a tenuous connection to the outside world.

The pictures the Kinseys took of camps closer up (figures 2.3 and 2.4) reveal another distinctive feature of timber country's geography that also shaped working peoples' relationship to the forest: in most of these towns no clear lines demarcated the human and nonhuman worlds. The camps taper off into the woods and gradually disappear into the mist-covered hilltops. Towns weren't so much built as woven into the forest. Buildings were tucked into small openings or dropped wherever the ground was clear enough and flat enough. The view from the front window of a home was typically the single-track rail line running through town, and the view from the back was most often acres of dense trees, making it not quite clear where the town ended and the forest began.

Figure 2.3. Simpson Logging Company railroad logging camp 7, Grays Harbor, Washington, ca. 1928. Clark Kinsey Photographs, Special Collections, CKK0764, University of Washington Libraries, Seattle.

Figure 2.4. Donovan-Corkery Logging Company railroad logging camp, Wishkah River Valley, Washington, ca. 1928. Clark Kinsey Photographs, Special Collections, CKK01917, University of Washington Libraries, Seattle.

Many memoirs written by the people who lived in these camps also describe a world where the boundary between the human and nonhuman realms was porous, both figuratively and literally. Rain and wind pushed their way through the cracks of homes, as did bugs and rodents. Deer routinely wandered through camp and tangled their antlers in the clotheslines stretching across people's porches. Squirrels and raccoons took up residence in the hollows under buildings. When a family of skunks moved in beneath the school Sam Churchill attended in a company town in northwest Oregon, the teacher instructed students to "tiptoe in and out" and "not make any sudden loud noises which would frighten the skunks and cause them to really smell up the place." Eventually, Churchill remembered, "the skunk family became good neighbors." Churchill's teacher was less accommodating when two of his classmates showed up one day with a bear cub they'd found in the woods. "We no longer have a school at the Western Cooperage Camp," Churchill recalls her saying, "we have a zoo."[7]

While people across timber country could probably share a story similar to Churchill's, it was likely workers' wives who were most conscious of a camp's isolation and the permeable boundaries between the human and nonhuman worlds. Like working-class women elsewhere, working-class women in logging camps were tasked with raising children, cooking, and housekeeping. Many also had to add routine medical care to their list of responsibilities. Hahn Neimand was born in a small logging camp in southern Oregon's Siskiyou Mountains, and she explained that the nearest doctor was at least a day's travel away, which meant her mother was regularly "stitching up wounds and delivering babies."[8]

Even activities less dramatic than childbirth posed unique challenges for women in timber country. Preparing the morning's coffee started with chopping enough wood to get the fire in the stove going, followed by a trip to the nearest creek for water. When she then opened a sack of flour to make breakfast, she hoped not to find a mouse or rat staring back at her. Once her husband was off to work and her children off to school, it was on to more wood chopping or a return to the creek to do laundry. Many of the pictures the Kinseys took of families outside their home show a broom resting against a porch support or in a corner (figure 2.5). The broom may be an easy detail to overlook, but it was indispensable to a woman in the Northwest woods, as important a part of her domestic labor as a saw was to her husband's wage labor. That broom was her first and often only line of defense against the nature that invaded her family's home, the mouse droppings that collected in corners, the mud tracked inside by her husband's boots, and the pollen that settled on nearly every surface during spring blooms.

Figure 2.5. Family outside their home in a Manley-Moore Lumber Company camp, Pierce County, Washington, ca. 1927. Note the broom perched on the right side of the picture. The broom was a timber-country housewife's first and often only line of defense against the dirt, dust, and pollen that invaded her family's home. Clark Kinsey Photographs, Special Collections, CKK0350, University of Washington Libraries, Seattle.

Those photographs of families reveal more than just the challenges of domestic labor, though. The pictures the Kinseys took from afar of company towns and lumber camps suggest life in these places was lonely and difficult, and in some sense that's accurate. But the pictures the Kinseys took of people closer up tell a somewhat different story (figures 2.6, 2.7, and 2.8). The people in these images appear content, even happy. There are multiple ways to explain this. Most timber camps were so remote that a visit from an outsider, any outsider, was cause for excitement and celebration. Moreover, by the 1920s the Kinseys had become something of regional celebrities, and people put on their best clothes and best faces when the couple visited. Even so, listen to the voices of people who lived in these tiny camps, and you'll hear stories that suggest the smiles on their faces were more than just performances for the cameras. "Mom liked the community of it," remembered Neimand. "Nobody had any real money, so they did lots of getting together. . . . Mom talked about how many kids there were, and there were lots of babies and, of course, that made everybody happy."[9]

Figure 2.6. Boys on steps of their home, unidentified railroad logging camp, 1928. Clark Kinsey Photographs, Special Collections, CKK0765, University of Washington Libraries, Seattle.

Figure 2.7. Children and their teacher in front of their school, St. Paul & Tacoma Lumber Company, Camp 1, Pierce County, Washington, n.d., possibly 1930s. Clark Kinsey Photographs, Special Collections, CKK0632, University of Washington Libraries, Seattle.

Figure 2.8. Family at Goodyear Logging Company camp, Clallam County, Washington, ca. 1919. Clark Kinsey Photographs, Special Collections, CKK0222, University of Washington Libraries, Seattle.

"We Were Poor But Never Hungry"

A major reason people were often content with camp life is because they rarely had to worry about their material needs. Like Pellegrini, Neimand remembered a bounty in the forests surrounding her home: "We were poor but never hungry," she said. The material needs of timber workers and their families were met not because of employers' policies but in spite of them. Lumbermen's approach to the families in their camps ranged from benign neglect to indifference, and this shaped every aspect of company-town life, basic subsistence most of all. Because of country musician Tennessee Ernie Ford, who famously sang of owing his soul to the company store, we tend to associate company stores with company towns. Yet, stores ranked among the many town features that lumbermen deemed an extravagance, and many camps in the Northwest woods simply didn't have them. Employers, instead, instructed families to order grains and durable goods from one of the large mail-order catalogues popular in the early twentieth century, like Sears, Roebuck, and Company or Montgomery Ward, and then hope their shipment arrived in a timely manner, which it rarely did. Towns often ran cookhouses for single workers, but when meals could cost the bulk of a day's wages, many men, single and married alike, preferred to look to the woods to fill their bellies.[10]

Spring marked the beginning of an annual pattern of subsisting off the forest. The end of winter can easily go unnoticed in the Northwest, where the heavy rains of late February continue well into April. The start of spring does bring increasingly longer days and warmer temperatures, though, which gently pull the forest from the dead months of winter. Those lengthening days also signaled to people living in lumber camps that after months of surviving on dried and canned goods, the first fresh foods of the year had become available. Ruth Manary lived much of her life in the logging camps of coastal Oregon, and she fondly remembered the early days of spring when people in her camp scoured the forest floor for berries, mushrooms, lady fern fiddleheads, sorrel, and edible roots, all of which she called the "gourmet food in our backyard." Manary was often on the lookout for morels, almond-colored mushrooms with a nutty flavor. If morels proved elusive, as they so often do, Manary considered camas a good consolation. Long central to Northwestern Native diets and economies, camas is a shrub that grows to about three feet high and in the spring explodes with brilliantly colored flowers. Buried in the earth beneath those flowers is a far plainer-looking bulb that when boiled or roasted turns from gummy and tart to tender and sweet. Depending on where and when it was picked, camas bulbs could be so sweet that they are used in place of sugar, which could be hard to come by in most logging camps.[11]

Spring also transformed waterways into crucial spaces of subsistence. The Northwest's rivers run low and clear for much of the winter, starved for the precipitation that falls as snow at higher elevations. The spring sun melts that snow and releases a rush of water, turning rivers from gin-clear trickles into torrents. Anglers in the Northwest refer to the color a spring river takes on as "steelhead green" because the deep emerald hue of a swelling waterway functions as a signal to anadromous fish congregated in the brackish water of estuaries that it's time to sprint upriver to the pebble beds of their natal spawning grounds. People in timber country celebrated the first returns of spring steelhead and Chinook alongside morels and camas. Remembered Sam Churchill of the Oregon camp where he grew up, "It wasn't unusual for half the one-room's school's enrollment of eight pupils to sneak out on a warm spring day and go fishing."[12]

Sometime in June, the rains of spring relent, and the days grow almost arctic in length. While the extended days of summer sun can be a refreshing change from the dark of winter, summer sun dries out the forest floor and returns rivers to trickles, making mushrooms, camas, and fish harder to find. In these months, people in company towns turned their attention to the vegetables they grew near their homes. "Clearing a place among the stumps for a small garden was regarded as a necessity," wrote Ted Goodwin, an itinerant preacher who traveled the lumber camps of southwest Washington. What was basic necessity to some was pure joy to others. As a child in the northern California town of Hilt, Louise Wagenknecht remembered joyfully running through "small dirt paths between raised vegetable beds" in her neighbors' gardens lined by "Swiss chard with leaves the size of palm fronds and parsley so lush and green that we picked off little pieces and nibbled them, the fragrance shooting up into our sinuses."[13]

Summer also brought the ripening of salmonberries, wild blueberries, and blackberries, which were widely celebrated throughout the Northwest woods. The blackberry most people are familiar with is the Himalayan varietal, an introduced, invasive, and excessively seedy species that pales in comparison to the varietal more commonly found in early twentieth-century woods, the Pacific or trailing blackberry. "Boy, oh boy!" remembered Ralph Darby when asked about picking blackberries around the Vancouver Island logging camp where he lived and worked. "We'd fill washtubs full!" People in logging camps would often spend entire weekend mornings in large groups, combing the edges of forests where blackberries grew and return to their homes in the afternoon to make preserves and pies. Melda Buchanan often organized those berry-picking parties. She lived in the same camp as Darby and shared his enthusiasm. Blackberries were "one of the biggest treats of our life," she remembered.[14]

The blackberries of late August and early September were prologue to the bounty of fall, the season everyone in timber country seemed to wait for. Northwesterners living in urban centers, today as in the past, tend to look on the shortened days of September with some regret and bemoan the weeks ahead, when dark clouds will again soak the landscape in the perpetual grayness this region is known for. But rural Northwesterners have long had a less-dour view of fall and have seen it as a time when the forests come alive. Rivers again swell with fall rains and bring new runs of anadromous fish. Small game animals start venturing out from the thickets where they've been hiding all summer, looking to pack on fat before winter. Ungulates enter the initial phases of the rut, their breeding season. Blacktail bucks, which are nocturnal for most of the year, shed the velvet from their antlers and start cruising the daylight woods in search of does, and the wraith-like bugles of

Roosevelt bull elk challenging one another for dominance in the herd fill the forest hollows.

The opportunity to hunt normally reclusive game was reason enough for people in the Northwest woods to get excited about fall and again an occasion for children old enough to carry a rifle or shotgun to duck out of school. Rabbit and grouse provided easy targets and an equally easy meal. Venison also filled the table of many families throughout the fall months. In October 1920, the *Camp and Mill News* (Seattle, WA), one of the many small newspapers that circulated throughout logging camps, reported that seventy-five deer had been taken by the residents of Bordeaux, Washington. "We ate a lot of deer meat in those days," a woman who lived in British Columbia timber country in the 1920s told an interviewer. "It was a necessity. We did everything imaginable with it—canned it, fried it, baked it, bottled it."[15]

Canned venison may not sound particularly appetizing, but it was among the many things people canned in the Northwest woods as winter approached, and they prepared for the sparse months ahead. The winter months are among the most difficult times to survive in the Northwest woods. Because the region is in a high northern latitude, the days become quite short when winter begins, and colder, filled with unrelenting rains in the lower elevations and regular snows up higher. The berries that in the summer months grew in excess on the edges of clearcuts disappear, and most game animals become reclusive. To subsist through the lean months of winter, people in the Northwest woods often relied on goods they'd preserved, pickled, and fermented in the waning days of the fall. In fact, they appear to have canned anything that would fit through the mouth of a jar, including but not limited to preserves made from berries harvested earlier in the year; the last vegetables in their garden; rabbit; grouse; and the aforementioned venison. When proper canning jars couldn't be found, people in the Northwest woods made do in other ways. One former resident of a southern Oregon logging community recalled that people in his town saved liquor bottles and patent-medicine jars and "filled them with fruit and sealed them with cloth by dipping them in sealing wax." Canning was so central to life in the early twentieth-century Northwest woods that besides abandoned logging equipment rusting into the earth, jar remnants remain the most ubiquitous physical evidence of life in the camps. A recent archeological investigation of a St. Paul & Tacoma Lumber Company camp in western Washington discovered 635 artifacts at the former camp site, 350 of which were pieces of glass jars that, researchers determined from makers' marks, were used in the canning process.[16]

The jars of preserves, vegetables, and game lining the simple plank shelves of a family's home represented more than just a winter survival strategy, though. Canned goods, alongside the vegetables from their gardens, fish in the rivers, game in the hills, and berries in the forest also represented economic independence. The lumber market of the early twentieth century was notoriously erratic. Full-time employment was never certain, and even when the market was good, wages were never high enough to guarantee a family's survival. Hunting, fishing, gardening, and forest foraging liberated timber-working communities from the vagaries of the market and freed them from their dependence on wages. The tiny towns strewn across the Northwest woods may have, indeed, been the antithesis of the working men's paradises common in other industries, but as both Pellegrini and Neimand had found, there was an abundance here that allowed for some measure of freedom and autonomy.

Bark Harvesting, Trapping, Beekeeping, and Moonshining

Of the many things a visitor to an early twentieth-century lumber camp might have noticed, one surely would've been the staggering number of things hanging from peoples' porches. Some of these things would've made sense to anyone, regardless of where they came from, like clothes washed in the nearby creek and drip-drying in the warmth of the noon sun. Other things might've looked odd to a visitor from a city but would've seemed perfectly normal to someone from a rural community, like the hindquarters of a recently killed deer hanging in the shade until cool enough to be butchered. Other things, though, would've made little sense to anyone not from timber country, like the long, thin, silver-gray strips of bark hanging next to the recently washed laundry on clotheslines.

Those strips of bark gently fluttering in the forest breezes came from the cascara tree, and they were evidence that, alongside subsistence, the forest provided families in timber country with opportunities for additional economic activity they used to supplement a husband's wages and further decrease reliance on their employers. A subspecies of buckthorn usually found on the sunnier south-facing slopes of hillsides, cascara (or chittem, as it's also known locally) is a deciduous shrub covered in a bark that when stripped, dried, and processed into a powder acts as a powerful laxative. Sometime in the late nineteenth century, pharmacists in Portland, Seattle, and Vancouver began shipping cascara powder to Europe. By the early twentieth century the export market had grown so large that pharmacists were

Figure 2.9. Logger Archie Adams (left) with beehives at Simpson Logging Company, Camp 5, Mason County, Washington, ca. 1940. Clark Kinsey Photographs, Special Collections, CKK0770, University of Washington Libraries, Seattle.

willing to buy as much as people could harvest. "We ranged far and wide to find it," remembered Leo Lind, a logging railroad worker from Nehalem, Oregon. Like many people in timber camps, Lind and his family stored up bags of dried cascara bark and sold them to local pharmacists on the family's periodic visits to town throughout the year.[17]

Jars of honey marked for sale to grocers often accompanied the sacks filled with cascara. Many people in camps purloined honey from what they called "bee trees," hives in cedar stumps easily identified by the marks of bears trying to claw their way to the honeycomb inside. Others cobbled together their own hives from scrap lumber and placed them near clearcuts where bees pollinated the wildflowers that blossomed every spring and summer (figure 2.9). Employers and camp foremen were largely indifferent to activities like cascara harvesting but tended to take a dimmer view of beekeeping because it posed potential health threats. In 1927 the Oregon-American Lumber Company ordered one of its employees to dismantle his beehive because, as a letter to the employee stated, your bees "run amok" and when "thoroughly aroused" had stung animals and children in the camp. The employee responded that surely the company was mistaken. His were "nice peaceable bees," and they never injured anyone "unless the other person starts the argument."[18]

The sale of pelts from beavers caught in the trap lines strung in the more placid and slow-moving portions of rivers also added to a family's income, as did the even more lucrative cougar pelts. Well through the 1950s most state and provincial game departments sought to limit predation by encouraging cougar hunting through bounty payments. Cougar hunting could be lucrative but rarely reliable. Among the rarest-seen animals in the Northwest woods, cougars possess a keen sense of smell and even keener sense of hearing, which allow them to slip away from approaching hunters, sight unseen. Few were as successful as Cecil "Cougar" Smith, a logger from Oyster River, British Columbia, who earned his nickname by killing an estimated one thousand cougars between 1900 and 1940. For each cat he killed, Smith collected a $40 bounty from the provincial game department, sold the skins to taxidermists for $10 each and the skulls to museums and collectors for another $5 apiece.[19]

The most common form of supplemental market activity in the Northwest woods was likely bootlegging and moonshining. Of course, determining the extent of any underground economy is a difficult task, and timber country's illicit liquor trade is no exception. But if anecdotal evidence is any guide, Northwest timber workers were as soaked in shine as they were the region's frequent rains. Even before Prohibition began in the United States in 1920, loggers were widely known to hide stills in the woods as a way around the bans most employers placed on alcohol in towns. Prohibition only encouraged more workers to take up moonshining. "When the nation went dry," remembered one man living in the Northwest woods, his town "went wet." Many American timber workers discovered that their isolated camps, far removed from the prying eyes of law enforcement, provided the ideal location for unlawful alcohol production. Several memoirs and oral histories tell of people tripping over barrels of liquor and beer hidden in the woods. Town postmasters recalled suddenly being asked to place orders for large sacks of sugar, the main ingredient used in mash. In 1928 a fire broke out in the Pacific Lumber Company's town of Rio Dell in northern California. The company exhausted its water supply fighting the fire, and the town appeared to be lost. It was only saved because of the efforts of Rio Dell's sizeable Italian immigrant community, who broke open barrels of wine illegally fermented in their cellars and doused the fire. Meanwhile, British Columbian loggers discovered that there was money to be made running Canadian spirits across the border.[20]

Like gardening, hunting, fishing, and forest foraging, activities like cascara harvesting, beekeeping, trapping, and moonshining shielded people in lumber camps from the uncertainties of the timber market and made it possible for workers to support families on the meager wages paid out by companies, orienting their social lives more toward the woods than to their employers. Work in the capricious early twentieth-century Northwestern timber industry could come and go, and mills could be shuttered as quickly as they'd been built, but through activities like these, people in the Northwest woods knew the forests would always be there to support them.

Working-Class Recreation

The forests also served as important recreational spaces for timber workers and their families. This was partly because housing in most camps discouraged people from spending much time indoors. There was "a lot of outdoor activity" remembered Shevlin, Oregon, resident Lois Gumpert. "Our houses were so small so everybody played outdoors." This was also because employers' frugality didn't leave much room for recreational facilities and company-sponsored activities. On Saturday nights a camp superintendent might make room in the company offices for a bridge game, though people had to bring their own playing cards. Companies sometimes hosted picnics but only on the rare occasions when a midwestern lumberman journeyed to the Northwest to survey his holdings and tour his camps and attempt to convince workers of his benevolence. There was one exception to employers' general lack of enthusiasm toward company-sponsored recreation: baseball. Like many industrialists in the twentieth century, lumbermen promoted baseball as a way to facilitate the Americanization of immigrant workers. Baseball was also cheap. It only required minimal equipment, and a clearcut could easily be transformed into a playing field. Employers were so committed to promoting baseball that they often gave employees who played on a company's team time off to practice or travel for games, which may explain why baseball was popular among many workers, as well.[21]

But for the most part, workers and their families were on their own when it came to recreation, just as they were on their own for nearly everything else. Even so, families seemed not to really notice that their employers provided few recreational opportunities because the forests provided plenty of amusements. Children, in particular, recalled that there was much to do in the woods. Gumpert fondly remembered the first snow of the year when the company's blacksmith would make skis for the children, and they would spend their days racing down the steep slopes of the High Cascade country. In the heat of the summers, those same children would crowd into the local swimming hole at the base of those slopes, in small plunge pools made by the cool waters of the spring-fed rivers. It wasn't just children who found respite in nature. Cookhouse waitress Anna Lind took joy hiking among the trees, which she described as "tall and beautiful."[22]

Things like Lind's walks through the woods were clearly forms of recreation. But just as often, the outdoor activities of people in timber country blurred the lines between recreation and subsistence, work and play, thereby suggesting that at least in the Northwest woods, people didn't draw hard boundaries between consumptive and productive uses of nature. At least Frederick Bracher didn't. A timber worker from Oregon's southern Willamette Valley, Bracher had a particular affinity for the North Umpqua, an emerald-green river that twists its way through lichen-lined canyons in Oregon's southern Cascades. Starting in the 1920s, the river became a premier destination for upper-class sportsmen from around the country, if not the world, something Bracher bemoaned. Looking at the finely dressed anglers in tweed jackets carrying split-bamboo fly rods that might cost a timber worker like him several months' wages, Bracher appeared to draw a distinction between the way he and these more-affluent sportsmen used the river. He wanted "no part of such effete pastimes," he stated. He was a "pot fisherman" and fished primarily to put food on the table. And yet, even as he rhetorically worked to separate himself from upper-class sportsmen seemingly more interested in style than substance, Bracher, too, remarked that what he enjoyed most about being on the water was that "fishing was a simple, natural pleasure." Bracher also expressed a concern for the aesthetics of fishing, making him sound very much like the upper-class sportsmen he grumbled about. He, for instance, dismissed hatchery-reared fish as "too synthetic" and admitted to enjoying fishing "Zane Grey style," a reference to the famous author of Westerns who popularized fly fishing in the West. "My all-time best trout," Bracher recalled, "was a seventeen-inch cutthroat, caught on a fly after a long cast across a pool."[23]

Louise Wagenknecht would also have agreed that the lines demarcating subsistence and recreation blurred in timber country. In her two memoirs of life in the Northwest woods, Wagenknecht emphasized the necessity of hunting and fishing to her family's survival. Yet, she was equally insistent that the hunting trips she followed her father on did as much to nourish her and her family's souls as it did their bellies. "What was really important," she wrote, was "the sitting, the listening, the sight of a doe clipping cautiously on a trail below us, or a jay swooping down, giving away our position with its shrieks." Pictures printed in camp newspapers echo Wagenknecht's belief that workers and their families derived great joy and pleasure from the same activities that sustained them. Men stand before a recently shot buck and grin ear-to-ear or proudly pose for the camera holding a salmon as long as they are tall. Women stand before baskets of blackberries, grinning just as joyfully.[24]

Those pictures reveal another reason why hunting, fishing, and foraging can't be narrowly categorized as just subsistence activities: rarely is an individual pictured alone. Those men standing in front of a buck stand close, with their arms around one another. Those women before the baskets of blackberries affectionately rest their heads on each other's shoulders. Rarely was a trip to the forest for morels, cascara, or anything else ever taken alone, and the communal aspect of these activities is what often made them enjoyable. Indeed, the central theme that emerges in nearly all the memoirs, oral histories, and recollections of life in the tucked-away timber camps of the early twentieth century is not the loneliness and isolation people felt but, rather, the deep sense of closeness and community they developed through their common use of the forests.

Such ideas figured heavily in Irma Lee Emmerson's memoir of her life in a logging camp near Coos Bay, Oregon. The people she lived with in camp, she said, became her "family," each one "hell-bent on helping you at great inconvenience to themselves." Sometimes this simply meant sharing some berries picked from the forest. In more serious times this could mean tending to a man who'd been injured in the woods or, worse, comforting a wife whose husband was killed in an accident. But what Emmerson made clear was that whatever challenges people in the Northwest woods faced, they faced them together, every person connected as much by proximity to one another as closeness to the forest. Some of Emmerson's fondest memories were of nights when people in camp gathered around a bonfire. Women brought baked goods laden with berries from the forest and sweetened with camas and honey, children worn out from playing in the forest all day gently dozed in their mothers' laps, and men swapped fishing tips and told stories of the proverbial one that got away while, it's easy to imagine, passing around a bottle of moonshine made in the still up the nearest creek. There, Emmerson recalled, the "dark green of Douglas firs covering the hills closed protectively around us."[25]

The picture Emmerson paints of the hills covering her community could easily be dismissed as mere poetics if not for how central the forest was to their lives. It was as much a part of this community as any person, did as much to take care of them as any relative, and was something people cared for as deeply and lovingly as any friend. In timber country the boundaries between people and nature disappeared much like the smoke from the campfire that Emmerson and her friends gathered around vanished into the cool forest night.

Logging and the Ecology of the Forest

Listening to people like Emmerson speak, it's easy to forget that the forests they described as lush and verdant had been significantly altered by logging. Even more confounding is that by the 1920s many outsiders visited the Northwest woods and saw a devastated landscape. Critiques of the environmental effects of logging predate the 1920s, of course. They can be heard in records left by eighteenth-century British settlers, the nineteenth-century transcendentalists, and early twentieth-century conservationists. But in the 1920s criticisms of logging became even more widespread, largely as a result of the expanding rate of automobile ownership. Cars allowed more urban people than ever, middle and working classes alike, to spend their leisure time outdoors, and the rural Northwest, with its salmon-filled rivers and game-filled hills, became a particularly popular destination for hunters and anglers. Yet, those hunters and anglers often didn't like what they saw when they got to timber country: cleared forests, trees burned in fires started by logging equipment, and rivers clogged with broken timber and sheered limbs. Most automobile tourists likely agreed with Stephen Mather, one of the early heads of the National Park Service, who, after his own car trip through Oregon timber country in 1920, told the *Oregonian* (Portland, OR), that much of the state's forest had been reduced to a "bare and desolate" region.[26]

The photos of Clark and Mary Kinsey provide some sense of what people like Mather encountered when they came to the Northwest woods (figures 2.10 and 2.11). Emmerson described the forests surrounding her home as rich and unbroken. These pictures suggest otherwise. Rather than the lush landscapes she described, the industrial forests of the early twentieth-century Northwest—if they could even be called forests anymore—were aggressively stripped of every living thing. Were the pictures in color, the apparent lifelessness of these spaces might be even more dramatic. An unlogged forest is awash in greens, from the dark-olive needles of conifers to the lighter hues of deciduous growth and almost neon lime of lichens. A clearcut is painted in darker hues: solemn browns and dour blacks. As alarming as the scenes in these photos may be, they don't even reveal the full extent of environmental changes that frequently accompanied logging. Landslides sometimes increased as a result of timber harvests, as did fires and wildlife habitat disruptions. Waste and silt washed downhill into rivers, clogging streams and causing floods that interfered with fish migrations. Clearcuts became prime

Figure 2.10. McCormick Lumber Company camp at foot of a logged-off mountain, southwest Lewis County, Washington, n.d., possibly 1920s. Clark Kinsey Photographs, Special Collections, CKK0335, University of Washington Libraries, Seattle.

Figure 2.11. St. Paul & Tacoma Lumber Company, Camp 1, with Mt. Rainier in the background, ca. 1922. Clark Kinsey Photographs, Special Collections, CKK0593, University of Washington Libraries, Seattle.

habitat for all manner of invasive species, from beetles to Scotch Broom, a particularly pernicious shrub that once established is nearly impossible to eradicate. That most logging camps and company towns would be surrounded by clearcuts makes sense. The towns had been built to facilitate aggressive logging, and that's precisely what they did. Still, it's hard to reconcile the descriptions offered by people like Emmerson with what we see in these pictures—or what we *think* we see.[27]

At their core, photographs, forestry reports, and the observations of tourists are stories about nature, and like all stories, they follow a certain narrative arc. Sometimes that arc is stated explicitly, other times it's just implied, but generally it goes like this: forests were created by natural processes that played out gradually over hundreds, if not thousands of years. Industrial logging brought an immediate halt to these processes with a few fell swoops of an axe. In this telling, a clearcut is the end of a long story, the elimination of both history and nature. Many environmentalists in the late twentieth century adopted new ways of describing forests that further entrenched this narrative in public consciousness. They described unlogged forests as "ancient," "primeval," and "prehistoric," suggesting forests had been millennia in the making and that clearcuts amounted to brief moments of hubris that forever and permanently erased that long history from the landscape. The problem with all these stories is that they assume forests are static environments. They ignore long histories of Indigenous forest management in the Northwest and the ways that Native burning and harvests constantly shaped and reshaped forests. The stories also ignore natural processes like fires, floods, landslides, windstorms, and even catastrophic events like volcanic eruptions that did the same. They ignore that forests are and have always been dynamic spaces, always in motion and always changing. This is true of the old-growth forests that latter-day environmentalists venerated, and, perhaps, even more so for the clearcuts they maligned. While there's no denying the destructive potential of industrial logging, especially as it was practiced in the early twentieth century, it's just as true that regenerative processes follow timber harvests. Logging certainly altered nature and the course of the forest's history, but it brought neither to an abrupt end. Because they lived and worked in the woods and saw how these regenerative processes unfolded in the days, months, and years after the trees had been felled, this was something people in timber country understood well, and they told a fundamentally different story about industrial logging and nature, one in which a clearcut was a new beginning, not an ending. Understanding how people like Emmerson could find beauty and bounty in the industrial woodlands of the Northwest requires listening to their stories.

The first thing that someone from early twentieth-century timber country would likely tell you is that "clearcut" is an imprecise term. Despite what the name implies, a clearcut is anything but clear. Even today, with production techniques far more efficient than in decades past, industrial logging leaves a lot behind: sheered limbs, shattered timbers, and bark stripped from trees as they're dragged up hillsides. Somewhat paradoxically, walking through a clearcut can be more challenging than walking through an old-growth forest. Viewed from above, the brush tops of firs and spruces make old-growth groves look impenetrable. But on the ground that same forest is fairly open, save for the clumps of deep-green ferns. A clearcut, on the other hand, is a horizontal labyrinth of gnarled branches, brush, and stumps. Moving across one requires more crawling than walking.

Dead branches and shattered limbs—known as "slash" in the logging industry—drying out on the forest floor pose a significant fire hazard. Companies have, therefore, long collected slash into giant piles that are then burned, typically late in the year when the rains of early winter decrease the likelihood of slash burns erupting into full-blown conflagrations. A forest in the middle of a slash burn is an otherworldly thing. The best place to watch one is from an adjacent hillside, on a day when the clouds blot out the sun. Seen from this vantage, slash fires are little pockets of dancing light that envelop the entire ridge in a soft glow. Smoke billows up from each little fire, creating thick smog that blends into the mountain mists, making it hard to tell where the land ends and the sky begins. It's tempting to liken these fires to funeral pyres, each solemnly marking the death of the forest.[28]

But slash fires are more properly seen as signs of life than symbols of death. If left to rot on the forest floor, slash would eventually decay and return nitrogen to the soil. Slash fires accelerate this process, turning nutrients into ash that is then washed into the earth by rain. If slash fires act as a sort of fertilizer, then the logging process, in a way, functions to till the soil. Trees crashing to the ground, root balls being unearthed, and trees bouncing up hillsides all loosen the ground that has compacted over years of inactivity, ultimately making it easier for new growth to take root. The final and perhaps most important ingredient in the recipe that will make a new forest is light. One of the main reasons an old-growth forest is relatively open on the ground is that so little light penetrates the canopy. Once that canopy is removed through harvests, the sun rays can at last reach the forest floor.[29]

Cleared forests—whether cleared by logging, fire, wind, or insects—go through a process that foresters call succession. No two forests follow the exact same path. Elevation, sun exposure, soil chemistry, rainfall, human intervention, and dozens of other variables affect how this process unfolds. Still, most forests follow a general pattern. First comes what foresters call the pioneer stage, when mosses, lichens, and grasses feed off the nutrients deposited by slash burns and begin covering the earth. These grasses and lichens harbor nitrogen-fixing bacteria that further enrich the soil and set the ecological stage for the next phase of succession, when brushes and shrubs take root. These brushes play a critical role in encouraging later tree growth. All trees need light, but too much light at the wrong time can kill a newly budding tree as surely as plucking it from the ground. The brushes that grow in this second stage let in just enough light to encourage alder and birch growth, which, in turn, provide the right balance of shade and sunlight for coniferous growth—firs, cedars, spruces, and hemlocks. As conifers grow larger, they begin battling deciduous trees for light and real estate. In the Northwest, it's most often conifers that win this battle, and if left undisturbed, they will eventually grow large enough to create a new old-growth-stand structure.[30]

Forest succession is what's long made human life in the Northwest's forests possible. An old-growth forest may be a beautiful thing, but it's also a relatively barren thing, at least in terms of plants and animals that humans can survive on. It's mostly fungi, lichen, mosses, and bugs that live in an old-growth forest; there's simply not enough light to support berries and deciduous growth, which means there's not enough feed for most animals. A regenerating forest, though, is different, teaming with flora and fauna. Small game animals are attracted to brushy growth, where they find shelter and feed. Larger game animals, like deer and elk, wander into regenerating forests to graze on berries, barks, and the tender shoots of budding conifers. This is why Indigenous communities in the Northwest, as elsewhere, routinely burned forests: those burns forced the forests into a succession process that then attracted many of the game animals central to their diets and economies.[31]

In size and scale, Native burning was nothing like early twentieth-century industrial logging. But both did reshape the forest and made it more conducive to survival. Timber workers and their families were conscious of the succession process, even if they never used the term, and often argued that they could survive off the forest precisely because it had been altered by logging. "None of these things can live in the shade. . . . In a big forest deer couldn't find anything to eat," said Vancouver Island logger Joe Cliffe. "But as soon as we cut the forest there were tens of thousands. The salal came back, and the berries, and bits of grass." Indeed, the abundance of deer in recently harvested forests was something that timber workers and their families commented on often, sometimes describing herds so large they moved through clearcuts like herds of migratory caribou. In the early twentieth century, loggers gained a reputation throughout the Northwest as expert hunters, and many upper-class sportsmen paid timber workers to guide them to deer. Timber workers' success during deer season probably had as much to do with their hunting abilities as with the fact that deer were just naturally drawn into industrial forests. Grouse could be even more prolific. After a clearcut there were "grouse on every stump," recalled one logger. Others described grouse flying through the open windows of homes. It wasn't just the game attracted to clearcuts that made subsistence in the Northwest woods possible. The berries timber-working families picked, the camas they harvested, and the cascara bark they stripped all required direct sunlight and, therefore, only grew in cleared forests.[32]

At its core, environmental history argues that humans shape nature, and nature, in turn, shapes human life. The relationship between early twentieth-century timber workers and the forests provides clear evidence of that synergistic relationship. Loggers transformed the forests through their work, and then the altered forests provided resources and spaces those loggers used to both form community and find some autonomy and independence in an industrial system that sought to deny them both. The relationship between people in timber country and the forests was not one of wanton destruction nor unbridled environmental exploitation but, rather, a more complex relationship in which logging altered the forests in ways that made life possible and sometimes even enjoyable. People like Emmerson could see beauty in the logged-over forests precisely because they understood that a clearcut was just a brief moment in time, and very soon the forest would spring back to life. Eva Bailey, who lived in a Vancouver Island logging camp, certainly thought so. Explaining logging, she said, "They'd burn the slash, and the next year you'd never know there'd been a fire gone over it. It was covered in purple fireweed which was absolutely gorgeous. And the next year, you'd see the young trees growing up—they'd seed themselves."[33]

In Pelle's Garden

Angelo Pellegrini would've likely appreciated that description. At the very least, he would dedicate a significant part of his later life to trying to convince people that there was much to admire in landscapes altered by human activity. Like Edward R. Murrow, Pellegrini left the woods in his teenage years and later gained some measure of class mobility and celebrity, even if he never achieved the name recognition of the famed CBS newsman. But while Pellegrini isn't as well known as Murrow, chances are you've directly encountered his ideas, at least if you've ever visited a modern, urban farmers market, shopped at an organic grocer, or dined at a farm-to-table restaurant. Pellegrini left the woods to attend college at the University of Washington in Seattle, where he remained to earn his doctorate in English literature and was ultimately hired as a professor. Though a scholar of Romantic poetry and one of the best lecturers on campus, Pellegrini—or "Pelle" as he was known to students and colleagues—would contribute far more to the field of American gastronomy. In 1948 he assembled several recipes handed down to him by his parents and wrote *The Unprejudiced Palate*. Though published as a cookbook, *Palate* was ultimately more than that. Part autobiography and part condemnation of the fast-food restaurants proliferating in postwar America, Pellegrini's writing sought to teach readers about the virtues of gardening, forest foraging, hunting, and fishing. He encouraged his readers to learn from his earlier life in timber country and rely on nature to fill their tables, rather than the sterile aisles of supermarkets. For Pellegrini it didn't matter that by the late 1940s most Americans lived in cities. Urbanization, like industrial logging, had transformed the environment but not destroyed it, and people could nourish their bellies and their souls if they knew where to look. He implored readers to scour strips of grass and urban parks, where they'd find edible mushrooms, berries, and "esthetic self-development." He asked readers to get their hands dirty gardening in their backyards and engage in "work that activates the bones and sinews and that at the end of the day, week, or month yields something for the worker to behold as entirely his own creation."[34]

In the decades following its publication, *The Unprejudiced Palate* resonated with environmentalists, activists, and chefs who would go on to significantly shape the food culture of the late twentieth and early twenty-first centuries. In the late 1970s the Italian activist Carlo Petrini, frustrated by the expansion of American fast-food chains into his native region of Cuneo, turned to Pellegrini's writings and increasingly began to argue for a food system based on gardening and forest foraging. In 1986 Petrini founded the International Slow Food Movement, an organization dedicated to advancing many of the ideas Pellegrini had advocated. Pellegrini's work also inspired chefs like Alice Waters and James Beard, both of whom popularized organic restaurants, and food writers like Michael Pollan, who criticized industrial food production. Likewise, Pellegrini's work was read by local food activists and small farmers who would create urban gardening programs and lobby city councils to support urban farmers markets. In no small way, modern middle-class urban American food culture has its roots in working-class life in the early twentieth-century Northwest woods.[35]

Pellegrini passed away in 1991, before many of these changes occurred, so we don't know what he thought about the farmers markets and organic grocers that now proliferate in many cities. On the one hand, he might celebrate the fact that so many people are today concerned with knowing where their food comes from and how it was produced (though, as a member of the Communist Party in the 1930s, he might also express some frustration with the poor labor conditions that exist on most farms, even organic ones). On the other hand, Pellegrini might argue that farmers markets and farm-to-table restaurants distort his vision. Pellegrini believed that his life in Mc-Cleary provided lessons about nature and autonomy. Just as he and his family found some measure of independence in the Northwest woods by relying on nature, he wanted postwar Americans to find freedom by cultivating their own gardens and searching their own neighborhoods for food. He most certainly would've bristled at the high prices so often charged for organic food and, more than that, argued that relying on chefs and restaurants, even well-meaning ones promising ethically sourced foods, still functioned as intermediaries distancing people from the landscape.

While Pellegrini's vision may no longer be alive in much of urban, middle-class America, it's still alive and well in working-class timber country. After World War II, most employers in the Northwest woods stopped operating company towns and lumber camps. Workers and their families transitioned to more-permanent communities, yet carried many of the traditions of earlier generations with them, continuing to hunt, fish, and forage, both to keep food on the table in hard times and to find an escape and solace. Like timber workers in the early twentieth century, subsequent generations of timber workers continued to assert that logging altered but did not destroy the forests, and this belief would go on to shape their unions in the Great Depression era, their conservation politics in the postwar era, and their bitter conflict with environmentalists in the late twentieth and early twenty-first centuries. You can get some sense that timber workers today continue to see logging as an activity that shapes but does not destroy forests when you drive the rutted logging roads of the Northwest woods and stop and talk with loggers. If it's the workweek, they may be carrying chainsaws, and if it's a weekend during hunting season, rifles. Ask, and they'll likely explain that both are crucial to how they know and care for the forest.

And what about the industrial labor represented by that chainsaw? To fully understand their relationship to the forest and understanding of place, we now must turn to that, too.

3

"A Goodly Degree of Risk"

When workers left the comfort of their camps and entered the woods to earn their formal pay, they crossed something of an ineffable line running through timber country's geography. Here, at work, the very same woods that sustained them with game, fish, and forage tried to kill them. In the opening decades of the twentieth century, lumbermen dramatically reshaped the productive process in the Northwest's timber industry. New, large, and powerful machines alongside a new managerial regime now facilitated the rapid liquidation of nature and ensured a steady flow of timber from forest to mill to market. Technological and managerial changes were exceptionally good for lumbermen's ledgers and helped transform the Northwest into the world's leading timber producer. But what was good for capital was exceptionally bad for labor. Managers pushed the pace of work, and machines made it possible to conduct logging operations on steep hillsides and muddy swamp bottoms, dangerous places that earlier generations of loggers had avoided. The result was that the accident rate skyrocketed, making logging and sawmilling two of the deadliest industrial occupations in North America by the 1920s. Sawyers sacrificed fingers, hands, and arms to the lumbermen's saws. Loggers were killed or mangled by falling timbers, snapping cables, and catastrophic machine failures. There was no shortage of ways to die in the early twentieth-century Northwest woods. As Dorothy Marie Sherman, a master's student writing her thesis on industrial relations in the Northwest timber industry, observed, "There are not a great number of 'soft' jobs around a lumber camp nor any that do not involve a goodly degree of risk."[1]

Perhaps, no one understood this better than Oiva Wirkkala. As a child of Finnish immigrants who started logging when he was just fourteen and barely big enough to fill out the baggy waxed-canvas pants often worn by Northwest timber workers, Wirkkala had encountered danger nearly every day of his life. Once, a cable attached to a log being hauled from the forest floor slipped loose and snapped back so close to him that he could feel the breeze on his face as it whipped past. Another time, a tree he was felling "barber chaired," splitting forty feet up its base as it toppled, crashing to the ground just an arm's reach from where he stood. Wirkkala would later state, quite matter of factly, that he never knew if he was going to walk out of the woods at the end of a day or be carried out on a stretcher. "It's a rough game, there's no doubt about it," he said.[2]

Wirkkala's closest brushes with death came when he was working as a high climber, the most prestigious and high-paying job in an early twentieth-century logging camp but also the most dangerous. With nothing but three-inch spurs strapped to their boots and a single safety rope tethering them to trees, climbers like Wirkkala ascended to heights of two hundred feet or more to rig spars, the tall trees that held the cables and pulleys central to an early twentieth-century mechanized logging operation. The job required incredible strength, marathon-like stamina, and, perhaps most crucially, a complete fearlessness of heights. Yet, it was rarely falls that killed climbers; there were other, more gruesome ways for them to die. The tops of conifers are extremely flexible, an evolutionary adaptation that allows the tallest timbers to survive through windstorms. To prevent the trees from collapsing under the tremendous loads they'd bear once fully rigged, these wispy tops had to be sawed-off by climbers, and doing so made for the riskiest part of the job (figure 3.1). Unlike workers on the ground, climbers suspended in treetops had nowhere to run if the unexpected happened. Workers were killed when an unexpected breeze pushed a tipping treetop back onto them. Others were crushed to death when the trees they were working split up their base and crushed them between the expanding trunk and safety line. Even when he dispatched a top without incident, a climber was not free from danger. The falling top would force the tree into a wild sway, and climbers had to dig in their spurs as deeply as they could and hold on with all their might to keep from being bucked off.[3]

In the early 1920s, climbers adopted a new technique that ostensibly made topping trees safer. "We shot 'em off with dynamite," Wirkkala explained. It seems like an odd adaptation, the addition of even more risk to an already risky job, and it says something about the nature of the work that explosives had the potential to make the job safer. From the perspective of climbers,

Figure 3.1. High rigger topping a Douglas fir, Clear Lake Lumber Company, Washington, ca. 1912. John D. Cress photograph. Panoramic Photographs, Special Collections, PPC033, University of Washington, Seattle.

though, blasting off tops made a certain sense. With dynamite, they could set the charge and with a long-enough fuse be safely on the ground when the blast ignited, thereby avoiding the dangers of topping by hand. And descending a tree quickly wasn't a problem for most climbers. Like many jobs in the early twentieth-century woods, climbing was part work, part performance. Climbers routinely rappelled down spars at terrifying rates, just for the thrill of it. Dynamite only added to the spectacle, timber country's version of a fireworks show. [4]

But nothing could be taken for granted in the early twentieth-century woods, safety most of all, as Wirkkala might be the first to explain. Wirkkala was working as a climber in a southwest Washington logging camp in the late 1920s. He ascended the spar he'd been tasked with rigging, augured a hole for the dynamite, and lit the fuse, just as he'd done hundreds of times before without incident. Only this time his safety line tangled as he started to descend from the tree. It was a bad spot to be in. Wirkkala had fallen too far to be able to reach up and snuff out the fuse but not far enough to be out of range of the impending blast, and the tangle prevented him from going either up or down. "I wasn't getting panicky yet," Wirkkala remembered. He tried finessing the line, flipping it gently to coax the tangle free. When that failed and with just one or two minutes before the charge went off, Wirkkala "started getting kind of a cold sweat a little bit." He now turned to brute force, trying to yank the tangle free, and that, too, failed. He began to prepare himself for the inevitable and dug his spikes into the trunk as deeply as possible, tucking his head beneath his arms in what was a valiant but likely futile effort to shield himself from the imminent blast. But before he did, he gave the rope one final "really heavy heave." Miraculously, the tangle snapped loose. Wirkkala didn't waste any time after that. He snapped his spurs free and let gravity carry him away from danger, falling ten or fifteen feet at a time, every now and then pulling his safety line taut to slow his fall. About twenty feet from the ground, he kicked his spurs in one last time to slow his descent, sending bark and wood shrapnel flying, and then crashed to earth in a hail of wooded debris. He looked up, just as the "blast went off, and the top went sailing."[5]

Safely on the ground, he stood up and brushed the bark and dust from his shirt. A coworker passed him a tin of Copenhagen, and Wirkkala filled his lower lip with a pinch of chewing tobacco. He then bent down, unbuckled his spurs, slung them over his shoulder, and headed down the landing for the next tree to be rigged. The day was getting late, and there was still more work to do, and it'd take more than a close call with death to keep him from doing it.[6]

Wirkkala's story begins to illustrate the dangers workers encountered in the early twentieth-century woods. But more fundamentally—in his ability to stay calm when danger loomed and in his willingness to immediately return to work once that danger had passed—Wirkkala's story functions as a window into timber country's work culture, one that still exists in many Northwest logging communities today and, quite likely, in many similar working-class and rural contexts that exist outside the middle-class mainstream of modern society, where struggle remains a verity and grit and toughness requirements for survival. It's a culture seeped in notions of independence and autonomy, one that accepts and sometimes celebrates risk and takes immense pride in the work, not in spite of its difficulties and dangers but precisely because of them. It's a culture born of the complex interactions between workers, technology, and nature. When lumbermen adopted new machines and managerial systems in the early twentieth century, they hoped to make the industrial woods function as smoothly and predictably as an assembly line in a factory. But workers understood something that their employers never did: Forests are complex environments, not so easily subordinated to managers and machines, and it was only workers' knowledge of the landscape that allowed this entire industrial system to function. And, if that was the case, then workers came to believe they should have first say in how the forests were managed. Indeed, the industrial union movement of the 1930s and, in a way, the environmental conflicts of the later twentieth century had their origins in the work culture of the early twentieth century and the ways that industrial labor imbued workers with a sense of ownership over the forest.

Wirkkala, though, put this in far simpler terms. Nearer the end of his life and gray-haired and thicker in the midsection now that his days of hard, physical work were well behind him, Wirkkala gave an interview in which he recounted the dangers he encountered on nearly a daily basis. Toward the end of that interview, he then said, "I enjoyed the woods, really." It seems like something of a curious statement, given that death and danger figured so heavily into his memories of work, perhaps explainable as misplaced nostalgia or time's tendency to erase the horrors and troubles of the past. But that's only if you don't understand that for men like Wirkkala, their dignity and power as workers rested in their relationship with the forest.[7]

Mechanized Logging in the Early Twentieth Century

By the early 1920s many Northwest forests ceased to look like forests at all. Complex snarls of cables attached to complicated rigging mechanisms, massive steam-driven engines spewing black smoke from their wood-fired boilers, thousands of miles of railroad track cutting across the land: these things, far more than trees, are what dominated the landscape. The sounds of an early twentieth-century logging operation were just as distinctive and offered audible signs that signaled the forests' industrial transformation. High-pitched whistles, the earth-shaking roar of engines, and frequent shouts of men warning each other of danger turned the woods into a cacophony of industrial clamor. In fact, it may have been the noises of timber production that left the most indelible impressions on the workers who were part of this system.

The loudest clamor came from steam donkeys, massive winches used to pull fallen timbers up hillsides that by the 1920s resembled wild smoke-breathing dragons more than the domesticated pack animals for which they were named (figure 3.2). At rest a donkey engine looked and sounded like a docile thing, several tons of passive black iron that emitted a rhythmic puffing from its stack. But like the huff of a thoroughbred lined up at the starting gate, that rhythmic puffing belied an almost uncontrollable power waiting to be unleashed. The moment the donkey puncher (the crewman operating

Figure 3.2. Donkey engine and crew, Saginaw Timber Company, Washington, n.d., probably early twentieth century. Clark Kinsey Photographs, Special Collections, CKK01336, University of Washington Libraries, Seattle.

the engine) leaned into a giant lever that engaged the machine's haulback drum, the puffing transformed into a baritone growl that shook the earth and rattled any bolts not firmly torqued down, adding a distinctive metallic melody.

Steam donkeys were as integral to early twentieth-century Northwest logging as the internet is to work today. If financial conditions made cut-out-and-get-out logging economically advantageous, the steam donkey made it possible. What the steam donkey did was solve a problem that had long restricted the industry's growth. The first thing that comes to mind when most people think of lumbering is an axe-wielding logger standing next to a tree as it plummets to earth. But felling timber is only one part of a labor-intensive journey that transforms standing trees into market commodities. In fact, felling is the easiest, relatively speaking, part of that journey. Yarding, the process of getting fallen timbers off the forest floor to a deck where they'll be loaded onto mill-bound trains, has long been considered by lumbermen, engineers, and workers the most arduous step in the entire process, "the most frustrating and irritating business that you could imagine," as one lumberman put it. The problem has always been one of rudimentary physics: a large log at rest on the forest floor wants to stay at rest, and it takes an incredible amount of energy to overcome that standing inertia. Up until the late nineteenth century, loggers had relied on waterways, pack animals, and raw determination to wrest trees from the forest, dragging timbers along skids greased with dogfish oil or dropping trees directly into rivers and floating them to mills, time-consuming techniques that limited logging operations to lowland valleys or tracts adjacent to rivers. A few committed teamsters and, one imagines, equally committed oxen had tried to yard timber on the slick slopes of more-mountainous forests, only to find that for every vertical foot of ground they gained, they slid back down two.[8]

The inspiration for change came not from the woods but from the sea. Sometime in 1881 a failed California gold-miner-turned-timber-investor named John Dolbeer was staring out over the small port of Eureka, California, when a ship pulling anchor caught his eye. It was a glancing observation that would revolutionize the logging industry, to say nothing of the forest ecology. Dolbeer salvaged a rusting steam-powered windlass that had once been used to hoist anchors, replaced the machine's chain with a rope, attached the terminal end to a fallen timber, and fired the boiler. The machine coughed to life, and much to Dolbeer's satisfaction, the log began slowly inching its way in. Dolbeer quickly filed a patent, and within a decade every logging camp on the Pacific Coast had replaced real donkeys with "Dolbeer's Donkey." Steam donkeys became so central to logging that many companies invested up to 75 percent of their initial capital or took out sizeable loans to purchase multiple units. Engineers continued to improve on Dolbeer's original design, expanding the size and power of boilers, adding larger haulback drums, and devising new gearing mechanisms. By the time the Lidgerwood Skidder went into production in 1913, steam donkeys had come to look like stationary versions of giant train locomotives, which in a way they were.[9]

Lumber-company owner George H. Emerson explained the advantages of steam engines in the logging process. With Dolbeer's Donkeys, he explained to readers of a prominent industry trade journal, there is "no ground too wet, no hill too steep. . . . They require no stable and no feed, all expense stops when the whistle blows, no oxen killed and no teams to winter. . . . It is easy to see they are a revolution in logging." Emerson might have also added that the steam donkeys allowed companies to log year-round, even in the heaviest rains that turned the forest floors into swamps that animals struggled to cross. And, just as important, steam engines allowed companies to move beyond lowland valleys and log in the mountain hillsides where teamsters and their animals were unwilling or unable to go.[10]

The roar of steam donkeys in an early twentieth-century logging operation were audibly rivaled only by the whine of cables racing through pulleys. Early mechanized operations dragged timbers through the forest using a ground lead, a single cable attached directly to the donkey's haulback drum. Although an improvement over pack animals, timbers yarded on ground leads still hung up on stumps and debris. As donkey engines increased in size and power, lumbermen searched for new cabling systems to make yarding more efficient. The pages of early twentieth-century industry trade journals often read more like technical manuals, with lumbermen explaining in excruciating detail new rigging plans that offered even the slightest increases in speed. By the start of World War I, the industry had largely settled on high-lead systems, complex networks of cables threaded through pulleys hung in spar trees that partially suspended a timber as it was being yarded, allowing it to skid and bounce over obstructions (figure 3.3). The pulleys used in high-lead systems also multiplied the mechanical power of donkey engines, making it possible to move even larger logs up even steeper slopes. By 1920 high-lead systems were capable of dragging logs up 30 percent inclines at more than 750 feet per minute.[11]

Railroads and mills also had to change and keep pace for steam donkeys and high-lead systems to translate into overall production gains. Larger boilers, complex gearing systems, and powerful braking systems developed in the early decades of the twentieth century allowed trains loaded down with

Figure 3.3. Loading logs with spar tree, unidentified logging operation, Washington, n.d., probably 1920s. Darius Kinsey Photograph Collection, Special Collections, KIN041, University of Washington Libraries, Seattle.

tons of freshly cut timber to climb up the most unforgiving grades, take tight turns, and race down mountainsides. Mill owners swapped water- and tide-driven saws for steam turbines capable of turning ever-larger and ever-more aggressive blades spinning on high-speed bearings made from complex alloys. In 1916 the average Washington sawmill produced 6.9 horsepower; by 1929 the average Washington mill produced 844 horsepower. That's the modern equivalent of trading a moped for a Lamborghini.[12]

Again, though, it was the sound of these new mills that often left the most distinct impressions. At the age of fifteen, Egbert S. Oliver went to work in a Cosmopolis, Washington, sawmill, a place he later called "the asshole of civilization, the sink hole of the lumber industry." As Oliver described it, stepping foot in the mill was to cross over into the "underworld" and navigate a "peril of whirring saws, clattering conveyors, and treacherous cogs." Of all the dangers that Oliver encountered, the massive bandsaw at the head of the mill stood out the most: "To say the bandsaw is huge is to say the obvious, . . . but to give an uninitiated person a valid conception of how it really operated is like trying to explain the power and immensity of the tidal surf to one whose experience with water is limited to the bathtub." When it hit a timber, the bandsaw was "traveling at a speed of about one hundred miles an hour or near a thousand feet a second. . . . It is of course invisible except as a motion like the wind, and it strikes the log in a hurricane of roar and whirr and the mill shakes and the floor vibrates until as you stand there your teeth chatter."[13]

Scientific Management in the Northwest Woods

Mechanization was only one change that transformed the woods and the way loggers worked. The other was a new managerial regime. Before steam donkeys and high-lead yarding systems, planning a logging operation involved little more than pointing a crew armed with hand tools and determination at an uncut stand. Decisions about which trees to fell and how to yard them were made by crews themselves; in terms familiar to students of labor history, the manager's brain was under the workingman's cap. But machine logging required far more detailed planning. Yarding cables, sometimes stretching over thousands of feet, had to be strung down hillsides and laced through narrow canyons. Railroad spurs needed to be snaked along the precipitous contours of mountainsides and over rivers. Forests had to be surveyed, stand densities documented, timber quality assessed, and harvests planned to maximize profits in a constantly changing commodities market.

In the opening decades of the early twentieth century, lumbermen increasingly turned to a new class of professionals to manage this ever more complex industrial system. This was hardly something unique to the Northwest woods. Throughout the Progressive Era, industrial employers started relying on a new class of managers to oversee work and workers. What was unique in timber country was that lumbermen drew their managers from the ranks of foresters and in the process fundamentally reshaped the profession. The earliest North American foresters who had studied at German universities or the first American East Coast forestry colleges had been reared in an empirical tradition. Whatever their faults and shortcomings—and they had many—early foresters prided themselves on their ability to craft management plans based on direct observations. As logging companies gradually took control of the profession, industry-employed foresters became less empirically oriented, and this would have profound consequence for the woods and the men who worked in them.[14]

The career trajectory of George Drake illustrates the new ways the lumber industry was using foresters. Born in rural Vermont in 1889, Drake spent much of his childhood outdoors, combing through the American Northeast's rich deciduous forests. Like many people raised in rural settings, he felt more at home outdoors than in. When he begrudgingly left Vermont for the confining classrooms of the University of Pennsylvania, he majored in forestry for no other reason than a friend had told him it would lead to a career "out West where you rode around on horses and had a perpetual picnic in the woods at Uncle Sam's expense." After graduating in 1912, Drake took a job with the US Forest Service (USFS) conducting fire surveys in Oregon, a task that, much to his pleasure, allowed him to spend weeks on end camped out in the backwoods. Shortly after World War I, Drake left the public sector for the private and accepted a job with the Simpson Logging Company in Washington, where he found himself spending far less time outdoors and much more time in the company offices, studying maps and developing yarding plans. "You're not just a straight forester," he said, describing the private forester's duties, "you're an engineer."[15]

Drake's comment hints at the ways the lines between forestry and engineering were blurring. This owed as much to the demands of lumbermen as it did the way those same lumbermen worked to reshape forester training. In 1909 George Cornwall, secretary-treasurer of the Pacific Coast Logging Congress, the major trade organization in the Northwest, began offering Northwest universities funds to expand their forestry programs in exchange for a say in curriculum development. Deans and university presidents eager to grow their fledgling forestry departments willingly complied. After accepting a donation from the congress in 1910, Oregon State University dean of forestry George Peavey announced that his school's new policy would be to "keep in close touch with the leading lumbermen of the state . . . [to] meet as fully as possible their special needs." University of Washington president Henry Suzzallo was no less direct when after accepting a similar donation in 1916, he said his forestry college would henceforth act as the "right hand of the lumber industry." The University of Washington's course catalogues show that in 1916 the forestry college added several new courses covering "the construction and uses of all types of logging machinery and equipment" and "topographic and railroad surveying applied to logging operations." Three years later, the college went further, adding two new programs: "specialization in logging engineering" and "specialization in the business of lumbering."[16]

Foresters trained in these new programs understood the woods more abstractly than their empirically minded predecessors. In particular, this younger generation came to rely on a new guiding text, the topographic map, which soon became as central to planning logging as the Bible is to clergy writing a sermon. Said one logging engineer recently graduated from the University of

Washington's School of Forestry, "The topographic map is the backbone of the whole scheme of logging. . . . Upon it, if reliably constructed, one can build the entire fabric of the operating details." Typically provided by outside companies that specialized in mapmaking, engineering maps were painstakingly thorough, far more detailed than the 7.5-minute US Geological Survey (USGS) topographic maps most hikers and backpackers are familiar with today. Contours were often marked in ten-foot intervals (for comparison's sake, a 7.5-minute USGS map usually has markings at forty-foot intervals) and different colors indicated varying stand densities and tree types. Logging engineers poured over these maps, using drafting tools to pencil in yarding layouts and using slide rules to calculate the deflection angles of cables.[17]

Logging engineers not only brought with them new ways of planning logging but also new ways of organizing labor. If the topographic map was their Bible, then Frederick Winslow Taylor's *Principles of Scientific Management* may well have been their hymnal. Influenced by Taylor and other Progressive Era "industrial scientists," who used time-motion studies to find ways to make work faster and more efficient, logging engineers meticulously examined the labor process, searching for ways to make the work faster or, as one employer stated, keep workers "constantly on the jump." With the advent of machine logging around 1900, logging companies segmented work crews into distinct units: Fellers would cut the standing timber, buckers would cut fallen timbers to the lengths demanded by mills, and yarders would do the work of dragging the timber off the forest floor. In the woods, engineers adopted a practice called busheling, basically a piece-work system that paid felling and bucking crews by the volume of wood they cut rather than an hourly rate. Several Northwest mills adopted the far more complex Bedaux system. Used widely in the southern US textile industry, the Bedaux system relied on complicated formulas to set production quotas, specified times in which those quotas should be met, and offered rewards or punishments for workers who exceeded or failed to meet those benchmarks. A 1930 investigation into scientific management in the Northwest timber industry commissioned by the American Federation of Labor found that "stripped of its pseudo-technical verbiage," the Bedaux system was "nothing more or less than a method of forcing the last ounce of effort out of workers at the smallest possible cost in wages."[18]

Measured in terms of production, mechanization and the managerial regime made logging operations more efficient and more lucrative than they'd ever been and ever would be. Between 1909 and 1929, the lumber industry in Washington, Oregon, and British Columbia collectively harvested 543 billion board feet of lumber. When the forest area lost to waste is factored in, this means that the industry cut through roughly fifteen thousand square miles of forest in this two-decade period. To put that differently, if all the clearcuts made between 1909 and 1929 were combined into a single landmass, it would roughly be the same size as Delaware, New Jersey, and Connecticut combined.[19]

Joseph Morgan, a student at the University of Washington majoring in logging engineering, celebrated these changes. Machines and scientific management, wrote Morgan, "makes for efficiency in all departments of the operation. The superintendent really superintends, the foreman sees that his crew produces maximum results." For Morgan, as well as many engineers and employers, the woods had come to resemble a perfectly functioning industrial system. Topographic maps tacked neatly to the walls of company offices, spreadsheets documenting harvest rates carefully stacked on the corners of desks, and neatly bound time-motion studies sitting on shelves told would-be managers like Morgan and the lumbermen who employed them that they had turned the forest into a space as predictable and orderly as any early twentieth-century factory. The problem was that maps, production figures, and time-motion studies were only abstract ways of knowing nature. For workers who experienced the industrialized woodlands of the early twentieth-century Northwest more directly, the only sort of factory the forests resembled was a slaughterhouse.[20]

Death and Danger

When Ellery Walter, a University of Washington undergraduate who signed on to a logging crew for the summer of 1921, showed up to the woods for his first day of work, he was told that in the likely event he saw a man die he was to leave the body where it lay. That way, the dead worker could still collect a full day's pay. Visitors to timber country like Walter were often greeted with this sort of dark humor. A reporter from the *Seattle (WA) Star* who wondered why none of the workers in attendance at a shingle weavers' union meeting had all ten fingers was told that a man had to surrender two fingers as the cost of employment—the rest were taken as needed. When a different reporter visiting Shelton, Washington, asked why such a small town needed two cemeteries, he was told that one was reserved just for body parts lost in logging accidents.[21]

Perhaps, such jokes say something about the fatalistic work culture of timber country, or maybe they were simply a way for workers to have a little fun at an outsider's expense. Whatever they might be, jokes like these begin to show that it was workers who paid the price for the industrial efficiencies created by mechanization and management. Timbers moving at breakneck speed along yarding systems slammed into their bodies. Pulled taut by the raw power of donkey engines, cables suddenly snapped and tore into men. Timbers rolled and pinned workers to the earth. Fellers needed to be on the constant lookout for toppling trees and errant branches that broke loose as timbers crashed to earth. Formalized speedups and foremen determined to exceed the day's production quotas only increased the danger as men were forced into ever more risky and dangerous situations. Quite simply, there was no shortage of ways to die in the industrialized forests of the early twentieth-century Northwest.[22]

It's impossible to fully document the extent of accidents because official records are incomplete and because deaths and injuries often went unreported. Even so, the records that do exist paint a horrific portrait, one that's alarming even by early twentieth century's more tolerant standards toward death in general and dying on the job. Between 1925 and 1929, 1,459 timber workers in Washington and British Columbia died as a result of industrial accidents. Most of those deaths—1,248—occurred in logging operations, with the remainder in milling and railroading operations. In that same four-year span, 47,528 workers were "temporarily disabled," 6,763 workers were "permanently partially disabled," and 138 workers were "permanently totally disabled." Because accidents frequently escaped the attention of official recordkeepers, the human toll of industrial logging was, in all likelihood, much higher than these figures represent.[23]

The other problem with statistics is that they don't capture the grizzly reality of accidents in the woods and mills. Take, for instance, accidents reported to Washington state's Department of Labor and Industries for just one month. On October 19, 1924, Joseph Shey, a feller working for the St. Paul & Tacoma Lumber Company was "crushed to death" under a falling tree. That same day, Arnold Eches was caught in a saw at one of the company's mills: "one leg was torn off, the other broken, and his skull fractured." A day later, William Edwards was killed when a timber "kicked back" into his head, "driving it against his left eye," and "cutting his face open." Six days later, a log fell on M. McMoen's leg. He was sent to the hospital, and the leg was amputated, but McMoen "failed to rally" and died a few days later. On October 30, Bruce Canning was crushed between two logs, and Fred Gakin fell from a logging train, "the engine passing over his body and death being nearly instantaneous."[24]

Official statistics also failed to capture the slower, less-visible ways this industrial system killed workers. Pneumonia and influenza became more commonplace as machine logging extended the operating season and forced men to work in the cold winter rains. Breathing in sawdust created tiny fissures in workers' lungs that made them more susceptible to tuberculosis. One 1931 study found that 6.6 of every 1,000 Northwest timber workers suffered from consumption. Shingle weavers regularly fell victim to a particularly pernicious respiratory illness called "cedar asthma." The sap that makes cedar naturally water resistant and an ideal shingling material is also deadly when inhaled. After just a few months in a shake-and-shingle mill, workers often reported difficulty breathing, increased phlegm, and what one journalist documenting the problem described as a severe "gripping at the throat." That same journalist found that the air in a shingle line could be so caustic that "several owners confessed they could not enter their own mills when the green timber was being worked on."[25]

The high accident and illness rates in the woods and mills were direct products of lumbermen's relentless quest for faster production and of the shortcomings of logging engineering. Ironically, lumbermen and the engineers they employed made the same mistake as the early twentieth-century preservationists who criticized them: they erred in believing that forests were static environments. What engineers looking at maps often ignored or didn't recognize was that the forest was constantly shifting, always moving, and that any map was obsolete the second it was printed. Even before the emergence of industrial logging, forests were constantly being reshaped by fire, landslides, and climatic changes. But industrial logging quickened the pace of change and with no shortage of irony. Mapping and industrial planning facilitated the rapid cutting of the Northwest's forests, hastening transformations to the landscape, and the more those landscapes changed, the more useless mapping and industrial planning became. Landslides, in particular, became a routine problem for logging engineers. Yarding layouts often failed because engineers didn't account for how soil disruptions had changed the topography. Weather did just as much to complicate things. The Northwest woods can be counted on to be rainy, but that rain varies a great deal, ranging from light mists to intense storms. The high winds that accompanied storms often changed the deflection angles of cables, sometimes leading to catastrophic failures. A hillside that on a map looked like a reasonable site for a log landing could during intense rain be turned into something resembling a waterfall, making logging safely nearly impossible.[26]

Scientific management and engineering had promised to take control of the labor process from workers and place it in the hands of rarified experts. "The one big feature" of centralized planning, one Northwest lumberman proclaimed, is that employers could "cease to rely upon the sole judgement of men . . . in the field." What employers often didn't see or perhaps refused to notice was that so-called centralized planning was an incomplete view of the landscape, and it was workers' knowledge of the environment and their ability to constantly adapt production to the ever-changing forest that was keeping their mills fed with lumber. Indeed, workers had to know forests and machines exceptionally well because this is how they stayed safe. It was yet another irony that a system designed to strip workers of their control and power created an industry where working-class autonomy was not just possible but necessary. In timber country, working-class power flowed through the forests.[27]

Nature, Skill, and Work Culture

By 1940 Roderick Haig-Brown was living a comfortable life in a small cabin nestled in the thick forests along the banks of Vancouver Island's Campbell River. The English émigré had come to British Columbia in the 1920s and worked in logging camps before he met and married a socialite from a wealthy family in Victoria, a good fortune that immediately increased his socioeconomic standing and gave him the opportunity to whittle away his days doing the two things he would soon come to be known for throughout the province: fishing and writing about conservation. While Haig-Brown took to this new life of leisure, nostalgia for his days working in the woods still crept into his writing from time to time. It was less the satisfaction of hard work that he longed for—though he could be nostalgic about that, too—and more the culture of the work that he missed. "Loggers," Haig-Brown wrote, "have all the clannishness and pride of good craftsmen."[28]

Haig-Brown's use of the term "craftsmen" to describe loggers warrants attention, in large part because historians who've studied the labor process in the woods have argued the exact opposite, that the large machines and managerial regimes that early twentieth-century timber workers like Haig-Brown encountered deskilled the labor process. Richard A. Rajala, for instance, has written that the new production systems brought "a progressive reduction in labour requirements, less reliance on physical and conceptual skills once considered essential to the industry, and a consequent loss of autonomy as loggers found themselves increasingly subject to the discipline of machine-pacing." That may be true if we only understand work as an activity shaped by machines and management. But work takes place in a technological, managerial, *and* environmental context. In timber country, it's often been that third context—the environment—that's mattered most and has been central to how Haig-Brown and the men he worked alongside defined skill. Even in the twenty-first century, when the job is far more mechanized than it was in Haig-Brown's era, there's no surer way to start a fight in a rural logging community than to refer to a timber worker as "unskilled." Today, as in the past, timber workers have measured their worth less by their relationship to machines and more by their ability to understand, navigate, and adapt to the vagaries of the forest.[29]

Skills and the knowledge of the forests were not gained incidentally. Rather, as Oregon logger Bill Inud explained, "men matriculated to this college of insane self-abuse." Specifically, young workers had to prove themselves by moving up an occupational ladder, very similar to the one that Thomas Andrews describes in his labor-environmental history of coal mining in early twentieth-century Colorado. And, just like the occupational ladder Andrews describes, timber country's informal apprenticeship system disseminated knowledge of the productive process, taught young workers how to keep themselves and their crewmates safe, and perhaps most important of all, functioned to help preserve working-class control of job sites.[30]

Workers typically began this occupational journey when they were still teenagers, often following their fathers and uncles into the woods. Boys new to the world of industrial logging tended to be steered toward more-menial jobs, doing tedious work under the direct supervision of older and far more experienced crewmembers like donkey punchers (donkey-engine operators), filers (saw sharpeners), iron burners (blacksmiths), and levermen (workers who operated the machines that loaded timbers onto railroad cars). Placing young workers with the recklessness of adolescent masculinity under the direct supervision of older crewmembers served a very important function in the woods. Drawing parallels between timber country's informal apprenticeship system and more formal educational structures, Washington logger John Liboky explained that one of the chief responsibilities of an older crewmember supervising a young worker was to put him "through school" and make sure they "would get nobody hurt."[31]

The most common place young workers could be found, though, was working as signalmen, operating the high-pitched whistle that relayed the orders of the hook tender (lead worker on a yarding crew) to the donkey puncher. Many boys "cut their teeth on the whistle wire as a family tradition," wrote Inud. In an industry defined by its sounds as much as anything else, the high-pitched squeal of the signal was (and remains) one the most distinctive noises made by a logging operation. Whistles had to be loud enough to reach across expansive yarding operations and pierce through the rumble of donkey engines. By the 1920s logging camps throughout the Northwest had adopted a standardized whistling code, a series of long and short bursts that told the donkey puncher when to slack the main line, come back on the haulback line, slack the straw line, and at least three dozen other commands. If early twentieth-century logging was a symphony, then whistle bursts were its main harmonies, the tones that everything else was timed to.

Despite the whistle's crucial function, working as a signalman wasn't prestigious, as the job's more colloquial title of "whistle punk" suggests. In the early twentieth-century working-class lexicon, explains historian Peter Boag, a "punk" was a "boy who submitted to the receptive role in sex with men." Trapped between the berating shouts of the donkey puncher on one side and the profane hand signals of the hook tender on the other, whistle punks did, indeed, appear to submit to the authority of more-experienced workers. But the whistle punk's lowly position had as much to do with human biology as anything else. Most jobs in the woods required marathon-like stamina and lightning-fast reflexes, and young men stumbling through puberty possessed neither. The whistle's location on the top of a landing afforded the signalman the opportunity to watch the yarding crew scurry over log piles below and gain an understanding of the process as his body caught up.[32]

Those yarding crews were often a young man's next occupational destination. Officially listed in employment records as chocker setters, the job's more colloquial title once again provides a better sense of what the work entailed. Commonly known as "chasers," men in yarding crews intercepted the wire loops (called chockers) zipping down the main line at high speeds and then slipped them over fallen logs so they could be hauled up to the landing. If working on the whistle wire functioned as a sort of a young man's baptism into timber country's work culture, then chasing was his sacrament of communion, his first real taste of the strength, stamina, and toughness it took to do this job. "Setting chockers will make or break a man," explained Walter.[33]

The job was challenging because forests actively being yarded were challenging environments. A dizzying maze of cables, brush piles, broken branches, and fallen timbers as wide as twenty feet in diameter, a freshly fallen forest looks as if it was engineered to be unnavigable. Frequent rains that turned steep hillsides slick only made this landscape more demanding. And yet, like a deer running through a thick coastal forest that somehow manages to find an unobstructed path through impenetrable brush, chasers dipped, dove, ducked, hurdled, and pirouetted across the hillsides, somehow managing to grab the fast-moving chockers just at the right moment. Thanks to pervasive popular cultural images (and the marketing department at Brawny Paper Towels), most people think of loggers as barrel-chested men, as stout as the trees they worked on. The opposite was typically true. Most loggers had the physiques of marathon runners rather than body builders, precisely because the job required haste, endurance, and nimbleness. In fact, larger men were often refused employment or at the very least looked at with suspicion by their crewmates. It was assumed they lacked that stamina to effectively work in the woods and the proper build to wiggle their way into and out of tight spots, which was a standard part of the job. Oregon logger Finley Hays explained, "A rigging man is at the mercy of the weather, gill poking sticks and limbs. . . . He stumbles and falls, dives into the mud and brush, squirms and kicks, forcing his way under a log, and in general works half the time with his hind end higher than his head."[34]

Watching an early twentieth-century yarding crew, it would've been difficult to tell where the work ended and the performance began. More-experienced chasers grabbed a chocker while it was "hot," still speeding down the main line, and then swung on the arcing cable. Haig-Brown explained that good chasers could "think ahead" of a log pile and scurry across it with grace and ease. Others leapt from log to log and somehow managed to land on a slippery timber no wider than a man's thigh, much the way a feline can jump great distances and still land confidently and gently. No surprise, then, that good chasers were often described as "catty," a term Haig-Brown defined as "a man who is quick on his feet and good on the job. This is about the ultimate expression of admiration."[35]

Chasers were taught important cultural lessons at the same time they learned to navigate the work environments of the early twentieth-century woods. The first of these was how to dress. The most important thing a logger wore were his caulks, high, thick-leathered boots with spikes on the bottom that gave workers traction as they scurried over log piles. Because a decent pair could cost nearly a week's pay, caulks were often the only footwear timber workers owned, which is why, even today, the surest way to tell you've wandered into a loggers' bar is a chewed-up floor. Most workers wore thick denim or canvas pants waterproofed with beeswax or linseed oil that'd been "staged," the bottom hem cut off to prevent it from catching on brush. Suspenders were the most distinctive item of a logger's dress (figure 3.4). "The reason you wore suspenders," explained Charles Ames, "was to keep your

Figure 3.4. Yarding crew, Tidewater Timber Company, Clatsop County, Oregon, ca. 1936. Note the men's suspenders, staged pants, and caulked boots. Clark Kinsey Photographs, Special Collections, CKK02908, University of Washington Libraries, Seattle.

pants up because you's runnin' all the time! You sure as the dickens couldn't run around through the brush with your pants a hanging down." Clothes also functioned as an important means of communication between workers moving from camp to camp. If a worker had the wrong boots or pants, then he likely lacked experience, which could be deadly. "If you went out there in the woods and [the boss] seen you with a belt on," continued Ames, "he'd know damn well you didn't know nothin.'"[36]

Chocker setters also learned how to talk like a logger. Like any tight-knit working-class subculture, timber workers had an esoteric language all their own. Many of their words referred to machinery and mechanisms unique to the industrial woods. To work effectively, young crewman had to learn the difference between a bull block and a cheese block, a tail-hold and a tail-tack, and a screw jack and a loading jack. Danger also had its own vocabulary. Workers had to know to avoid "widow makers" (branches that unexpectedly fell out of trees), "schoolmarms" (double-crowned trees that could fall unpredictably), and "barberchairs" (trees that split up their base as they fell). "Crotchline" probably required no further explanation. Logger talk also extended beyond the vocational. If, for instance, a young worker was called a "beaver" or a "woodpecker," he had to know if he was being complimented or insulted (in these cases, the latter). Always he was to refer to himself and his fellow crewmembers as loggers and the place they worked as a logging camp. "It is safer to call a sailor a marine," explained Elrick B. Davis, a linguist studying Northwest logging terms in the 1940s, "than to refer to a logging camp as a lumber camp." Calling a logging camp a "show" was also acceptable, and men looking for new work were always advised to avoid "haywire shows" (camps with poor equipment) and look for "candy shows" (camps with good equipment). Many terms were taken from Chinook jargon, a pidgin language developed during the Northwest's fur-trade era to facilitate communication between English-speaking merchants and Native trappers. To be *skookum* was to be good at your job, a *tyee* was a foreman, and *ki'-noos* (often abbreviated as "snoose"), depending on context, meant chewing tobacco or power, as in the donkey engine needed more snoose.[37]

If the whistle wire was a worker's baptism and chasing his first communion, then felling and bucking were his confirmation, his transition into manhood, and his opportunity to demonstrate all the knowledge he gained about the woods in his previous jobs. At first glance, felling a tree appears to be a straightforward task in which gravity does most of the work. But it's actually a job that requires a deep understanding of the environment and an excruciating eye for detail. As Washington logger Jasper Chase explained, "there is a lot to knowing which way a tree goes and where to fall it." One British Columbia logger was more direct: "It's not a job you want to bullshit your way into." That's because felling trees could be incredibly dangerous and because doing the job right required that trees not shatter when they hit the ground, no easy task when timbers weighed several hundred tons and crashed into the earth with unrivaled force. "If you didn't save your timber," recalled one feller, "why, you didn't last long."[38]

Felling was, therefore, a job requiring care and craftsmanship. Fellers generally worked in teams of two, and the process began with those crewmen using axes to carve an undercut into the tree, then sawing through the back, and finally slamming wedges into the crevice to finish the job. At least that's the way it worked in theory. In practice, each tree was a unique engineering problem requiring workers to make dozens of calculations, accounting for the slope of the hillside, the natural lean of the tree, the wind, and the amount of internal rot running up the center of the timber's trunk. What separated good fellers from great ones was something that loggers referred to as "bush sense." The best workers could make all these calculations in a second's time and intuitively know how deep to cut a notch, what saw angle would steer the tree safely to the ground, and when to drive another wedge into the cut and when to let gravity take over. Watch a logger fell a tree today, and you'll notice that he spends less time looking at his saw and more time looking up. This is, in part, because fellers are often killed by falling branches but more because the wispy top of a tree broadcasts what that tree is going to do: if it's about to tip or if a wind is about to push it in an unexpected direction.

Like chasing, there was a performative aspect to felling. For much of the twentieth century, fellers in coastal forests used springboards—stiff, six-inch-wide boards reinforced with an iron footing—to elevate themselves above the saw-gumming sap and pitch that collects in a tree's base. Most trees only required fellers to use two or three springboards and raise themselves just five or six feet off the ground. But fellers often created makeshift scaffoldings of ten or twelve springboards reaching twenty feet up a tree's trunk simply for the thrill of it (figure 3.5). Men on felling crews regularly competed with each other to see who could springboard his way up a tree higher and faster. Another common competition in the woods was to place a stake a hundred feet from a tree being felled and then see which crew could come closest to

Figure 3.5. Fellers in the woods, Saginaw Timber Company, Washington, n.d., possibly 1910s. Clark Kinsey Photographs, Special Collections, CKK01337, University of Washington Libraries, Seattle.

hitting that stake with their tipping tree. The best crews could land a timber directly on the stake.[39]

A handful of workers graduated to the upper echelon of timber country's occupational ladder and became hook tenders, donkey punchers, and high climbers. Precisely because they required the most knowledge of the productive process and the forests and because workers in these positions often held the safety of the entire crew in their hands, these jobs were often reserved for experienced crew members. A hook tender was the leader of a yarding crew, and according to most employers, his main job was to make sure younger men didn't slack. In practice, a hook tender's real job was to manage the risks younger chasers took, allowing a certain level of daredevil behavior and stopping it short before anyone became truly imperiled. Donkey punchers had to know exactly how much power to give the engines they worked, constantly balancing the vagaries of the machine with the vagaries of the forest. Too much power applied at the wrong time and a lumber could hang up and snap the cable it was attached to, endangering workers on the hillside.

A select few workers became high climbers, like Oiva Wirkkala. More than just about any job in the woods, the work of climbers, or riggers, shows that nature helped preserve the autonomy of workers. Climbers were supposed to set cables and pulleys according to plans crafted by logging engineers. Those plans rarely reflected the realities of the woods. Engineers often assumed that donkeys were operating at peak horsepower, which they rarely did, and that hillsides and soil compositions were static, which they never were. So the first thing a climber did after strapping on his spurs and ascending a tree was disregard the engineers' plan and implement his own. This is why the job only went to the most experienced crew members. A good rigger had to have a fine-grained understanding of the forest and hillsides and know how high to set cables and what particular system of pulleys would most effectively and most safely allow yarding systems to function. Climbers actually became the unofficial leaders of logging operations, and workers often took their orders from riggers more than employer-appointed foremen. "[The rigger] is one of the most respected and considered of the buffaloes," wrote one man observing a logging operation in 1929, "and he shows it."[40]

Indeed, in a work culture that valued performance, climbers' daredevil acts were often the most dramatic and certainly the riskiest. Riggers regularly sat on freshly crowned treetops with their feet dangling in the air, smoking a cigarette while waving to crewmembers below. Some would do handstands or jumping jacks while perched on treetops, while others enacted performances that tended more toward the profane. A logger speaking with folklorist Robert Walls remembered one climber in his camp: "While everybody was busy underneath the tree getting things ready to send up to him, he'd wee-wee on ya'. He'd stand there and let you have it." There are multiple ways of reading such performances: as a gendered assertion of dominance over nature or as a way for men in a dehumanizing industrial system to assert their masculinity. Such explanations likely have a lot of merit. But for climbers themselves and the younger workers who observed their treetop performances, Walls's analysis probably would've rung the most true: The climber created "a domain of spontaneity and defiance within a context of managed regimentation and compliance. . . . The climber's exceptional physical abilities and proven technical understanding of high-lead logging questioned the arbitrary authority of less-experienced foremen who often originated from bureaucracies outside the ranks of seasoned woodworkers." A timber worker who spoke with Walls, though, put the matter more bluntly, as timber workers are often wont to do: "Climbers had an attitude."[41]

That attitude pervaded all aspects of timber workers' culture. Because workers believed it was their teamwork and knowledge of the forests that allowed the entire productive system to function, they showed little respect for foremen, engineers, and lumbermen. Quite simply, they believed the bosses needed them, but they didn't need the bosses. And at times, workers reminded their employers of that. Labor economists and industrial relations experts of the early twentieth century often noted the infrequency of strikes in the early twentieth-century woods and concluded that lumbermen had effectively created a loyal workforce. It's true that strikes were a relatively rare thing in early twentieth-century timber country because, in part, employer policies had so effectively circumvented labor radicalism. But as generations of labor historians have shown, a strike is only one tool that workers use to protest their conditions. In timber country, as elsewhere, workers turned to other, sometimes more informal forms of protest that demonstrated they never fully accepted employer controls.

Perhaps, the most common form of protest was one of the oldest forms of protest, one employed for as long as people have worked: timber workers labored at their own pace. Hook tenders were often the subject of employer scorn for their refusal to push the pace of their crews. One lumberman complained that his operations often failed to meet production goals because of the "caprices" of his hook tenders. When five veteran hook tenders at the British Columbian firm Bloedel, Stewart, and Welch were working too slowly for the foreman's liking, the firm fired all five. If hook tenders routinely worked their crews at their own pace, not what employers demanded, why weren't such firings more routine? The answer is that skilled workers with knowledge of the forest and the productive process were hard to replace. Though lumbermen, like employers in other industries, often had an unwavering faith in the power of technology and managerial systems to regiment work and deemphasize skill, there were times when they grudgingly admitted that there were limits to their systems of control. As one Washington state lumberman lamented, his operations would've been far more profitable "if not for the ever present human element to contend with."[42]

Timber workers engaged in another long-standing form of protest: they quit. This practice was not nearly as widespread because lumbermen's policies, like bonus and incentive systems, provided material benefits to workers staying in their jobs, and the necessity of supporting a family made quitting difficult. Yet, highly skilled workers at the top of timber country's occupational ladder, who could often easily find a job elsewhere, had few reservations about walking off the job. As one logger explained, workers may have been able to assert their independence by quitting, "but you had to be a good worker to get away with this." Therefore, often the most skilled and experienced workers employed quitting as an assertion of independence. Because nearly everything in an early twentieth-century logging operation depended on the high climber, many an operation was temporarily hobbled when a rigger up and quit because the pay was too low or conditions too dangerous, or he didn't like the foreman working over him or the crewmen under him. Again, hook tenders were a source of frustration. Employers often liked hiring Scandinavian immigrants to serve as hook tenders because Scandinavia's timber industry adopted machine logging systems nearly a decade before North America's, and many had experience working in mechanized logging operations. Yet, in 1909 foremen in the Merrill and Ring Lumber Company's camps reported they were having "trouble in keeping a crew" because so many men began to quit after the company adopted a new skidder system. It is "almost impossible to keep Finns," the foreman lamented, adding that his plan was to work "in some white men on the skidder" to solve the problem of labor turnover.[43]

Perhaps, the best evidence for the ways in which work in the woods preserved skill and fed into an oppositional work culture comes from the voices of the workers themselves and in the way they described their jobs and their positions in the industrial system. Quite often, when describing their work, timber workers consciously juxtaposed logging with what they saw as more-mundane and less-autonomous work in factories. "The work is never the same like, say, in a factory," said one British Columbia timber worker. "It's a man's work and is risky." Likewise, workers often explained that it was their on-the-ground knowledge, more than the foreman and engineers, that kept this system running. Inud said as much when he wrote that logging is "a science without a formula, a combination of skills and a glomeration of dirty hard jobs and it can't be done by those who never studied to set chockers and tighten guylines." Hays, who worked alongside Inud in Oregon's coastal rainforests, agreed with his friend, saying that the culture that emerged around work in the Northwest woods emphasized rather than diminished workers' autonomy: "The woods are full of power and the logger is the boss of that power. Loggers have a fierce independence . . . [and] resist mightily [when] forced into the detestable mold of conformity." But A. J. Larson, a logger from Washington's Kitsap County, captured this sentiment the best. He explained that he learned many things in the Northwest woods, but two stood out the most. The first was what it meant "to be a man working in the woods." The second, a statement that hints at the conflict on the horizon, was to say "to hell with the boss."[44]

Indeed, the experiences of timber workers and their communities in the opening decades of the twentieth century laid the foundations for the labor unrest of the Great Depression era. Although the company-town system and the mechanization and management of work had been designed to strip workers of their independence, those workers and their families found ways to preserve that independence in the woods. In work, like subsistence and recreation, they found community, closeness, and a common cause that would facilitate the growth of organized labor over the course of the next decades. Just as important, they developed an attachment to the woods, an understanding that their well-being and the forests' well-being were fundamentally linked, and to protect themselves, they had to protect the landscape. This would be reflected in their union movements, too.

PART II

Power

4

"Conservation . . . from the
Guys Down Below"

Northwest timber-working communities had always lived at the whims of capricious market forces. The regional lumber industry's origins in a failed speculative market made financial instability a regular feature of timber country's economic landscape. Chronic overproduction and erratic lumber commodity prices were endemic to the industry, and workers and their families regularly contended with shortened hours, reduced pay, or layoffs during periods when the market slumped. Still, nothing in timber country's past prepared its people for the dramatic upheaval that was the Great Depression. In just the first four years of the economic crisis, more than half of all sawmills and logging camps in the Northwest closed. Communities were scattered and families fractured as men took to the road in search of work. For those that remained in the woods, the accompanying cultural changes were nearly as significant as the economic changes: the Depression fundamentally reshaped the way people in timber country saw the forest.

That's what Sam Churchill remembered most about the hard years of the 1930s. He could almost remember the exact moment when his understandings of nature shifted. It was the summer of 1933, and Churchill was about ten. He and his mother had set out early in the morning, hoping to find some ripe blackberries and cool air in the steep hillsides that surrounded their tiny logging camp in the northwest corner of Oregon. The network of game trails they followed out of town wound through logged-over forests scattered with rusting steel cables, broken chockers, and giant piles of slash waiting to be burned in the fall, over abandoned railroad spurs and across landings where the acerbic smell of donkey-engine smoke lingered. For most of his life, Churchill had found nothing particularly distressing about this industrialized landscape. It'd provided his family with game and forage they used to fill their table, and his father, a logger directly responsible for some of the stumps Churchill now stumbled over, with a steady paycheck. For much of his life, this landscape represented stability for Churchill and his family.[1]

But dire economic times have a way of shifting perceptions. Work for Churchill's father had become increasingly uncertain over the past few years as buyers canceled their lumber contracts with the company. Churchill's father still awoke every morning and laced up his caulks with the hope of heading into the woods, but usually just ended up idling in front of the company offices with the other loggers from town, who anxiously smoked cigarettes as they waited and worried. Churchill could see other, equally distressing changes throughout his community. Many of his friends had left, following their parents out of town as they hoped to find work elsewhere. Gone were the shouts of children playing in the dirt road that ran alongside the rows of company houses, as were the sounds of the forest he'd grown accustomed to. The usual clamor of industrial logging that functioned as the backdrop to Churchill's life—the high-pitched screams of the whistle, the growl of the donkey engines, the rumble of trains careening down the mountainsides loaded with freshly cut timber—had mostly disappeared.[2]

Though he was just a boy with no understanding of the complex financial forces that had created the Depression, Churchill still understood that the unsettling changes his town was undergoing had much to do with the state of the land he was now walking across. Reaching the ridgeline above his camp confirmed that notion. Here, he had an unencumbered view of the vast clearcuts below, acres of barren earth cracking in the summer heat. "It reminded me of pictures of battlefields," he later wrote, "it looked as though the big guns of war had been here." For Churchill, the connection between his town's troubles and this landscape was perfectly clear. The community depended on timber, and as there was no timber left, soon there'd be no community. Churchill began to cry as he was overwhelmed by these thoughts. His mother leaned down to offer comfort and, hugging him tightly, told him, "Trust in God and the mountain." It was a refrain that he'd heard time and time again from his parents, their reminder that nature and the divine—if they even distinguished between the two—would see them through whatever difficulties they encountered. This might've been true in earlier years, before the Depression, but now it was difficult for him to see how this forest would ever again support his family, and he remained unmoved by his mother's words. "To my way of thinking," he later wrote, "God hadn't been as thorough in His planning as He might have been."[3]

Like Churchill, people in Depression-era timber country came to sense that their larger economic and social problems were rooted in the misman-agement of the Northwest's forests. Churchill had blamed the Almighty's lack of foresight for his community's problems, but most would find fault with actors in more corporeal realms. Lumbermen and their cut-and-run logging were clearly the most culpable, but the state was equally at fault. Though the Depression offered new opportunities to create more democratic forms of resource management, both the American and Canadian states would ulti-mately concede control of forest management to private companies. If neither employers nor the state would take responsibility for protecting forests and rural communities, then people in the Northwest woods would have to do so. Like millions of workers in the 1930s, Northwest timber workers turned to the labor movement with hopes of creating more-democratic workplaces. What was unique about timber country's Depression-era labor movement is that it reflected the concerns someone like Churchill expressed on that ridgeline, and it would aim to democratize workplaces at the same time it democratized forest management. If life in company towns and patterns of work in earlier decades had convinced timber workers and their families that they had a special connection to the forest, the Depression now convinced them that they had a special obligation to protect it. As a result, the union they'd build would be equal parts labor movement and environmental move-ment.

Experiencing the Depression in Timber Country

Nearly everyone in timber country suffered as a result of the Depression, but the specifics of suffering differed from place to place. Most lumber companies responded to the market crash by shuttering their camps and mills and laying off large percentages of their workforces. Just in Oregon, employment in the timber industry fell by more than 60 percent between 1929 and 1933. Wash-ington's and British Columbia's employment figures were similar. But some companies did find creative ways to keep men employed. In the north-central Oregon town of Shevlin, the company paid men to do odd jobs around camp, like painting and repairing houses. Other companies transitioned to four- or six-hour shifts, in an effort to spread around what little work remained. In some cases, companies stopped charging rent and allowed families to stay in their homes, even though men weren't working.[4]

Men lucky enough to keep their jobs worked for far less. In January 1930, the Oregon-American Lumber Company started hook tenders at $9.60 a day. Ten months later, hook tenders at the company were working for $4.60

a day. But even at reduced wages, work was never reliable. "There wasn't any sawmills that were steady at all," remembered Bill McKenna, a timber worker from Coos Bay, Oregon, "most of the people would work for a few weeks, and they'd be off for a while." Nor did work necessarily guarantee a paycheck, as many companies prioritized repaying creditors over paying their workers. Victor West, another Coos Bay sawmill worker, remembered that throughout the 1930s, his paychecks were "bouncing all over the place."[5]

While work could be unsteady or nonexistent, when given the choice, many people preferred to stay in camps and company towns, if they could, and weather the Depression among friends and family. That's what Curt Beckham found. After Beckham lost his job at a sawmill in Powers, Oregon, he headed for Portland, where he found work as a gas-station attendant. That job lasted only a few months. He then found work as a hosiery salesman but was again laid off after a few months. Not having eaten in days, Beckham used his last seventy-three cents to buy a train ticket back to Powers. The town was struggling, he remembered, but at least there "you weren't alone." Like Beckham, others discovered that timber country's community and kinship networks were the only certain thing in the larger uncertainty of the Depression. Ted Goodwin, an itinerant preacher who delivered religious services to company towns in southwest Washington, recalled an old chewing-tobacco tin in the church at Ryderwood where people dropped whatever coins they could part with to help out neighbors. Residents in Longview started a relief fund and encouraged workers who still had jobs to donate $1 month. Julia Bertram, the wife of a sawmill worker in a company town just south of Portland, organized the other women in camp, and together they went into the more affluent neighborhoods of the nearby city and sought donations for children's clothes.[6]

In camps and company towns, unemployed loggers and millworkers could also continue to rely on the forest. A visitor walking into Oregon logger Cliff Thorwald's home at the peak of the Depression would've found a deer in the bathtub waiting to be dressed, several large salmon waiting to be cleaned, a stringer full of trout waiting to be gutted, or several gunny sacks full of clams. "There was no reason to be hungry," Thorwald explained, "if you could get around or if you had friends who could get around." Logger Dow Beckham, Curt's brother, agreed. "Here," he said, speaking of his coastal Oregon logging camp, "the Depression hardly touched people as far as eating is concerned. [People had] a big garden. They had deer. They had fish. But the money part, they didn't have."[7]

The New Deal That Never Was, or Mr. Greeley Goes to Washington

Surviving the Depression may have strengthened timber country's communities and their reliance on the forest, but as Churchill had realized on that ridgeline, the forest was in trouble, which meant their communities were in trouble. He certainly didn't know it at the time, but the anxiety he felt was a product of political developments that occurred far outside the Northwest. A year earlier, Franklin D. Roosevelt had entered the White House, promising a New Deal for the "common man" and in just a short time had spearheaded new legislation to make natural-resource management more sustainable and democratic. Canada had no equivalent of the New Deal, and the country's progressives often complained that the government in Ottawa had met the Depression with a "No Deal." Still, even north of the forty-ninth parallel, land managers and political radicals hoped to use the Depression to usher in new land-management regimes that would abate the anxieties of Churchill's Canadian counterparts. Yet, despite the reform and conservationist impulses of governments on both sides of the border, Churchill could see nothing from his perch on that ridgeline that was new and certainly nothing that represented a deal for him and his community. The reasons why had much to do with the outsized political influence of lumber-trade organizations and, at least in the United States, one man in particular, William Greeley. Churchill had most certainly never heard Greeley's name, but by the mid-1930s, no one was more responsible for the anxieties and economic problems experienced by people in timber country.

To be perfectly fair, not even Greeley himself knew that he would be responsible for shaping Depression-era forestry policy when he was summoned to the White House in the summer of 1933 to discuss plans for stabilizing the failing lumber industry. Rather, he had every reason to believe that his influence in forestry was rapidly coming to an end. Greeley had long believed that restrictions on timber harvests unnecessarily burdened the industry that was the economic engine of the far West. As the third chief forester of the United States, Greeley had departed from his predecessors, Gifford Pinchot and Henry S. Graves, in seeking looser conservation standards in the nation's public forests. In 1928 Greeley left the USFS to head the West Coast Lumbermen's Association, then the largest lumber-industry trade organization in the Pacific states, where he continued to lobby against state intervention. But the new president who'd summoned him to the US capital was a conservationist more in the vein of Pinchot and Graves. Roosevelt proudly referred to himself as a "tree planter" after overseeing the reforestation of his family's Hyde Park estate and had already said on campaign stops that he wanted to do the same for the Northwest's forests. Indeed, as Greeley's train departed Seattle, location of the association's headquarters, for Washington, DC, he had every reason to believe he was racing toward the end of the laissez-faire environment that he and his industry had long enjoyed.[8]

We don't know exactly what Greeley was thinking as he sat on that East Coast–bound train, but his thoughts may well have turned to significant changes in the forestry profession. A small but vocal group of foresters had begun to call for more federal oversight of the nation's woodlands. Forestry is as much a physical science as a social science, they said, and foresters had a professional obligation to protect rural communities from the devastating effects of resource exploitation. Robert Marshall was at the forefront of this new movement. A hypermasculine adventurer who often spent months on end trekking through Alaska's wilderness, Marshall's rugged demeanor masked a deep sympathy for people like Churchill, whose lives were too easily thrown into disarray by the vagaries of the marketplace. "Private profit and future welfare are not compatible," Marshall wrote in a 1930 pamphlet calling on the federal government to expand the public ownership of forests and free them from the profit-seeking motives of Greeley and the lumbermen he represented.[9]

Greeley could dismiss Marshall as a sentimental radical, but the politicians who appeared to take his ideas seriously were another matter. In 1932 New York senator Royal S. Copeland authorized an intensive study of the nation's forests to "insure all of the economic and social benefits which can and should be derived from forest products." The final, two-thousand-page report, though, went well beyond this initially limited mandate and evolved into a scathing indictment of the lumber industry, private forest management, and even Greeley's tenure as chief forester. Cut-and-run logging had, according to the report, led to "far-reaching and utterly demoralizing economic and social losses to dependent industries, to local communities, and to entire forest regions." In the end, the Copeland report recommended that the government use its purchasing power to acquire more than two hundred million acres of private forestland and manage it on a more sustainable basis.[10]

Greeley's train most likely raced north out of Seattle, hooking right near Bellingham and following the American-Canadian border, a route that would've reminded him that he had to be concerned with political developments in British Columbia, as well. In 1932 Canadian Socialists founded a new political party, the Co-operative Commonwealth Federation (CCF). The CCF shared Marshall's and Copeland's belief that resource mismanagement had caused widespread social problems in rural communities, though its proposed solutions were decidedly more radical in nature. "There is no solution possible to the problem of preserving our major resources," stated Colin Cameron, a CCF member of the Legislative Assembly of British Columbia, "unless private ownership of forest lands is abolished."[11]

Greeley's train would've passed by many other scenes that also suggested the order he represented was under assault from the New Deal. The earliest Civilian Conservation Corps (CCC) camps had already been built, where young men hired by the federal government replanted forests, repaired levees, and built hiking trails. In the Columbia River Gorge, civil engineers were planning for the massive concrete dams that would soon span the river's turbulent waters and send cheap water and electricity flowing into the dry and dusty fields of the High Desert. Past the Rocky Mountains, government soil scientists were starting to bring life back to the denuded farms of the Great Plains.

Yet, even as these scenes portended a new world of democratized resource management that threatened the new empire of Northwest lumbermen, Greeley also understood there were ambiguities in New Deal resource policies that he could exploit in the interest of capital. New Dealers faced a question when it came to America's forests: How should timber be categorized for the purposes of recovery efforts? Should they be regulated as agricultural goods, similar to wheat and corn, or as industrial commodities, like coal and ore? The question mattered because the Roosevelt administration had dramatically different approaches to each. While the nation's agricultural lands were the targets of massive federal programs, New Dealers took a more hands-off approach to industrial commodities, pursuing a policy of self-regulation. Do your own "housecleaning," Roosevelt urged America's industrialists in one of his famous fireside chats, "and thus avoid oppressive federal regulation."[12]

As Greeley saw it, the timber industry's best hope for warding off oppressive federal regulation, or worse, the radical proposals of Marshall and Copeland, lay in convincing the administration that timber was an industrial commodity and, thus, eligible for inclusion in the National Industrial Recovery Act (NIRA). One of the Roosevelt administration's first attempts to stabilize Depression-riddled industries, the NIRA worked by issuing a series of rules and production quotas intended to end the cycles of overproduction that had brought the nation to the brink of economic collapse. New Dealers believed that the best, and really only, way to ensure compliance was to allow industrialists to draft the codes themselves. While the administration had given steel, coal, and manufacturing magnates a good deal of latitude in preparing their codes, Roosevelt had indicated that he'd only sign a lumber code if operators agreed to conservation guidelines. Lumbermen initially scoffed at the notion, but at an emergency meeting of lumber-trade representatives earlier in the year, Greeley had made a compelling case that the industry would be best served by seeking an NIRA code. Lumbermen could refuse to work with Roosevelt and hope that he didn't listen to the likes of Copeland or Marshall, or they could, in Greeley's words, beat the more radical conservationists "to the draw." Over the course of the next several weeks, Greeley and lumbermen "wrote and tore up and wrote again drafts of many sections" until they finally settled on con-servation language they could at least live with.[13]

That draft was ultimately a political gambit, an attempt to use vague and flexible wording to convince conservation-minded politicians that lumber-men took industry sustainability seriously, even as they followed their usual cut-and-run practices. Indeed, the draft code that Greeley carried with him as he ascended the steps of the White House to meet with Roosevelt required operators to undertake replanting programs but offered easy paths for opting out. It required companies to leave seed trees to facilitate the natural regen-eration of cutover stands but only "as far as practical" and "so far as feasible." It mandated sustained yield—basically, only cutting timber at the same rate it grew back—but allowed operators to make their own calculations to de-termine sustainable yields. And finally, the code contained no enforcement mechanisms.[14]

We have no record of the meeting between Greeley and Roosevelt, only what Greeley recorded in his autobiography. By that account, though, what-ever anxieties he might have felt about trying to slip ineffectual conservation standards into the NIRA were unfounded. "The President beamed his ap-proval," Greeley wrote and Roosevelt agreed to adopt the lumber code into the NIRA without any further augmentations. "We left the Capitol with shiny new halos on our heads," he remembered. "The proceeding reminded me a bit of the baptism of armies of Franks and Gauls in the Middle Ages, by the simple rite of wading through a river."[15]

The NIRA Lumber Code would be a relatively short-lived piece of forestry policy. In 1935, two years after it was implemented, the US Supreme Court found the entire NIRA unconstitutional. Yet, the longer-term importance of the lumber code lay less in its specific mandates and more in the way it reshaped New Dealers' view of the industry. Today, it might be called a good bit of corporate branding. As Roosevelt's glowing endorsement suggests, the code helped lumbermen convince politicians that the industry recognized the folly of its past practices and they could be trusted to correct course entirely on their own, even as they continued to harvest as recklessly as they'd always done. A clear measure of the effectiveness of Greeley's gambit could be seen in subsequent New Deal forestry policies, most of which continued to pursue industrial self-regulation as the salve to the long-standing social and ecological problems of the industry. As one progressive forester would describe the code's effects years later, it had all amounted to "a publicity stunt to convince the indignant public that operators had finally found religion."[16]

As Greeley made the return trip home from Washington, DC, his train once again swung near the Canadian border, and soon he would be able to rest easy that the threat of socialized forests had been averted there, too. Like the USFS, British Columbia's Ministry of Forests was (and is) funded almost entirely through timber sales. While many British Columbia foresters believed that the Depression provided a new opportunity to enact harvest restrictions and new rules regulating overhead logging systems, the rapidly declining budget of the ministry that resulted from decreased timber sales in the early 1930s led to massive layoffs within the ministry that made it nearly impossible to enforce existing rules, let alone implement new ones. Much like in the United States, lumbermen operating in British Columbia filled the regulatory void by proposing industrial self-regulation.[17]

Greeley finally returned to Seattle content and confident that he'd warded off federal intervention and assured his industry's future. Roughly two hundred miles to the south, Churchill and, most likely, the other men, women, and children living in the mill towns and lumber camps of Northwest timber country continued to worry about what the future Greeley had forged meant to them. Few likely knew of his trip and the consequential deal he'd struck with the administration. Nor, for that matter, did they know about other missed opportunities articulated by people like Marshall and Copeland. Perhaps, they knew about the new concrete dams being strung across the Columbia, the irrigation canals being dug into the desert, and the CCC enrollees and farm scientists working to pull other rural communities up from poverty. And if they had, this likely only added to their feelings that they'd been left behind. What they could see more definitively—the continued layoffs, declining wages, the cutover forests, and the once-thriving communities being turned into ghost towns—perhaps told them that if timber country was going to get a new deal, then they would have to do it for themselves.

But this would require a coordinated movement of workers. And how could the organization of the industry proceed when timber workers were spread out across a landscape that had been expressly designed to inhibit the growth of unionism? This was the question radical timber workers asked themselves in the early 1930s as the shadow of the Depression continued to creep across timber country.

Early Organizing in the Timber Industry

Ernie Dalskog had an answer to that question, though it wasn't a particularly romantic one: walking. Quite simply, this is how the union movement was built in the early years of the Depression, by organizers like Dalskog who wore down their shoes beating their way through thick forests, sneaking into logging camps and company towns under the cover of night, carrying stacks of unsigned union cards. Dalskog was an organizer for the Canadian Communist Party's Lumber Workers International Union (LWIU). By the start of the Depression, the LWIU and its counterpart on the south side of the American-Canadian border, the American Communist Party's National Lumber Workers Union (NLWU), were Northwest timber workers' only real hope for organization. The Industrial Workers of the World never had all that much of a presence in the Northwest woods—or, at least, not the presence Wobblies claimed—and what little presence it did have had largely faded by the mid-1920s. In 1933 the American Federation of Labor (AFL) founded a new union in the Northwest woods, the Sawmill and Timber Workers Union (STWU), but this was more of a strategic move to head off the growing influence of the Communist Party than a real effort to organize the industry. The only established union remained the Loyal Legion of Loggers and Lumbermen, the company union founded just after World War I, and just as in the past, workers only joined when forced by their employers.[18]

Looking at Dalskog, it would've been difficult to fathom that he possessed the fortitude and physical stamina required to infiltrate the company towns of timber country. Short and chubby with thick, wire-rimmed glasses that slumped down his nose, Dalskog looked more suited to office work than long treks through the woods. But his bookish appearance belied a toughness and radical political persuasion that he'd carried with him from his native Finland, both of which were further honed in his years working as a timber feller on Vancouver Island throughout the 1920s. And it was that toughness that sustained Dalskog as he took part in an organizing drive that the LWIU initiated in 1934, one that illustrates the geographic challenges radicals encountered as they undertook the task of organizing timber country.

The drive began in early spring, just after the winter snows receded, and organizers could access the province's high-mountain camps. In April, Dalskog and fellow LWIU organizer Jack Brown rented a boat and headed for northern Vancouver Island to, as Dalskog later explained, "get to the camps where roads were inaccessible." The pair found a welcome audience in several camps and signed "at least three dozen men" to the union. From there, Dalskog and Brown hiked thirty miles up a decommissioned railroad and held several "productive meetings" with workers in the camps near Campbell River. Brown remained in the Campbell River area, and Dalskog hitchhiked in the direction of Brown Bay. Unable to find a ride to cover the last few miles and with night quickly approaching, he began jogging and arrived "just in time" to talk with loggers as they were finishing supper. A few days later, Dalskog joined up with LWIU organizer Arne Johnson, and the pair set out for a logging camp near Englewood. They were met at the camp's entrance by company security guards and were given a thorough beating before being turned around. Undeterred, Dalskog and Johnson waited until the following evening and then cut a path to the camp through the thick forest to elude the guards. "I just had ordinary oxfords," remembered Dalskog, and "had a hell of a time keeping up."[19]

While Dalskog's story certainly speaks to the difficulties and dangers union organizers encountered, it also speaks to the advantages they enjoyed. Dalskog discovered that workers often needed little convincing to sign a union card. That had much to do with the strong communities that had coalesced in the previous decades and the work culture in the woods that made people in logging camps disposed to a sort of class consciousness that enabled union organizing. Dalskog likely encountered other evidence of this, as well. The wives of timber workers often facilitated the success of organizers like Dalskog. Because employers believed that women were naturally anti-union, women assisting in organizing efforts could often remain hidden in plain sight. It was often women who met organizers like Dalskog on the outskirts of camp and snuck them into towns. When organizers were deterred by security guards, women often took those organizers' union cards and went door-to-door signing up men to the union. Women also covertly snuck union newspapers into camp in hat boxes and sewing baskets. Organizers like Dalskog didn't so much foment radicalism in the Northwest woods as they functioned as something akin to power lines, connecting isolated pockets of energy into a broader network capable of emitting a power greater than the sum of its parts.[20]

Communism was a less-important ingredient here. Despite directives from party leadership that LWIU and NLWU operatives engage in "agit-prop" work and "come forward as the political leaders of workers," organizers like Dalskog were often resistant to do so. Dalskog recalled that workers tended to look at him "goofy" when he gave lessons on Marxist economics. The messages that resonated more were the ones about protecting communities, towns, and forests. Fellow LWIU organizer J. M. Clarke was even more resistant than Dalskog in adhering to the party line. After being admonished by the Canadian Communist Party's leadership for refusing to distribute party literature in camps, Clarke fired back a missive questioning the leadership's understanding of the timber industry's workers. "What in the hell is the need of trying to persist and subjecting yourself to unlimited hardships in the face of Goddam driveling shit like this?" Clarke asked the party's leaders. "Words, words, words," he continued, "oceans of verbosity; miles of trollop; reams of junk; hours of scatter-brained blah that in no way indicates the slightest understanding of conditions as they actually exist in the country among rank-and-file workers." For most of the NLWU's and LWIU's organizers and members, communism was the means, not the end.[21]

By the end of 1934 the LWIU and NLWU had signed roughly five thousand members to their unions, just a small fraction of the Northwest lumber industry's workforce. But the new networks they created would significantly shape the course of timber country's labor movement in the following years, as would broader developments in the ranks of organized labor. In the spring of 1934, longshoremen from San Diego to Vancouver shut down docks in what was, at the time, the largest strike in the Pacific Coast's history. Though the strike failed to achieve many of its goals, it, nevertheless, suggested new possibilities for other workers. The following year, the Communist International instructed its affiliates to abandon independent unions and join existing AFL unions as part of its Popular Front strategy for combating the global rise of fascism. Soon thereafter, both the NLWU and LWIU disbanded, and their members turned to the AFL's Sawmill and Timber Workers Union (STWU).[22]

If the 1934 longshoremen's strike and the party's Popular Front strategy provided a new political atmosphere that promised to abet unionization in timber country, then it was the tear-gas canisters arcing through the air during the spring and summer of 1935 as timber workers faced down National Guard troops in the largest strike in the Northwest lumber industry's history that provided the final catalyst. The NLWU and LWIU members who joined the STWU provided the union with an immediate infusion of radicalism. In the spring of 1935, the STWU issued a call for a new region-wide contract that included union recognition, a six-hour day, five-day week, worker-controlled hiring halls, and a seventy-five-cents-per-hour minimum wage and then set a strike deadline of May 6 if those demands were not met. At the same time, the STWU's leaders established "roving committees" responsible for infil-trating camps, recruiting workers, and asking them to sign on to the union's demands. It was basically the same work that Dalskog had been doing in the years before but now on a much-larger scale made possible by the STWU's larger budget.[23]

Northwest timber operators resoundingly ignored the STWU's demands, and convinced a strike was imminent, workers began walking off their jobs even before the May 6 strike deadline. When that deadline passed with no further movement from lumbermen, even more workers joined the strike. By mid-May, newspapers in Seattle and Portland were reporting that more than twenty thousand workers were on strike and by the end of the month were running stories claiming that nearly every logging camp and sawmill in the region had been idled by pickets. Violence followed tightly on the heels of the industry's shutdown. Wielding batons and bats, mill security guards tried to break picket lines and open up mills and camps to scab labor. As reports of violence spread, Washington Governor Clarence D. Martin called up the National Guard to restore order to the embattled timber industry, which only escalated the violence.[24]

As striking STWU members battled police, company security guards, and now National Guard troops on the picket lines, Abe Muir, president of the United Brotherhood of Carpenters and Joiners (UBCJ), arrived in the North-west, intent on bringing an end to the strike. Muir's UBCJ had jurisdiction over the STWU, and the relationship between the two unions had always been fraught. Muir came from the more conservative craft-union tradition in the American labor movement and believed that the immigrants and so-called unskilled workers in the STWU were a stain on his union's prestige. In a series of backroom meetings that began in mid-July, Muir negotiated deals with the region's timber operators that fell far short of the STWU's initial demands and then threatened locals with expulsion if their members did not vote in favor of the new agreements. A committed group of radicals within the STWU attempted to keep the strike going, but by early August, most Northwest timber workers had returned to work.[25]

The strike failed to achieve many of its initial objectives, and about the only thing STWU members won for enduring months of violence on the pickets was a nominal wage increase. In purely material terms, the strike was a failure. But strikes are not so easily measured in material terms. The

STWU had about fifteen thousand members when the strike began. By the time the strike ended in August, its ranks had swelled to roughly thirty-five thousand, and in a year's time the union would count more than seventy thousand members, making it the largest union on the Pacific Coast. Perhaps more important, the strike created a new sense of purpose among the region's timber workers. What had launched the union movement in the Depression-era woods was a belief that timber-working communities, not lumbermen, should be able to determine the fate and future of the forests where they lived and worked. Now, timber workers added Muir and the AFL to the list of forces they believed were inhibiting their control of their own futures. And as workers picked up their tools and returned to lumber camps and mills in the summer of 1935, they now increasingly grumbled about the need for an independent union. For many of them, the 1935 strike wasn't an ending but a beginning.[26]

The IWA and Labor Environmentalism

One of those timber workers was Harold Pritchett. In December 1936, Pritchett boarded a train bound for Washington, DC. Other than leaving from Vancouver, British Columbia, rather than Seattle, he likely followed the same route that William Greeley had three years earlier, and Pritchett could see many of the same things that Greeley had seen: the CCC camps, the new irrigation networks, and the new power lines stretching from dams to rural communities. But Pritchett certainly envisioned more possibilities in these scenes than Greeley. Like many radicals of the 1930s, Pritchett saw hope in the despair of the Depression, the opportunity to build a new and more just world from the ashes of the old. That's a goal he'd been working toward for much of his life. Pritchett had been born in Birmingham, England, and immigrated to British Columbia in 1912 at the age of eight. Though his teenage years were spent in the dark confines of a Port Moody, British Columbia, shingle mill, tending a conveyor for ten cents an hour, he never lost his "Birmi" accent, the lilting brogue of Birmingham's working class. By the 1920s he'd moved to a mill town near the Fraser River, working eleven-hour days and then staying up late in the night discussing radical literature in a Marxist reading group. He joined the Communist Party sometime in the late 1920s, and when the Depression began shortly thereafter and workers in his mill started talking about a strike, they elected Pritchett to lead their efforts. He continued to rise through the ranks of the Northwest's nascent labor movement, and by the time the timber workers' strike ended in the summer of 1935, he'd become a leading proponent of a timber workers' union free of AFL control.[27]

The audience Pritchett sought in Washington, DC, was also quite different from the one that Greeley had sought. A year earlier the US government had passed the National Labor Relations Act (NLRA), a monumental piece of labor legislation that made it far easier for American workers to organize unions. Afterward, John L. Lewis, the pugnacious leader of the United Mine Workers of America, helped spearhead a new labor federation called the Congress of Industrial Organizations (CIO) to take advantage of the opportunities the NLRA afforded. The CIO was different from the AFL in nearly every respect. The CIO advocated a broad industrial unionism rather than a narrow craft unionism. It opened its ranks to immigrants, women, and Black workers and the so-called unskilled. In its first few years the CIO had achieved gains for workers in the mines of Appalachia and steel belts of Pennsylvania and Ohio, and now Pritchett hoped to extend the new federation's influence to Northwest timber country by convincing Lewis to grant woodworkers a CIO charter. And though Pritchett, like approximately one-third of the STWU's members, was a Canadian who would be unprotected by the NLRA's provisions, he believed that the best hope for increasing the power of timber workers was in a transborder union that would allow British Columbian workers to leverage the gains made by their NLRA-protected American brethren south of the border.[28]

Lewis had plenty of reasons to entertain the idea of a CIO timber workers' union, as well. Though the new federation had made spectacular gains in the industrial Midwest, it had yet to establish a strong presence on the Pacific Coast. For the time, longshoremen were remaining in the AFL, and craft unions had a firm grip in Portland and Seattle. A CIO timber workers' union would help the federation spread to a new jurisdiction and begin a move into Canada. There were other reasons, too, for Lewis and Pritchett to be allied. Both men had worked in resource-extraction industries, dominated by company towns and shortsighted operators more concerned with immediate profits than the long-term health of workers and their communities. And though Lewis was a stout, heavy-set man with thick eyebrows and a lifelong Republican, and Pritchett a tall and lean Communist, the two men shared a vision of progressive, social-movement unionism that certainly facilitated their conversations. At the end of their meeting, Lewis agreed to offer a CIO charter to timber workers.[29]

In the months after the meeting, Pritchett traveled across timber country, speaking with union locals and shoring up support for CIO affiliation. On

July 16, 1937, lumber workers from across the Northwest and a handful from the Midwest met in Tacoma, Washington, to formally vote on the issue. A clear consensus emerged with just a handful of more-conservative locals from Portland voicing any objection: timber workers would abandon the AFL and join the CIO, and Pritchett would be named president of the new union, now called the International Woodworkers of America (IWA).[30]

The creation of the IWA marked the beginning of organized timber workers' problems, however, not the end of them. Shortly after the echoes of delegates chanting "Go CIO!" at the IWA's founding convention faded, Pritchett found himself helming an embattled union under attack on multiple fronts. On one flank were the operators. Like employers in other industries where the CIO attempted to extend its influence, Northwest lumbermen refused to recognize the new union, and in the first few months of its existence, the majority of the IWA's locals were forced to the picket lines in recognition fights. Closing in on the IWA's opposite flank was an embittered AFL, angry that it'd lost approximately seventy-thousand dues-paying members to its CIO rivals. In the days before the CIO affiliation vote was taken, UBCJ leader Frank Duffy had promised the woodworkers "the sweetest fight of your lives" if they left the AFL, and the rocks that UBCJ loyalists hurled at IWA members now holding picket lines showed that Duffy's threat had not been made in jest. Indeed, violence was more the rule than the exception in most of the IWA's early conflicts. IWA picketers fought with company security guards, dodged bullets fired from the guns of local police, and grappled with AFL members. Northwest timber country had simultaneously erupted in both class war and civil war.[31]

Julia Bertram was on the frontlines of these wars, and her experiences once again reveal that the effort to build a union in the Northwest woods involved women and other community members, not just the men who worked in the mills and camps. Bertram stood no more than five feet, two inches tall and possessed a fierceness disproportionate to her size. When the IWA was founded, Bertram had urged her husband, a sawmill worker, to join. "This is industrial war and we belong in it," she'd told him. Afterwards, she became one of the most productive union organizers in her company town of Linnton, just outside of Portland, where she went door-to-door encouraging men to join the union and then impugning their masculinity if they refused. When AFL members attempted to break an IWA picket at Linnton's mill, Bertram gathered a contingent of wives to walk the pickets, reasoning that even the most violent of men wouldn't attack marching women. The picture that appeared in the IWA's newspaper afterward showed Bertram and several other women holding the picket line and carrying baseball bats, rolling pins, and whatever else they could find to defend themselves. The photo carried the caption, "IWA women don't fear AFL goons." That likely pleased Bertram. "Women are more radical than men," she would say years later when recounting this story. "I really believe that."[32]

Scenes like the one in Linnton played out across timber country throughout 1937 and 1938. Yet, in reading the IWA's main newspaper, the *Timber Worker*, what's most remarkable is that the union's members seemed less concerned with the immediate threat posed by employers and the AFL and more concerned with the longer-term threat posed by overcutting. And as IWA members ducked bullets fired by mill security guards, dodged the bats of AFL loyalists on the picket lines, and endured months without paychecks as strikes and lockouts stretched on, the question they seemed most concerned with was this: what were these sacrifices for if the timber industry had no future? Union members certainly worried about the ways that continued overcutting would impact immediate employment opportunities but also their towns, communities, and future generations. Calling conservation an obligation "to posterity," union member G. D. Meek argued that the union had "a duty to our children" to fight for a sustainable industry. A timber worker said much the same thing in the IWA's British Columbia paper: These are "our forests, and we must take pride in perpetuating them so that our children and our children's children might know of the majestic grandeur of our wooded places before the Mackens, M[a]cMillians and the Filberts [British Columbian lumbermen] get a hold of them."[33]

Such comments hint at a new consciousness that began to emerge in the IWA during the union's formative years. Timber-working communities had long recognized that they had a special relationship to the forest. Now they began to see that that relationship came with a unique obligation, if not duty, to work toward forest conservation. Lumbermen clearly had no long-term interest in the forest, and the foresters and politicians who did had been silenced by the industrial self-regulation fervor of the early New Deal. This left only the industry's workers as the last line of defense to prevent Northwest woodlands from, as IWA member Don Hamerquist said, being "turned into a Gobi desert." What was beginning to be articulated in the *Timber Worker* and in union halls and logging camps in the late 1930s was labor environmentalism: a belief that healthy forests could only be achieved through a powerful union, and a powerful union could only be achieved through healthy forests. It was a vision that linked working-class economic security to environmental sustainability. This idea was, perhaps, most directly and forcefully stated in an editorial in the union's newspaper. "We shall unite in every honest effort to save the forest," it read. "Real conservation, selective logging, sustained yield, reforestation, fire prevention—coupled with union recognition, union wage scales, means sustained prosperity in the lumber industry for all!"[34]

Olympic National Park

If fears over the industry's future had initially encouraged IWA members to articulate labor environmentalism, it was a political battle over the creation of Olympic National Park that suggested a political strategy for integrating labor environmentalism into regional and national forestry policy. It was wildlife, more than trees, that first encouraged conservationists to take notice of the roughly nine-hundred thousand acres of temperate rainforest nestled between Washington's Olympic Range and the Pacific Ocean. Lurking in those forests is a subspecies of elk found only on the Pacific Coast, one that excited the imaginations of hunters and wilderness advocates, most nota-bly President Theodore Roosevelt. In the early twentieth century, Roosevelt visited Washington's Olympic Peninsula and observed the elk. Much larger-bodied than their Rocky Mountain cousins, mature bulls could weigh more than a thousand pounds and carried chocolate-black antlers from rubbing pitch-laden firs. These elk are also less likely to bugle—the high-pitched squeal bulls emit to attract cows and challenge other bulls during the fall rut. Instead, they rely on something called a chuckle, a series of short, guttural bleats that are downright terrifying when heard up close. Roosevelt was so moved by the elk that in 1909 he passed a national monument designation for the peninsula herd's subalpine calving grounds, and later the species was officially named Roosevelt elk in his honor, though most Northwesterners today refer to them just as "Rosies."[35]

Teddy Roosevelt and the conservationists who created Mount Olympus National Monument had another factor working in their favor to preserve the area: geology. The ring of mountains surrounding the monument formed a sort of natural rampart that kept many of the peninsula's forests safe from the axes and plows of late nineteenth-century White settlers and lumber-men. But by the 1930s, timber-industry operators were threatening to crest the mountain range and descend into the timbered valleys below, assisted by improvements in railroad technology and driven by the rising price of Sitka spruce, a high strength-to-weight-ratio lumber used in airplane manufac-turing, which grew in dense groves within the monument's valleys. Already, foresters and rangers had discovered illegal logging operations within the protected area's borders, suggesting to many conservationist-minded politicians that the monument's future was in a precarious position.[36]

One of those was the representative from Washington's Third Congressional District, Monrad Wallgren. Before becoming a politician, Wallgren had been an optometrist in Everett, a career that served him well in politics, he'd say, because it allowed him to see the shortsightedness of his opponents. At the very least, Wallgren could see the shortsightedness of lumbermen clamoring for access to the peninsula's forests, and in 1935 he introduced legislation adding 440,000 protected acres to Mount Olympus National Monument and transforming the site into a national park. Wallgren was motivated by a desire to preserve the uniqueness of the landscape—its old-growth trees, its wildlife, and the crystal-clear waters that filled Lake Crescent and bubbled up from Sol Duc Hot Springs. But he had other motivations, as well. Like many New Dealers in the Northwest, Wallgren believed that the Roosevelt administration had missed an opportunity to implement sustainable forestry policies when it sanctioned industrial self-regulation. Locking up a significant portion of forestland within the boundaries of a national park, he believed, would decrease harvestable acreage and force lumbermen to manage existing productive stands more sustainably. Put differently, his goal was to achieve conservation through preservation.[37]

Wallgren had several allies on his side, like Harold Ickes, a Progressive Era reformer turned preservationist and wilderness advocate, who now oversaw the nation's public lands as secretary of the interior. Joining Wallgren and Ickes were several members of Washington's congressional delegation and a nascent wilderness movement led by the Emergency Conservation Committee. Opposing Wallgren were the timber industry and the USFS, which controlled the lands surrounding the proposed park's boundaries and which saw Wallgren's proposal as a direct challenge to its authority and control over the nation's public forestlands. Sitting on the fence between these two battling factions was Franklin D. Roosevelt, who by 1937 had yet to publicly come down in favor or opposition to the proposed park.[38]

As with so many debates over natural resources, both past and present, the debate over Olympic National Park centered on jobs. Though employment in the timber industry had improved since its nadir four years earlier, by 1936 when the House Committee on Public Lands called a public hearing in Lake Crescent, Washington, to hear testimony on Wallgren's legislation, the unemployment rate in Northwest logging remained much higher than the national average, a fact that provided the park's opponents with convenient arguments. Lumbermen testifying before the House

Committee claimed that a park would bring an end to logging on the Olympic Peninsula. The Chambers of Commerce in the nearby logging towns of Aberdeen and Hoquiam agreed. C. J. Buck, the USFS regional forester who oversaw the Olympic Peninsula, testified that keeping the area open to logging "would mean year-long employment for 600 men in the woods and 600 more family men working in five mills with 120 thousand per day cut, 200 days a year. A total community of 1,200 families from now until Gabriel blows his horn." For the park's proponents and Ickes, in particular, the industry and the USFS's sudden concern for jobs and timber-working communities rang hollow, belying their true motives. After all, it was their policies that had created widespread unemployment in the industry in the first place. Ickes testified they "see no wrong in destroying a national treasure so long as a profit may be taken."[39]

This was the political battle that the IWA waded into when it came out in favor of Olympic National Park in the spring of 1937. Like Ickes, the union supported Wallgren's legislation because it believed that the cut-and-run logging of the past several decades, and not preservation, was responsible for the high unemployment in the industry, and it further shared Wallgren's belief that expanding protected areas would force the industry to manage existing stands more sustainably. Yet, the IWA's support for the park went beyond mere economics to the varied ways timber-working communities had long known and used the forests. Speaking at the IWA's October 1937 executive board meeting, Ted Dokter, representing the union's Puget Sound District, encouraged the IWA to "vehemently petition" politicians and "press for early enactment of the bill" because of the proposed park's "unique flora and fauna" and the "essential primitive natural conditions now prevailing in that area." The executive board agreed with Dokter's assessment, and in the weeks after the meeting, the IWA became a vocal advocate of the Wallgren bill, lobbying local politicians and encouraging members to write their representatives and tell them that the park was necessary "to conserve the timber and other natural resources from greed and rapid depletion."[40]

The debate over the park was finally settled later that fall, when Roosevelt visited the Olympic Peninsula and in a cabin on Lake Crescent hammered out a compromise with Wallgren, Ickes, and USFS and timber-industry representatives, ultimately agreeing on the national-park designation with a slightly smaller boundary than originally proposed. Though the bulk of the political lifting on the bill was clearly done by Wallgren and Ickes, the fledgling IWA's vocal support played a role in the park's creation, a fact not lost on Northwest New Dealers. Speaking at the union's 1938 convention, John Coffee, a US Representative from Washington, commended the union for the stand it'd taken on the park, even as it battled employer security guards on the picket lines across the region. "I want to congratulate the IWA on having supported the creation of Olympus National Park," he said. "This great organization believes thoroughly in the principle of conservation. And who more than anybody else should believe in conservation than those who are employed in the lumber industry." Coffee concluded his remarks by saying that both Roosevelt and Ickes had taken notice of the union's stance and its "temerity to stand up and fight for conservation of one of the most beautiful things that God ever created—and that's an old growth virgin fir tree."[41]

For IWA leaders, the accolades visited on the union by New Dealers like Coffee suggested a new political strategy for realizing labor environmentalism. The union's leaders could now see that plenty of people in the nascent wilderness movement and many politicians disagreed with the control granted to lumbermen by early New Deal policy, but just remained politically isolated. Thus, the IWA could act as a lynchpin connecting these disparate groups and uniting them in a powerful coalition capable of finally passing real forestry reform in the Northwest woods. Pritchett laid out this vision at the union's 1939 convention: "Organized labor must arouse public opinion to a great degree and weld it to political and community leadership to obtain correlation and integration in the use of the forest resource, wood products, pure water, electric power, wild life, recreation, forage crops, through the application of the multiple use principle."[42]

Pritchett's words are noteworthy because in them, he articulated a vision of forest management that would shape the IWA's environmental politics for the next several decades and can still be heard throughout timber country today. He was advocating for multiuse forestry, policies that conceive of the forest as neither a purely productive space nor a purely consumptive space but, rather, a combination of both. It's a vision that makes room for work and recreation, the tangible economic value of timber, and the less-tangible—but no less-important—aesthetic, cultural, and social values of forests. In one sense, Pritchett's was a forward-looking vision, one that anticipated the economic pressures that would be placed on forests as the economy rebounded after the Depression and then called on policy makers to tread carefully as harvests increased. In another sense, though, this vision was rooted in the culture of timber country and the ways timber workers and their families had long known and used the forests. It represented a concern to protect their jobs and a concern to protect the forests they hunted, hiked, and fished in. In short, Pritchett's concept of multiuse forests, if not the IWA's labor environmentalism more broadly, represented the political articulation of ideas of place that emerged decades earlier.

World War II and the New Culture of Conservation

This vision, however, would have to wait, as suggested by the high-pitched hum of electricity coursing from the New Deal dams on the Columbia River and the industrial rumble of factories turning out airplanes and ships as the region mobilized for war. Not a month before Pritchett stood before the delegates at the union's 1939 convention, Canada had entered World War II, and in two years' time the United States would also join the Allied forces. World War II was the most mechanized war fought in human history up to that point, but the Allied war effort still required an incredible amount of good old-fashioned lumber. Forty-thousand board feet of timber went into every C-62 cargo plane; 140,000 board feet went into every aircraft carrier flight deck. In 1942 alone the US military used 9 million board feet just for ammunition crates and another 25 million board feet for road beds and bridges. A 1943 report by the War Manpower Commission concluded that timber was the Allied forces' most important strategic asset, surpassing steel and nonferrous metals in terms of military need. Wartime industry had an equally voracious appetite for timber and used billions of board feet in the construction of new factories and worker housing. In 1942 Washington's and Oregon's timber industries set new production records, producing more than 36 billion board feet, 90 percent of which went directly to supplying the military and wartime industries. Given the centrality of lumber to national geopolitical interests, forest protections quickly became anathema to patriotism, and in the interest of supporting the Allied cause, the IWA signed a no-strike pledge and sidelined its conservation efforts.[43]

Even if the war complicated the IWA's future political plans, the increased demand for lumber gave the union an incredible amount of power that it leveraged to expand its membership. A 1942 report conducted by the National War Labor Board predicted a looming timber shortage that threatened to undermine the war effort. The report pointed to several problems, from the cut-and-run logging of the previous decades to labor shortages created by timber workers leaving the woods and mills for more-lucrative jobs in airplane manufacturing and shipbuilding. Yet, the most immediate problems it identified were the strikes, lockouts, and jurisdictional disputes that continued to idle logging camps and mills. A year after the report was issued, the National War Labor Board assigned arbitrator and future Oregon US Senator Wayne Morse to the Northwest woods and tasked him with bringing some order to the industry's labor relations. In late 1943 Morse convinced both operators and the IWA to sign an industry-wide master agreement that mandated across-the-board wage increases and, more important, automatic recognition in camps and mills organized by the IWA. British Columbia had no equivalent of the National War Labor Board, but the Canadian military's demand for lumber likewise gave timber workers north of the border considerable leverage: given a choice between strikes that shut down production or union recognition that allowed lumbermen to continue to fill wartime contracts, many British Columbian operators chose the latter. As a result of the war, the IWA's membership ballooned, going from roughly seventy thousand members before the war to over one hundred thousand immediately after. And while strikes and lockouts were not entirely a thing of the past, they now occurred less often.[44]

As timber workers felled the trees and milled the timber that would soon be woven into ships and aircraft destined for the Pacific and European theaters, they increasingly talked with optimism about their futures at the war's end. The sense of uncertainty that someone like Churchill had expressed just a decade before had now been replaced by a belief that organized labor could guide the industry in more-sustainable directions. This was an optimism shared by the Progressive movement throughout the region. In the late 1930s and early 1940s the Northwest's literary left produced no fewer than a dozen novels, stories, and plays prophesizing that timber workers would be the architects responsible for building a more just, post-Depression world. Aberdeen, Washington, author Robert Cantwell's *Land of Plenty* was, perhaps, the most famous of these literary products. "Suddenly, the lights went out," reads the highly allegorical novel's opening line. The mill's workers amble around in the dark, confused about what direction they should take. Over the course of the novel, the workers slowly realize their commonalities and that the difficulties they face, from low pay and regular injuries, are all the fault of the mill's owners. And when the lights come back on in the second half of the novel, workers have a newfound sense of collective power that leads to a strike.[45]

But it was *Timber*, a novel written in 1943 by Roderick Haig-Brown, the logger-turned writer-and-conservationist, that, perhaps, best captured the hope that many proletarian authors of the Depression era saw in timber country's working class. The story takes place in a fictional logging camp in the Northwest's coastal rainforests and opens with the main characters, Johnny Holt and Alec "Slim" Crawford, debating the high accident rate in the woods. Slim, the voice of labor radicalism, believes accidents will continue until the men in camp get a strong union. "It's just a racket," he tells Johnny, "and you guys fall for it. You keep falling for it and making money for the companies."

Johnny, the more naturally skilled logger, resists unionization out of a sense of frontier independence and deep-seated nativism. "We'd have a bunch of foreign bastards telling us what to do," he says, opposing unionization. While Johnny and Slim disagree over politics, they find common ground in a shared love of the forest. On one of the pair's frequent backpacking trips, both are shocked to find that a small trout stream they loved to fish has been filled in by a landslide caused by overlogging. At that moment, Johnny sees that the same industrial forces injuring loggers are the very same forces responsible for destroying the forest, and he begins to see that unions are the best hope for protecting workers and nature. "Conservation will have to come from the guys down below," he says, "the owners will never do it."[46]

Haig-Brown's story captured the essence of working-class culture and politics in the Northwest woods of the 1930s and 1940s: a love of the forest born equally of work and hunting, fishing, and hiking. More than that, though, it captured the essence of labor environmentalism: that human and environmental exploitation are not distinct processes but linked and that strong unions hold the potential to address both. The notice that authors like Haig-Brown, conservationists like Ickes, and politicians like Coffee had taken of the IWA portended a new coalition on the immediate horizon.

5

"The Many Uses and Values of Forests"

Ellery Foster must've felt a little out of place every time he attended an IWA convention or visited one of the union's halls, which, by the time he was hired as the director of the union's Education and Research Department in 1945, existed in nearly every logging camp and sawmill throughout the Northwest. A tall man with an athletic build, Foster certainly could pass for a timber worker but only from a distance. Up close, anyone would've noticed small yet distinct markers of class status that signaled he was an outsider. Unlike most IWA members, who only reluctantly traded their staged pants and caulked boots for slacks and dress shoes to attend formal union functions, Foster wore a suit and tie with confidence. Then there were his hands, which still had all ten of his fingers. Few IWA members who'd lived their lives inches from saws could say the same. The more consequential differences, though, had less to do with appearances and more to do with vocation. Foster had spent most of his adult life working as a forester and resource manager. After graduating from the University of Michigan's School of Forestry in the 1920s, he worked in the US Forest Service as a ranger, timber cruiser, mapmaker, and silviculturist. In 1935 chief forester of the United States Ferdinand A. Silcox handpicked Foster to lead the agency's Division of National Planning. In 1937 Foster left the Forest Service to head his home state of Minnesota's Department of Natural Resources. In 1940 Foster returned to federal work when he took a position in the US Department of Agriculture's Cooperative Land Use Program, and in 1942 he began working for the War Production Board as a timber analyst. So Foster had worked in the woods, in a sense, but the sort of labor he did—and the ways he knew the woods—were categorically different from the sort of labor IWA members did and knowledge of the forest they had.[1]

Yet, despite what his resume suggests, Foster would soon prove to the IWA's members that he had a view of forestry more resembling their own. He was highly critical of lumbermen, whom he routinely called "timber butchers," and equally critical of the members of his own profession who served them. Industrial forestry, he once wrote, is "a colossal hoax by which the lumber barons hope to lull an uneasy public into complacency long enough to finish their wasteful exploitation of old growth forest for the benefit of a privileged few." But perhaps the most important thing about Foster, and the one quality that would, more than any other, help him meld into the IWA's ranks was his firm conviction that foresters needed organized labor, and organized labor needed foresters. "Against the forces of entrenched interests that grow fat by exploiting scarcity," he said, "foresters and woodworkers should be natural allies."[2]

Though Foster would only work at the IWA for three years, his tenure as the head of the union's Education and Research Department would be hugely consequential and guide the union's environmental politics well into the 1960s. The IWA's early intervention in the Olympic National Park debate had suggested a way for the IWA to push for conservation while building its power and influence in the industry. World War II had disrupted the union's political plans, but as the war wound down in 1945, IWA members once again began talking with renewed enthusiasm about a future of democratized forestry. Foster played a crucial role in these efforts, gilding the union's working-class environmentalism with the language of New Deal conservationism. This new articulation of labor environmentalism proved politically powerful in the postwar years and created new opportunities for the IWA to build partnerships with sympathetic politicians and an increasingly powerful environmental movement. This coalition would successfully protect millions of acres of forest through wilderness designations in the 1950s and 1960s and, in so doing, attempt to ensure that there'd be forests for jobs and recreation for subsequent generations of timber workers and their families.

Postwar Timber Country

Timber country emerged from the war a new and transformed place. The unprecedented demand for lumber created by wartime mobilization helped lift struggling timber communities from the depths of the Depression, and this demand continued unabated into the postwar years. Cities and suburbs were expanding throughout North America, and millions of new homes were being built as a result of new housing policies intended to democratize homeownership. Europe was also rebuilding after the war, and much of the lumber used in those rebuilding efforts came from the Northwest. By 1947 the Pacific Coast states produced upward of 13 billion board feet of lumber a year, which accounted for more than 38 percent of total US softwood lumber production, and the wage rates the IWA negotiated for its members helped ensure that workers benefited from the industry's postwar expansion. Jurisdictional conflicts between unions also abated in the postwar years. The IWA and Carpenters battled one another to something of a truce by the start of the war, and then in the postwar years both unions began to bargain jointly with employers.[3]

The postwar timber boom owed as much to large economic factors as it did new productive technologies. Sawmill owners swapped steam power for diesel motors, logging operators replaced old and worn donkey engines for more-reliable and far-faster steel spars—large, extendible metal poles mounted on the back of large trucks that allowed companies to speed up the yarding process and move operations more quickly and frequently. And most timber fellers allowed their old crosscut saws to rust as they picked up new chainsaws produced by German manufacturers. Yet, the biggest change of all came with the ways lumber was transported from forest to mill. Logging railways had always been expensive to build and maintain. New improvements in diesel engines and transmissions combined with an extensive network of logging roads built by state and provincial forestry departments now allowed logging trucks to do what locomotives once had, at a fraction of the cost (figure 5.1).[4]

Truck logging changed lumber production, and it changed where workers and their families lived. Roads and trucks made traveling across timber country more reliable, which allowed workers to live a bit farther from job sites. Many timber companies had shuttered their towns and camps during the Depression, but now, after the war, new transportation technologies encouraged even more companies to abandon the landlord business. In some cases, owners simply razed their camps and instructed families to move to the nearest town. In other instances, towns were converted into independent municipalities, and workers were offered the opportunity to purchase their homes. That was the case in McCleary, once home to Angelo Pellegrini. At the start of World War II, Henry McCleary sold his mills and town site to the Simpson Logging Company. At war's end, Simpson announced that McCleary would be converted into an independent town, and workers would be

Figure 5.1. Logging trucks, North Bend, Oregon, 1943. Industries and Occupations Photographs, Special Collections, INDo233, University of Washington Libraries, Seattle.

allowed to buy their houses for what amounted to eighteen months of rental payments.[5]

Even if the ownership of many logging towns changed, people in these towns continued to use and rely on the forest. If anything, the rising affluence of workers and the shorter hours they now worked, both a result of growing IWA power, encouraged people in timber country to spend even more time outdoors. Some of the best evidence for how hunting and fishing remained part of timber country's identity can be seen in the pages of the region's labor press. In the early 1950s, the editors of both the IWA's and Carpenters' papers made space for columns by famed Oregon outdoor writer Fred Goetz. A native of Baltimore, Maryland, Goetz had first come to Portland during World War II as a merchant marine. He remained in the Northwest at war's end and began writing outdoor columns for the *Portland (OR) Reporter* as well as several regional hunting and fishing journals. While most of Goetz's pieces involved discussions of various sportfishing tactics or offered lessons in basic elk and deer biology, he also picked fights with chemical companies that dumped industrial effluents into Oregon's rivers and was a fierce critic of the region's pulp and paper industry, which he blamed for singlehandedly causing declining salmon runs. Goetz's columns for the IWA and Carpenters continued in this tradition. He reported on union members' successful hunting trips, published photos of loggers holding freshly caught salmon, and offered advice on the best outdoor gear, all while condemning a timber industry that too often harvested timber with little regard for wildlife and hunting opportunity.[6]

Yet, the Depression still loomed large in the collective memory of the IWA, and as many of the union's members understood it, without responsible forestry policies, the economic security many timber workers now enjoyed could end in an instant. In the union's paper in 1945, newly minted IWA president James Falding reminded readers that the companies they worked for had little interest in the sustainability of forests and rural communities and that the high wages and steady employment of the postwar years shouldn't blind union members to the fact that all this was fleeting without meaningful forest conservation standards regulating the actions of logging companies. "The operator lives a thousand miles from the forest," Falding said, "no Weyerhaeuser has slept in a log cabin for more than a generation. But the lumber jacks [sic] and their families, after the trees are gone, find themselves inhabiting ghost towns. The mill machinery rusts and the schools close."[7]

In some ways, though, making the political case for sustainable, socially oriented forestry was more difficult after the war than it'd been before the war, for reasons having to do with changes in North American forestry. The profession experienced something of a schism in the late 1930s. Socially conscious foresters like Bob Marshall, who'd argued for a resource policy rooted in rural economic stability, had become disillusioned with the outsized influence of industry in forest management. They fled the ranks of public agencies and, instead, turned to what was, at the time, a nascent wilderness movement, where they hoped their ideas could be put to better use. In their place, a new generation of more-technocratic foresters emerged. Wielding scientific authority and increasingly arcane theories, they made little space for working-class environmental concerns, leading Falding to complain that when it came to forestry, workers were treated as "interested but technically uninformed." This is why the IWA ultimately turned to Foster. In his formal training and vast experience in conservation bureaucracies, the IWA saw someone who could help convince politicians and land mangers that union members weren't, as Falding continued, "shooting in the dark."[8]

The schism within the forestry profession also helps explain why Foster turned to the IWA. Like many progressive foresters of the Depression era, Foster had become disillusioned with the forestry profession, and he just saw organized labor, more than wilderness organizations, as a more effective vehicle for change. Foster's thinking was best articulated in an article he published in the *Journal of Forestry*. He argued that despite their scientific training and fancy degrees, most American foresters understood little about the nation's woodlands. Certainly, Foster argued, new methodologies and experimental techniques had allowed foresters to learn a lot about things like forest succession and regeneration rates. But, he said, "meager progress" had been made in putting all that science to "use for the common good." Foster believed that all land managers and foresters, in particular, had a professional obligation to work with rural communities and take their ideas about land use as seriously as the most rigorous scientific studies, and then work with those communities to implement management plans that would simultaneously conserve resources and economically benefit people.[9]

Foster's views on the relationship between planners and rural communities had been shaped by what sociologist Jess Gilbert has called the "agrarian intellectualism" of the New Deal. The agrarian intellectuals believed that expert knowledge was as much to blame for the Depression as anything else. They said that conservation agencies, state planning boards, and farm scientists had been so convinced of the infallibility of their scientifically guided land-management strategies that they'd failed to listen to farmers and workers warning of critical environmental problems, like topsoil erosion and deforestation. The agrarian intellectuals saw in the New Deal a promise of more-democratized land management, where planners listened to, rather than dictated to, rural producers. This view informed Foster's view of how forestry should function. "Research may be done by the expert alone," Foster once wrote, "but planning *ought* to be done with the people." The role government should play in resource policy was, thus, to limit the power of industry and experts and ensure land managers listened to farmers, loggers, and all rural producers who, as Foster stated, "have shown capacity to think in broad terms of the general good, and not merely of selfish interest."[10]

Lumber Snafu

In Foster the IWA had found an effective advocate to give voice and scientific credence to its ideas, and in the IWA Foster had found an organization willing to commit its membership and resources to finally realizing a more socially conscious forestry. It would be an intellectual and political marriage that would shape the IWA's forestry politics for the next two decades and, in the immediate future, encourage the union to charge headlong into private-forestry policy. Foster's first major act as director of the Education and Research Department was to assist the IWA's officers in drafting a series of resolutions to be introduced at the union's 1945 constitutional convention. Other than its founding convention in 1937, perhaps no other convention was as important in the IWA's history. Meeting in Eugene, Oregon, delegates endorsed a platform that committed the union to an ambitious postwar social agenda, from expanding Social Security and veterans' benefits to increased international oversight of atomic energy. It was environmental concerns, however, that dominated the proceedings. J. Alfred Hall, director of the USFS's Pacific Northwest Range and Experimental Station, gave a keynote address that celebrated the union's work toward creating a "permanent forest industry, based on permanent forests." In their official report, the IWA's officers called on the union's membership to continue "developing and maintaining contacts with interested groups, agencies, and individuals whose interests in forestry and wood utilization are similar to those of woodworkers." And delegates passed five forestry resolutions calling for increased regulation of private-lands logging, more funding for silviculture research, improvements in wood utilization, and better fire protection.[11]

The most important of these was resolution 29, Regional and Local Natural Resources Planning. At its core, resolution 29 committed the union to a political campaign to democratize sustained-yield forest management. Sustained yield is almost as old as the forestry profession itself. The basic idea, as the name implies, is to harvest timber at roughly the same rate it grows back, in theory ensuring timber supplies in perpetuity. Foster and the IWA agreed with the concept of sustained-yield management, just not the ways it'd been implemented. In forestry, as in life, the devil is always in the details. Who, exactly, should determine harvest rates, regeneration rates, and the size of sustained-yield units? Should foresters only count the most-marketable species of timber, like Douglas fir, and ignore less-desirable species, like hemlock, when making their calculations? What time frame should foresters manage for? A fifty-year cycle? A hundred-year cycle? Even longer? The industry had long used its economic and political power to answer these questions in ways that affirmed cut-and-run logging. Resolution 29 proposed a radical and far more democratic way of addressing the ambiguities inherent in sustained-yield management. Drawing connections to the public boards that'd been created to market the electrical power created by the Tennessee Valley Authority and Columbia River Dams, the union argued that sustained-yield units should be determined and managed by committees composed of workers and rural community members. "Sustained yield forestry has little meaning for woodworkers unless it is achieved locality by locality where woodworkers live," the resolution stated.[12]

Following the 1945 convention, Foster authored a pamphlet that distilled the union's new forestry resolutions down into a cohesive policy statement, further articulating the union's forestry politics in the language of agrarian intellectualism and New Deal conservationism. The title of the piece, *Lumber Snafu*, taken from Foster's observation that Northwest forest management was "situation normal—all fouled up," added Foster's own rhetorical flair to the otherwise lackluster language of union convention proceedings. Detailing the ways that policy makers had ignored land speculation and land consolidation in the early twentieth century, and the ways that the Roosevelt administration had endorsed industrial self-regulation in the early years of the New Deal, Foster concluded that the state had simply created a "paradox of excessively inflated lumber prices along with a preponderance of substandard wages for lumber workers." Breaking that cycle, Foster argued, would require policies that made forestry look more similar to New Deal farm programs, like technical assistance for small-woodland owners, funding for research into more-effective resource utilization, and most important of all, more community-based participatory forms of land-use planning. "Most of what the government does about lumber production is to issue news releases," Foster wrote. "Contrast this with the farm program. The government has a genuine program . . . aimed at improving life in the farming communities."[13]

What Foster effectively did in *Lumber Snafu* was revisit that consequential meeting between West Coast Lumbermen's Association president William Greeley and Franklin Roosevelt more than a decade prior. Greeley had effectively convinced the president that timber should be administered like an industrial commodity, not an agricultural good. Foster now argued the exact opposite: the nation's forests would be better protected by thinking of them as agricultural goods and managing them with the same concerns for rural communities and the "common man" that were so central to the New Deal farming programs. "Lumber and the forests which grow the lumber are so important for the present and the future as well, that we must do what it takes both to produce the lumber and at the same time conserve and build up the forest," Foster concluded. "It will cost money, but the investment will add to our national wealth, just as the national farm program does."[14]

It was a message that many were willing to listen to. Following the initial publication of *Lumber Snafu*, the IWA printed several thousand copies and distributed them to union locals, urging rank-and-file members to use the text as a basis for forestry discussions. "I want to urge every local union to take up this problem," Falding instructed, "and organize its own program to make every member familiar with the IWA forestry plan and to make the whole community familiar with it. It is our job—the organized woodworkers' job—to lead off in the forestry fight." Foster also published a condensed version of the piece in the *Journal of Forestry*, and the IWA sent copies to foresters and political allies. By early 1946, the *International Woodworker* was reporting that the union's offices had been inundated with letters from conservationists and politicians thanking the union for their stand and asking what could be done to support the union in its efforts, including Gifford Pinchot, who offered his "hearty thanks" for their work. Conservationist and soon-to-be US senator Richard Neuberger (Oregon) published an endorsement of *Lumber Snafu* in the *New York Times*, while US senators Wayne Morse (Oregon) and Henry "Scoop" Jackson (Washington) praised the IWA's forestry policy in the local press. Finally, *Lumber Snafu* found its way to the desk of the House member from Michigan's Twelfth District, "Fightin'" Frank Hook.[15]

The Hook Forestry Bill

Fightin' Frank had been given his nickname by teammates during his high school wrestling days. Still, it was a handle he did his best to live up to for much of the rest of his life. He'd worked for a time in Michigan's logging camps, and though he later turned to the more genteel world of politics, he always retained something of a logger's belligerent edge, particularly, when it came to defending workers and organized labor. In 1940 Hook gained national attention when he publicly claimed that Martin Dies, the infamous anti-Communist and anti-labor senator from Texas, was a member of the fascist Silver Shirt Legion (Hook later apologized for the accusation after it was shown that the documents he'd based his claim on were forgeries). Five years later, Hook again gained national attention when he interrupted an anti-CIO statement being given by Mississippi US representative John Rankin. The verbal dispute escalated, and before anyone could intervene, Hook had wrestled Rankin to the floor of the House chamber.[16]

Hook was as fierce a defender of organized labor as he was of conservation. By the time he entered politics in the 1930s, he could look out over the rolling hills of his home district in Michigan's Upper Peninsula and see the once-thriving rural logging communities now stripped of their forests and their livelihoods. Like many New Dealers, Hook believed that the best thing he could do for his constituents, as well as other rural communities, was press for more-conscientious conservation policies. He'd been an early supporter of Olympic National Park in 1938, a stalwart supporter of New Deal rural-improvement programs, and had in 1940 authored and introduced the legislation that created Michigan's Isle Royale National Park.[17]

Hook was, therefore, receptive to the IWA's message when the union sent him a copy of *Lumber Snafu* in early 1946. The following April, Hook read the pamphlet into the *Congressional Record* and a few weeks after that introduced H.R. 6221, the Forestry Conservation and Development Act, to the House Agricultural Committee. What quickly became known as the Hook Forestry Bill adopted nearly all the IWA's recommendations. Mirroring the language of New Deal farm programs, the legislation proposed a federal forest-insurance program, similar to the crop-insurance program, and subsidies and planning assistance for forestland owners to implement replanting programs. Hook's draft bill also allocated funds for research into forestry, workers' safety, and more-efficient wood utilization. Those were the relatively uncontroversial elements of the legislation. Two additional proposals included in the bill were far more contentious and ensured that Hook's legislation would face significant opposition from the industry. First, the draft bill required that *all* timber harvests, on public and private lands alike, be approved by a federally licensed forester. Second, it called for the creation of "cooperative forest management committees" to manage sustained-yield units. Together, both provisions aimed to reshape the management of the nation's forests, taking control out of the hands of the industry and placing it in the hands of the federal government and rural communities.[18]

In an *International Woodworker* analysis of the bill, the IWA's leaders explained why its passage was crucial to the union's future. According to IWA leaders, the bill's call for more-cooperative forest management would expunge the "monopolistic evils" inherent in land-use policies and create a more democratic landscape, leading to a more stable industry that would ensure both trees and jobs well into the future. But the IWA's support for the bill wasn't based on economics alone. Rather, the union also evoked timber workers' deep sense of place and promised that Hook's legislation would protect the many ways they had long known and used forests. "The IWA wants a broad-scale forestry program, one that makes provision for the many uses and values of forests, and not just for saw logs," the union's officers explained. "We want our forests and forest waters to be good places for hunting and fishing, we want to see more of the attractive spots in the woods developed for family outings, where we and anyone else can come on holidays and vacations to have a good time outdoors."[19]

The Hook Bill became the topic of fierce debate among foresters, workers, timberland owners, and industry representatives in the months after its introduction, in both predictable and unpredictable ways. Industry opposition was likely expected by Hook and the IWA. "Important facts you need to know about the hook forest dictatorship bill" reads the headline of an advertisement taken out by a trade group in Hook's hometown newspaper, the *Escanaba (MI) Daily Press*. The article warned timber landowners, large and small alike, as well as hunters and anglers, that under the provisions of the bill, "You could be sent up for as many years as the Bureaucrats wanted to send you in jail, for any number of years, up to life." What was likely less expected was that the bill created fissures in the house of labor and strained the IWA's relationship with one of its staunchest allies on the Pacific Coast, the International Fishermen and Allied Workers of America (IFAWA). Both the IWA and IFAWA were CIO affiliates organized in the Depression era, and both represented workers in resource-extraction industries known for dangerous work. Even so, by 1945 the two unions were speaking in remarkably different tones about conservation. That year, and much to the Fishermen's frustration, the Woodworkers had strenuously supported an Oregon referendum to ban commercial steelhead fishing in Nestucca Bay, arguing that protecting the few remaining fish in the watershed outweighed whatever minimal job losses the ban might cause. Now, a year later, the IFAWA came out against the Hook Bill, a position that the IWA's members saw as a violation of CIO progressivism. The Fishermen had been "duped by their employers into believing that conservation and employment were mutually exclusive propositions," one IWA member told a local journalist, going on to suggest that the IFAWA hire its own biologist "to put you fellows on the beam the way Ellery Foster has done for us."[20]

Even as the IWA found itself now entangled in resource debates with allies, the Hook Bill also created new opportunities for partnerships. The emphasis the IWA had placed on healthy forests for hunting and fishing resonated with members of the United Auto Workers (UAW). By the postwar period, rising rates of affluence and car ownership among autoworkers—the result of hard-won victories at General Motors and Ford during the Depression—allowed UAW members to spend more time in the outdoors, creating a conservationist ethic within the union. Shortly after the Hook Bill's introduction, the UAW overwhelmingly agreed to commit resources to push for its passage. Ivan Brown, president of UAW Local 9 in Hook's home district, led these efforts, and on a return trip from Washington, DC, to lobby for the bill, he explained the rationale for autoworkers' support. "Congressman Hook has recognized the deep-seated American love of our forests," Brown said. "He knows that his constituents have always considered it their right to go into the forests to hunt, to study nature, to picnic or camp out." The UAW's support of the Hook Bill proved vitally important to rallying the entire CIO, as well. The CIO didn't have a stellar record on environmental issues prior to the postwar period. John L. Lewis, the federation's figurehead and former president of the United Mine Workers of America, had opposed many New Deal hydropower programs out of fear they would replace coal. And, in 1945 at the CIO's constitutional convention, anticonservationist delegates had nearly succeeded in defeating a resolution in support of a forestry program. But a year later, the IWA, then the largest union on the Pacific Coast, and the UAW, then the largest union in the industrial Midwest, succeeded in shifting the CIO's environmental stance. At the UAW's behest, delegates at the CIO's 1946 convention nearly unanimously passed a resolution in support of the Hook Bill, stating that its provisions to "protect and preserve selected areas of forest wilderness and virgin timber for public enjoyment and recreation" were of vital concern to all American workers.[21]

Beyond the ranks of organized labor, support for the IWA and the Hook Bill, again, played out in unpredictable ways, drawing the support of organizations that had long been indifferent to unions. Officially, the USFS remained silent on the bill, but at the IWA 1946 executive board meeting, union officers reported that they'd received the widespread, if silent, support of public-lands foresters. The Oregon Grange also supported the Hook Bill. "We have a big stake in forestry," grange leader Morton Thompkins told the *International Woodworker*. The IWA's newspaper also reported that the union had received support and endorsements from the Seattle Mountaineers and the Sierra Club, two organizations that largely drew membership from the urban middle class. In *The Nation*, Neuberger summed up the ways the Hook Bill was creating new environmental coalitions. "Various outdoor clubs fought the conservation battle for decades without labor's assistance," he wrote, ultimately concluding that, with their support for the Hook Bill, "labor is the newest recruit in the camp of the conservationists."[22]

By the fall of 1946 the IWA officers were predicting the imminent success of the Hook Bill. They had good reason to be optimistic. The bill marked one of the first times in the history of environmental politics that such a broad array of people and groups—from workers to more traditional conservationists and newer wilderness advocacy organizations—were all standing together behind a single piece of legislation, and the IWA believed that no politician could reasonably ignore such widespread support. Writing in the IWA's newspaper, the normally cynical Foster spoke in uncharacteristically sanguine tones about a future of democratic forest management portended by the Hook Bill: "That's the kind of thing this country has needed for a long time, . . . and we're certainly glad to see a Congressman with the brains and the push to throw it in the legislative hopper."[23]

Postwar Forestry in British Columbia

Foster focused most of his efforts on reforming American forestry, though he did frequently offer analyses of British Columbia resource policy in the pages of the IWA's newspaper. Yet, even if Foster wasn't as directly involved in the Canadian IWA's postwar forestry campaigns, the union's British Columbian district council would pursue many of the same ideas he advocated. This had much to do with Colin Cameron. Cameron wasn't exactly the Canadian version of Foster (nor Foster the American version of Cameron). Unlike the American forester, who'd been born into a solidly middle-class family and had spent his formative professional years in the ranks of conservation agencies, Cameron was born into a solidly working-class community in the coal and timber country of Vancouver Island and spent his early years working on the docks where he'd acquired a socialist strain that ultimately pushed him toward the Co-operative Commonwealth Federation (CCF). Shortly after the CCF's founding, Cameron had won a seat representing the party in the Legislative Assembly of British Columbia and in 1937 was appointed to be the CCF's chief forestry critic. For all their political differences, though, both Cameron and Foster shared a disdain for the technocratic directions the forestry profession had moved in, an agrarian intellectualism, and a belief that New Deal conservation programs could and should guide postwar forest management.[24]

Cameron's ideas about forestry were most clearly articulated in his 1941 pamphlet, *Forestry . . . B.C.'s Devastated Industry.* Cameron argued that the wanton waste and environmental destruction that characterized the province's timber industry had been created by professional foresters who, alongside lumbermen, had traded long-term social stability for short-term economic gains. British Columbia, he wrote, "has been conducting her affairs like an exiled Russian Grand Duchess who sells her jewels bit by bit to get the more prosaic but more useful necessities of life, and like the Grand Duchess we are rapidly getting down to the last necklace." Cameron believed that resource policies south of the border offered something of a guide for British Columbian land managers, particularly, the democratic resource-management provisions of the Tennessee Valley Authority (TVA). Detailing the ways in which New Dealers had begun to lift poor Appalachian communities up from poverty by giving them control of the water and electricity spilling out of the TVA's dams, Cameron saw the project as "the most significant social experiment in North America," an experiment that promised to play "a more important part in the development of a new order of society than all the books and all the speeches in the socialist arsenal."[25]

Repeated calls by the CCF for forestry reform combined with the party's growing popularity among the province's farmers and industrial workers forced the legislative assembly in 1944 to convene a committee tasked with examining the province's forestry system. Led by Chief Justice for the Court of Appeals Gordon McGregor Sloan, the commission heard testimony from hundreds of individuals, foresters, industry representatives, and workers. Predictably, industry representatives argued for maintaining the status quo and against any new conservation standards. Roderick Haig-Brown, the timber-worker-turned-conservationist and author of fishing books, told the committee that saving the province's salmon required a more conscientious forestry program. Harold Pritchett, the IWA's former president who'd been forced to step down from his office after the United States denied him an entry visa because of his communist affiliations but who remained the leader of the union's British Columbia district council, said that the province's forests could "provide a livelihood to thousands of people," if "steps are taken to bring an end to the waste that has characterized lumbering in the past." Cameron's testimony was perhaps the most radical. "The only way out of this impasse," he said, was an entirely "provincially owned and operated industry."[26]

Few likely expected that the politically moderate Sloan would take Cameron's calls for socialized forestry seriously, but what the IWA and CCF presence at the hearings did do was help shift Sloan's centrism leftward. As E. T. Kinney, British Columbia's Minister of Lands and Forests, later explained, testimony given by timber workers and CCF Socialists forced Sloan to tilt toward "a compromise between rigid government regulation and outright exploitation of the forest resource." At the end of the hearings, Sloan recommended that the province adopt a new conservation program. Those recommendations, which ultimately became the basis of the 1947 British Columbia Forest Practices Act, created a new system of auctioning off the province's public timber that echoed some of the proposals in the Hook Bill. Specifically, the new legislation created what were called "forest management licences" (FMLs). Any company harvesting Crown timber would have to have an FML, which would require a provincial forester to approve all harvesting plans.[27]

Although the IWA and CCF press lauded the 1947 Forest Practices Act as legislation that would reduce "wanton waste and ruthless destruction" on public lands, both worried about continued overharvests on private lands. Still, what timber workers saw in postwar British Columbia was a crucial step in the right direction and an acknowledgment by state actors that forests were, as one rank-and-file IWA member said in the pages of the union's British Columbia paper, "basic natural resources that cannot be left entirely in the hands of private interests, but must become the responsibility of the government, acting in the interests of the people." Indeed, for timber workers on both sides of the border, the postwar years marked a period of optimism, a moment when working-class power was growing on job sites and, more significantly, appeared to be growing in the domain of resource politics. After decades of cut-and-run logging and the failure of Depression-era politicians on both sides of the border to address the ways resource mismanagement negatively impacted rural working peoples, timber country finally seemed to be getting its long-awaited New Deal.[28]

From New Deal Conservation to Wilderness

Events of the late 1940s, however, would prove this optimism was wildly misplaced. The political landscape was changing in the postwar era, moving away from the very sort of New Deal liberalism that IWA forestry proposals on both sides of the border were rooted in. The consequences of this political realignment would be most damning for the Hook Bill. Hook had introduced the Forestry Conservation and Development Act in the spring of 1946, and by fall he still hadn't been able to push it out of committee to the floor for a vote. Preventing the bill's movement was the political faction in control of the House Agricultural Committee: the Dixiecrats, southern Democratic Party members committed to upholding Jim Crow segregation. The Dixiecrats had long seen organized labor as a threat to the White supremacy they sought to maintain, but by 1946 they'd come to see the CIO and the IWA, in particular, as existential threats. Earlier that year the CIO had initiated Operation Dixie, a massive effort to organize Black workers in the region's textile mills, docks, tobacco processors, and cotton gins. The IWA was at the forefront of this effort and committed two hundred organizers to bring mostly Black southern timber workers into the union's fold. By September, the IWA had organized twenty-six new locals in southern pine country and had earned the ire of the Dixiecrats, who, in retaliation, now refused to move the Hook Bill.[29]

Southern Democratic intransigence was just one factor working against the Hook Bill. Another was that the bill's sponsor was up for reelection, and if recent history was any guide, it was going to be a tough race. Hook had never really had a firm grip on his congressional seat. He'd first won it in 1934 after defeating Republican John Bennet by a 5 percent margin. He lost the seat to Bennet in 1942 and regained it in 1944. And now, in 1946, Bennet was again challenging Hook. Each race had been tight, but recent events guaranteed that the 1946 race would be especially so. A national strike wave earlier in the year had made even liberal voters wonder if the Democratic Party was doing too much to coddle organized labor. Growing tensions between the United States and the Union of Soviet Socialist Republics (USSR) also fueled fears that both the Democrats and the CIO were trying to sneak communism into America. Hook could still count on the lumber workers and miners in his district to cast their ballots in his favor, but as polls opened on Election Day, he likely wondered if this would be enough to counteract the growing conservativism of his district, if not the nation. If Hook did indeed express those concerns, they were well founded. In the days after the 1946 election, voters opened their newspapers to find that Hook had again lost his seat to Bennet, by a 3 percent margin. After his defeat Hook told the local press that he still believed his bill had a chance to be passed into law. The IWA echoed Hook's optimism in their newspapers. Both were wrong. After Hook's defeat, the Forestry Conservation and Development Act died the same death that much of the rest of the New Deal order was now dying in more reactionary postwar America.[30]

The loss of one of their stalwart congressional allies was the beginning of a period of struggle for the IWA, if not all of organized labor. Like Hook, many prolabor Democrats lost their seats in the 1946 midterms. Voters had resoundingly turned control of the House over to Republicans, who now used their majority to push an antilabor agenda. In the 1947 legislative session, the majority Republican Congress dismantled many of the protections that organized labor had been afforded by the New Deal's Wagner Act with the passage of the infamous Taft-Hartley Act. Among its many provisions aimed at weakening radical unions, Taft-Hartley required all elected union officers to sign affidavits that they were not members of the Communist Party. The IWA's American locals grudgingly complied with the new guidelines, though it meant the ouster of many of their leaders in the Communist-led locals of northern Washington. British Columbian IWA members claimed that they were outside the purview of American labor law and refused to comply with the new anti-Communist policies of Taft-Hartley. Fearing that noncompliance of even the Canadian locals would expose the union to legal troubles, IWA leaders required British Columbian union officers to sign the affidavits.

British Columbian IWA leaders remained adamant in their refusal and in 1948 led an ill-fated attempt to secede from the international and establish their own autonomous union. British Columbian employers quickly refused to recognize agreements that had been negotiated with the IWA, and given the choice between the affidavits and protracted contract fights, members of the British Columbia council voted to return to the IWA, though they would now have do so without many of the Communists who'd helped build the union in the Depression years.[31]

That schism would affect forestry politics in British Columbia, too, and, specifically, undermine the future of the 1947 Forest Practices Act. Capitulating to political pressures placed on it by operators hoping to turn massive profits in the postwar timber boom, the British Columbia Forest Service had issued more FMLs than it could adequately manage. Companies were allowed to harvest timber without the mandated government oversight, and in a few widely publicized cases, foresters even accepted bribes to ignore harvest quotas. In 1954 the province's legislative assembly convened a second Sloan Commission with the hopes of salvaging the licensing system. Organized labor and the CCF had played a crucial role during the first commission, but both were conspicuously absent during the second. The British Columbian IWA's secession had created a massive fissure in the CCF, with some party members supporting the break and others opposing it. On the national level, CCF leadership denounced the secession move, and many IWA members loyal to the union left the party. As a result, the CCF went into a brief period of decline in British Columbia, and it wouldn't see a resurgence until it reorganized as the New Democratic Party in the early 1960s. In the more immediate future, the schism meant that neither labor nor the left had much representation during the second commission hearings, and Sloan ultimately recommended that the province abandon the licensing system and revert to older models of issuing forest contracts that contained little oversight.[32]

Adding to these problems was that Foster unceremoniously left the IWA. He seemed drained of much of his enthusiasm after the defeat of the Hook Bill. He remained director of the IWA's Education and Research Department for two more years, but it was clear in his regular columns in the union's newspaper that he now lacked much of his characteristic fervency. Over the course of 1947 those columns became shorter and eventually nonexistent. Late in 1948 Foster resigned his position as the union's head of the Education and Research Department without so much as an announcement in the IWA's paper, though he did continue to occasionally correspond with the union's leadership well through the 1960s. Reportedly, Foster returned to his home state of Minnesota, where he and his wife became back-to-the-land proponents.[33]

By the mid-twentieth century, the Northwest's lumber industry was also changing in ways that threatened to undermine many of the economic gains the IWA had made for workers over the past two decades. The 1950s were the boom years of Northwest logging, and the industry's growth had, indeed, helped bring about increased wages and benefits for union members. But starting in the late 1950s, more and more timber was increasingly being cut on public forests. Nationally, the harvest on USFS lands increased by roughly 250 percent in the postwar period, climbing from 2.7 billion board feet in 1946 to 6.9 billion board feet in 1956. Logging in the Northwest followed this general trend. Over that same ten-year period, public-lands harvest in Oregon climbed from 794 million board feet to 1.8 billion board feet. As harvests increased, so, too, did the number of people working in the Northwest's woods. Between 1947 and 1950, the number of wage workers employed in Oregon's wood-products industry skyrocketed from just over sixty thousand to about eighty-five thousand. Increases in IWA membership over this period, however, were not commensurate, as much of this work was being done by "gyppo" loggers, independent contractors who were harder to unionize because of their small crew sizes and frequent labor turnover.[34]

The industry's increasing orientation toward public lands threatened the IWA's bargaining power but also created new opportunities to press for democratized forest management. Unlike private companies that made forest-use decisions shielded from public view, the USFS was a public agency managing a public resource, and this provided all citizens with opportunities to intervene in management decisions. Since the 1920s USFS foresters had divided lands under their control into three management categories. Large-scale industrial logging was permitted in "intensive management" areas, limited logging was allowed on "primitive use" areas, and no logging was allowed in "wilderness" areas. Starting in the 1950s, the IWA increasingly turned its attention to these land-use categories and began pressuring the USFS to reclassify many "primitive use" areas as "wilderness."[35]

At first glance this shift in tactics appears to represent a significant break from the sort of conservationism the IWA had pursued over the past two decades. But as a 1951 resolution passed at the union's constitutional convention reveals, the IWA's leaders saw fights for wilderness as an extension of their earlier efforts. Employing a rationale similar to the one used in the Olympic National Park debate more than a decade prior, IWA leaders argued that creating new wilderness areas would force operators to manage private stands more sustainably while also creating "good outdoor country for recreational purposes." Put differently, wilderness became a way to achieve the ends of labor environmentalism through new means. Pivoting toward wilderness politics would also allow the IWA to continue building the broader coalition that it believed was necessary to shift public consensus toward more-sustainable harvesting. Indeed, while the Hook Bill was most certainly a legislative failure, it wasn't entirely a political failure. The union had established connections to environmental organizations, and it would now increasingly rely on one organization, the Wilderness Society, to push for more-democratic forestry.[36]

From the vantage of the present, when workers and environmentalists are far more likely to fight than cooperate, the IWA's desire to ally with the Wilderness Society appears somewhat odd. But in the 1950s both groups had ways of thinking about forests and rural workers that made them well suited to a partnership. Many of the society's founders and early members, like Robert Marshall and Aldo Leopold, had been public-lands foresters, and whatever their eventual critique of industry and USFS policy, they, nevertheless, recognized that regulated timber harvests had a legitimate place in forestland management. Others, like Benton MacKaye, had worked in natural-resource planning in New Deal conservation agencies and believed rural poverty could be best addressed through responsible resource policy. And others still, like eventual Wilderness Society president Howard Zahniser, who was raised in Pennsylvania coal country, hailed from rural communities, and they retained an affinity for the rural working-class. In short, the Wilderness Society of the 1950s, like the IWA, believed that protecting wilderness was just one part of a larger multiple-use land-management strategy that preserved some forest areas for recreation and wildlife habitat and others for sustainable production. "Our hope in preserving areas of wilderness free from lumbering," commented Zahniser in 1958, "is dependent on our ability to achieve a prosperous lumbering industry based on sound timber management within the forests and woodlots outside the wilderness."[37]

Shared beliefs about the merits of multiuse forest policy formed the basis for a partnership that throughout the 1950s had both Wilderness Society members and IWA members jointly supporting changes to Forest Service land classifications. The coalition won an early victory when it blocked a planned reduction to Olympic National Park. At stake were two large tracts in the Hoh and Bogachiel rain forests. In 1953 Washington governor Arthur B. Langlie, a friend of neither organized labor nor wilderness, announced his intention to reduce the park's boundaries and turn control of the forestland over to the USFS for intensive use. Reading the testimonies of witnesses opposed to the park's reduction, it's hard to tell exactly who were the workers and who were the environmentalists. The former often focused on the innate beauty of the park and the need to preserve recreational opportunities, and the latter talked about the need for sustainable logging practices outside the park's boundary. "The old-growth forests in the park are perhaps unique in the Northwest," IWA president Al Hartung told the committee, "which can provide great enjoyment for large numbers of people." Members from the Wilderness Society, in turn, testified that "more effective and permanent alternatives exist in a better defined and dynamic application of proven modern forestry practices on commercial forest lands outside the park." The outpouring of opposition the IWA and Wilderness Society organized helped sway public opinion against the reduction, and Langlie soon dropped the plan.[38]

The IWA and Wilderness Society, however, would be far less successful in blocking another proposal to open a section of Oregon's Three Sisters Primitive Area to logging, three years later. Named for a trio of now-dormant volcanoes that jut up from the forested hills of the Willamette National Forest, the woodlands surrounding the Sisters are unlike just about any other in the Northwest. Not quite the rain-soaked Douglas-fir stands of the western slope nor the arid pine forests of the eastern slope, the forests of the Sisters are a unique blend of both, a place where open wildflower fields more typical in central Oregon blend with the towering trees more commonly found in the western part of the state. It was the uniqueness of this place that encouraged chief forester Silcox to designate 190,000 acres of Sisters forest as primitive use in 1937. Two years later and shortly before his untimely death, Marshall, then serving as the head of the USFS's Division of Recreation and Lands, convinced Silcox to add another 55,000 acres to the Three Sisters Primitive Area. The addition contained Horse Creek and French Pete Creek, two drainages that sit on the outside shoulder of the Cascades, each made from relatively recent (in geological time) lava flows that created broad alpine valleys, which, Marshall had argued, were ecologically unique and worthy of protection.[39]

These 55,000 acres would significantly reshape American environmental politics and land management. As public-lands harvests increased in the early 1950s, timber operators increasingly clamored for access to the Three Sisters, specifically, the densely packed timber in the addition. In 1954 the USFS offered a solution intended to appease both the industry and wilderness activists. It would switch the designation of the original 190,000-acre parcel from primitive to wilderness but retain the primitive designation in the addition, thus keeping it open to logging. Both the Wilderness Society and IWA were quick to protest the addition's exclusion from the wilderness designation. If "they get this 50,000 acres," IWA President Al Hartung said, "then they can say, with much justification, that the remaining 200,000 acres could just as well be pared down further—a little here and a little there." At public hearings convened to debate the future of the Three Sisters, the same dynamic that had emerged in the Olympic Peninsula hearings played out once again, with IWA representatives stressing the recreational value of the Horse Creek drainage and the environmentalists stressing the need for more-sustainable logging practices outside the wilderness. The Three Sisters is a "great tourist attraction," Hartung told the committee, while Karl Onthank, Wilderness Society member and dean of students at the University of Oregon, instructed the committee that "this industry will have to find other solutions, the first of which will doubtless be better utilization of the wood now cut, such as is already being done by the more efficient operators."[40]

Unlike the Olympic National Park campaign, though, these arguments failed to sway the USFS. In 1957 the agency went ahead with its plans to keep the addition open to logging. The problem that the Wilderness Society and the IWA were up against was the undemocratic nature of decision making within the Forest Service. The USFS was required to take public comment, but it didn't have to listen. After the final ruling had been issued, Onthank penned a letter to his fellow Wilderness Society members: "The decision certainly points up the importance of passing a 'Wilderness Preservation Bill,' which will give substantial and durable protection. . . . If it is not passed we can take it for granted we will have this kind of battle on every one of the primitive and the limited areas found" in the Northwest's public forests. The local press agreed. If the USFS wouldn't act to protect sensitive forest areas, opined the *Redmond (OR) Spokesman*, the newspaper in a town not too far from the Three Sisters, "then the job should be given to some department that does." The editors of the *Eugene (OR) Register-Guard* agreed, as well. Similarly bemoaning "the ease with which such areas can be opened to logging," the editorial staff at the paper concluded that "what is needed . . . is a national wilderness system."[41]

What the editors at the *Spokesman* and *Register-Guard* did not know was that Wilderness Society president Zahniser had been quietly drafting legislation that would take control of wilderness designations from the USFS and turn it over to Congress. The conflict over the Three Sisters had now energized enough wilderness advocates and sympathetic politicians that Zahniser believed the time had come to more strenuously push his legislation. In 1958 Idaho Senator Frank Church took Zahniser's draft legislation and introduced it as a bill called the National Wilderness Preservation Act. The IWA played a crucial role in the public hearings that followed, providing a counterweight to industry representatives who claimed that the Wilderness Act would cost jobs. In written comments submitted in support of the bill, the IWA stated that its analyses did not show that wilderness would cost jobs, and even if it did, those few jobs would be well worth the price of more forest protections. If Congress did not act, the union concluded, future generations would "hold us responsible for having cheated them of part of their birthright as Americans." The final bill went forward and was signed by President Lyndon B. Johnson in 1964. The act did much of what the Wilderness Society and IWA had requested. It turned control of wilderness designations over to Congress and created a national wilderness system that preserved more than 9.1 million acres of federal forestland, including the Three Sisters.[42]

Several environmental historians have understood the 1964 Wilderness Act as a turning point in the history of American environmental politics, a moment when the environmental movement began to turn away from the conservation-oriented policies of the New Deal era and more toward the politics of preservation. But from the perspective of the IWA and many timber workers, the 1964 Wilderness Act represented less a break from previous struggles and more an extension of them. Since its founding in 1937, the union had called for more-democratic oversight of the nation's forests and pursued policies intended to give local communities more control of forest resources. For the IWA, turning control of wilderness designations over to elected members of Congress, who were ostensibly accountable to their constituencies, was a crucial step in this same direction. And, the union's members continued to hope that expanding wilderness would force lumbermen to manage existing productive stands more effectively and efficiently.

"Daylight in the Swamp"

The IWA's belief that wilderness could represent New Deal–style conservation by another means would, however, in the very near future, usher in a host of problems for the union, if not people in the Northwest woods, more broadly. Timber workers and even some wilderness advocates may have seen new wilderness areas as a means of democratizing forest management, as a way of achieving timber country's long-held goal of finding a way to manage forests for harvests, recreation, and aesthetic and biological values. But environmentalists who would soon join the movement, particularly, in the years after the Wilderness Act passed, would not be so interested in managing forests for multiple uses. They would increasingly take the act's central provision, that wilderness amounted to "untouched" nature, as their guiding principle of forest management and turn away from multiuse forestry and toward an exclusive focus on expanding wilderness, ultimately bringing an end to the partnership that had defined Northwest forest politics in the postwar era.

The changing nature of the environmental movement and new definitions of forests and wilderness are largely to blame for the dissolution of the relationship between timber workers and wilderness advocates but not solely to blame. The other, potentially more significant and intractable problem, one that would be at the center of timber country's problems for the foreseeable future if not up to the present and shape the fissure that emerged between environmentalists and workers, involved the ways environmentalists came to *see* workers. Just before the war, novelists like Robert Cantwell and Roderick Haig-Brown had celebrated the Northwest's rural working class as the vanguard of progressive conservation and had heralded timber country as the social and political force that would guide the region away from decades of wanton resource exploitation. Later generations of writers, however, would not say the same thing, and this would make it easy for subsequent generations of environmental activists to believe that timber workers were as ecologically unconscientious as the lumbermen they worked for.

It would be countercultural and New Left authors of the 1960s and beyond who would do the most to engrain this view into the public consciousness. Yet, those very countercultural authors often understood the rural working class based on the writing of a small cadre of Northwest journalists who became popular in the 1950s. Stewart H. Holbrook and Murray Morgan were among the most prolific of these journalists. Both were writing at a time when the Northwest was dramatically changing. Cities were growing. Industrial manufacturing had replaced resource extraction as the driver of the region's economy. Ports expanded, helping link the Northwest to the global economy, and the growth of aerospace companies like Boeing turned the region into a center of Cold War science. The postwar Northwest, in short, was becoming a modern, urban, technologically advanced region, and neither Holbrook nor Morgan wanted any part of it. Both believed the Northwest's identity was rooted in its frontier character and that regional modernization amounted to a loss of regional distinctiveness. In their writings, Holbrook and Morgan attempted to preserve this imagined frontier past and remind their readers that though they may be living in cities and working high-tech jobs, they, nevertheless, descended from more heady, independent, and masculine stock. They told stories of Oregon Trail migrants who battled harsh conditions and American Indians to bring civilization westward. The authors said that Portland and Seattle had been far-better places when brothels and flophouses outnumbered churches and family homes. Loggers played a starring role in their mythic pasts. Like the gunfighters in the stories of Zane Grey (who, perhaps not coincidently, wrote some of those stories from his fishing cabin on Oregon's Rogue River), loggers for Holbrook and Morgan were the shock troops of American civilization, rough and rugged men who didn't fit well into polite society but who, nevertheless, cleared the trees and as Holbrook put it in one of his more popular stories, "let daylight into the swamp," thus, clearing the way for civilization.[43]

Disney animators also helped cement this view of timber workers into public consciousness with their 1954 animated short *Paul Bunyan*. Paul Bunyan mythology dates back to at least the early nineteenth century and likely emerged in the woods of Quebec. Early nineteenth-century Paul, though, was nothing like the Paul most are familiar with today. He wasn't a giant of a man but normal size, and he wasn't a frontiersman but a working-class trickster who regularly played pranks on employers. Over the course of the nineteenth century and into the early twentieth century, Paul grew in size, though he still retained something of his proletarian politics and was depicted in Depression-era art and writing as a committed and often radical unionist. That had all changed by the time Disney got ahold of him, and the company's animators further did away with his working-class politics. Paul, as Disney presented him, was the same sort of frontier logger as Holbrook and Morgan had written about. "North America was a great big land with a great big job to be done," goes the song that opens the film, "a job that needed a great big man. Paul Bunyan was the one." The film centers on Paul's exploits as he cuts nearly every tree from Maine to Washington and, in the process, makes room for pioneers, churches, and schools. It was the cartoon version of Frederick Jackson Turner's infamous frontier thesis, which argued that fur trappers and gunfighters cleared the way for civil society and, ultimately, American democracy, and like Turner, Disney's animators lamented the loss of that frontier. Upon finally arriving on the westernmost coast, Paul has no trees to cut; he's become a logger without forests to log. "Look, bub," a townsperson says to a despondent Paul as he encourages him to finally settle down and start a family, "you got to get with the times, become modern." But Paul is too big in size and spirit to be contained by civilization. In the film's final scene, Paul marches off into the sunset (just like every gunfighter in nearly every Western movie made in that era). A group of more modern loggers looks on as Paul departs, making the message of the film clear: Paul may be gone, but those modern loggers maintain something of his spirit and, in also knocking down trees with reckless abandon, preserve the frontier character that the rest of society had lost.[44]

The irony in all of this was that at the very moment when the Northwest's timber workers were being portrayed in culture as part of a frontier past of reckless resource exploitation, they were charging into a future of conservation and democratized land use. These cultural images and many more to follow would blind much of the rest of society to timber country's environmental politics and convince many environmentalists that workers, alongside the companies they worked for, were directly complicit in the ecological decline they saw in the Northwest's forests. If Cantwell's and Haig-Brown's writings had portended a new era of conservation and cross-class environmental partnership, then these newer cultural products signaled derision and division, a new and prolonged era of problems in timber country. In 1949 the editors of the IWA's newspaper had counseled the union's members to "forget this proneness to emulate Paul Bunyan and remember that we are human, our families are human and that Paul Bunyan and his mighty feats of prowess are just a myth." It was a message much of the rest of society would not receive.[45]

PART III

Problems

6

"Strong Winds and Widow Makers"

Timber country, like the whole of the Northwest, if not industrialized world, changed dramatically in the 1970s. The decade's sweeping economic realignments upended traditional labor relations and weakened organized labor's power. The regional economy pivoted more decisively toward urban manufacturing and a budding high-tech industry, leaving resource-extraction industries like logging behind. The unemployment rate in cities like Portland, Seattle, and Vancouver reached all-time lows at the same time unemployment in timber-dependent communities spiked to levels not seen since the Great Depression. The demography of the Northwest changed, as well, and along with it the region's political priorities. Affluent newcomers from southern California along with aging hippies and countercultural types began moving to the Northwest in unprecedented numbers and, as they did, began calling for restrictions on logging. In short, the regional character of the Northwest was changing. It was in the 1970s that the Northwest began to develop its reputation as a high-tech, thoroughly modern, and ecologically oriented region, a place that logging and timber workers fit into awkwardly, if at all. Politicians, policy makers, environmentalists, and the urban affluent all began to see people in timber country as relics of the region's ecologically destructive past, and, for their part, people in timber country began to see outsiders as a threat to their continued existence. And, like all important historical stories—or at least the most interesting ones—the story of this emerging social and cultural divide begins in a bar.

That bar is the Timbers Restaurant and Lounge, located in the coastal Oregon town of Toledo. The Timbers went out of business in 2003, but descriptions suggest it resembled any of the working-class bars you can still sometimes find in the Northwest's logging towns today, or at least the ones valiantly fighting off the specter of twenty-first-century rural gentrification: chewed up floors from loggers' caulked boots, a well-worn bar carrying the stains of spilled beer, and darkly lit atmosphere, save for the neon signs promoting the well-known domestic beers, which is all that's on tap because that's all that people in these sorts of places drink.

One common feature found in most working-class bars that a visitor to the Timbers would not have seen after 1970, however, was a pool table. The story of the pool table's demise, along with the larger story of the Northwest's emerging social and cultural divides, begins in the spring of that year, on an exceptionally rainy night, when a stranger wandered into the Timbers. His identity was initially obscured by dim lighting, but the regulars occupying the well-worn stools along the bar could see that he was on the taller side, with a slim, athletic frame, perfectly silhouetted by the glow from the streetlights outside.

We'll never know what people inside the Timbers that evening found more surprising once the man wandered a bit farther in and revealed his identity: that this stranger was Paul Newman, arguably the most recognizable Hollywood actor of the era, or that he was carrying a massive chainsaw.

The story, as it's told, is that Newman was drunk and stood wobbling and disoriented in the bar's entranceway for some time, not sure how he'd gotten there or why he'd come. Then suddenly, seeming to recall his purpose, Newman strode over to the Timbers' pool table, fired the saw, and methodically cut off its legs. After the table crashed to the ground, Newman cut the power to the saw and, apparently having done what he'd come to do, calmly exited and vanished into the night. All, again, without saying a single word.

At least that's what some say happened. The story has become part of the lore of coastal Oregon. Find the right bar, with the right clientele, and for the cost of a round for the regulars, you can hear the story told today, as if it were gospel. But press for more information, and the details begin to become murky and contradictory. Matt Love, a historian from nearby Newport, spent considerable time looking into the story, and he could only come up with the most circumstantial evidence in support of its veracity. Newman was in Toledo in the spring of 1970. That much is undisputed. He was there directing and starring in the Hollywood adaptation of *Sometimes a Great Notion*, Ken Kesey's 1964 novel about a family of Oregon loggers. Newman denied vandalizing the pool table although also admitted that his memory of the early 1970s was clouded by heavy drinking. Some claim that the Timbers' owners displayed the detached legs above the bar, next to a sign that read, "Paul Newman was here." But by the time Love started investigating, the Timbers had closed, and the legs had disappeared, if they ever existed. Nor could Love track down any eyewitnesses. He'd hear of someone who was there the night it all happened, only to find that the supposed witness heard the story from a friend or relative who also heard it from a friend or relative, and so on. Ultimately, Love concluded that the story is likely the result of people conflating reality with a scene in the eventual movie, where Newman, playing Hank Stamper, storms into a union office and takes a chainsaw to the president's desk.[1]

But this is one of those instances where fiction may reveal more than fact. What makes the story particularly interesting is that Newman reportedly got along splendidly with Toledo's loggers when he was in town shooting the film. He cast many locals as extras, visited several logging sites, and joined loggers in the bar after their workday had ended. The final film, though, displayed little of Newman's affinity for rural Oregon. The movie, like the book it was based on, portrayed timber workers as part of a dead and dying culture that refused to change, even as it rotted from the inside. The existence of the story of Newman and the pool table likely speaks to the ways that memory reinterprets the past through the lens of subsequent events. It's evidence of the betrayal some in Toledo may have felt after Newman ingratiated himself to them in person and then denigrated them on the movie screen. In this interpretation, Newman's vandalism of the pool table is a metaphor for his broader cultural disfigurement of the rural Northwest.[2]

If nothing else, the story is evidence of the ways that popular culture be-came a battleground during a time of immense and, ultimately, disruptive social and economic change in timber country. The economic stability of the 1950s and 1960s gave way to record unemployment rates as large timber companies began fleeing for the South. The IWA's ranks, along with its bar-gaining power, collapsed. Smaller, family-owned mills and largely nonunion-ized independent contract loggers replaced the larger companies, and as they did, some of the class antagonisms that had once defined labor relations in the Northwest woods began to diminish. Logging towns changed, in part because of the larger economic upheaval of the era and in part because af-fluent newcomers started buying up homes in rural communities. Timber workers took the animosity they once directed at their employers and redi-rected it toward these newcomers and an increasingly active environmental movement, which many in the rural Northwest blamed for timber country's broader social and economic problems.

Northwest timber workers were not alone in confronting strange and un-settling changes in the 1970s. Across North America, working people stumbled headlong into a perplexing economic world where corporations turned record profits at the same time they issued layoff notices, where the Old Left of organized labor went into decline, and the New Left of the civil rights and the antiwar movements was on the rise, and where new conflicts emerged, ones focused less on class politics and more on ineffable cultural politics. The social and economic changes of the era reverberated through popular culture and spawned new, cold portrayals of the working class. No longer the proletarian heroes they'd been in the Depression era, academics, politicians, and young activists now described the working class as bitter and reactionary. People in Northwest timber country were just as affected by these cultural changes. Books and films like *Sometimes a Great Notion* marked the end of a regional cultural consensus that had once imagined timber workers as the vanguard of conservation, and the beginning of a new consensus that suggested timber workers were among the greatest threats to the forest. Timber workers turned to their own cultural products, too, particularly, a regional variant of country music that articulated a disaffected ruralness and viewed environmentalists, or any outsiders for that matter, as a threat.[3]

Environmental conflict in timber country would not reach its apogee until that late 1980s, when debates over the northern spotted owl and so-called ancient forests sparked a social war, pitting environmentalists against rural timber-working communities. To make full sense of those conflicts, though, we have to start in years before that conflict reached its most divisive heights. It was the social, economic, and cultural changes of the 1970s and early 1980s that laid the foundations of a new and acrimonious relationship between timber workers and environmentalists, the rural working class and the urban middle class. By the time activists filed the first petitions seeking an endangered listing for the spotted owl in 1987, both workers and environmentalists had already become thoroughly convinced that each posed an existential threat to the other.

The Changing Timber Industry

Standing nearby any Northwest sawmill at the dawn of the 1970s, it would've been difficult to tell that economic hard times lay in timber country's immediate future. There, just beyond the chain-link fence of the mill gate, young men, many still in high school, lined up looking for work. Few of them carried resumes because few had any formal work experience. The only thing most knew about the inner workings of a mill came from stories told to them by their fathers and grandfathers. But that didn't matter much to the company officials doing the hiring. Applicants were simply looked up and down, and as long as they were reasonably well put together and appeared to possess the willingness to punch in every day roughly on time, they were given high-paying union jobs, complete with full benefits, on the spot.

The reasons why had everything to do with what was happening at the shipping docks of those mills, where steady processions of trucks and railway cars, overflowing with freshly milled lumber, departed for any one of the Northwest's ports, where white-hatted longshoremen would then tightly pack it into the hulls of ships, bound for the opposite side of the Pacific Ocean. Starting in the early 1960s, cities and industries across Asia and Japan, in particular, began to rapidly expand. Factories, apartment buildings, research complexes, and new subdivisions sprang up nearly overnight as Asian policy makers and planners turned the corner on the economic lethargy of the post–World War II era and moved their countries into the new era of postwar prosperity. The leaders of Asian countries may have hoped to build an economic and industrial system that could compete with the global superpowers of the West, but they relied on solid American lumber to do so. Softwood lumber producers in the United States went from exporting roughly 210 million board feet in 1960 to exporting more than 2,316 million board feet in 1969, the bulk of which (roughly 2,000 million board feet) went to Japan. What was good for urban planners in Asia was equally good for organized labor in the Northwest. The overwhelming majority of young workers who entered mills and logging operations during the export boom signed union cards, and by 1970 the IWA had more than 117,000 members across the United States and Canada.[4]

Those young workers had every reason to expect a future of steady work, high pay, and union protections, because that's what their fathers had. What few realized was that as they crossed over the gates of the mill for the first time, they were crossing over into a new economic world, one that was fundamentally different from their fathers'. Across the developed world, corporations and states were abandoning an economy rooted in production and turning their backs on the implicit social contract they had with workers. Since roughly the 1940s, the global economy had been anchored in the production of consumer goods. Corporations turned out billions of automobiles, home appliances, and electronics and, in the process, turned record profits. Redistributive tax policies and high wages negotiated by organized labor helped funnel some of those profits to working people, preserving their purchasing power and keeping inflation in check, even as production surged. Beginning in the 1970s, however, states began relaxing trade barriers and deregulating markets, opening the door to new forms of accumulation. Trading in arcane financial markets, manipulating currencies, leveraging pensions—these, more than production, were the ways corporations turned profits in the 1970s and beyond. As manufacturing declined, so, too, did industrial employment and the ranks of unionized workers. The working class lost wages and its purchasing power. Inflation surged while the economy stagnated, what economists in the 1970s would call "stagflation." In futile attempts to prop up flailing labor markets, state and municipal governments reversed course on those redistributive tax policies, cut social programs, and funneled money toward corporations. Neither country nor city went unscathed, but rural communities lost just a bit more. Because corporate profitably was no longer directly linked to production and, hence, a specific place, resource-extraction industries in rural communities fled for the professionalized workforces and favorable tax policies of cities.[5]

In short, capitalism was changing across the industrialized world in ways that favored corporations over workers, cities over the countryside, and the middle class over the working class. The Northwest lumber industry stumbled into this strange new economic world in the summer of 1969 when, nearly a half continent away, a trader on the floor of the Chicago Mercantile Exchange purchased a contract for the future delivery of Oregon plywood. Commodities markets like the Chicago Mercantile had been trading futures contracts for nearly a century at that point. And like the plywood contract, earlier forms of futures trading rarely involved the actual exchange of goods. Rather, when contracts came due, traders would collect on the difference between the contract price and prevailing market price. Still, the plywood contract represented something new: one of the Chicago Mercantile's first forays into nonagricultural commodities. Soon, commodities traders in Chicago and elsewhere would be dealing in oil, steel, and other Northwest lumber products alongside more-traditional futures in corn, wheat, and pork bellies. Traders exchanged all manner of nonagricultural goods in the 1970s and beyond, and Northwest timber became a particularly hot commodity. The export boom inflated timber prices, and as a result, trading swelled.[6]

This created something of an odd financial situation for Northwest lumber companies. Global lumber consumption remained relatively static, even as futures trading pumped up the price of lumber and, more than that, the price of the land where it grew. It was a brave new financial world that, nevertheless, encouraged many timber companies to revert to land speculation, the oldest form of profit seeking in the North American lumber trade. Across the Northwest, timber companies effectively became forestland brokers and sold off tens of thousands of acres to hungry real estate developers. What happened at Brooks-Scanlon, once central Oregon's largest timber producer, was typical. A 1971 profile of the company in a local trade journal explained that executives had recently concluded that "a substantial amount of its holdings were better suited for land development than timber management." The company scaled back its logging operations at the same time it created a new corporate subdivision called Brooks Resources, which now employed foresters to devise plans to "make the land more attractive to homebuyers."[7]

Companies that continued to produce lumber increasingly did so outside the Northwest. The export boom had initially led to record employment in mills. But soon corporate executives realized they could increase their margins by shipping unprocessed timber to Asia and mill it with nonunion labor. Nor was a return to land speculation the only reversal of history that occurred in timber country. Lumber firms that had migrated to the Northwest in the early twentieth century now shifted production back to their home regions, marking what the *Seattle (WA) Post-Intelligencer* described in 1984 as "an ironic retreat to the nation's early days when the lumber industry was concentrated in the Northeast and Midwest." The piece didn't mention the South, but it should have. Southern companies like Louisiana-Pacific and Georgia-Pacific, which had shifted operations to the Northwest in the 1950s, now shifted their operations back to the South. A company didn't have to originate in the South to turn there, though. The region's yellow-pine forests regenerated quickly and offered shorter harvest cycles and, thus, a quicker return on investments. And, the South's largely union-free workforce offered an effective way to control labor costs. In 1972 timber workers in the South made, on average, $2 an hour, which compared favorably with the $3.44 an hour made by Northwest timber workers, on average. By 1975 more than half of Weyerhaeuser's landholdings were located in the South, and the company was preparing to build its largest-ever mill in Columbus, Mississippi.[8]

Real estate speculation and capital flight cut short the hiring boom of the early 1970s. Just after the unemployment rate in the rural Northwest reached an all-time low, it spiked to an all-time high. All of timber country suffered, but it was Oregon that suffered the most. Declining private-forest reserves after World War II increasingly pushed Washington and British Columbian operators into the still-dense stands of western Oregon, and by 1970 the state had become the region's top lumber producer, which made its economic fall

all the more devastating; between 1970 and 1980, employment in Oregon's timber industry declined by roughly 32 percent. High unemployment rates affected more than just workers. Small, family-owned stores along rural main streets and diners that catered to timber workers posted out-of-business signs and were replaced by pawn shops and payday lenders. Completing his study of Coos Bay, a once-vibrant logging town on central Oregon's coast, historian William Robbins looked out on a town fundamentally transformed by the larger economic changes of the era. "Empty office buildings and storefronts and vacant automobile dealerships are becoming regular features of the land-scape," he wrote. "The area once billed as the 'Lumber Capital of the World' is now taking its 'turn in the bucket.'"[9]

There had always been differences between the American and Canadian timber industries, many of them rooted in land-ownership patterns. But the broad economic changes of the 1970s now accentuated those differences. As the timber industry in Oregon and Washington crumbled, their economies diversified. By 1980 both states were dominated by industrial manufactur-ing and an emerging high-tech industry; timber accounted for less than 30 percent of their domestic product, and many politicians, responding to the new environmental concerns of voters, were happy to let mills close. Tim-ber remained king in British Columbia and by 1980 still accounted for 80 percent of the province's overall economy, which gave Canadian lawmak-ers more incentive to try and prevent closures and layoffs, which they did by reducing harvest fees. Moreover, by the early 1980s, the US dollar rose roughly 18 percent against Canadian currency, giving British Columbian timber producers an advantage in the global marketplace. The result of it all was that the decline of the American timber industry was propping up British Columbia's timber industry. In the late 1970s the province exported 79 percent of all its lumber and 83 percent of all its newsprint to the United States, which, somewhat paradoxically, meant Oregon timber workers read about layoffs in newspapers that'd once been British Columbian trees.[10]

As the industry on both sides of the border diverged, so, too, did the political culture of the IWA's American and British Columbian district councils. British Columbian IWA leaders leveraged the vested interest pro-vincial politicians had in maintaining the timber industry to combat con-cessions demanded by employers. When employers insisted on rollbacks, rank-and-file unionists voted to strike, and they often won. In 1986 British Columbian lumber operators demanded that the provincial IWA district council reopen its contracts and accept significant reductions to hours and wages. Reporting back on the first meeting between IWA negotiators and employer representatives, one union bargaining-team member stated that it was a "short-lived" conversation: "Industry was requested by the spokesman, Brother [Jack] Munro, to take the proposals and insert them in a highly unlikely place. The Union Negotiating Committee also questioned the ancestry of some of the industry negotiators." After negotiations predictably broke down after that initial meeting, IWA members overwhelmingly voted to strike. At five months, it was one of the longest strikes in the history of the British Columbian timber industry, and when it was over, workers returned to work with no wage or benefits reductions and new rules banning the industry's use of nonunion subcontractors.[11]

Meanwhile, on the other side of the forty-ninth parallel, unionized timber workers were moving in more-conciliatory directions. New rules enacted by President Ronald Reagan's administration allowed employers to discharge workers on strike and replace them with nonunion workers, a policy American lumber operators used to significant effect. In 1983, for instance, a strike at Oregon's Louisiana-Pacific operations abruptly ended when the company fired all the workers on the picket lines and replaced them with strikebreakers. A year later, the National Labor Relations Board decertified the IWA at Louisiana-Pacific's plants. In 1986, at roughly the same time the British Columbian strike was beginning, Weyerhaeuser demanded that IWA locals representing workers at more than thirty of the company's sites in Washington and Oregon reopen their contracts and agree to new wages and benefits concessions. Workers voted to strike, their first at the company in more than thirty years, but the strike vote represented less a resurgence of working-class radicalism and more the fact that by the mid-1980s workers had been so economically damaged by a decade of hard times they had little more to lose. "I've already lost my house," Brad Rhodes, a logger from Washington told a reporter. "How is a strike going to hurt me?" For five-and-a-half weeks, workers like Rhodes walked picket lines until Weyerhaeuser threatened to hire replacement workers. Strikers returned to work in April of that year, now working for far less an hour and with their health care and pension plans gutted. Over the next several years, Weyerhaeuser shuttered many of its operations anyway.[12]

It was more than just new labor policies reshaping the American IWA, though. Something less tangible was going on here, a new dour mood across Oregon and Washington timber country. That's what Jim Lowery, business manager of the IWA local in Shelton, Washington, remembered of these years. Union leaders like Lowery initially responded to the economic crises of the 1970s and 1980s with the same rhetoric as the union's leader had in the

Depression era: criticizing the forest mismanagement of timber capital. The union's paper charged companies with trying to cut "every available stick of lumber" and blamed mill closures on corporate "rape and ruin"–style forestry. Yet, as Lowery explained it, this rhetoric now resonated less with the rank and file. Younger workers hired during the late 1960s and early 1970s timber boom hadn't been politically seasoned by decades of acrimonious labor relations and were unwilling to accept the leadership's radical analysis. Older members critiqued the younger generation's political ambivalence, but they often didn't see that recently hired workers had good reasons to be frustrated. Like many unions suffering layoffs, the IWA focused most of its efforts on protecting older workers with seniority, not younger ones. Nor did those older workers recognize that their own commitment to radicalism was waning. Lowery remembered having trouble getting any members, young or old, out to union meetings by the early 1980s, let alone engage in more confrontational forms of activism. Workers concerned with layoffs now started to believe that the union was "too radical," Lowery said, and that more needed to be done to work with management, not against it.[13]

In the end, the diverging political culture of the American and British Columbian IWA district councils, along with the wildly different political and economic climates they now inhabited, brought an end to the cross-border partnership that had defined the union since its founding. In 1987, after nearly a half century of sustaining itself as equal parts American and Canadian, the IWA split into two independent unions. American and Canadian IWA leaders asserted that the split was a strategic response to the anti-union politics of America in the 1980s, that combating anti-union policies forwarded by the Reagan administration was soaking up too much of the IWA's resources. But this was as much about culture as anything else. The British Columbian IWA continued to voice a strong opposition to timber companies at the same time it expanded its jurisdiction and adapted to the new economy of the late twentieth century. By 1989 what was now being called the IWA-Canada had organized workers in nursing, plastics manufactures, and in Quebec a hockey-stick manufacturer. Meanwhile, south of the border, leaders of the IWA (the Americans got to keep the original name) continued to bemoan the waning radicalism of the rank and file as layoffs at large companies continued apace. In 1994 membership in the union fell so low that the IWA merged with the International Association of Machinists (IAM). What was renamed the IAM Woodworker Division did little of the normal work of a union. It existed mostly to manage the pensions of older workers, some of whom likely looked back with nostalgia to earlier decades, when wages were high, rural communities were bustling, organized labor was powerful, and workers harbored a healthy distrust of employers. For them, timber country of the late twentieth century probably felt like a foreign place.[14]

"I'm a Logger"

If that's indeed true, then it had as much to do with the types of forests that loggers in Oregon and Washington were increasingly working as it did with broader economic changes. In the late twentieth century, the American timber industry became more dependent on public forests and federally owned timber than it'd ever been. The cut on American public lands had been steadily increasingly since the 1950s, driven both by the postwar housing boom and the budgetary models of federal land-management agencies, which incentivized timber sales. Public harvests again expanded in the 1970s and 1980s when federal foresters began auctioning off ever-more public timber to fill the gap left by large companies abandoning their Northwest production facilities. By 1984 public timber accounted for over 60 percent (4,643 million f.b.m.) of Oregon's total timber harvest (7,550 million f.b.m.).[15]

The increase in public-lands logging helped offset some of the economic problems of the 1970s and 1980s, but it hardly represented a return to the old days of big companies and equally large unions. Quite to the contrary. The industry looked and functioned very differently on public lands than it did on private lands, and the shift to the former ultimately ushered Washington's and Oregon's timber country into a new era of labor relations and, consequently, new articulations of working-class identity. Most public timber was cut by independent contract loggers, commonly known as "gyppos," small crews of roughly five to fifteen workers using lighter and more-mobile machinery better suited to the smaller tracts auctioned off in public-timber sales. Independent contractors have worked in the Northwest woods since the early twentieth century, though for decades most workers saw signing on to a gyppo crew as a lower-paying and often more dangerous alternative to work in the larger, unionized companies. Perceptions shifted as those large companies began laying off workers by the thousands. In 1920 just about 15 percent of all Northwest loggers worked for or as independent contractors. The rest, 85 percent, worked for larger firms. By 1990 those figures had flipped, almost exactly: 85 percent worked for or as independent contractors while 15 percent retained their jobs at the big companies.[16]

Independent contract loggers existed in British Columbia's woods, too. They just were far fewer. Canadian IWA locals forced timber operators to include in contracts provisions prohibiting subcontracting and independent contracting, meaning that loggers continued to work directly for companies. For American timber operators unburdened by similar contract language, independent contract logging offered a way to transition to the more flexible forms of labor relations characteristic of the 1970s and beyond. Because "gyppos" worked under short-term contracts, companies were freed from longer-term union contracts that committed them to costly wages and benefits packages. With independent contractors, companies simply paid a crew's leader an agreed-upon fee and left it to him to compensate his workers. Contracting also shifted much of the financial risk and legal liability away from corporations. The owners of independent contracting companies, not the companies they contracted with, had to purchase and maintain machinery, pay workers' compensation and unemployment insurance, and were often legally culpable when accidents occurred.[17]

Yet, many workers who signed on to independent contracting crews or, just as commonly, started their own outfits, didn't necessarily see all this as an unwelcome change. At least Dick Gilkison didn't. A tall man with a logger's characteristically broad shoulders who, even today in his eighties, still sometimes puts in a full day in the woods, Gilkison began in the industry in the 1950s, while still in high school. His first job was working at a sawmill near his hometown of Cottage Grove, Oregon. An uncle later got him a job setting chockers in the woods, and by the 1960s he was working as a high climber for Weyerhaeuser. Gilkison loved the work and the woods, which, he explained wryly, "must have something to do with the big vacuum between my ears." Still, by the 1970s, he, like many Northwest timber workers, began to worry about his future in an industry that now looked to be failing. Organized labor did little to allay those fears. Gilkison had been an IWA member since he started back in the 1950s, but by the 1970s he'd come to feel that the union had "worn out its welcome." He worried about his own future at the same time he worried about the future of his two sons, both of whom also worked as loggers. Rather than be kept awake at night by thoughts of layoffs and concessions, Gilkison and his boys decided to go into business for themselves. In 1984 they took some money they'd saved up, bought some well-worn logging equipment, and started their own independent contracting company. They called it Gilkison & Dad, a play on the "———& Sons" name common in many male, family-owned businesses.[18]

A desire for more autonomy, as much as financial worries, drove Gilkison's decision, though. Unlike loggers employed at larger companies, Gilkison and his crew could avoid jobs they deemed too dangerous or too low paying. "We could pick where we worked and who we worked for," he said. Environmental concerns also played a role in pushing Gilkison and his sons into contracting. Working for large companies, Gilkison had often been told to ignore both formal and informal conservation standards in the woods, all in the interest of speed and production. As his own boss he could slow down and take the time to do what needed to be done to steward the forest. "We tried to leave ditches open, and pile the brush, and not leave a bunch of garbage laying around," he explained, "we always tried to do a clean job. I think a logger like me is a true conservationist. . . . We don't want to ruin what we're working on."[19]

It's an interesting comment, one that begins to reveal that although the IWA may have been in decline, ethics of forest stewardship and conservation remained central to timber country's culture. Even so, it now became a culture easy for outsiders to ignore. The IWA had given voice to timber workers' environmental concerns on regional and national stages. Nonunionized independent contract loggers may well have had the same concerns as their unionized brethren of decades past, but they now lacked a sufficient vehicle for articulating and politically mobilizing in the interest of those environmental concerns.

There were other changes as well—changes that, in the minds of many Northwesterners, distinguished workers like Gilkison from the earlier, potentially more class-conscious proletarians who once worked in the woods. Indeed, independent contractors like Gilkison often articulated a new sort of class identity, one that's nearly impossible to pin down. He owned his own company, yet often contracted with mills and small landowners making him something of their employee. Day in and day out, he worked right alongside the men he hired and came home just as tired and just as covered in sweat, sawdust, and rain. As the company's owner, he did collect a larger share of contract payments but spent a significant portion of contract proceeds maintaining expensive equipment prone to breakage. Nor did his status as an employer shield him from the dangers of the woods. "I've had my back broke . . . my leg broke," he said. Once, when working on a steep hillside, a falling snag caught him and punctured his kidney. Unable to muster the breath to scream for help, he had to crawl up the hillside to his crew before he could be taken to the hospital. Doctors later told him he'd never log again. He was back in the woods a year later. When asked if he saw himself more as worker or boss, company owner or struggling timber worker, he shot back a quizzical stare, as if to say that's a question that only matters to ivory-tower academics or anyone else who doesn't know the verity of hard work. "I'm a logger," he ultimately answered, and did so with a confidence and authority that suggested follow-up questions on this topic would be unwelcome or, at the very least, yield no additional insight.[20]

Class identities were changing just as labor relations did, and like Gilkison, people in rural timber-working communities of the 1970s and beyond were drawing their identities more from their association with the industry, rather than their specific economic position within that industry. The lines between employer and employee were blurring, and that was as true in mills as it was logging operations. As big timber firms fled the region, it was often smaller, family-owned mills that began processing public timber. In the 1940s the IWA had criticized lumber companies for being absentee landholders that cared little for the land and local communities. Workers employed at these smaller mills in the 1970s couldn't necessarily say the same thing. Roseburg Lumber, operating out of Roseburg, Oregon, was a case in point. The company had been started in the 1930s by Kenneth Ford, an unemployed logger struggling through the Depression who cobbled together a mill from spare parts he salvaged from a junkyard. Ford invested his early profits in buying up cutover lands abandoned by larger companies and he then nursed them back to health through aggressive replanting programs. In the 1950s Ford started a philanthropic foundation and then later donated millions of dollars to local schools facing budgetary shortfalls as a result of the timber industry's decline. A mill owner like Ford couldn't credibly claim to be of the working class, even if that's where he'd started off, but owners like him could claim something of a rural, timber-working identity that, at the very least, helped smother some of the class divides of old. Indeed, workers at companies like Roseburg often saw kindred spirits rather than heartless lumbermen in employers like Ford. One man living in rural southern Oregon said that small mill owners were, like workers themselves, local people who "just tried to make a buck." And, by replanting forests and providing jobs, that same worker continued, these smaller companies would "guarantee the future of this area." By the 1970s many workers began to believe that their interests and their future depended more on aligning with their employers, rather than opposing them.[21]

"Don't Californicate Oregon"

At the same time the changing structure of labor relations in the Northwest timber industry pulled employers and employees closer together, they were pushed into a new relationship by their shared frustrations with the changing demography of the rural Northwest. Rural real estate prices plummeted in the 1970s as a result of an oversupply of land created by lumber companies that sold off their holdings to real estate developers, who then turned them into sprawling subdivisions. Collapsing real estate prices created new financial opportunities for affluent investors looking for new homes or vacation properties in the economically damaged but still beautiful Northwest. The arrival of these more affluent newcomers created new social tensions in many of the region's rural communities, turning rural working people into outsiders in towns where they'd resided their entire lives and, perhaps more significantly, sparking new debates about forest management and logging that portended more acrimonious environmental conflicts.[22]

The change was most evident in southern Oregon, a place plagued by a particularly pernicious breed of real estate speculator: the California "equity migrant." Beginning in the early 1970s, upwardly mobile professionals, many from Orange County and suburban Los Angeles, realized that they could sell their homes in California's grossly inflated real estate market, buy cheap land just across the state border in rural Oregon, and live comfortably off the difference between the sales. Between 1970 and 1980, the population of southern Oregon's Josephine County grew by more than 40 percent, and bumper stickers that read, "Don't Californicate Oregon," began appearing on rural residents' pickups. Rural Oregonians weren't alone in disparaging Californians. It became something of a statewide pastime and has remained so ever since. The *Oregonian* newspaper regularly ran jokes about Golden State refugees, suggesting that the US Department of Transportation build a tunnel the length of Oregon to funnel Californians directly into Washington or reintroduce grizzlies along Oregon's southern border to ward off would-be residents. In 1967, a desire by all of Oregon's voters to limit in-migration led them to elect Thomas Lawson McCall, Oregon's famously antigrowth governor, who once quipped, "Come visit us again and again. This is a state of excitement. But for heaven's sake, don't come here to live." At the state border, along Interstate 5, the Oregon Department of Transportation erected a new sign reading, "Welcome to Oregon. Enjoy your visit," a subtle invocation of McCall's and Oregon's message that tourists and their money were quite welcome in the state but permanent relocation, not so much.[23]

While many Oregonians complained about Californians, it was rural people whose lives were most affected by their presence. Victoria Sturtevant, a sociology professor from Southern Oregon University, explained that affluent Californians often made little effort to fit into rural towns and disrupted the strong sense of community that many rural people held dear. "They've established who they are, they don't need to be accepted, they don't have to assimilate to get what they want," she said. Outsiders also brought new ways of seeing nature. Many had moved to rural Oregon to enjoy forests and mountains, not clearcuts. Even some newcomers from California's Orange County, the seat of the conservative revolution of the 1960s, suddenly became strident environmentalists when it came to protecting the views they enjoyed from the windows of their new rural homes. They strung fences up along their property and closed off access to lands that rural residents had long used. "Anymore you try and go back to some of the places where we used to go and fish, or we used to go and swim. Somebody's down there and they're calling the cops. They siccing the dog on you, they're pulling a gun on you," one southern Oregon timber worker explained. Another lamented the ways that the sprawling estates built by Californians intruded on rural lands. "There was a spot right up on this mountain that I used to go to, because the calypso orchids were so beautiful there," he said. "Those spots are gone now because of encroaching civilization. It's sad, because I just really have a connection with the woods. I don't go back to those spots. 'Cause people live in some of those spots. And they're damaged. They're scarred now. It's hard to go back and be reminded of that."[24]

Californians weren't the only invaders. In the 1970s and 1980s, rural Northwesterners also had to contend with back-to-the-landers who, like the equity migrants, were drawn to the region by cheap land. Between 1965 and 1975, San Francisco Bay Area hippies and countercultural types seeking more-pastoral living established over one hundred communes throughout Washington and Oregon. Nearly all embraced values, ideologies, views of nature, and "all sorts of weird shit," according to one rural Oregonian, that put them into conflict with local communities. Some were run according to the principles of Buddhist theology, others championed transcendental meditation, and a few embraced occultism and mysticism. Others still, like the Oregon's Women's Land Trust, accepted only lesbians and promoted ecofeminism. Like the Californians, the back-to-the-landers maligned clearcuts, industrial logging, and resource extraction. Unlike the Californians, though, the back-to-the-landers often celebrated labor. A *Life* magazine profile of one Oregon commune explained that members "regard chopping wood, planting seeds, and washing clothes as acts of creative meditation which contribute to the spiritual wellbeing of the workers and to the good of the commune. They say that work strips them of their city frustrations." It's tempting to believe that the back-to-the-land movement's veneration of labor provided some common ground with rural workers, who also celebrated hard work. But the counterculture saw tilling gardens, clearing streams, and replanting forests as categorically different than rural resource work, and the emphasis they placed on labor exacerbated, rather than alleviated, growing tensions.[25]

This was most evident in Hoedads, a tree-planting cooperative founded in Oregon in 1971 by ex-hippies and former Peace Corps volunteers. Taking their name for the tool used to dig holes for seedlings, Hoedads worked on a contract basis, replanting logged-over public and private lands. The group tended to attract young, idealistic, middle-class kids committed to environmentalism and a communal spirit. Members adopted new names like Moon Child and Elf, lived in yurts during the planting season, and in their off hours read the organization's newsletter, which critiqued American foreign intervention, patriarchy, racism, and, most of all, capitalism. Yet, ironically, Hoedads became successful in the most capitalistic of ways: by skirting labor laws and underbidding competitors. Hoedads claimed it was a cooperative, not an employer, and that its members were independent contractors, not employees. They therefore did not have to pay minimum wages or workers' compensation insurance and were able to offer far-cheaper rates on replanting work. That work was often done poorly and slowly. Hoedads claimed they offered "quality over quantity," but according to foresters and rival companies, Hoedads achieved neither.[26]

But that really didn't matter to Hoedads members, who tended to believe that the purpose of work wasn't productivity or even a wage but "healthy consciousness raising." In the group's newsletter, one member explained that the real value of the group's labor lay in the opportunity to restore the damage done by the "ravenous" timber industry. "Most of us are Hoedads," he opined, "because treeplanting [sic] is RIGHT ON. Trucking on to the woods and laying those baby trees on those nasty desolate clear cuts feels real good—like we're the storks delivering the forest babies. Getting nature back in balance." If tree planting brought nature back into balance, it was only because logging had disrupted forest ecologies, and Hoedads made little distinctions between employers and the workers who carried out their orders. As one member explained, loggers "rape the forest and leave their slash and trash." Perhaps, the most significant evidence that Hoedads saw themselves and their labor as distinct from loggers came in 1979, when the IWA, in an effort to bolster its declining numbers, offered to incorporate the Hoedads into the union. While some of the cooperative's members supported the idea, the bulk of the membership voted against it.[27]

"Never Give a Inch"

The refusal of the Hoedads to join the IWA, along with their more disparaging views of loggers, hints at a larger and even more significant change in the ways that environmentalist thought and activism were turning against timber workers in the late twentieth century. Interviews with environmentalists conducted by anthropologists in the 1970s and 1980s reveal that a cultural shift was underway, one that increasingly took a dim view of the Northwest's rural working class. "Many of these workers are ignorant," one environmentalist in southern Oregon told Theresa Satterfield. Another environmentalist she spoke with referred to timber workers as "uneducated dolts," while another spoke of "dumb loggers." Yet another described timber workers as "piggish louts whacking down trees with reckless abandon, rubbing chain saws in glee at the destruction of the forest and its wildlife." Independent scholar Beverly Brown, who also conducted several interviews in southern Oregon, heard similar descriptions. Brown summarized her findings: "In the minds of many environmental activists, the trees were being saved from the ignorant 'rednecks'—read: local working-class people—who, it was assumed, were dupes of the transnational forest companies and captives of an outmoded frontier mentality."[28]

This all marked a significant departure from the Depression and New Deal eras, when foresters like Bob Marshall talked about the virtuousness of the rural working class, authors like Roderick Haig-Brown and Robert Cantwell championed timber workers as the vanguard of progressivism and conservation, and wilderness activists like Howard Zahniser talked about the need to preserve rural working-class communities alongside forests. This new cultural consensus was a product of the ways the environmental movement had changed between Zahniser's time and the later twentieth century. What, in earlier decades, had been a movement largely led by rural and working-class people became, in the 1960s, a movement led largely by urban, middle-class people. Rachel Carson's *Silent Spring* (1962) told city dwellers that they weren't safe from agricultural pesticides and helped mobilize millions of urban people to fight for clean air and water. Paul Ehrlich's *Population Bomb* (1968) warned of sprawl and overpopulation, helping turn middle-class homeowners into fierce critics of consumerism and development. Events like the first Earth Day in 1970 further drew urbanites and suburbanites into organizations that had once been dominated by rural conservationists, like the Sierra Club and Wilderness Society. Environmentalists also started to come from new political spaces, less from the Old Left of the Communist Party and organized labor and more from the New Left of the civil rights and antiwar movements.[29]

What the shifting political, social, and geographic loci of environmentalism meant in the Northwest was that an environmental activist was unlikely to know a real timber worker and far more likely to know his cultural analogue, and this mattered because culture was not kind to the working class in the 1970s and beyond. The working class fell from grace in that decade, losing the esteem and privileged place it once held in the minds of politicians, academics, and the Left, more broadly. Gone were John Steinbeck's Joads and Clifford Odets's Lefty. They'd been replaced by Norman Lear's Archie Bunker. The 1970s swapped Woody Guthrie for Merle Haggard, John L. Lewis for George Meany, and picket lines for hardhat riots. Cultural products from and about the Northwest reflected the emerging cultural consensus that timber workers, like workers more broadly, were reactionary to their core and then blended that critique with environmentalist thought.

In his 1960 collection *Myths and Texts*, for instance, Beat poet Gary Snyder lamented,

> Someone killed and someone built, a house,
> a forest, wrecked or raised
> All America hung on a hook
> & burned by men, in their own praise.

Snyder didn't identify loggers specifically, but it was likely clear to readers who, exactly, was responsible for the forest wreckage he described. David Shetzline's 1969 novel *Heckletooth 3*, likewise, situated loggers at the center of a narrative of forest destruction. In many ways a modern Melvillian narrative about humankind's hubris toward the natural environment, the story focuses on three men trapped in a Forest Service lookout tower as a massive fire consumes the surrounding woods. The story's antagonist, a logger named Replogle, has shot an elk out of season and hopes to use the conflagration as cover to sneak the animal out of the woods. He's so independent he can't effectively work with the other two men to escape the blaze, and much like Melville's Ahab, so intent on exploiting nature (in his case, getting the elk out of the woods) that he cannot see that the world around him is collapsing.[30]

Yet, the most enduring cultural product to deal with Northwest loggers, and the work most singularly associated with the region, is Ken Kesey's 1964 novel, *Sometimes a Great Notion*. Set in the fictional Oregon logging town of Wakonda, Kesey's book tells the story of the Stampers, a fiercely independent family of loggers who work through a strike, despite the desperate objections of friends, townspeople, and union officials. Hank Stamper, the main character, is both protagonist and antagonist. He is proud and obstinate and justifies his decision to work through the strike by evoking the Stamper family motto (handed down to him by his equally obstinate father): "Never give a inch!" But deep down, Hank is troubled and broken, too insecure to realize that his fierce determination is tearing his family apart. In the novel's final, memorable scene, Hank is floating a raft of logs down the river. He's hung his father's disembodied arm (lost in a logging accident) in the window of the Stamper family home, its middle finger raised in defiance of the union members and townspeople who said he'd never get his lumber out of the woods and to the mill on his own. Hank believes he's won. He's too blinded by pride to see that he's really lost. Both his father and brother-in-law have been killed in logging accidents, his wife is leaving him (but not before sleeping with his half brother), and the Stamper family home is disintegrating into the rising Wakonda Auga River. Even the book's title, taken from an old blues song, speaks to the tragic nature of the Stampers' story. "Sometimes I get a great notion," Lead Belly sings in "Good Night, Irene," "to jump into the river . . . an' drown."[31]

Like many cultural products of the 1960s, *Notion* inverted the themes of 1930s proletarian literature. Unions are weak instead of strong. Workers are at war with each other rather than their employers. And working-class resiliency and defiance, once seen as righteous and virtuous, is now anachronistic. Identifying a single, central theme in *Notion* is difficult, if not impossible. The story is massive, sprawling, nonlinear, and told from the perspective of multiple narrators. It evokes themes that are not just central to 1960s literature but to all American literature, including (but not limited to) the complexities of families, the seemingly intractable conflict between old and young, and the tensions between tradition and modernity. Yet, if there is an overarching theme, it's that the Stampers and by extension Northwest timber workers are too hardheaded to realize that their world of resource extraction is rapidly coming to an end and are too consumed by an antagonistic spirit to change. "Many oldtimers from bygone times," Kesey writes, "are reluctant to admit those times are gone by."[32]

The irony of *Notion* is that at the time Kesey wrote it, the real timber country was the opposite of his fictional timber country in almost every conceivable way. The IWA was at the peak of its power, and its members were not stuck in a frontier past of wanton resource exploitation but trying to create a more sustainable future by actively supporting wilderness expansion. Part of the reason Kesey so missed the mark was because he had little connection to the Northwest woods and its workers. Though Kesey would become synonymous with the Northwest and Oregon, in particular, his connection to the region at the time he wrote *Notion* was relatively tenuous. He was born in Colorado in 1935 to a family of Dust Bowl refugees, and for much of his life he identified more as an Okie than a Northwesterner. Kesey's family did move to Springfield, Oregon, in 1946, and he did attend the nearby University of Oregon, but he left after graduating in 1957 to attend Stanford University's prestigious writing program. Kesey wrote *Notion* while still living in the San Francisco Bay Area, surrounded by Beats and members of the burgeoning hippie movement. His understanding of the rural Northwest was, in all likelihood not based on any actual interactions with Oregon loggers but rather on the writings of Stewart Holbrook, Murray Morgan, and the 1950s journalists who celebrated loggers as heady frontiersmen. That's something worth critiquing. The only problem is, Holbrook's and Morgan's loggers were fictitious in nearly every way, meaning Kesey culturally lashed out at a rural working-class culture that never existed. And famously, of course, Kesey was under the influence of more than just Holbrook and Morgan when he wrote *Notion*. His writing sessions were fueled by massive amounts of lysergic acid diethylamide (LSD) and then supplemented with amphetamines to counteract the fatigue brought on by the hallucinogens. Shortly after publishing *Notion*, Kesey and a group of like-minded hippies piled into a dayglow-painted van and toured the country, attempting to turn the world on to the liberating effects of LSD. Kesey hoped that drugs would make the world more connected and communal, and he saw the frontier ethic of the rural working class, imagined as it might've been, as a barrier to that goal.[33]

The films of young, New Left auteurs made in the late 1960s reinforced the narratives first articulated by countercultural writers. Directors and television producers had never really portrayed rural America in a flattering way. The Ma and Pa Kettle movies of the 1940s and 1950s alongside television shows like *Petticoat Junction* and *The Beverly Hillbillies* depicted rural folk as simple and bumbling. But at least these characters were likeable and well-meaning. By the late 1960s, however, affable country bumpkins had been replaced by violent and dangerous others, like the rednecks who murder the protagonists in Dennis Hopper's *Easy Rider* or kidnap and sexually assault the main characters in John Boorman's *Deliverance*.

In the late 1960s Newman secured the rights to Kesey's book and traveled to Oregon in the spring of 1970 to shoot the Hollywood adaptation and vandalize the pool table in the Timbers. Maybe. Kesey's original story already echoed the portrayals of rural America being offered by directors like Hopper and Boorman, but Newman further emphasized the cold-hearted nature of the Stampers through casting. Playing the father, Henry Stamper, was Henry Fonda, who, on the tail end of his distinguished acting career, captured the inherently angry nature of the Stamper family patriarch through long, piercing stares into the camera. Lee Remick played Viv Stamper, Hank's wife, and she, too, delivered a memorable performance, capturing the heartbreak of her character in passionately delivered monologues. And finally, Newman himself played Hank, marshaling much of the same aloofness he'd brought to many of his earlier roles. True, the rural America that Newman portrayed in his film wasn't as violent as Hopper's or Boorman's, but his Stampers were just as cold and uncompromising. Newman initially wanted to call the film "Never Give a Inch," after the Stamper family motto. The studio rejected the title, although it would've perfectly communicated what he and young film-makers like him now thought about rural people.[34]

The Stampers were, of course, fictional characters, stitched together from Kesey's LSD-induced hallucinations and Newman's New Left politics. But in the early 1970s, Americans could look at a young long-distance runner from the logging town of Coos Bay, Oregon, and reasonably conclude that Kesey and Newman had accurately captured the character of the rural Northwest.

His name was Steve Prefontaine, though fans and opponents alike simply called him Pre. He'd been a champion runner in high school and in his first few years at the University of Oregon but remained largely unknown outside the small world of Americans who followed track and field. This changed during the five-thousand-meter finals at the 1972 Munich Olympics. Even casual observers tuning into the television broadcast would've noticed that Pre was clearly outgunned as he took the starting line. He was much shorter and much younger than the rest of the field, and the broadcast's announcers frequently pointed out that he was flanked on all sides by world champions and former Olympic medalists. But what Pre lacked in size and experience he made up for in grit. Most long-distance runners approach a race as some-thing of a chess match, carefully vying for a position that will put them in a place to contend for the win in the final fast-paced laps. Pre approached races as wars of attrition and won by seizing an early lead and then pushing the pace faster than his competitors could bear. "Someone may beat me in the 5,000 meters," he'd told the local press a few days before leaving for Munich, "but they're going to have to bleed to do it." When the starter's gun went off, Pre charged out to an early lead and, much to the shock of the audience and announcers calling the race, still held it in the final laps. Only in the closing meters did he start to stumble and falter, collapsing across the finish line in fourth, just a few lengths from a podium position.[35]

Sportswriters who interviewed Pre afterward suggested that had he run a more conservative race he could've easily taken the bronze, maybe even the silver. But that wasn't Pre's style. Anything short of decisive victory was a loss, and the strategy-based game most other runners played was as feckless as it was cowardly. "A lot of people run a race to see who's fastest," Pre once said. "I run to see who has the most guts, who can push himself into exhausting pace, and then at the end, punish himself even more."[36]

It was colorful comments like these that made Pre popular with many Americans and helped spawn a national running craze that ultimately launched a small shoe company that Pre owned with his University of Oregon coach Bill Bowerman and teammate Phil Knight called Nike. But it was sportswriters who were perhaps most taken with Pre. Indeed, his was a story that journalists just couldn't resist: a tough, rough-around-the-edges, working-class kid who fought his way up to the highest levels of competition and came close to victory, only to lose in heartbreaking fashion (this same narrative arc would be further inscribed into popular culture by Sylvester Stallone's *Rocky*, released two years after the Munich Olympics). Profiles of Pre in the press suggested that it was his hardscrabble upbringing in working-class Coos Bay that had turned him into the fierce runner he was, and ultimately journalists turned Pre's story into a much-larger story about the uncompromising culture of the rural Northwest. Like many papers, the *New York Times* noted that Pre's father worked in a sawmill and explained the runner was a product of Coos Bay's "aggressive loggers, longshoremen, and fishermen." *Life* magazine echoed this sentiment. It described life in Coos Bay as "tough" and "elemental," painting a picture of a proudly blue-collar community where loggers drove battered pickups, drank cheap beer, and made no apologies for it. Pre himself did much to cultivate his image as a working-class kid hardened by life in Coos Bay. He said that he drew inspiration from the folks he saw on his early-morning training runs, when the only other people awake were sawyers headed for the first shift at the mill or logging-truck drivers headed to the woods. "My people," he called them, "the working-class, plain-spoken people who really appreciated someone being tough."[37]

Put differently, journalists made Pre into a real-life version of the Stampers, too stubborn to give in or give up. In a eulogy written by his friend and former teammate Jerry Van Dyke, that comparison was made explicit after Pre's untimely death in a 1975 car accident on the outskirts of Eugene: "Whenever I think of Pre, I think of Hank Stamper. . . . Pre is the same independent, obstinate, tough lumberjack. . . . He was naïve, unsophisticated, and unafraid of anything." True as that might've been, comments like these, reinforced the view that the Northwest's rural communities were tough but perhaps too tough for their own good—too strong-willed and stubborn to ever compromise, even when or maybe especially when it came to deciding the future of the Northwest's forests.[38]

"Where There Walks a Logger, There Walks a Man"

Environmental activists and the Northwest's urban middle class were hardly the only ones increasingly taking their cues from popular culture in the late twentieth century. To make sense of the topsy-turvy world they increasingly encountered—a world in which the timber industry appeared to be in decline and the lines between employer and employee were blurring, creating new and ambiguous social identities—people in timber-working communities also looked to new cultural products. Like the films and novels of the counterculture and New Left, cultural forms popular in the Northwest woods emphasized the tough, independent character of its rural communities. Indeed, the major difference between the cultural tropes that emerged from within timber country and the cultural tropes that emerged from without had less to do with the specific qualities ascribed to rural people and more to do with how those qualities were interpreted. Kesey and Newman had suggested that the obstinance of the rural Northwest was something to be condemned, even feared; rural Northwesterners said their uncompromising attitude was something to be venerated. In their eyes, hard work, determination, and independence were the sinew holding the Northwest if not the entire modern world together.

This new identity was articulated most clearly in a distinct subgenre of country music that could be heard spilling from the staticky speakers of loggers' pickups in the 1960s and beyond. Certainly, some of the great outlaw country musicians of the era, like Merle Haggard and Charlie Daniels, also held prominent places in timber country. But the more popular musicians were local acts who sang about loggers and sawyers. Given that timber country is so far removed from the folkways of Appalachia and gospel revivals of the South, where country music originated, it may seem odd that Northwest timber workers adopted the music as their own. But culturally and even demographically, the Northwest woods were similar to these more distant regions in ways that helped country music take hold. Many early twentieth-century Northwest timber workers had come from the South and brought their musical tastes with them. These transplanted Southerners then provided aspiring country musicians with a marketplace to launch their careers. Though most people knew her as a coal miner's daughter from Butcher Hollow, Kentucky, Loretta Lynn actually wrote her most famous song while living in Custer, Washington, where her husband and future manager worked part-time as a logger. Tennessee native Dolly Parton received her first-ever standing ovation while singing a concert in Eugene, Oregon, and later expressed her gratitude in a song named for the town. Lynn's and Parton's early recordings were given airtime by a disc jockey in Vancouver, Washington, who had his own dreams of making it big in country music. His name was Willie Nelson. Finally, country music likely became popular in the Northwest woods because, as many scholars have recently shown, the genre gave voice to the frustrations and fears of the late twentieth-century working class. And in the 1970s and 1980s, Northwest timber workers were certainly frustrated and fearful.[39]

Lloyd Earl "Buzz" Martin became the most prominent singer to come out of the Northwest woods. Like all country music greats, Martin's life was filled with considerable hardship that would later be expressed in his music. Even the name of his birthplace, Coon Holler, Oregon, a small logging town roughly twenty miles east of Salem, sounds more Appalachian than Northwestern. Martin developed debilitating cataracts shortly after his birth in 1928 and was sent to live at the Oregon School for the Blind as a teenager. Both his parents died when he was away, and he was sent to live with his older sister and her husband, a struggling logger constantly out of work, in a home with neither electricity nor indoor plumbing. It was his older sister that first encouraged Martin's interest in music. "Keep a song in your heart and on your lips," she once told him, "even the toughest burdens are easier to bear when you sing." She taught the teenage Martin how to pick a guitar, and both often stayed up late into the night listening to broadcasts of the Grand Ole Opry when their small, battery-powered transistor radio could pick up the signal. If Martin's sister taught him to love music, then his brother-in-law taught him to love logging and the woods. "God made the logger to be a guardian of the forest," he told a young Martin, "so care for it well and it will always be here for others to share with you."[40]

Martin's cataracts miraculously disappeared in his early twenties, and he followed his brother-in-law into logging camps to help the family make ends meet. At the end of a workday, Martin would often grab his guitar and spend a few hours entertaining his fellow crewmembers, singing Hank Williams country classics alongside a few tunes he'd come up with on his own, most of which focused on logging. News of Martin's musical talents quickly spread, and by the late 1950s he was earning a little extra money singing in dance halls and honky-tonks up and down the Oregon coast. In 1962 Buddy Simmons, the host of Hoedown on Portland's channel 2, heard Martin perform and offered him a guest spot. Martin's reoccurring appearances on Hoedown earned him the attention of local recording studios, and in 1967 he signed a recording contract with Oregon's Lavender Records. While Martin achieved neither the popularity nor album sales of some of the great country musicians of the era, he had a strong and loyal following in timber country and gained something of a reputation outside the Northwest as a country musician's musician. George Jones, Nelson, and Haggard were reportedly fans. In 1972 Johnny Cash invited Martin to perform on *The Johnny Cash Show*. Though the performance never aired, Cash saw a kindred spirit in Martin. "The only difference between me and Buzz is that he's singin' about lumberjacks and I'm singin' about cotton pickers," Cash said.[41]

Indeed, much like the Man in Black, Martin's music found humanity and dignity in the lives and labor of rural people. "I've seen two loggers stand toe-to-toe and slug it out in a free-for-all-fight," sings Martin on the title track of his debut album, *Where There Walks a Logger, There Walks a Man*, "and when it was over, they'd get up and shake hands and laugh and drink together all night." Here in Martin's music was timber country's response to Kesey. Hard work and tough demeanors didn't tear families and communities apart, it held them together. "I think a logger loves his family just a little bit more than most men," Martin continues in the song, "because he knows if he makes just one mistake, he'll never see them again." Martin also pushed back against the counterculture's suggestion that loggers didn't care for the forests, often highlighting the ways work inspired a love of the forest and highlighting timber workers' care and concern for nature. "I've seen a logger pick up a baby bird, and put it back into its nest," he sings. In Martin's world, a logger's life was worthy of respect and admiration, not derision.[42]

For all its sentimentality, however, Martin's music could also strike a combative tone. This was apparent on his most famous song, "Strong Winds and Widow Makers," which appeared on his 1969 follow-up album *Logger's Reward*. Like nearly all of Martin's music, "Strong Winds and Widow Makers" was about doing hard work in dangerous conditions. What made the track unique, and perhaps popular, was that Martin seemed to be directly confronting the rural Northwest's critics, specifically, affluent urbanites who failed to understand that loggers provided the raw materials that made their modern lives possible. "We're the Northwest's unsung heroes, the backbone of this land," Martin sings on the track, further reminding listeners that there'd be no timber for homes and buildings "if we don't cut 'em down." That same confrontational stance is evident in the song's chorus, which embraces the very sort of hard, physical, and dangerous labor that middle-class city dwellers seemed so intent on avoiding. Martin sings,

> Strong winds and widow makers don't bother us at all.
> We don't complain if the timber's small or the ground is steep.

Hard work don't scare us.
We can lay right down beside it and go to sleep.

Pride in place, pride in community, and, above all, pride in the ability to do a hard job and do it well: these are the central themes of the song if not all of Martin's music.[43]

Subsequent musicians from timber country, like Hank Nelson, Bob Antone, and Craig & Terry (Craig Jenkins and Terry McKinnis) would continue articulating similar themes. Part of what made the music popular was that Northwest-woods country singers often sang about local folks, turning hardworking loggers who might've otherwise toiled in obscurity into celebrated regional heroes. Gilkison was one of those. "All things considered, I guess this ain't too bad," Craig & Terry sing on their 1989 album *The Snag Fallers Ball*, "this here workin' for Gilkison & Dad." Yet, despite their often intensely local focus, Martin and his fellow Northwest-woods country singers did the same cultural work as the nationally popular country musicians like Haggard. Their music ascribed new cultural borders around rural communities, rejecting modern urban life in favor of simpler, more-honest country living. Martin may have identified as a "poor old gyppo logger, trying to make ends meet," and Haggard as an "Okie from Muskogee," but both suggested that the real America, the hard-working, genuine America, was found in its rural communities and, perhaps, only in its rural communities. Both effectively sang about working-class struggle, but theirs was a definition of class loosed from history and economics and focused much more on geography; ruralness became synonymous with working-class identity. They celebrated working-class tradition but excluded legacies of labor radicalism. They were populists but directed their populist rage more at cities than corporations. Explicitly stated in Haggard's music and implicitly in Martin's were exclusionary understandings of class. Martin's Northwest woods like Haggard's Muskogee was uniformly White and overwhelmingly male. The main social divisions both imagined weren't between worker and boss but between country and city, between hard-working White men and effete urbanites, a category that, for them, included both the affluent middle class and the imagined and racialized "welfare queen."[44]

The Witches of Wolf Creek

The rural culture that Martin sang about—a culture emphasizing pride, toughness, and grit—was hardly new to timber country. That's a culture that'd been born in the early twentieth century in hardscrabble company towns and dangerous work conditions. That's a culture that, in part, propelled the growth of organized labor and sustained workers on the picket lines of the Great Depression. If the elements of that culture weren't new, where it was being directed was. Martin, if not White, rural, working-class culture more broadly, refocused the angers, fears, and frustrations of working-people away from employers and capital and toward urbanites and the environmental movement. Speaking in 1980 before the Oregon Logging Conference to a group of mostly independent contract loggers and small landholders, Betty Dennison, president of Oregon Women in Timber, articulated timber country's problems in a new way, reflecting new identities, that may well have been lyrics in one of Martin's songs: "You produce and they consume. They are parasites and you are creators. They have been brought up in remote cities, unaware of the need for basic resources, unaware that their comfort and affluence is paid for not just with their desk jobs, but ultimately by the sweat of your brow." This was an articulation of class but one that swapped differences between boardroom floor and shop floor for differences between city and country.[45]

The conflicts portended in Dennison's comments were still a few years away when she spoke in 1980. Still, her speech speaks to how, well before that conflict came, anger and animosity had thickened the social atmosphere of Northwest timber country. Increased environmental activism, largely on the part of more-affluent urban environmentalists, couldn't alone be blamed for timber country's problems in the later twentieth century, even if the environmentalists bore a modicum of responsibility. High unemployment, social problems in rural communities, the uncertainty that seemed to constantly loom over people's lives—these things had much more to do with corporate policy and broader economic changes than increasing environmental activism. Still, urbanites and environmental activists, the parasites Dennison talked about, appeared to people in the rural Northwest as the personification of the broader and more intangible cultural, social, and economic forces now seemingly allied against them.

There were other signs, as well, that timber country was on the verge of a new sort of conflict, one pitting rural against urban, worker against environmentalist. One of those signs could be seen in a Hoedads camp perched in the hills above the tiny meandering drainage of Wolf Creek, not too far outside Roseburg, Oregon. In March 1980, four men from a nearby rural community loaded into two pickup trucks and drove the rutted logging roads to the Hoedads camp. According to reports later offered by Hoedads present, the men were intent on running the tree planters off the land because the four believed the camp was home to a coven of witches engaged in the ritual sacrifice of children. Whether or not the four men actually believed that is uncertain, as that's a detail provided only in the Hoedads' account. In 1980 much of the United States was on the verge of the so-called satanic panic, when widespread charges of child sacrifice were levied against otherwise law-abiding citizens. And some Hoedads did, indeed, dabble in occultism and Wiccan religion, meaning it might've been easy for the four men to get swept up in the hysteria of the era. What is, perhaps, clearer is that the four men didn't want the Hoedads there and let it be known. Upon arriving in the camp, the four men spilled from their trucks and started firing rifles in the air. One man approached a Hoedad and pointed a rifle directly in her face. According to her later statement, the man said, "Look, lady, I see a dear [sic]."⁴⁶

No one was injured, and the four men left camp having terrified the Hoedads but doing no physical damage. In a letter to local law enforcement, Greg Nagle, then president of the Hoedads, summed up the meaning of what the Hoedads' paper would later call "the Wolf Creek incident": "What worries us is an attitude that 'our type' are not welcome in Josephine County."⁴⁷

Nagle was right, though he conveniently ignored that the Hoedads and other newcomers to timber country had done little to ingratiate themselves to rural Oregon. Regardless of who's to blame for the escalating tensions in the Northwest woods, what's clear is that at least by the spring of 1980, if not before, environmentalists and workers were looking upon each other with increasing suspicion, distrust, and animosity. The region appeared to be on the precipice of a war, and all it would take is something to push both sides into more-open conflict. That something would be a diminutive bird that, in the early 1980s few people had heard of, and fewer had even seen. It would flap its wings and fly off its perch of obscurity and land directly in the middle of a contentious social landscape, transforming it into a battleground.

7

"Tie a Yellow Ribbon
for the Working Man"

The photographer from *Life* wanted Wilbur Heath to smile, but Heath wasn't in a smiling mood. As the sixty-two-year-old owner of an independent contract logging company who'd been seasoned by decades of hard work in the woods, smiling wasn't something that came naturally to him. Then there was the weather. It was early in the winter of 1990, and the air was filled with a stinging rain. Heath was used to that. Logging often had to happen in inclement weather because inclement weather was all the Northwest had. But usually the work kept him warm—traversing steep, muddy hills, wrestling chockers and cables, leaning on saws as they chewed through trees. Now, he was being asked to stand still for hours on end as the photographer, in no apparent hurry, snapped, as he'd later complain, "a million damned pictures."[1]

Really, though, Heath's refusal to smile had less to do with his disposition or the weather and much more do with the creature perched on his shoulder: a northern spotted owl.

Just five years ago, few people had heard of the owl. By 1990, however, the bird had become something of a celebrity. It was the focus of multiple scientific studies and the subject of too many newspaper articles to count. A few months before the journalist and photographer from *Life* came to timber country, the bird had appeared on the cover of *Time* and in headlines printed in the *Guardian* (UK edition). Schoolchildren from across the United States and as far away as Germany wrote letters to the US Forest Service, imploring the agency's land managers to save the owl. The actions of environmentalists, though, were far more consequential. Activists claimed that the owl was endangered and that saving the few that remained required significant reductions to logging on public lands. Land managers often agreed, if not in principle then at least because they feared lawsuits threatened by lawyers working for the environmental movement. As a result, work was becoming increasingly harder to find for loggers like Heath. Just a few weeks before the *Life* shoot, he'd been forced to lay off about a third of his crew, and he feared more layoffs would be necessary in the very near future. In his hometown of Creswell, Oregon, a small, easy-to-miss community of loggers and sawmill workers roughly ten miles south of Eugene, the unemployment rate was skyrocketing to rates not seen since the Great Depression. Families were losing their homes, the town was losing money for social services and education, and the rural Northwest was, in many ways, losing its very identity. All this was responsible for his dour mood. "It wasn't a fun time," Heath remembered, "it was a very serious time."[2]

Heath's frustrations are clearly visible in the final picture *Life*'s editors chose to print. In it, he stares coldly at the camera, the anger and anxiety he experienced over the last few years apparent in his chilling gaze, firmly clenched jaw, and tightly pursed lips. For readers of *Life*, Heath may well have appeared as the personification of rural outrage that by 1990 had been well documented by journalists. They called it the spotted-owl conflict or the timber wars, a somewhat hyperbolic appellation that, nevertheless, had a ring of veracity to it. Over the past several years, normally lackluster public hearings on land-management decisions had erupted into shouting matches as loggers and environmentalists debated the future of the owl and the rural Northwest. Large protests led by people from the rural Northwest and massive convoys of logging trucks flying yellow ribbons—the symbol many in timber country adopted to represent their anger—created chaos and disorder at state capitals in Olympia and Salem. Loggers hung dead spotted owls from fence posts on the outside of their towns and plastered bumper stickers with slogans like "I like spotted owls . . . fried" on their battered pickups. Like a good deal of the reporting covering the conflict, the text that accompanied Heath's picture in *Life* explained that rural animus was an expression of rural economic anxiety, that it was fears over job losses that'd spawned the disruptive protests now routine throughout the region. For the text's author—no byline was given and to this day, Heath doesn't know who wrote it—the acrimony of the past several years had proven that balancing the economic needs of the rural working class and the habitat needs of wildlife had proven as "tricky as staying upright in a logrolling contest." The Northwest, if not the entire region, was now at a crossroads and had to make a "tough choice: jobs or the environment."[3]

Figure 7.1. "Endangered Species. An Owl and a Logger Symbolize the Nation's Tough Choice: Jobs or the Environment." Courtesy LIFE magazine and Brian Lanker Archives. LIFE and the LIFE logo are registered trademarks of TI Gotham Inc., used under license. © 1991 The Picture Collection Inc. All Rights reserved. Reprinted/Translated from LIFE and published with permission of The Picture Collection Inc. Reproduction in any manner in any language in whole or in part without written permission is prohibited.

But rural outrage couldn't so easily be explained by timber country's rapidly rising unemployment rate, even if that was a large part of it. The more central source of their collective anger had to do with the dichotomous ways of thinking articulated in the text of the *Life* piece: jobs *or* the environment, loggers *or* owls. It was a framework that invalidated the direct experiences of timber workers like Heath, and the longer history of forest stewardship in timber country, one that had always sought a balance between work and nature, jobs and the environment. Certainly, complex policies and understandings of forest ecologies were necessary to adequately strike that balance, but it was hardly as tricky as the author at *Life* had suggested. It was the refusal of policy makers and environmentalists to listen to working people in the Northwest woods that fueled their frustrations.

Indeed, insofar as the spotted-owl conflict amounted to a war, it was more a cultural one than the sort of class war that earlier generations of loggers and millworkers had fought. It wasn't a war between workers and bosses but, rather, a war between country and city, between enlightened urbanites and narrow-minded rural folk, or honest, hard-working loggers and effete environmentalists, depending on your perspective. It was a war about the future of the Northwest and what place rural communities had, if any, in that future. More than anything, it was a war over competing definitions of environmentalism and which of its forms—the middle-class environmentalism of the urban Northwest or the working-class environmentalism of timber country—would guide forest management. These battlelines had started to take shape in the 1970s in the cultural forms of the counterculture and rural working class alike. But the spotted-owl conflict ultimately cemented them into the Northwest's social and political landscapes, hardening the divides between the urban and rural, relegating timber country to the silent fringes of the region's environmental politics and making the sort of partnerships that had existed between wilderness activists and timber workers in the mid-twentieth century all but a political impossibility.

The spotted owl would cast a long, dark shadow over much of the rural Northwest. It would have devastating economic effects that timber-dependent communities are still reckoning with today, and just as significantly, it would shape the course of subsequent land-use debates, many of which have exacerbated timber country's economic, social, and political marginalization.

As the photoshoot with *Life* was ending, Heath, too, could sense that the bird would forever change the Northwest, and he seemed to understand that from that point on, everyone would understand him and his relationship to the forest through the owl. Sitting on Heath's shoulder, the bird had dug her sharp talons into his skin, and hours later he could still feel the scrapes and gouges, like a phantom presence reminding him he'd never be able to detach himself from the owl. At home, Heath poured himself a Scotch, hoping to dull the pain in his shoulder and the deeper pains of the past several years. Then his wife noticed something on his back. Heath removed his shirt to look. "Damn," he said, when he realized what it was, "that's the second time the spotted owl has shit on me."[4]

Spotted Owls and Ancient Forests

Heath's picture in *Life* raises several questions. Should ecological or economic considerations guide land-management decisions? How do we balance the nation's need for lumber with wildlife's need for habitat? What do we owe workers, and what do we owe forest fauna? But, perhaps, the more basic question it raises is this: where, exactly, does one find an ostensibly endangered species to pose for a picture? The answer to this last question is the only one that's easy to answer. Her name was Hazel. She'd been abandoned as a hatchling roughly fifteen years earlier in a forest near Corvallis, Oregon, and then found, rescued, raised, and brought to the *Life* shoot by a Forest Service wildlife biologist named Eric D. Forsman. By the time the shoot took place in 1990, Forsman had become the nation's foremost spotted-owl expert. He'd published dozens of scientific papers documenting the owl's population status and habitat needs and provided expert testimony in several court hearings that resulted in new logging restrictions. But Forsman never intended to become a central player in a debate over the future of the forests and logging communities. He came from rural Oregon and had family members employed in the timber industry, and while he often counseled caution and sometimes recommended modest harvest restrictions in the interest of protecting the owl's habitat, it was environmentalists, more than scientists like Forsman, who effectively wielded the owl as a political and legal tool to limit and in some cases completely end logging. Perhaps, the most important thing to understand about the campaign to save the spotted owl is this: it was never really about the owl.[5]

For most of the twentieth century, no one really paid much attention to the spotted owl. Wildlife biologists, especially those at federal land-management agencies, focused their research on game animals. This began to change in the late 1960s as a new generation of younger scientists trained in what was then the young field of ecological science entered agencies like the Forest Service. This younger generation said you could learn a lot about forests by focusing on the smallest and seemingly most insignificant flora and fauna. They began to study things like fungi, rodents, and microorganisms and, of course, owls. Forsman was part of this new generation. His early research revealed that the owl had an incredibly delicate life cycle. Although spotted owls live fifteen years on average, females typically only lay eggs once every two years. Hatchling survival rates are also astonishingly low. Baby owls often attempt to leave their nests before they're ready to fly and then plummet to their deaths. For reasons that scientists still don't understand, mothers regularly abandon their brood, making newborn owls easy targets for tree-dwelling predators. Some studies estimate that fewer than 10 percent of hatchlings survive into adulthood. It's something of a wonder how evolution saw fit to preserve the owl. But for Forsman, the owl's fragility was precisely why it was worth studying. Because its life cycle was so frail, it needed a perfectly functioning ecosystem to survive. Biologists began calling the owl an "indicator species" and said the forest's overall health could be measured by the owl's overall health. The spotted owl became the proverbial canary in the coal mine.[6]

Assessing the status of the spotted owl required finding and counting owls, which proved to be tricky. The bird is small and mostly nocturnal, with (as its name implies) speckled plumage that allows it to disappear into the treetops where it nests. Wildlife biologists developed all sorts of methods to locate owls, from mimicking calls to creating traps intended to humanely capture birds. By the early 1980s, biologists had directly observed about three thousand nesting pairs across the bird's native range, which stretches from northern California to the southern tip of British Columbia. But given the difficulties of locating owls, just how many actually existed remained something of a mystery. Lacking observational data, scientists turned to projections, based on what they believed was the owl's preferred habitat: old-growth forest. The problem was that, as late as 1989, the Forest Service had yet to conduct a comprehensive survey of forest stand structures in the Northwest and, thus, didn't know how much old-growth there currently was nor how much there'd historically been, which meant biologists like Forsman couldn't say how many owls there currently were or how many there'd historically been. Scientists *suspected* the owl's numbers were in decline but admitted they weren't confident enough in their data to make policy recommendations. Even by 1992, two years *after* the spotted owl had been listed as a "threatened" species by the US Fish and Wildlife Service, Jack Ward Thomas, lead Forest Service biologist and future chief forester of the United States, admitted in a public hearing that his agency had based owl-management plans on projections, not hard data. Nor were biologists confident that the owl exclusively relied on old-growth forests. "We cannot say with absolute certainty," read a 1987 Forest Service planning document, "what kind of habitat the owl needs in order to survive."[7]

If scientists had so many questions about the owl's overall population, how was it that late twentieth-century activists became so certain the owl was in need of saving? The answer has less to do with science and more to do with the politics of the environmental movement and one activist, in particular, Andy Kerr. Kerr is likely the most hated environmentalist in timber country. At the very least, he has the unusual distinction of being hung in effigy—twice—by people in rural communities. For Kerr, though, his reputation in the rural Northwest was more a product of his birthplace than his activism. Kerr was born and raised in Creswell—the very same town Heath came from—and he believes this is why he was (and is) so loathed. "Every movement needs a demon," he said, "and I was particularly demon-esque because I was from timber country . . . so I was a traitor."[8]

Kerr's transition from son of timber country to one of the industry's fiercest critics came while he was a student at the University of Oregon in the early 1970s. Kerr happened past a wilderness protest in front of the Forest Service office in downtown Eugene. "What a novel concept," he said to himself at the time, "part of the national forest you should leave alone." Wilderness movements were nothing new in the Northwest, but the protest Kerr encountered did represent something new in American environmental thought, what historian Keith Woodhouse has termed "crisis environmentalism." A product of the Cold War arms race, when the complete annihilation of all living things appeared to be a distinct possibility, crisis environmentalism held that global ecosystems were on the verge of breaking down and that radical action was needed to reverse course. Kerr, like the wilderness activists he'd seen in downtown Eugene, applied this same rationale to the Northwest's forests. The region's woodlands were teetering on the edge of a collapse, he said, and broad prohibitions of logging were needed to prevent that collapse. There could be no middle ground here, and certainly no compromising. "Don't ask me to compromise," Kerr said. "The forests have been compromised, and there's not enough left."[9]

Shortly after leaving the University of Oregon, Kerr helped found the Oregon Wilderness Coalition, which changed its name to the Oregon Natural Resources Council (ONRC) soon thereafter. Throughout the 1970s and into the early 1980s, Kerr and the ONRC initiated several court cases looking to block public-lands timber sales and aggressively lobbied politicians for expanded wilderness designations. Yet, for every fight the ONRC won, it lost a dozen more. The ONRC was a small organization with limited financial resources going up against powerful timber-industry lawyers and politicians weary of disrupting the state's economy. Expecting Oregon's congressional delegation to expand wilderness, Kerr once famously told the press, "would be like expecting the Mississippi delegation to solve segregation in 1959." What Kerr wanted was the support of the larger and much better funded national environmental organizations. His problem was that until the 1980s, those larger organizations were mostly focused on protecting what he described as "rock and ice," that is, high-elevation wilderness areas and bucolic mountain vistas, not the forests that grew at lower elevations on those mountains' slopes.[10]

Kerr learned about studies documenting the owl's habitat needs and overall population status in the late 1970s. For many of the biologists who'd completed those studies, this research was a story about the complexities of ecosystems and the uncertainty undergirding all scientific inquiry. Kerr saw something different. He saw data that confirmed his belief in an ecological crisis. More than that, he saw an opportunity to convince the broader environmental movement to care about the Northwest's forests. "It was something you could see," he said, speaking of the owl, "it was easy to make the case." What the owl had going for it was charisma. Spotted owls have small, boxy frames that make them look almost human-like in silhouette, and their deep black eyes suggest, to many, a capacity for human thought. Owls also have something of an esteemed reputation in Western lore and religion. Athena, the Greek goddess of wisdom, is often depicted beside an owl, as is Merlin, the learned wizard of Arthurian legend. For a generation of Americans familiar with these stories and then raised on the anthropomorphized animals in Disney cartoons, the spotted owl appeared almost designed by nature to elicit sympathy.[11]

Getting environmentalists from outside the Northwest to care about the owl may have been a relatively easy sell. Making the case that saving the owl required limitations on logging proved to be a somewhat-thornier issue. Biologists said the owl needed old-growth forests to survive. But preserving old growth didn't necessarily equate to prohibiting logging. Since the term first came into usage in the late nineteenth century, foresters have never had a clear definition of "old growth." Sometimes foresters used the phrase as a synonym for "never been logged," but that only created more confusion. An unlogged forest that regenerated after a windstorm or landslide in the mid-twentieth century might contain trees that were, on average, far younger than a forest that'd grown back after being actively logged in the mid-nineteenth century. Then what about Indigenous land management? Were forests that'd been burned by Native peoples "old growth" or not? To clear up some of the confusion, foresters sometime in the 1970s began to use "old growth" less to refer to age and more to refer to overall stand structure. An "old-growth forest," they said, was one dominated by late-successional species, such as fir, pine, and cedar. According to this definition, a logged-over forest could, with time and proper management, become an old-growth forest, which meant protecting old growth didn't necessarily require banning harvests, and this was Kerr's problem.[12]

It was James Monteith, Kerr's partner at the ONRC, who came up with a solution. In 1986 Monteith suggested that henceforth the ONRC link the owl's survival not to "old growth" but to "ancient forests." It was a genius, if fundamentally misleading, rhetorical shift. Historians tend to define "ancient" as everything that came before 500 C.E. While Northwest forests could be old, none were that old. But historic accuracy wasn't the ONRC's goal. Appealing to emotions was, and in that sense, "ancient forests" was an ideal term. Unlike "old growth," "ancient forests" suggested that the Northwest's woodlands were irreplaceable. Forests could be returned to old-growth status after logging, but once "ancient forests" were gone, they were gone for good. More than that, "ancient forests" suggested that the Northwest's forests were part of the world's shared history, something akin to an antiquity, and that saving the owl and the "ancient forests" upon which it depended was an act of preserving our common global heritage.[13]

The timing here was critical. Had Monteith come up with his idea a few years earlier, or a few years later, the idea of "ancient forests" still may have caught on in environmental discourse. But something happened in 1986 that helped cement the term in the consciousness of the Northwest's environmental movement. In the mid-1980s, the federal government lowered interest rates, which led to new housing and construction starts, which created new demands for Northwest lumber. Responding to that demand in the spring of 1986, Willamette Industries harvested a public-timber-sale site it'd been holding for several years. It was a roughly forty-five-acre patch of forest outside of Sweet Home, Oregon, containing some trees more than five hundred years old and potentially a spotted-owl nest. Willamette Industries' decision to cut the stand quickly provoked environmentalists. Here was proof that the timber industry was indeed destroying owls and the "ancient forests" they depended on. The ONRC sought (but failed to win) an injunction stopping further harvests at the site. Protesters camped out in front of the Forest Service office in Eugene and demanded that the agency intervene to prohibit future harvests. On Memorial Day, a new group called Cathedral Forest organized a protest in front of the Sweet Home Forest Service Ranger Station. Jazz musician Paul Winter played for the protesters, weaving recorded spotted-owl calls into his saxophone performance. "Incorporating animal songs and calls into music is his way of giving voice to creatures otherwise left out of natural resource debates," explained a journalist covering the protests.[14]

It's difficult to pinpoint an exact moment when the spotted-owl conflict began. Its roots lie equally in the social, cultural, economic, and demographic changes of the 1970s, the rise of ecological thinking in wildlife biology, and the emergence of the crisis environmentalism represented by a group like the ONRC. But if there was a single moment that helped galvanize antilogging sentiment in the Northwest and reframe it as about owls and "ancient forests," it was most certainly the Willamette Industries' harvest. "A lot of people all over Oregon, and particularly in the Portland area who seldom pay attention to the timber industry," stated an editorial in *Oregon Business*, suddenly started "talking about the cutting of those trees, and they are mad about it." Following the protests, the Forest Service was inundated with over thirty thousand letters, most of which now demanded new guidelines protecting owls and ancient forests. Partly in response to public pressure and more as a preemptive move to avoid litigation, the Forest Service identified 550 spotted-owl nests across Oregon and Washington and issued new rules prohibiting logging within roughly two thousand acres of those nests, which amounted to a roughly 20 percent reduction in timber harvests.

The decision set a precedent, one that would be repeated time and time again. Federal land managers responded to public pressure that environmental activists created without giving much thought to the economic impact on rural communities. The life of the owl was becoming more of a management priority than the lives of rural working people. "I am a housewife with three kids to raise. My husband owns his own small business—auto repair—and he relies on loggers and millworkers for a lot of his business," wrote Christy Duncan in a letter to the editors of the *Albany (OR) Democrat-Herald*, "All this fuss about saving the spotted owl, I think, has hidden the real endangered species—the great Oregon working man and woman. . . . All of us who live in timber towns are environmentalists, but we have no kinship with those radicals who want to stop all logging." As Duncan's letter indicates, in 1986 new questions started to percolate to the surface of land-management discussions. It was partly a question of what land managers should prioritize: jobs or ecology? But it was, perhaps, even more fundamental than that. Whose vision of environmentalism should be reflected in land management: the more urban and middle-class environmentalism of the people who'd written into the Forest Service demanding rule changes or the more working-class environmentalism of people like Duncan?[15]

"Room Enough for Loggers and Owls"

Heath's *Life* photoshoot had taken place in the Siuslaw National Forest, just a few miles west of Philomath, Oregon. Environmentalists concerned about owls and "ancient forests" told a story of decline, one in which both charismatic wildlife and its habitat were in crisis. Yet, things looked a little bit different from where Heath stood, and understanding the emerging conflict requires some understanding of what loggers like him saw when they looked at the Northwest's forests. What Heath might've pointed out was that traveling just a bit farther west from where he was standing would've taken a visitor to the Rock Creek Wilderness, an area that the Forest Service today describes as one of the Northwest's "most remote" wilderness areas, a place with "pristine rain forest canyons" and small creeks running with "crystalline water." Rock Creek was added to the American wilderness system as part of the 1984 Wilderness Act, and driving north along Highway 101 from Rock Creek would take anyone to several more wilderness areas also added in 1984, including Cummins Creek and Drift Creek. Heading east would've revealed more wilderness areas still, like the Menagerie and Three Sisters Wilderness, which the IWA had helped create.[16]

What a journey through the Northwest's public forests would've revealed was that by 1986, right when environmentalists were claiming that wilderness and old-growth forests were disappearing, the region had protected more old-growth stands through wilderness designations than at any other point in history. That's not to say environmentalists didn't have cause for concern. Public-forest harvest rates had remained relatively consistent throughout the 1980s. The issue, though, is where public-lands managers were allowing harvests to occur. Responding to economic and industry pressures, the agency increasingly sold off timber in places they probably shouldn't have. The Willamette Industries case was just one example. Indeed, a few years later, in 1989, after a group of concerned public foresters started a new group, Forest Service Employees for Environmental Ethics (FSEEE), some of the excesses of the public-lands managers would become even more apparent. FSEEE's members claimed they'd been instructed by supervisors to ignore the agency's own conservation guidelines and federal soil and water standards and authorize harvests that shouldn't have been greenlighted. Heath also remembers questioning some timber sales in the mid-1980s and then declining to bid on timber he thought was too close to streambeds.[17]

Even so, forest management in the 1980s couldn't so easily be summed up by public-agency malfeasance. In the final picture that *Life's* editors chose to run, Heath and the owl are in clear focus, but the forest background is blurry. Had the photographer brought that forest into sharper focus, though, the final picture might've captured a the more complex relationship between forest ecologies and logging. In the 1980s, as in the past, timber workers described the ways in which logging removed dead and dying trees, opened the forest floor to light, encouraged new growth, and created new wildlife habitat. "The timber industry has done more to perpetuate our natural resources than any other group I can think of," said logger Jim Standard at a 1989 public hearing on the spotted owl. "Ask any logger who daily shares his lunch with a raccoon, a chipmunk, a raven, or even a doe and her fawn if he is destroying habitat or enhancing it." Loggers often added owls to the species that may have benefited from logging. Loggers claimed to have seen owls in second- and third-growth forests and speculated that owls did perfectly fine in industrial woodlands because they could effectively hunt in clearcuts. "We know there are more owls than once thought!" wrote one man in a rural paper. "We know that their habitat is much more diverse than we once thought! I simply feel there's enough room in the woods for Loggers and Owls. Don't make us the owl's enemy. We wish to coexist with it as we have for so long."[18]

Here, in many ways, is what it came down to for many people in timber country. There was already plenty of wilderness in the Northwest, and this would remain, as one man opined, "spotted owl habitat forever." The environmental movement was now starting to seek, and the Forest Service implement, broader protections that limited logging outside of wilderness areas. This threated the economic health of timber country *and* the ecological health of forests. What environmentalists adhering to the "ancient forest" concept assumed—and what the concept itself *encouraged* people to assume—is that the Northwest's forests were static, unchanged until people with saws changed them. It ignored how natural disturbances, including floods and fires, and Indigenous land management had constantly shaped and reshaped the forests, creating a diversity of stand structures. Long before the rise of industrial logging in the Northwest, most of the region's forests were a complex matrix of stand structures, where patches of older trees intermixed with patches of far-younger trees. Rather than an unbroken sea of old-growth forests or so-called ancient forests, Northwest woodlands prior to the era of Euro-American settlement contained, according to some studies, no more than 40 percent of what in the late twentieth century would be considered old growth. The rest was transitional forest in various stages of succession. That stand age diversity was critical for the forest's overall ecological health, in no small part because it provided a range of habitats for wildlife. Logging helped preserve some of that overall diversity, and by shutting down logging, environmentalists weren't so much trying to preserve the forest as they were creating one that'd never existed. "I'm not sure what 'primeval forests' are," wrote forester David Keiser, offering a basic lesson in land management to the readers of the *Eugene (OR) Register-Guard*, "but the Coast Range [of the early nineteenth century] only had a few pockets of old-growth timber, while the vast majority of the forest was Douglas fir that seeded the area after a disastrous fire swept the whole Coast Range." Keiser concluded, "Since nature herself did not see fit to 'save the old growth,' it seems a little presumptuous of man to advocate it."[19]

The movement coalescing around the spotted owl and "ancient forests" in 1986 wasn't just ignoring the extent of wilderness and the complicated ecologies of forests, it was ignoring the culture of stewardship in timber country. What got quickly ignored in the aftermath of the Willamette Industries' harvest was that some critics of the company's decision could be found in rural communities. Comparing the company's actions to one of the more publicized atrocities of the Vietnam War, one logger told a reporter from *Oregon Business*, "In one fell swoop that company did as much for the public image of the timber industry in Oregon as My Lai did for the image of the U.S. Army." Loggers in Washington noticed much the same thing. One Forks-area timber worker speaking with sociologist Matthew Carrol complained, "They [environmentalists] are depicting us as barbarians and idiots, that we are raping the forest, but the majority of loggers are much more environmentally conscious and much more concerned with the woods than the average person." Heath can't remember the Willamette Industries' decision specifically, but he does remember he was open, at least before the late 1980s, to discussing harvest reductions that might've protected sensitive forest areas. "We in the industry were certainly willing to talk," he said. "We could've come to a pretty happy medium, really. We could've probably found a good compromise."[20]

"Spike a Tree for Jesus"

If workers in the industry were, indeed, willing to compromise, as Heath suggested, those feelings would not last long past 1986. That year, three interrelated changes occurred that turned debates over forest management into an irreconcilable conflict. The first thing that happened was that, as Kerr had hoped, large, national, environmental organizations became involved in Northwest environmental politics. As they did, they helped legitimize the idea of "ancient forests" in the broader public consciousness, making more-nuanced conversations about forest management and the complicated ecologies of logging less likely. By early 1987, the Audubon Society was warning its members that "ancient forests" that had existed since "the time Columbus made landfall in the New World" were quickly disappearing. That same year, the Wilderness Society struck a similar tone and published a policy paper that warned of the "end of the Ancient Forests," and the Sierra Club Legal Defense opened a new office in Seattle with the express purpose of saving the last of the Northwest's "ancient forests." Two years later, in 1989, the Sierra Club, Audubon Society, and National Wildlife Federation joined forces and established the Ancient Forest Alliance. "In the time it takes to read this brochure," read a pamphlet issued by the new group, "several acres of irreplaceable virgin forest will be clearcut. These are the original, untouched forests that existed when the first white settlers arrived in North America, *and only five percent is left*."[21]

The second thing that happened was that as large environmental movements became involved in the effort to save spotted owls, they began to chart a new course of legal activism. Initially, smaller environmental groups like the ONRC were hesitant to seek an "endangered" species listing for the spotted owl under the terms of the 1973 Endangered Species Act (ESA) because, up until that point, the ESA was legally untested. It'd been signed by President Richard M. Nixon largely as a symbolic gesture, and for most of its existence it'd only been used to prohibit the importation of animal parts from foreign countries. Lawyers for large environmental organizations were far more willing to brave the ESA's uncharted legal waters. In 1987 lawyers representing the Sierra Club, National Wildlife Federation, Wilderness Society, and several others filed petitions with the US Fish and Wildlife Service (FWS) asking the agency to list the owl as an "endangered species." If the agency agreed to listing the owl, it would force public-lands-management agencies to adopt new management plans that prioritized the owl's survival over harvest rates.[22]

The third thing that happened was that radical environmental groups became more active in the Northwest woods, and as they did, they opened up new legal and political space that made it easier for lawyers in the environmental movement to more effectively make their case. There was some irony here, precisely because some of those radical environmentalists explicitly rejected legal activism as a tool of environmental protection. At least that was the case for Earth First!, a group that was the very embodiment of crisis environmentalism. Founded in the southwest United States in 1980 by radical activists dismayed by what they described as the mainstream environmental movement's willingness to capitulate to industrial interests, Earth First! members, instead, maintained, as one of their oft-used slogans put it, there could be, "No compromise in defense of Mother Earth!" Alongside compromise, Earth First! rejected political lobbying and legal activism. The group's members said that industrial interests were too entrenched in the country's legal and political systems, and, thus, other forms of activism were necessary. Their chosen method was what they called "monkeywrenching" after Edward Abbey's *Monkeywrench Gang*, a novel about a ragtag group of environmentalists who plot to dynamite Arizona's Glen Canyon Dam. A form of industrial sabotage, monkeywrenching involved sneaking into resource-extraction operations, often under the cover of night, and destroying access roads, equipment, and tools. Earth First! had no unifying political ideology. Some of its members were anarchists, others ecofeminists, and others still something like libertarians. What tied the group's activists together, though, was an adherence to ecocentrism, the belief that all living things had equal value and that humans deserved no more consideration or protection than trees and wildlife.[23]

Earth First! arrived in the Northwest in 1984, when activists were drawn into the region by an effort to block a timber sale near southern Oregon's Bald Mountain. Soon thereafter, Earth First! activists began appearing at logging protests throughout the region. The group employed many of the same monkeywrenching tactics in the Northwest as it did elsewhere, though it added some new tactics, as well. One of those was the tree sit, in which activists occupied platforms high up in old-growth trees, forcing loggers to choose between felling the tree and sparing the life of the activist. Because they were often such dramatic affairs, tree sits attracted the attention of journalists and helped further popularize the campaign to save "ancient forests." But it was another activity, done more clandestinely, that often garnered more attention: tree spiking. Described as an "extremely effective method of deterring timber sales" in *Ecodefense: A Field Guide to Monkeywrenching*, a how-to guide for activists edited by Earth First! cofounder Dave Foreman, tree spiking involved driving large metal nails into trees with the hope the nails would then damage saws and, as *Ecodefense* continued, "bring operations to a screeching halt." Earth First! claimed that its war was with timber companies and not workers, and some of the group's members would later denounce spiking as unnecessarily alienating loggers. But the group's music sometimes told a far-different story. Many of Earth First!'s songs, like "Earth

First! Maid," (set to the tune of Woody Guthrie's "Union Maid"), "They Sure Don't Make Hippies the Way They Used To," and "Ballad of the Lonesome Tree Spiker" identified workers as the target of tree spiking. "Spike a Tree for Jesus" was most direct. The conceit of the song is that because Christ was nailed to a cross made of lumber, "'twas the loggers [who] killed Jesus, and it's time that we got them back good."[24]

Indeed, for every Earth First! member that claimed spiking amounted to an unnecessarily violent practice, there was another who saw it as an effective form of activism. One of those was "Bonnie Abbzug," a pseudonym of an Earth First! member active in Oregon's woods in the 1980s. "Tree spiking made sense," she explained, "tree spiking was something that could be done safely, any time you wanted, under the cover of darkness, and not face any serious repercussions." Spiking may have shielded activists like Abbzug from repercussions, but loggers could hardly say the same thing. Mark Keiser, a timber feller from Oregon, explained that hitting a spike "would cause the saw to kick back violently, probably into my chest or legs. . . . I don't like to think about it, but I guess every timber feller does. This is pretty scary business." In actuality, only one timber worker was ever injured by a spike, a sawyer from northern California, and it's likely that the spike was placed by a disgruntled landowner, not an Earth First! member. Moreover, companies quickly installed metal detectors in mills that found spikes before they became a problem. In short, tree spiking probably didn't have the economic effects Abbzug claimed—but it most certainly had an effect. Spiking convinced many timber workers that environmentalists cared little for their safety, and this was a movement that couldn't be reasoned with. Spiking also threatened to create rifts and divides within the broader environmental movement. William Turnage of the Wilderness Society, for one, worried that radicals running through forests with spikes made the entire movement look like "irresponsible and rather bizarre characters."[25]

But in ways someone like Turnage may not have initially recognized, Earth First! actually helped legitimize more mainstream groups like the Wilderness Society. As Kerr explained, for most of the twentieth century, federal land managers, politicians, and the courts had always been reticent to implement policies that threatened the economic foundations of the Northwest. "It was considered radical to stop cutting old-growth forests," he said. But now, Earth First! made a group like the ONRC look downright reasonable. What Earth First! did was effectively shift the landscape of environmental politics in the region, situating itself on the radical fringes and making harvest reductions and spotted-owl set-asides look like a reasonable alternative to spiking and tree sits. David Brower, a former director of the Sierra Club, agreed with the assessment offered by Kerr: "Earth First! now makes us look reasonable."[26]

And, indeed, the courts and land-management agencies appeared more responsive to mainstream environmental demands after 1987 or, at the very least, began implementing new changes intended to avoid litigation and lawsuits down the road. After establishing two-thousand-acre set-asides for spotted owls in 1986, the Forest Service and federal Bureau of Land Management (BLM) increased the buffer around known spotted-owl nests to three thousand acres in 1987 and five thousand acres in 1988. Also in 1988, as the FWS status review of the spotted owl was ongoing, environmentalists brought a suit before the federal courts, claiming that logging should be halted until the FWS came to a final decision. A year later, in 1989, Judge William Dwyer largely agreed and issued an injunction blocking 163 timber sales on federal lands.[27]

"The People Environmentalists Don't Want You to See"

Forest Service administrators and the courts were effectively responding to the ecological concerns and considerations of the environmental movement, but they were increasingly ignoring the social and economic concerns of timber country (not to mention their ecological insights). Driving home from his photo shoot, though, Heath would've found it far more difficult to ignore what was going on in the region's timber-working communities. His drive home would've taken him first through Philomath, a small logging town home to several small, independent contract loggers who, like Heath himself, were likely struggling to find work. Boarded-up storefronts on the town's main street would've spoken to the ways in which rising unemployment in the timber industry reverberated throughout entire local economies. His next stop would've been Corvallis. Timber workers were struggling here, too, but this town was larger, with a much more diversified economy, and the jobs provided by Oregon State University helped many in town ignore some of the problems that its working-class residents were experiencing. After turning south on Interstate 5, Heath would've sped past smaller logging towns tucked into the hills just beyond the Willamette Valley, places like Sweet Home, Marcola, and Mohawk. Things were especially bad in these places, where their economies rested entirely on public timber. Heath's trip home would've taken him next to Eugene. Like Corvallis, a major university helped keep Eugene an economically thriving city, even if the sawmills on the north end of town and many of the mill workers living in adjacent

Springfield didn't share in that prosperity. Finally, Heath would've arrived in his hometown of Creswell, and things here looked similar to Sweet Home and Mohawk. The drive amounted to a relatively short one and probably took Heath not much longer than an hour. Still, in that time he'd experienced two Northwests, one prospering and the other faltering, and a growing economic divide increasingly reshaping the region.

Determining the relationship between the rural Northwest's economic problems and new harvest reductions was and remains incredibly fraught. There are almost too many variables to account for here: logging restrictions, yes, but also national and global lumber demands, competition from other lumber-producing regions, automation and technological changes that impact overall employment figures, the inherent volatility of the lumber market that has impacted employment figures since the early twentieth century, and the unreliability of economic data, to name just a few. In short, it is impossible to definitively say whether the spotted owl was responsible for exacerbating the Northwest's economic divide. But that didn't stop people at the time from making assertions with absolute certainty (a trend that has continued well into the present), and whether someone believed that the owl was or was not to blame for the rural Northwest's high unemployment figures was less a function of the methodologies they used and far more a reflection of their political allegiances. A 1988 report published by the Wilderness Society claimed that spotted-owl set-asides had only cost the Northwest timber industry about three thousand jobs. The American Forest Resources Council, an industry trade group, claimed that set-asides were responsible for the loss of more than eighty thousand jobs. Environmentalists countered that, yes, the timber industry had lost an incredible number of jobs in the past decade, but this had more to do with capital flight and automation. Several economists—some working for or with the timber industry, others independent—argued that the environmental movement significantly overstated the effects of automation and that job losses caused by the adoption of labor-saving technologies were significantly lower than many assumed.[28]

While most in timber country certainly agreed with industry assessments that spotted-owl protections had, indeed, led to job losses, the larger issue was that the debate hinged on data in the first place. "This isn't about numbers. It's about people's lives," said timber worker Michael Harris in an op-ed responding to an earlier editorial authored by an ONRC member that claimed automation, not the spotted owl, was responsible for timber country's economic woes. Harris continued, "We are the people the environmentalists don't want you to see. We are the ones who will pay the price for their actions." Harris had a point that neither environmentalists nor land managers rarely considered in the spotted-owl era. Whether or not the owl had cost the timber industry jobs (and, to be clear, Harris argued, it most certainly had), making the debate about numbers and labor statistics masked deep and troubling economic problems in the rural Northwest. It directed the sympathies of many in the urban Northwest, land managers, politicians, and judges toward the owl and "ancient forests" and oriented them away from rural communities.[29]

Indeed, while the labor-market effects of the spotted owl got debated, what quickly got ignored was a clear and far less ambiguous social and economic consequence of reduced public-lands harvests: the rapid decline of rural county budgets. Because many counties in Oregon and Washington contain large amounts of public lands, county governments cannot collect property taxes to fund municipal and social services. To make up for the reduced tax base, federal land-management agencies have, since the late nineteenth century, shared a portion of timber sales with counties. In some cases, timber payments made up close to two-thirds of a rural county's total operating budget, and dollars acquired through timber-sharing agreements fund law enforcement, social services, and education. The loss of those payments as timber sales were canceled created several vicious social and economic cycles in timber country in the late 1980s. Crime rose as people lost their jobs, yet county sheriffs were forced to lay off deputies, which only led to more crime. Social-service providers eliminated staff and closed offices, even though more people were now seeking out services. Rural school districts also contended with budget shortfalls and laid off teachers, consolidated classrooms, and cut extracurricular programs. The high school dropout rate in many rural communities rose in tandem with the unemployment rate. For Ellen Tigart, the lack of attention to all this seemed to signal the ways the environmental movement cared more about the owl than the rural Northwest. "The environmentalists—I think that everybody needs a cause, but it would have been nice if they had looked a little further for one," she commented. "There are big things to be concerned about, you know? Saving an owl isn't one of them. We've got kids starving to death. We've got kids that are getting into some serious trouble. We need work."[30]

Cherie Girod of Mill City, Oregon, might have agreed. At the very least, she understood better than just about anyone else the social crisis timber country experienced in the late 1980s. Girod ran the Canyon Crisis Center, a social-services provider in Mill City. Throughout the 1980s, most of her clients had been women who were victims of domestic abuse. But, she said that starting in 1989, "we would get men into our office who would not normally come. Loggers, people of the earth, are stoic, very proud, and these men would come on the pretext of using the coffee machine." She explained that after milling around for some time, those men would start to "talk of problems with the industry, then talk of friends who were having difficulties, then start to relate these to their own families and finally themselves." She remembers counseling loggers who worried they were drinking too much, who described more frequent fights with spouses over past-due notices from utility companies, who were kept awake at night, anxious about their children's futures. "These things that so embittered these men and churned in their stomachs would start to come out," she said. Just after Judge Dwyer issued his injunction, Girod recalled a man who came into her office and asked, "If I kill myself, will my family get my insurance?"[31]

As Heath might have noticed on his drive home, the rural Northwest's economic decline occurred alongside the urban Northwest's rise. Both Seattle and Portland experienced high unemployment rates in the 1970s, but things had turned around as both cities began to attract new, high-tech industries and electronics manufacturers, in particular, that provided plenty of high-paying jobs for the urban middle and working classes alike. Demographics and the real estate market also played an important role in the urban Northwest's late twentieth-century economic transformation. New workers flocked to cities to take advantage of high-paying jobs, and they needed places to live. Developers in Seattle quickly built out to the edges of Puget Sound and Lake Washington while developers in Portland bumped up to the edges of the city's urban-growth boundary. Soon there was more demand than supply. Looking to boost the prices of their homes further, homeowners renovated and built additions. Portlanders of the late 1980s spent more time remodeling their homes than residents of every other American city.[32]

The contradictions of this growth were not lost on James Petersen, the editor of a small trade journal called *Evergreen*. "The very visible results of Portland's economic boom," he wrote, "have overshadowed the power *behind* the city's rebirth," which for him was timber country. And yet, Petersen continued, even as timber workers in the rural Northwest supplied the raw lumber that facilitated homebuilding and urban economic development, environmentalists had built "overwhelming urban support for its proposed ban on the harvest of old-growth timber." We don't know if he was a fan of Buzz Martin, but the analysis Petersen offered was the same exact one the country singer had articulated decades prior: that outsiders disparaged timber country and denied the dignity of rural labor, even as they reaped some of the economic rewards of that labor. Indeed, Petersen concluded his piece with words that may well have appeared as lyrics in one of Martin's songs. What the spotted-owl conflict amounted to, Petersen said, "was an urban-inspired quest to control rural Oregon, as though rural Oregon were Portland's playground; when, in fact, rural Oregon is Portland's workshop. It is where goods are fashioned from natural resources, where the good citizens of rural Oregon fashion our state's riches from the sweat of their brow."[33]

Petersen imagined something of a coordinated conspiracy or, at the very least, a conscious strategy on the part of environmentalists to mobilize urban sentiment against timber country. Perhaps. But the larger issue was likely that just as Petersen had taken his cues from the ideas and identities articulated in popular culture from years before, so, too, did environmentalists and urban-ites. Indeed, when confronted with questions about the social consequences of spotted-owl protections, environmentalists often responded with indiffer-ence or, sometimes, downright disparaging comments that reflected some of the cultural tropes articulated in earlier decades. "I personally look around at a lot of these loggers, and I feel sorry for them because of their lifestyle," one environmentalist told environmental policy researcher Steven Yaffee. "They're uneducated, they're crude, they're not people that I would choose to be around. . . . I don't think there's a defensible reason to keep these people doing what they're doing and in their state of ignorance. . . . Bring them up so that they can spell, talk, and get along like the rest of us." Former Sierra Club leader David Brower was perhaps more direct: "People being out of work because of [the] spotted owl is, in my eyes, no different than people being put out of work after the furnaces at Dachau shut down."[34]

To make sense of comments like Brower's, as well as the experiences of people in Northwest timber-dependent communities more broadly, sociolo-gist Robert Lee, who conducted field research in rural Washington during the height of the spotted-owl conflict, employed the concept of "moral exclu-sion," the idea that moral considerations don't apply to those living outside an imagined moral community. "Moral exclusion of those who 'harm or abuse the environment,'" wrote Lee, "has been one of the most prominent expressions of the emerging cultural theme associated with environmental preservation." Environmentalists "fret about owls and trees," he continued, "but reveal indifference to rural peoples' plight." What historian Jefferson Cowie has argued about the American working class more broadly is equally applicable: namely, that starting in the 1970s, workers were cast out from social and civic life, blamed by establishment liberals and the New Left for their own economically precarious positions. But, as usual, timber workers themselves had a far clearer way of summing up what was going on. What timber country was up against in the spotted-owl era, wrote Robert Heinlein, a tree planter from southern Oregon's Willamette Valley, was "hard realities and harder institutions indifferent to our humanity."[35]

Environmental Conflict in British Columbia

By the late 1980s, a great deal separated an Oregon logger like Heath and his counterparts in British Columbia, much of it rooted in the economic disruptions of the 1970s that sent the American and Canadian timber industries, along with their workers, in wildly different directions. In a way, though, environmental conflict of the late 1980s and early 1990s again tied American and British Columbian woodworkers together, if not in a direct, material way, then at least in a common set of experiences with the environmental movement. It didn't have to do with the owl, specifically. The spotted owl's native range barely extends into British Columbia, and starting in the mid-1980s, new regulations intended to protect the owl's habitat implemented by provincial foresters had no appreciable economic effects on harvest levels and rural economies. But "ancient forests" became a rallying cry for British Columbian environmentalists all the same, and starting in the mid-1980s, the province's timber workers also found themselves struggling to contend with the same sort of moral and social exclusion that an American timber worker like Heinlein described.

The province's first visible "ancient forest" campaign occurred on Haida Gwaii (then called the Queen Charlotte Islands). In 1985 several local environmental groups started pressuring the provincial government to create a new national park that would protect roughly 147,000 hectares on the archipelago's southern tip. After years of pressure, in 1987 the Legislative Assembly of British Columbia passed a law establishing a new park. Unlike courts in the United States, British Columbia's politicians appeared more cognizant of the potential impacts on the island's timber workers and, at the same time they established the park, created a compensation commission to provide financial assistance to timber-working communities negatively impacted by preservation efforts. At least that's what was promised. Ultimately, the compensation commission refused any direct payments to workers displaced by the park's creation, though it did award more than $31 million to the logging companies that'd lost their timber leases. "This is a complete sellout of workers," complained IWA-Canada member Norm Rivard, "to provide compensation for the companies and to provide no protection at all for the people who make their living on the land—that's not acceptable."[36]

Complaints like Rivard's went unheard. Indeed, IWA members again found themselves paying a steep price for preservation efforts in Clayoquot Sound, a grove of massive, low-elevation trees on Vancouver Island's west-central coast. Starting in 1988, Canadian environmental organizations began organizing massive protests, calling for the elimination of harvests in the Clayoquot. A year later, the provincial government responded by conveying a task force, composed of representatives from several environmental organizations, First Nations communities, and industry representatives and tasked it with arriving at a solution. Organized labor was also given several seats on the task force, and Dave Haggard was chosen to represent the IWA-Canada. After a year of contentious meetings, he reported in the union's paper that little progress had been made because representatives of the environmental movement remained adamantly opposed to any logging whatsoever. "This has been frustrating as hell," he said, but added, "I still remain optimistic that we are going to accomplish something." That optimism was misplaced. In 1993 the provincial government disbanded the task force and reduced harvests in Clayoquot Sound by more than 40 percent, which led to massive layoffs and a severe unemployment spike in western Vancouver Island. Summarizing the government's decision a few years later, IWA-Canada member Kim Pollak argued that the government had capitulated to environmentalism, which "has turned into a highly codified ideology that originates not with the working class, but largely with the professional middle classes. As such, it is an ideology that often neglects the needs and interests of working people."[37]

"Ecotage," likewise, became something British Columbian timber workers had to contend with. Earth First! was active in British Columbia's woods, and so, too, was Greenpeace, another radical environmentalist group founded in the province in 1971. Greenpeace had made a name for itself mostly in protests involving whaling and fishing and became widely known for using small inflatable rafts to get between harpoon ships and whales. But starting in the 1980s, the organization turned its attention to terrestrial realms, and its members became vocal advocates for "ancient forest" protection. British Columbian workers, like timber workers to their south, now had to worry about tree spikes, broken logging equipment, and protesters occupying trees. In November 1990, IWA members arrived at a forest in British Columbia's Tsitika Valley to find that radicals had strung nearly a mile of heavy-gauge fishing line at ankle and neck levels, creating a dangerous situation for a feller or bucker who had to quickly dart from a falling tree. In April 1992 IWA member Ken Nickell struck a spike with his saw. He described the incident in the pages of the union's paper: "It's just the psychological factor knowing there are spikes and losing concentration and being unable to control the environment. You're wondering what the hell will happen."[38]

At the very moment environmentalists were arguing for significant harvest reductions in Clayoquot Sound and more-radical activists were stringing fishing line through the Tsitika's forests, Dave Luoma, Don Zapp, and Dave Morrison had wandered into the grove near the White River and then risked their jobs to protect it. Stories like this were easily ignored in the contentious land-use debates of the late twentieth century.

Yellow Ribbons and Spotted-Owl Stew

If the spotted-owl conflict more or less began in 1986 and became more contentious after 1987, the spring of 1989 marked another major turning point. Events of those months would transform debates over spotted owls and "ancient forests" from a conflict into what forester Norm Johnson would later call a "holy war" and what the press would begin calling the timber wars. Judge Dwyer had issued his injunction in early March. A few weeks later, environmental groups filed a new petition seeking a wilderness designation for Opal Creek, a long-fought-over area in Oregon's Santiam Valley. At the end of the month, Earth First! gained national media attention when it led a several-days-long protest at a logging site on the Santiam Valley's Breitenbush River. Covering the protest for the *New Yorker* magazine, journalist Catherine Caulfield portrayed Earth First! activists as members of the local community, people with "ordinary lives," who'd taken a valiant stand to "preserve what remains of our ancient forests." The actual local people, the loggers at the Breitenbush River site, whose work had been significantly disrupted by Earth First!'s activism, went unquoted and largely unmentioned in the piece. Finally, in early June the FWS completed its status review of the owl and recommended listing it as a "threatened" species.[39]

After the events of spring, the tenor of rural sentiment changed. "People were out for total retribution," Girod later said. Logger Doug Hirons remembered, "We were willing to compromise. But that spring we realized environmentalists weren't interested in compromise. They wanted the whole pie." A new and acrimonious mood was especially evident in the pages of rural newspapers. "Enough is enough," wrote one man, "if this continues, it will turn Oregon into a ghost state." It was an interesting choice of words—words that harkened back to the rhetoric of the Depression-era IWA. It's tempting to see in the events that would come after 1989 timber country's repudiation of the traditions of forest stewardship that had long been central to this place's culture. But, as a comment like this begins to suggest, there was something connecting the labor environmentalism of the past with timber country's outrage in the late 1980s. In earlier eras, timber workers had organized, in part, to rein in the timber industry's cut-and-run practices because that's what threatened the stability of their communities. For people in late twentieth century, injunctions and spotted-owl set-asides now threatened to do the exact same thing, and they would again organize, even if the forms that organization took reflected the ways the Northwest's social landscapes had changed in the preceding decades. Indeed, this would not be a movement of workers opposed to bosses but, rather, a movement of workers and bosses opposed to environmentalists. It would seem that the environmental movement of the late twentieth century was able to do something that employers of the early twentieth century had only dreamed of, and that was create a culture of unity between labor and capital.[40]

The most visible sign of that new organization could be seen fluttering from the antenna of Heath's pickup in the late 1980s, if not nearly every pickup in the Northwest woods: foot-long ribbons of canary-yellow vinyl. By 1989 yellow bows and ribbons were everywhere in timber country: tied to trees that lined rural highways, fluttering from logging trucks, waving from town welcome signs, and dangling from the awnings of small businesses along rural main streets, next to signs with slogans like, "We support the timber industry, and the timber industry supports us." If the spotted owl had become the environmental movement's symbol of an ecological crisis, here in these ribbons was timber country's response, its symbol of a social and economic crisis.[41]

Those yellow ribbons were the official symbol of the Yellow Ribbon Coalition, a group started by James Petersen, editor of *Evergreen*, and logger Bob Sagle. Petersen and Sagle believed that the political system's unwillingness to listen to rural people had everything to do with the fact that they were, well, rural—isolated from centers of power, out of sight and out of mind of decision makers. Hoping to increase the visibility of loggers and highlight the ways new logging restrictions were negatively impacting rural communities, in the spring of 1988 Sagle and Petersen organized the Silver Fire Roundup to be held in southern Oregon's Josephine County Fairgrounds. They invited anyone and everyone who'd been negatively affected by court rulings and harvest restrictions and asked those coming to fly yellow ribbons like the ones many Americans had displayed ten years earlier when the

Iranian government detained several American embassy officials. Loggers, like American diplomats, Sagle and Petersen said, were being held hostage by a foreign government. Just before the roundup was scheduled to take place, logger Gregg Miller hiked Interstate 5 from Grants Pass to Eugene, a roughly 140-mile journey, tying yellow ribbons to mile markers to guide out-of-state timber workers and their families to the fairgrounds. Miller's efforts helped popularize the yellow ribbon as a symbol of rural identity, and, as Sagle and Petersen hoped, the three thousand people who showed up to the roundup on August 27, 1988, wore yellow ribbons pinned to their shirts, leading one observer to claim that it represented "the biggest show of solidarity" in timber country's history.[42]

Afterwards, so-called yellow-ribbon rallies became commonplace throughout the Northwest. Timber workers and their families packed into high school gyms or the basements of churches and took turns decrying the environmental movement, Earth First! monkeywrenching, and the courts. The rallies were, in large part, attempts by rural people to voice their angers and frustrations. They also represented an effort by people in rural towns to hold on to and restore the sense of community they felt was being lost as a result of harvest restrictions. And, at times, the rallies could look more like picnics than political events. Children played games, and women brought dishes for potluck lunches. In between fiery speeches denouncing environmental activists, men played cards and drank beer. As many workers told it, this, more than anything else, was what the Yellow Ribbon Coalition was all about. "When we pass a car or truck that is also flying yellow ribbons," explained one timber worker, "a bond is formed that cannot be separated by words or deeds of our preservationist adversaries. Our timber industry, our homes, our families, and our communities are at risk. We are united."[43]

Statements like these abounded in letters to the editor and in editorials written for small rural newspapers. Workers saw in the yellow ribbon a sign of rural solidarity, community pride, and, perhaps even more than all that, a working-class pride that had long been central to the culture of timber country. This was evidenced not only in public statements but in what, perhaps, became one of the more popular signs appearing in rural communities: "Tie a yellow ribbon for the working man." What those statements and signs obscured, however, were the fundamental ways that the community and solidarity that members of the Yellow Ribbon Coalition envisioned often included their employers. Indeed, those employers, like their workers, saw in the spotted owl a manufactured crisis intended to economically hobble the timber industry. "I am being put out of business by a surrogate species that will never be extinct and the goddamn preservationists know it. . . . It's a damn ploy to stop cutting trees," said the owner of a small mill to the *Eugene (OR) Register Guard*. In fact, the existence of the Yellow Ribbon Coalition owed as much to labor as it did capital. Many of the group's community gatherings and rallies were funded by employers. When hundreds of timber workers and their families traveled to Salem, Oregon, in 1989 to protest the creation of the Opal Creek Wilderness, many workers had been given the day off by their employers to do so. That same year, the Freres Lumber Company of Lyons, Oregon, paid its workers to attend a rally in Salem. By April 1989, eleven county governments, four members of the state's congressional del-egation, and too many sawmill owners to count had signed on as members of the Yellow Ribbon Coalition. That same year, the coalition received a size-able donation from the Western Public Lands Coalition, a Colorado-based nonprofit organization representing mine owners and energy companies.[44]

What statements about rural solidarity and community also obscured was the often-divisive nature of yellow-ribbon activism. The group often claimed that its primary purpose was to draw attention to the economic struggles of rural communities and highlight the culture of stewardship in timber country, to show, as one of the group's publications said, timber workers' commitment to "productive forests and a clean, vital environment." Yet, the actual actions of many within the coalition often told a somewhat different story. In April 1989, newspapers across the United States reported that a tavern in Coburg, Oregon, had placed "pickled spotted owl eggs," "roasted spotted owl," and "spotted owl stew" on its menu (diners ordering any of the above would've, in fact, been served chicken). *Time* reported on loggers who'd hung a dead spotted owl swathed in yellow ribbons from a fence post. In the Sierra Club magazine, Sallie Tisdale wrote, "Spotted owls have been shot, crucified, hung and their corpses mailed to various people perceived as environmentalists." Bumper stickers started appearing on trucks with slogans like, "Save a logger, eat an owl." Some members of the Yellow Ribbon Coalition began a cam-paign to ban from schools Dr. Seuss's *Lorax*, a parable about the decline of forests. And, the Forest Service decided to forgo participating in Portland's annual Rose Festival Parade after the agency received death threats aimed at the actor who was going to appear in a Woody the Owl costume, next to Smokey the Bear.[45]

In many ways, actions like these played right into urban people's and en-vironmentalists' perceptions of timber country. If people in the Northwest woods wanted to convince the rest of the world they weren't heartless loggers who lacked an ecological consciousness, then dead owls hanging from fence posts was an ineffective way of showing it. Indeed, precisely for this reason, not everyone in timber country supported the Yellow Ribbon Coalition. One of those was Steve Rood. "We don't really appreciate owl-bashing. People who wear T-shirts about fried owls and things—well, it's funny, but it's not what we are all about," he said to a reporter from the *Los Angeles Times*. Other workers described to journalists feeling pressured to fly yellow ribbons or post signs declaring support for the timber industry. "There was a big ditch," remembered Girod, "you were on one side or the other, and you had to make clear where you belonged." In 1989 people in Santiam Canyon established a new organization, Greater Communities of Oregon (GCO) that sought to be a less-confrontational and less-divisive version of the Yellow Ribbon Coalition. The group also adopted public education as its primary focus and seems to have been more committed to it than the Yellow Ribbon Coalition. Its newsletters struck a far less confrontational tone and described the various conservation and replanting efforts many companies had undertaken. It organized mill tours aimed at teaching people about "the wise use of our public lands, specifically timber."[46]

The more moderate and potentially more constructive voices of people like Rood and members of the GCO were, however, easily drowned out as the Yellow Ribbon Coalition began organizing large convoys and protests in the region's cities. Called the Yellow Ribbon Express, the first convoy took place in Olympia, Washington, on February 28, 1989, and then spread throughout much of the Northwest and became a regular occurrence in large cities, state capitals, and smaller rural towns from northern California all the way to western Montana. The largest Yellow Ribbon Express started on May 6, 1989, when logging trucks met in Grants Pass, Oregon, and set out on a two-thousand-mile-long journey through timber towns, all the way to Missoula, Montana. Several hundred logging trucks joined a convoy that ended up stretching for miles. In small rural towns they were greeted by cheers and people waving yellow ribbons, and in larger cities they were greeted by counterprotesters hurling rocks. In Eugene, the convoy stopped, and several hundred loggers and their families rallied downtown. One of those convoy members and protesters in Eugene was a logging truck driver named Dave Snyder, and he explained the purpose of the event to the local press: "If we lose the timber industry, it will affect everybody. With the convoy, something this big, drawing this much attention, we hope people will take notice of what we're doing and what the downfall is going to be if the timber industry is reduced."[47]

But few in the environmental movement, legal system, and land-management agencies were willing to listen to workers like Snyder. In 1990 the FWS formalized its earlier recommendation and listed the spotted owl as threatened species under the ESA. Public land-management agencies significantly expanded set-asides surrounding known owl nests to ten thousand acres. As a result, public-lands harvest fell to their lowest levels in more than a century. Employment in Oregon's timber industry fell to fifty thousand, its lowest level since the Great Depression.[48]

In the end, the yellow ribbons that timber country displayed throughout the final years of the spotted-owl conflict were less symbols of solidarity and working-class power and more evidence of this place's social and political marginalization. The spotted-owl conflict really took place in the courts and halls of land-management bureaucracies, terrains that the well-funded environmental movement backed by upper- and middle-class donors was more suited to win. Working and rural people simply had no representation here, and all they could do was stand outside of courtrooms and federal buildings and shout. Perhaps, the most accurate analysis of the yellow-ribbon campaign was offered in an editorial by Don Brown, editor of Coos Bay's *World*. People in the rural Northwest were up against a political system that didn't hear them, a region with an economy that no longer relied on lumber production, and large, powerful, and national environmental organizations, Brown wrote, and against these odds, "all the yellow ribbon in the world won't be enough to save the timber industry."[49]

The Northwest Forest Plan

The rallies and convoys may have done little to sway judges and federal land managers, but they did help attract the attention of a young and charismatic politician running for the presidency in 1992 named Bill Clinton. The incumbent, George H. W. Bush, had largely steered clear of Northwest forest politics, appeasing the industry with supportive statements but ultimately deferring to the courts. Yet, Clinton saw in the conflict an opportunity to keep the environmental movement firmly within the Democratic coalition and potentially win back some of the White working-class voters his party had been steadily losing for roughly two decades. On campaign stops in the Northwest, Clinton talked about his affinity for nature and old-growth forests *and* having been born to a single, working-class mother in rural Arkansas. In short, Clinton said he could understand where people on both sides were coming from and promised, if elected, to bring the timber wars to an amicable resolution.[50]

After winning the election, Clinton appeared to make good on his promise and in early 1993 convened a timber summit in Portland. For three days, Clinton alongside several of his cabinet members heard testimony from loggers, biologists, company owners large and small, environmentalists, and representatives of tribal nations. Those hearings formed the basis for the 1994 Northwest Forest Plan (NWFP), a series of guidelines intended to restructure public-forest management and bring an end to the spotted-owl conflict. It's sometimes said that the sign of a good compromise is that all sides feel as if they were shorted, and if so, the NWFP may have been one of the best compromises ever. The plan reduced public-lands harvests in Washington and Oregon by upwards of 88 percent while still allowing a harvest of 1.2 billion board feet annually. Environmental groups claimed that this was still too much logging to effectively protect spotted-owl habitat and quickly filed a host of legal challenges aimed at preventing its implementation. Timber workers, people from rural communities, and industry representatives countered that the plan allowed for too little logging and would mean the end of much of the rural Northwest. While no one appeared happy with the NWFP, it did ultimately end the spotted-owl conflict. Legal challenges made by the environmental movement continued, but the courts sided with the Clinton administration and instructed public-lands-management agencies to abide by the NWFP's mandates. People in rural logging communities, meanwhile, unceremoniously removed the yellow ribbons from their homes and trucks and quietly conceded defeat.[51]

And that, at least in most histories of the Northwest timber industry, marks the end of the story. However, ending with the NWFP suggests that timber country died in the years after the plan was implemented. While it's certainly true that people in the Northwest woods encountered severe social and economic difficulties throughout the 1990s, if not up until the present, it's just as true that they're nothing if not survivors. The story of timber country after 1994 is, in part, a story of economic depression and dislocation, but it's also a story of how people in the Northwest woods remain committed to the forests and protecting their place within them. Put differently, ending the story in the 1990s is part and parcel to the larger patterns of marginalization that drove the spotted-owl conflict in the first place, an excuse to not acknowledge people in the rural Northwest and continue to exclude them from forest-management decisions.

While timber country remains important and relevant in the present, the survival of the industry and its workers has, nevertheless, played out in the shadow cast by the spotted-owl conflict of thirty years prior. Disparaging attitudes about timber workers first articulated in the popular culture of the 1970s and then reinforced by the events of the 1980s and 1990s have been a difficult thing for people in the Northwest woods to shake, and continue to impact how they're regarded by environmentalists and policy makers. As Heath had sensed on his drive home from the *Life* photo shoot, the owl had become part of him and the rural Northwest. Even today, residing in an assisted-living facility in Cottage Grove, Oregon, he keeps a framed copy of his *Life* magazine photo on his wall. It's displayed among many other pictures of Heath's years spent in logging, pictures of crew members and loggers he's worked alongside over the years, many gone now, some to old age and others to tragic logging accidents. In some, a younger Heath stands proudly with crew members before a recently fallen timber, with huge grins after having done a hard, dirty job and having done it well. His wife, who passed away several years ago, appears in many, in the woods alongside her husband, just as happy and seemingly just as connected to the forest. These are photos of happier times and evoke themes of community and an affinity for the forests, the very themes at the center of timber country's story. I asked Heath why he would keep the *Life* picture so prominently displayed alongside these other images, why he would want to be reminded of a troubling time and events that threatened to undo all that those other photographs represented. Heath stared at his wall of photographs for a long time, and I suspected he was searching his soul for a thoughtful answer, as he'd done many times throughout our conversation. Then he responded. "Well, I would've preferred to have been a centerfold in *Playgirl*, but *Life* isn't too bad."[52]

8

"We Keep Carbon-Eating Machines Healthy"

Payton Smith probably isn't the sort of person who comes to mind when you think of a Northwest timber worker. Tall, blonde, and in her mid-twenties, Smith looks a lot like she hails from one of Portland's more affluent suburbs. But despite what her appearance might suggest, Smith is a proud daughter of timber country. Born in Coos Bay, Smith has been around the timber industry since the day she was born. She spent her formative years at the mill of Southport Lumber, a small company co-owned by her father. "I would run there after school," she remembered, "and hang out with the secretaries or just wander around." In high school she started working at the mill, and the experience excited her. "I liked it. I liked the people. I wanted to be in this industry," she said. After graduating from the University of Oregon in Eugene, Smith went to work at the headquarters of Roseburg Forest Products in Springfield, Oregon, where today she works in the company's shipping and logistics department.[1]

Smith isn't supposed to exist, at least according to some. Historians and economists who've written about the Northwest timber industry and its workers typically end things abruptly in 1994, after the Northwest Forest Plan (NWFP) was put into place. The suggestion, whether explicitly stated or not, is that people like Smith don't matter. Journalists have done a better job of covering timber country in the late twentieth and early twenty-first centuries, but not by much. While a handful of reporters have made at least some attempt to document life in the Northwest woods since the end of the spotted-owl conflict, the stories they've told are often ones of declension and decline. Typical are articles like one that recently ran in the US edition of the

Guardian, titled "The Job No One Wants: Why Won't Young People Work in Logging?" The article details how logging is dirty, dangerous work that younger generations of rural people are avoiding, instead seeking out safer and more comfortable jobs in cities.[2]

These scholars and journalists haven't met Smith. Her experiences in the timber industry directly challenge the larger cultural perception that timber country is dead or dying. Certainly, in the years following the Northwest Forest Plan, people in the Northwest's timber-dependent communities faced significant social and economic challenges, ranging from a high unemployment rate to steep declines in social services and educational funding. But people in the rural Northwest changed, adapted, and survived, often by relying on the ethic of forest stewardship that's long been central to timber country's culture, and they still have much to teach us about how we can more effectively manage the Northwest's woodlands in ways that protect both rural economies and forest ecologies. And those are lessons that those outside the rural Northwest would be wise to pay attention to. Though the spotted-owl conflict effectively ended more than two decades ago, environmental conflict remains as persistent as rain in the Northwest. Owls and "ancient forests" aren't fought over as vociferously as they once were, even if species habitat is an issue that's constantly debated. Rather, new forest-use debates centered on the larger issue of climate change have pushed the Northwest to the precipice of a second timber war that listening to the voices of people from timber country may help us avoid.

Following Smith as she navigates her way through the modern Northwest timber industry provides a window into how timber-working communities have changed since the end of the spotted-owl conflict and how, more importantly, we all might think in more politically productive ways about the relationship between work and nature. Smith's story, of course, isn't necessarily typical. As the daughter of a company owner and a woman in an industry that's long been dominated by men, she's had experiences not necessarily shared by most. Still, her experiences show that, just as in the past, the Northwest doesn't have to choose between a healthy environment and rural economic stability. In fact, each one may depend on the other.

After the Owl

Smith became acutely aware at the University of Oregon of how many people from outside the rural Northwest tended to view those from the rural Northwest. Many of her friends came from Portland or California's San Francisco

Bay Area and were somewhat surprised to learn she'd come from Coos Bay. Several had not heard of the town, and those that had associated it with an older generation, nostalgic for bygone times and bitter over their passing, not college-bound young people. What frustrated Smith more, though, was the widespread assumption that places like Coos Bay were responsible for their own demise—that had people in the town possessed just a bit more foresight and a bit more of an ecological consciousness, the town and the forests it depended on would be just a bit healthier. For Smith, like many from present-day timber country, the narrative was backward. It was environmental politics and the NWFP, in particular, that created the social and economic problems that people in Coos Bay had to contend with.[3]

The specific management strategies the NWFP prescribed were developed by a team of biologists and foresters called the Federal Ecomanagement Assessment Team (FEMAT). After he created FEMAT, President Bill Clinton issued the team five principles that, he said, should guide its work. The first of these stated, "We must never forget the human and the economic dimensions of these problems. Where sound management policies preserve the health of forest lands, sales should go forward. Where this requirement cannot be met, we need to do our best to offer new economic opportunities for year-round, high-wage, high-skill jobs." The scientists and researchers Clinton appointed to FEMAT suggested that the team would take this mandate seriously. All had reputations as moderates with no particular allegiances to either environmentalists or the industry. Jack Ward Thomas, then the USFS lead biologist, chaired FEMAT. Eric Forsman, the nation's leading spotted-owl expert also served on the team, as did Brian Greber, a forest economist who'd previously argued that preservation, not automation, had done more to create economic dislocation in rural logging communities. After months of meeting and debating various plans, in late 1993 FEMAT delivered to the president ten different management options, all of which varied widely in the amount of harvests they allowed. Clinton ultimately chose option 9 as the basis for the NWFP. If remembering the "human and economic dimensions of these problems" was Clinton's goal, then option 9 was an odd choice. Four years earlier, a committee Thomas led had issued a report claiming that the spotted-owl population could be protected by reducing harvestable acreage on Northwest public forestlands by roughly 25 percent. Yet, option 9 more than tripled that number, reducing harvestable acreage from previous years by 88 percent. The remaining land was included in what the NWFP called "the matrix," forests where logging was allowed but highly contingent on multiple factors, including spotted-owl nesting.[4]

Historian Daniel Nelson has argued that the NWFP was more a product of politics than the expertise of FEMAT's members. For years, Nelson
writes, "Thomas and his colleagues had battled politicians who thought they
were saving too many trees. Now they had to satisfy politicians who were
concerned about saving too few, thereby inviting new rounds of litigation,
injunctions, and layoffs." And, indeed, the threat of litigation, perhaps more
than any other single factor, was responsible for Clinton's choice. Rather
than decrease the number of suits brought by environmental groups against
public-lands-management agencies, the spotted owl's ESA listing in 1990
emboldened environmental-movement lawyers, who now recognized that
endangered species could be wielded as powerful tools to reduce forest harvests. In 1992 environmental activists successfully pressured the US Fish and
Wildlife Service to list the marbled murrelet, a seagoing bird that also requires
old-growth forests to nest, as an endangered species. And, in the years immediately afterward, environmentalists submitted more than a dozen more
petitions seeking ESA listings for ostensibly old-growth–dependent species,
many of which were accompanied by requests for injunctions or set-asides
halting timber sales and harvests. In the early 1990s the Northwest's public
forests became the most litigated public lands in the United States. One study
found that though USFS Region 6 (Oregon and Washington) contains just
12.8 percent of the nation's public forests, it's been the subject of 21.9 percent
of all USFS litigation between 1989 and 2008.[5]

The emergence of new and radical environmental groups, alongside the
legal activism of the more mainstream environmental movement, likewise
pushed Clinton toward option 9. One of these was the Native Forest Council, a group started by Oregon environmentalist Tim Hermach in 1988. The
council was, in many ways, a more legally oriented version of Earth First! It
relied more on court filings than tree spikes but still shared radicals' belief
that compromise amounted to defeat. Hermach and his organization advocated for what they called "zero cut," a policy that, as the name implies,
would mandate absolutely no harvests on public lands. By 1993 Hermach
had successfully pressured the Sierra Club, Audubon Society, and National
Wildlife Federation to also adopt zero cut as their guiding principle.[6]

In a sense, option 9 *was* the compromise Clinton had sought between industry and environmentalists, but a compromise that reflected the political
realities of the late twentieth century: the growing political and legal power
of the environmental movement, the waning economic power of the timber
industry, and, ultimately, the increasing silence of working people in forest-
management decisions. Indeed, the complete absence of timber workers in

the NWFP drafting process ensured that the entire plan reflected environmentalists' understandings of forest ecologies, not workers', and this would
prove to have some devastating consequences for both rural communities
and the forests they've long relied on.

In theory, NWFP management guidelines were based on the principle of
"ecosystem management," the idea that foresters should consider the needs of
wildlife and forest biota alongside the needs of industry and rural communities. In practice, the NWFP was a policy of preservation, one that assumed
human intervention of any kind was anathema to forest protection. Not only
did the final plan limit most logging on Northwest public lands but it also
put severe limitations on noncommercial active-management strategies, like
undergrowth thinning, controlled burns, and invasive-species management,
actions that allowed foresters to mimic the natural processes of disruption
that were central to the forest's ecological health. In the end, the NWFP didn't
so much protect the forest as it created a new forest, one where the natural
dynamism was interrupted or altogether halted.[7]

Environmental historians say it's possible to read landscapes the way other
historians read archival documents, as a record of past choices and decisions.
If so, then a walk through the Northwest's forests today reveals many of the
problems of the policy of benign neglect mandated by the NWFP. Those
who've only experienced the region's public forests from the vantage of a
well-maintained trail could be forgiven for believing the timbered landscapes
here are healthy and that prohibitions on active management are doing some
ecological good. But wandering off those trails tells a different story. Not that
you can wander very far. As soon as you do, the forest quickly becomes so
clogged and chocked full of undergrowth that it becomes nearly impossible
to walk. Ferns, rhododendrons, vine maple, manzanita—these and hundreds
more species have long been a part of the understory ecology of the Northwest's forests and are crucial pieces of the much-larger forest ecosystem. But
historically, understory was kept at bay by fires, both naturally occurring and
human caused, and later by logging and commercial and noncommercial
thinning. Prohibitions on controlled burns and active management now
mean that many of the Northwest's forests have too much of a good thing:
in many places the understory has grown so thick and gnarly that it's thrown
the entire landscape out of balance. Really, the only way to navigate many
timberlands is on hands and knees, crawling through thorny bushes, snarls
of invasive species, and prickly brambles. But don't stray too far from the
trail, as the understory is often so thick that finding your way back becomes
difficult.

The problems of runaway understory growth are hardly limited to aesthetics. All that dense brush makes it difficult for trees—the very trees environmentalists were hoping to save—to survive. Trees need room to grow. But understory growth denies them that space. More than that, it sucks up nutrients and water from the soil, and as a result, trees stunt and die. Dead and dying trees then attract diseases and bugs, which creates a vicious ecological cycle. Those diseases and bugs kill more trees, which attract even more diseases and bugs, which kill more trees. As a result of this cycle, something started to happen in the Northwest's forests in the late 1990s, something that, as far as most foresters could tell, was unprecedented in the region's environmental history: timber mortality began to exceed timber growth. Put differently, the forest wasn't springing to life as a result of the hands-off approach mandated by the NWFP. It was slowly dying.[8]

Trees withering as they succumb to diseases or are starved of nutrients aren't the only way forests in the Northwest are deteriorating—and certainly not the most dramatic way. Wildfires in the region have increased significantly in the past few decades. "Since the 1980s," reads a report issued by Oregon State University's extension service, "the number and size of large (>1,000 acres) wildfires and the total area burned in the western United States has increased." Simple numbers and figures, though, fail to truly capture what a typical Northwest fire season is like today. Skies turn a postapocalyptic shade of brownish-gray as the smoke from fires blends into the atmosphere and covers the entire region—and sometimes, depending on the winds, the entire North American continent. Ash covers the ground like snow, and spending time outside, especially for those with respiratory-health issues, becomes difficult if not dangerous. Air-quality warnings become regular features of news reports, as do updates on evacuation orders being issued to the rural communities most at risk of wildfire danger. Fire, of course, has always been part of the Northwest forest ecology. Naturally occurring and Indigenous fire regimes played a role in processes of regeneration and succession. But wildfires today are unlike fires of the past. They burn hotter, are more destructive, and inhibit rather than encourage regeneration. Prohibitions on active management are part of the problem. The dead and dying trees proliferating as a result of runaway understory growth provide ample fuels that contribute to the size and intensity of fires. Equally problematic is that the NWFP has sought to return all forests to a uniform late-successional stand structure. A major reason that fires of the past were smaller was because stands were more varied. Wildfire burns differently in different sorts of forests. A fire that starts in a late-successional stand has difficulty jumping to an early-successional stand, and vice versa. But now, as the NWFP has created a more uniform forest, fire expands with few interruptions. This became painfully apparent in Oregon in the summer and fall of 2020. It was the state's second-worst fire season on record. Between August and October, more than one million acres of the state's forests went up in flames, and the rural towns of Talent, Phoenix, and Blue River were completely consumed.[9]

Post-1990s forest management isn't the only reason for the rising frequency, size, and intensity of wildfire in the Northwest. Low rates of precipitation and warming temperatures, both caused by climate change, are doing just as much to exacerbate the wildfire problem. But the relationship between wildfire and climate change is again another vicious ecological cycle: the climate is warming because of increased carbon in the air, and there's more carbon in the air, at least in part, because of wildfires. One study found that just one fire in Oregon—the 2003 B&B Complex Fire near the Metolius River—released 600 percent more carbon into the atmosphere than all other energy and fossil fuel used in the state that year.[10]

If they could speak with us, animals might also register complaints about the consequences of late twentieth-century forest management. Wildlife, like trees, also have difficulty surviving in forests now clogged with undergrowth. Prohibitions on active management have disrupted game-migration pathways, eliminated birthing and calving grounds, and made it difficult for many species to find adequate feed. This is especially true when it comes to deer and elk, both of which require open lands to graze. The clearcuts that environmentalists often decry were once the primary feeding grounds of the Northwest's deer and elk herds. As logging declined, so, too, did available land for deer and elk to survive. A 2008 study conducted by Oregon's Department of Fish and Wildlife, for instance, found that the state's Columbian blacktail deer population has fallen by more than 30 percent since 1980, in large part because of the "reduction of habitat availability associated with the decline of timber harvest activities on federal lands." Reductions in the state's deer population has as much to do with a rapidly expanding cougar population, and the cougar population is increasing, in part, because they can now more easily stalk and prey on deer feeding in dense forests rather than more open clearcuts.[11]

The cruelest irony of the NWFP is that the very species that prompted its adoption—the northern spotted owl—may have suffered as a direct result of its guidelines. Like deer and elk, spotted owls have difficulty surviving in the Northwest woods of today. One species of owl better suited to this landscape is the barred owl. Indigenous to the US East Coast, barred owls first began appearing in the Northwest in the 1970s. Larger and more aggressive than their spotted-owl cousins, barred owls can more effectively hunt in the Northwest's overgrown forests. As their population has expanded in the past several decades, they've begun to cross breed with spotted owls and outcompete them for habitat. As a result, the spotted owl's overall population has continued to decline, at about 3 percent a year, according to some studies.[12]

But it's likely people from rural logging communities who've suffered the most. As a result of NWFP-mandated harvest restrictions, the Northwest's timber industry lost something in the neighborhood of thirty thousand jobs in the late 1990s and early 2000s, though saying exactly how many jobs is difficult. As it was during the height of the spotted-owl conflict, the economic data is awash in assumptions and political biases. Scholars who assert that the spotted owl's ESA listing and NWFP amounted to good environmental policy tend to blame timber country's economic woes on capital flight and automation, while scholars who see the NWFP as bad social policy link the depressed state of the rural Northwest's labor market directly to preservation efforts.[13]

What is clear and not debated even among scholars who see the NWFP as sound environmental policy, is that the plan's social provisions were sorely lacking. Job-retraining programs were woefully underfunded and poorly administered. As a later Forest Service report found, most of the money allocated for job retraining went instead to infrastructure projects that provided few and only short-term employment opportunities for former loggers and millworkers. FEMAT predicted that restoration and replanting work would provide new jobs in rural communities. But the Forest Service's and Bureau of Land Management's budgets declined significantly as timber sales declined, and as a result, restoration and reforestation programs were slashed, and the anticipated work never materialized.[14]

The NWFP contained no financial provisions to make up for the money rural counties lost as a result of declining timber sales, and schools and county social-service providers suddenly had to deal with severe budget shortfalls. During Clinton's 1993 timber summit, Robert Lee had told the president and his advisers, "We're seeing the collapse of families, disintegration of families, disintegration of communities, loss of morale, homelessness, stranded elderly people, people whose lives are in disarray because of substance abuse." The problems that Lee identified in the mid-1990s only intensified in the years afterward. Indeed, look at any negative social indicator—crime, homelessness, substance abuse, high school dropout rate, people living below the poverty line—and all are higher in the Northwest's timber-dependent communities than they are in the region's cities. It wasn't until 2000 that Congress passed emergency funding for rural school districts in the Secure Rural Schools and Community Self-Determination Act. But the legislation didn't entirely make up for the money rural schools had lost as a result of declining timber sales, nor did it do anything to help social-service providers. In April 2007, southern Oregon's Josephine County was forced to eliminate the jobs of 250 of its 650 county workers, close several sheriff's offices and all of its public libraries, and end funding for multiple drug-and-alcohol-treatment centers, prompting one county commissioner to lament that Josephine County could no longer provide "what normal American citizens expect in a First World nation." By the early 2010s, Josephine County had been forced to also eliminate many emergency services. Afterward, people calling 911 with potential life-threatening emergencies outside the standard business hours of 8 A.M. to 4 P.M. were forwarded to the state police, who were often too far away to respond in a timely manner.[15]

Sympathy for timber country's plight, like money for rural schools and social-service providers, was also in short supply the 1990s. This had much to do with the changing economy of the region. Politicians and policy makers could easily ignore the staggeringly high unemployment rate in the rural Northwest because a boom in Seattle's and Portland's high-tech sector drove the overall region's economy and employment rate to new heights. Many of those cognizant of what was going on in timber country met the demise of the rural Northwest with indifference, in ways that reflected popular culture's broader ambivalence toward the White working class in the 1970s and beyond. At the same time, new cultural narratives emerged in the late 1990s that for many in the Northwest's urban middle class justified the absence of any political or social response to timber country's problems: the rural Northwest was dying as a result of its own archaic narrow-mindedness, and the region was better off for it.

This new narrative was told most potently through the stunning rise and dramatic fall of a wayward kid from the sawmill town of Aberdeen, Washington, named Kurt Cobain. Cobain was the reluctant front man of the Northwest punk band Nirvana. It was no more polished than a high school garage band, and Nirvana's members made no apologies for it. Cobain didn't so much sing as wail, making many of his lyrics unintelligible. But understanding the band's lyrics wasn't important. Nirvana communicated through volume and amplifier static, and you didn't have to hear Cobain's words to know that this music was about frustration and pain. It's precisely the type of music that parents hate and angst-ridden suburban kids with too much disposable income love, and those angsty kids ultimately purchased more than thirty million copies of Nirvana's records and transformed what'd been a small, regional punk act into a national phenomenon.[16]

Rock critics had a hard time describing Nirvana's music because it sounded unlike anything else popular at the time. The search for the origins of what the critics dubbed the distinctive "Northwest Sound" eventually led journalists to Cobain's hometown of Aberdeen, and it didn't take long for reporters to connect Nirvana's music to timber country's landscape. In particular, two prominent features of Aberdeen were employed to explain the anger and hopelessness Cobain expressed in his music: gray skies and high suicide rates. "Pervasive unemployment and a perpetually rainy gray climate have led to rampant alcoholism and a suicide rate more than twice the already high state average," reads a profile of the band in *Rolling Stone*. The connections were also easy to make because Nirvana looked a lot like unemployed loggers. Indeed, the aesthetics of Nirvana and similar bands made in its image—what rock journalists would later dub "grunge"—was a product of Aberdeen's thrift shops, where Cobain had procured the disheveled flannel shirts and torn blue jeans sold by unemployed timber workers who needed a few extra dollars. Nirvana sounded and looked like Aberdeen felt, journalists said, and the band's music and style seemed to reflect the town's collective despair.[17]

In some ways, this is the same narrative arc that journalists had used to tell long-distance runner Steve Prefontaine's story in the early 1970s, roughly two decades earlier. Both were tough kids from tough towns who appeared unexpectedly on the national stage, propelled there by the hardscrabble realities of their rural upbringings. There was, however, one key difference: Prefontaine celebrated his working-class roots, Cobain scorned his. "I felt more and more alienated," he told *Rolling Stone* journalist Michael Azerrad, describing his early life in Aberdeen. "I couldn't find friends whom I felt compatible with at all. Everyone was eventually going to become a logger, and I knew I wanted something different." He described how the town objected to his punk sensibilities and told stories about being beat up in high school by the sons of timber workers who didn't like his long hair. "Real narrow-minded people," he said, describing Aberdeen's working class, "they look at something they weren't used to as being bad." Although, by the release of the band's third album in 1993, Cobain had achieved widespread fame and no small amount of fortune, journalists, nevertheless, described him as a lost youth, unable to escape Aberdeen's vortex of hopelessness. Widespread rumors of Cobain's heroin use and suicidal tendencies only further suggested that the rural Northwest was a cancer eating away at hope. Those rumors were soon confirmed. On April 8, 1994, Cobain locked himself in his large Seattle home. He cooked up $100 worth of black tar, more than enough to guarantee an overdose. But just to be certain, and before the heroin rendered him motionless, Cobain reached for the shotgun at his side. The *Seattle Times* said the final scene was too gruesome to describe.[18]

Before the suicide, *Rolling Stone* had sent Azerrad to Aberdeen to corroborate Cobain's descriptions of Grays Harbor County. Azerrad arrived on a particularly gray morning when the rain fell in sheets, and dense clouds floated low, almost in arm's reach. The clouds blended seamlessly with the brown-washed clearcut hillsides and the dull, blue expanse of the Pacific Ocean to the west. Rainfall pooled in the streets below businesses that'd been boarded-up and abandoned. Only neon-bright signs advertising low-interest payday loans broke up the monochromatic landscape. Azerrad stepped into a bar to escape the rain. Inside, unemployed loggers hunkered over their beers, and though it wasn't yet noon, many were on their fourth or fifth drink. He struck up a conversation and asked the out-of-work logger on the adjacent barstool about Nirvana's appearance on *Saturday Night Live*, a few days earlier. Cobain had kissed bandmate Krist Novoselic after the last set—what Cobain later described as a middle finger to all the homophobic loggers back home in Aberdeen. "Yea, I know the Cobain kid," the logger said to Azerrad, pausing to drain his beer. "He's a faggot. We *deal* with faggots here. We run 'em out of town." Later, this would be all the evidence that journalists and Cobain's largely middle-class fans needed. Cobain may have spiked his own vein and pulled the trigger of the shotgun, but it was rural backwardness that had really killed him. In a different world, Cobain's suicide might have sparked a conversation, if not actual policy, intended to address the social problems forest management caused in the late twentieth century. But that would've required compassion, and it was hard to be compassionate toward the sorts of people Azerrad described.[19]

"People in Our Industry Have Sawdust in Their Veins"

This is the timber country Payton Smith was born into: a place with failing schools and few social services, where the number of people collecting Social Security often eclipsed those earning a paycheck, and where years before the rest of the nation acknowledged an opioid crisis and so-called deaths of despair, drug overdoses and suicides were well above what they were in other parts of the country. None of those problems have gone away, but things have improved slightly in the past few years. At the very least, the unemployment and poverty rates are trending downward. Several factors explain why. Harvests have increased slightly since their nadir in the mid-1990s. Some, though certainly not all, former logging communities have turned toward the tourist economy, which has created new service-sector jobs. But companies like the one Smith's father owns, Southport Lumber, are also an important part of the story.[20]

Payton actually started working at Southport when she was eight years old, and her father tasked her with grabbing tickets from the logging-truck drivers delivering lumber to the mill. Later, when she started high school, he promoted her to the mill's production line. "I had to have my Danner boots and my Hickory shirt," she remembered. "I looked very out of place." However, she was more concerned with her safety than her appearance. The mill's loud machinery and whirling saws seemed threatening to a high schooler, just as they would to anyone not accustomed to this occupational world. After her first day she complained to her father, "This is really not a safe place for me." He responded with the time-honored parental retort: difficult, dangerous work "builds character."[21]

Smith didn't know it at the time, but her early work experience actually reveals a lot about how the timber industry has changed in recent decades, how it's adapted to the post-NWFP Northwest, and how and why timber country has been able to recover some of the social and economic stability it lost in the 1990s. Much of that had to do with the nature of the job she did inside the mill. Despite her fears, Southport's mill, like most modern sawmills, was a relatively safe place to work. That's largely because Smith actually had little contact with saws. At most modern mills, humans barely touch lumber. As timber moves along automated conveyors, it's scanned by several lasers that tell those saws how and where to cut. Smith's job was to simply sit on a stool nearby the conveyor and clear jams when they occurred. What she remembers most about the work was how monotonous it was and how the piercing volume of the saws prevented her from reading, listening to music, or anything else to pass the time. Since the 1980s, environmentalists have often argued that it's intense automation in a mill like Southport that has led to so many job losses in the Northwest's timber industry. But the fact of the matter is that without technology a mill like Southport and the jobs it provides simply wouldn't exist. Indeed, technology may be saving the timber industry.[22]

The story of Payton's father, Jason Smith, and how he came to start South-port speaks to some of the reasons why. Although the elder Smith is co-owner of a modern mill and lumber company, he has one foot firmly planted in timber country of the past. "You hear the expression, 'People in our industry have sawdust in their veins.' I come from many generations of people in the forest-products industry," he explained. His paternal grandfather had worked in a Louisiana sawmill and then as a timber cruiser for Weyerhaeuser's North-west operations. His father worked in an Oregon pulp mill, and even though he was killed in an accident when Jason was young, there was still a "family attraction," he said, that pulled him into the industry. But Jason never set out to own his own company. Rather, after college, he got a job with one of the Northwest's larger timber companies, working on a reforestation crew. It was "grunt work," he said, days of excruciating labor, scrambling up steep hillsides and fighting mud and rain to plant seedlings. Still, it was work he liked, and he may have stayed there for some time except that his first months at the company "happened to be the summer the spotted-owl crisis hit." Jason, along with all of the company's reforestation workers, was laid off. Though he'd only spent a few months in the job, it'd, nevertheless, given him an idea. In addition to planting seedlings, reforestation crews also conduct precommercial thinning operations, removing small trees to give the trees left standing more room to grow. The small trees removed during precom-mercial thinning are too small to effectively mill, and so they've historically been discarded, burned with logging slash, or turned into wood chips or pulp.[23]

Jason believed these tiny trees could be turned into construction lumber. As an industrial engineering student at Oregon State University, he'd heard about sawmills in Germany and Denmark using new technology to process small-diameter logs. He expected to find similar mills in the Northwest. But after doing some research and finding none, he decided to build one. Starting a new company was a difficult process, given that Jason had no background in business and didn't really know how to put together an investment pro-spectus. The process was made even harder given the year. It was 1994. The NWFP had just been implemented, and the industry was preparing to deal with a future of timber shortages. Other sawmill owners said he was foolish to try and start a new company. Banks and lenders wouldn't even meet with him. "People looked at me like I was crazy," Jason remembered. Eventually, in 1997, he was able to convince a small bank in Coos Bay to issue him a loan. "We got a shoestring budget, and we built this little mill," he said, "and after a year the thing was humming along and making a little money."[24]

Today, Southport's mill employs about two hundred workers and can process up to two-hundred million board feet a year, much of it small-diameter lumber that would have once been discarded. Without the technological developments Jason had learned about in college, the mill and its jobs wouldn't be here. Even the most skilled sawyer can't remove the small fractions of an inch required to turn small-diameter lumber into a merchantable commodity. The scanners and computer-controlled saws at Southport are better suited to the task. But even if it's computers that are doing a job that people once did, humans are still integral to the company's daily operations. As everyone who uses modern technology knows, sometimes painfully well, computers can be finicky. The computers running Southport's production line are no exception. Jason thus employs a small army of technicians, computer programmers, and maintenance staff to keep the saws turning. He explained that he's had difficulty hiring recent college graduates with computer-programing degrees because he can't compete with the salaries offered by the Northwest's large tech companies, and even if he could, few young, upwardly mobile professionals want to live in Coos Bay. So, instead, many of his employees are older workers who learned to use technology or are their sons and daughters born in Coos Bay who grew up with smartphones and personal computers and can pick up the ins and outs of the mill's computers relatively quickly.[25]

But Jason doesn't just like hiring local people because they're less likely to flee for Portland or Seattle the moment a better job comes along. He believes that providing jobs for people and families that struggled as a result of environmental legislation is helping to bring life back to the rural Northwest. And this may explain why labor relations at Southport seem relatively cordial. If changes to the industry in the 1970s diminished some of the class divides that had long defined the social landscape of timber country, and if the spotted-owl conflict eroded class boundaries further, a collective effort by owners and workers to save rural communities from ruin seems to have diminished class antagonisms altogether. Workers joke and rib Jason as if he were still one of them. The company's summer picnics and holiday parties are well known throughout Coos Bay as raucous affairs where workers and managers alike try to drink each other under the table. Payton went to high school with the children of men who worked at Southport and still considers many of them to be close friends, a few of whom even now work at her father's company. Many of those workers explain that they feel that an employer like Jason is the only person looking out for them and that the state and people in cities are indifferent to their problems.[26]

Another factor that likely explains the close relationship between Jason Smith and his employees is Southport's approach to forest management. When the company began, Jason purchased most of the company's logs from industrial timberland owners. But in recent years Southport has been expanding its own landholdings, purchasing formerly denuded forests and nursing them back to health through aggressive reforestation programs. Both Jason and the people who work for him are extremely proud of this. "We manage the forests for future generations," he said, "people don't even know we replant." Jason doesn't identify as an environmentalist. Far from it, in fact. He generally has a dim view of environmental legislation, if not all legislation. Payton compared her father to Ron Swanson, the libertarian character from NBC's *Parks and Recreation*, known for his strident critiques of government and state regulation. Yet, even as he rejects the title of environmentalist, Jason has, nevertheless, begun experimenting with wind power to run the company's operations and has expanded reforestation efforts on Southport's lands. Southport's mill may also benefit the entirety of the Northwest and its forests. By turning once-discarded, small-diameter logs into construction lumber, the company is filling consumer demand while decreasing the economic pressure on older stands. In many ways, Southport is what Ellery Foster, the IWA's forester in the 1940s and 1950s, envisioned as the model of a healthy Northwest forest industry: a small, family-owned company, responsible to land and rural communities.[27]

Changing Forests and a Changing Climate

That's a vision that Payton shares, too, and it's one of the reasons she decided to take her current position at Roseburg after college. She knew her father would give her a job, but she didn't want to be seen as the "boss's kid," getting special treatment. More than that, she was attracted to Roseburg because of the company's reputation for sustainable forest management. In the 1940s, long before it was required to do so by Oregon law, the company voluntarily replanted many of its properties. Throughout the 1960s and 1970s, Roseburg's foresters experimented with selective harvests and longer forest rotations. It was one of the first American lumber companies to be certified as sustainable by the Forest Stewardship Council (FSC), a global nonprofit forestry agency created by the World Wildlife Fund in the 1990s to limit deforestation. And today, it has the distinction of being the longest continually FSC-certified lumber company in North America. While Payton's current job in shipping and distribution affords her little opportunity to learn about forestry, she hopes to one day transition to a new job within the company that allows her to learn more about Roseburg's land-management practices and to, perhaps, bring some of those lessons back to Southport if she decides to return.[28]

But Payton's interest in forestry extends far beyond helping her father's company become more sustainable. She's driven by a deeper concern, one that Roseburg's early twentieth-century foresters and earlier generations of timber workers were not burdened with: climate change. Like many young people, Payton is deeply concerned with rising global temperatures, increasing levels of atmospheric carbon, and how all this might affect her future. Unlike many young people, she believes that sustainable timber harvests and active forest management may be some of the best ways to address the climate crisis. Her arguments, widely shared among people currently working in the timber industry, show some of the ways ideas of environmental stewardship remain central to timber country's culture, and how they've changed in response to new ecological threats.[29]

Understanding the arguments that Payton and people like her make requires some understanding of Northwest tree-growth dynamics. A tree grows throughout its entire life, but not uniformly. The most rapid growth occurs during its first forty to fifty years. Older trees still capture and convert carbon, just not as quickly. Thus, one of the more effective ways to reduce atmospheric carbon levels may be to manage stands on forty- to fifty-year rotations—that is, harvest trees just when they reach the end of their peak carbon-capturing years and replace them with younger trees that will again grow fast and capture more carbon. Several climate scientists and foresters agree. One study conducted by researchers at the University of Washington found that industrial forestlands in Washington managed on thirty- to fifty-year rotations annually remove 4.3 million tons of atmospheric carbon dioxide (CO_2). When accounting for carbon emitted in the production process—running equipment, saws, trucks, and mills—the study found that Washington's timber companies still annually remove 1.7 million tons of atmospheric CO_2.[30]

Expanding logging could benefit the climate in other ways, including reducing fires that release carbon and helping to clear the forest of dead trees, which capture no carbon. Timber is also a unique industrial commodity in that, as long as it isn't burned for fuel, it continues to store carbon, even after it's harvested and milled into construction lumber. This makes it a far more environmentally conscious building material than many alternatives, especially concrete. Environmentalists continue to decry the Northwest's timber industry, but it's the global concrete industry that should really concern them.

A 2019 article in the *Guardian* (UK edition) explained that concrete is "the most destructive material on Earth." Producing concrete monopolizes water, often in drought-ridden developing countries, pollutes the air, and creates 4 to 8 percent of all the world's CO_2 emissions. Only the coal, oil, and gas industries are responsible for flooding the atmosphere with more carbon. As environmental journalist John Vidal has said, "concrete is tipping us into climate catastrophe."[31]

For most of the twentieth century, though, concrete was the only viable material for large-scale construction projects, and timber could only be used in smaller buildings and homes. But technology is changing that and again helping to create new jobs in the Northwest's timber industry. Specifically, engineered lumber, the broad name for a host of forest products, now makes it possible to build large commercial buildings out of timber. Making engineered lumber involves gluing together several boards and alternating the direction of the grain to produce remarkably strong panels. Entire buildings can be built of nothing but engineered lumber. Payton's eyes lit up when she talked about the new building material. "It's so cool," she said, drawing out the "so" in an elongated crescendo. She quickly cited for me all the statistics about cement and how it adds carbon into the atmosphere and how we can easily replace it with engineered lumber. Then she explained how engineered lumber is yet another technological innovation that has the potential to help fuel the timber industry's recovery. American and Canadian lumber companies are finding it difficult to compete with Asian plywood and multidensity fiberboard manufacturers. Chinese plywood suppliers, in particular, have recently been undercutting American suppliers, forcing Roseburg to close its plywood facility in Dillard, Oregon. But at the same time, the company just opened its first engineered-lumber facility. "What can we be the best at?" Payton wondered, "We're not going to be the best at making plywood. But we can be the best at making engineered wood."[32]

Payton isn't the only one excited by the potential of engineered lumber. Recently, several architects interested in promoting sustainability have begun to make more use of it in their building projects. Benton Johnson, a materials engineer who works at a New York architecture firm, recently told the *New York Times* that engineered lumber has the potential to simultaneously address building shortages and climate change. "We know that we need to build a lot more buildings," he said, "and we know that we need to lower CO^2." Engineered lumber provides a way to do both. But increasing the use of engineered lumber will require that we allow for more logging. That's become an unpopular proposition in the last three to four decades. And recent events have made it even more so.[33]

"A Bunch of Neanderthals"

Payton has long recognized that she and people in her industry are fighting a difficult battle when it comes to convincing the broader public that logging may help mitigate climate change. No one questions the relationship between logging and forest health in her hometown of Coos Bay. But she realized just how opposed to logging many people are when she left her rural community to attend college in Eugene. Professors often peppered their lectures with subtle yet stinging antilogging comments. Students organized protests of timber companies who were recruiting job candidates on campus. For years Payton resisted telling even her close friends where she was from and what her family did. When some of those friends learned, they then recoiled at the thought of logging. "They will say to me, 'You know, that's kind of bad, you guys cutting down all those trees,'" she remembered. Payton was always frustrated by this. "People have this idea that we're going in and cutting down every last tree in the forest," she said, "people conflate what's happening in South America's rainforests with what's happening in the Northwest. Really, we have so many rules and regulations that's never going to happen here." Public-opinion polling confirms what Payton believes: most in the Northwest take a rather-dim view of the timber industry. One 2006 poll found that more than 70 percent of Oregonians felt that logging needed to be severely restricted. More recently, a 2016 poll the Wilderness Society conducted found that 79 percent of voters in California, Oregon, and Washington felt that rules and regulations governing the timber industry weren't strict enough.[34]

Payton's employer, Roseburg, is acutely aware of opinion polls like this and, like many present-day Northwest timber companies, has actively tried to distance itself from the sort of cut-and-run logging practiced in the early twentieth century. "In the past," Payton explained, "people in the industry have been like, 'Fuck you guys. You need wood and paper and blah, blah, blah.' I think the industry now is realizing that they need to change how they present themselves." She said that she believes this is why Roseburg was so eager to hire her. Initially nervous about being a young woman going to work in what has traditionally been a male-dominated industry, Payton explained that many in the company, from executives to logging-truck drivers, were really excited to see a young person interested in the industry, and all have gone out of their way to make her feel welcomed and comfortable. Roseburg has also tried to reach ecologically-minded young people in other ways, though, perhaps, with less success. Smith said the company's foresters have recently started posting pictures on Instagram of reforestation operations, hoping to show young people that modern timber companies often plant more trees than they harvest. I asked her if she thought it was effective. She just rolled her eyes and sighed, much the way many younger people do when older people try to use social media. Still, she thought Roseburg's heart was in the right place and hoped the efforts would pay off. "I see the industry really trying to manage its image," she said. "I think the industry is going to appeal to people who really care about the environment."[35]

Perhaps. But it's going to take more than just increased social-media savviness for companies like Roseburg to shift the conversation about logging. Recent portrayals of timber workers and their industry have continued to rely on disparaging tropes that reinforce long-standing narratives about rural backwardness. Television shows like David Lynch's *Twin Peaks* or Cheryl Strand's memoir of hiking the Pacific Crest Trail, *Wild*, have portrayed people from rural timber-working communities as dangerous and mysterious others. Academics have done little to dispel these images. Most recently, in her study of Oregon mushroom pickers, anthropologist Anna Lowenhaupt Tsing described the Northwest's forests as a "ruined" landscape caused, in no small part, by "reckless loggers."[36]

The greatest offender of all, though, may well be the History Channel series *Ax Men*. Premiering in 2008 and running for ten seasons, *Ax Men* was a reality show chronicling the work of several active logging crews (most, though not all, in the Northwest). At first glance, the show appeared to mark the potential cultural revitalization of timber country, challenging narratives of backwardness articulated by the counterculture of the 1970s and of rural death articulated during the grunge movement of the 1990s. Here, ostensibly, was a show that highlighted the unsung labors of rural people and their day-to-day struggles to bring timber to market. It promised to chronicle the verity of work in a resource-extraction industry and honor the quiet dignity of rural communities, a reminder to audiences that the rural Northwest had not faded into obscurity after the timber wars of the previous decades but remained a potent part of the region's social landscape and continued to provide the very lumber that we all use in our modern lives. It promised to be a more up-to-date, twenty-first-century take on the same stories that regional popular-front authors like Robert Cantwell and Roderick Haig-Brown had told in the Depression era. But good proletarian drama *Ax Men* was not. In the end, the show did much more to reinforce disparaging tropes than dispel them. Indeed, for a series that purported to be about the nobility of work, the show only rarely showed loggers actually working. Instead, a typical episode opened on crew members arriving at a job site and then fighting and cussing each other out for the next hour. If there was a star of the show, it was clearly Dwayne Dethlefs, a feller who worked for Pihl Logging out of Vernonia, Oregon. He wore tattered flannel shirts, sported a bushy red beard, was (by his own admission) often hungover, and whenever given the opportunity told viewers at home exactly what he thought of environmentalists and the do-nothing bureaucrats who wanted to shut down logging. Dethlefs's more colorful commentaries, however, were often cut short, presumably by producers with advertising dollars to think about. *Ax Men* was less a show about the realities of logging and more a distorted caricature of rural America. As one critic opined, it all amounted to "let's-laugh-at-the-white-trash-hixploitation."[37]

I asked Payton if she'd seen the show, and that was probably a mistake. She shot me a hard, disapproving stare, as if to say, "Are you really asking me that?" While, at its peak, more than 2.8 million people tuned in weekly to watch *Ax Men*, very few, if any, of those were loggers. In fact, people employed in the industry have been among the show's fiercest critics. "It's a crock," Archie Dass, a retired timber feller living in Portland, told the *Oregonian*. Dass objected to the ways *Ax Men* made loggers look reckless and careless. In every episode he could count a dozen times when loggers violated safety rules. "They wouldn't last 15 minutes in the woods with me," he said. Jay Browning, whose logging crew was featured in early seasons but then left the show for the way it portrayed loggers, agreed. "The show has taken on a whole different direction of guys fighting and arguing and all this screaming and yelling and all of this cussing," he told a reporter from his hometown paper in Astoria. "It makes us look like we're a bunch of Neanderthals." Several loggers also pointed out that *Ax Men* reinforced perceptions that timber workers don't care about the environment. Said Don Nomad, another retired feller from Portland, "We wish it showed more of what we really do—the replanting, taking care of the land. We wish it showed the big-city people that we're not just out there clear-cutting and wiping out the trees." After *Ax Men*'s second season, Jim Geisinger from the Association of Oregon Loggers met with History Channel representatives and asked them to include more images of loggers doing conservation work: "We sat down with the producers last summer and asked them why they didn't show loggers planting trees or protecting streams, instead of all that danger and drama. They just looked at us and said, 'Because we want people to watch the show.'"[38]

#TimberUnity

The broad cultural consensus that timber workers and their industry are fundamentally destructive likely explains why a good deal of recent legislation, particularly state-level policies aimed at reducing climate change, have sought to restrict logging. To be perfectly clear, the science on the relationship between timber harvests and climate change is far from conclusive. While several credible studies do indeed suggest that regulated timber harvests may mitigate climate change, an equal number of credible studies suggests that timber harvests contribute to climate change. Even so, legislatures have only tended to pay attention to the latter. Just as problematically, politicians have largely failed to consult representatives from the timber industry or rural communities and created climate-change policies that threaten to again disrupt logging towns that have just clawed their way back from the economic doldrums of the spotted-owl era, and many from those towns are angry. Much of the Northwest, and Oregon, in particular, appears to be on the verge of a second timber war.

The opening salvo in this new conflict came in early 2019 when politicians sent HB 2020 to the house of the Oregon State Legislature, an act creating a cap-and-trade system to reduce statewide carbon emissions. The legislation had a lofty and commendable goal, but many people in rural communities claimed it went about achieving that goal in a problematic way, burdening rural businesses more than urban ones. Based on a California law, HB 2020 set an annual statewide carbon-emissions cap and then required businesses and industries producing more than their share of greenhouse gases to purchase carbon credits. The legislation targeted the gas and oil industries more than the timber industry. Still, many economists predicted that energy companies would pass on the cost of carbon credits to consumers. By effectively imposing a new tax on fuel, timber-industry representatives claimed that rural resource industries, which tended to rely more on gasoline and diesel in production and shipping, were being unfairly targeted. Why weren't real estate developers using concrete in cities also being taxed? Why wasn't the considerable carbon footprint of Portland's tech industry also being considered? Why, when the timber industry had a net mitigating effect on carbon emissions, as timber workers claimed, was the industry being made to pay more for the fuel it needed to do that work? In short, many people in rural communities believed that HB 2020 required sacrifices on their part while allowing business as usual in cities.[39]

Despite these criticisms, the house approved the bill and sent it to the senate for a vote. What happened next became national news. Republican state senators demanded changes to the bill, and when the senators in the Democratic majority refused, the Republican caucus walked out of the capitol, denying the senate the quorum it needed to move the bill. Oregon Democrat Governor Kate Brown threatened to mobilize the Oregon State Police and, if need be, forcibly return the Republican senators to Salem. In response, several well-armed militias, most notably the Three Percenters, a group active in the occupation of the Malheur National Wildlife Refuge three years earlier, vowed to defend the Republican senators from the state police. Fearing violence, the governor backed off her threat. Republicans continued their walkout until the legislative session ended, preventing any further action on HB 2020 and effectively killing the bill.[40]

The failure of HB 2020 had as much to do with protests organized by timber workers as it did Republican recalcitrance. Throughout the summer of 2019, a new group called Timber Unity organized multiple logging-truck convoys and rallies that effectively shut down the streets of Salem and provided the Republican senators the political support they needed to maintain their walkout. Like many twenty-first-century social movements, Timber Unity was born on social media. In early 2019, as HB 2020 was working its way through Oregon's house, a handful of people from rural communities put together a Facebook group to discuss and criticize the cap-and-trade legislation. Someone from the group started posting on Twitter using #TimberUnity. The hashtag quickly caught on, and the numbers of subscribers to the Twitter feed and members to the group's Facebook page rapidly expanded. By the summer the group counted more than twenty thousand members.[41]

Timber Unity's rallies look remarkably similar to the rallies the Yellow Ribbon Coalition held during the spotted-owl conflict, from the use of logging trucks to clog streets to the protesters who wear hardhats and work clothes to mark their membership in the industry. Signs at the rallies contain phrases that sound like they could've come from thirty years ago: "Stand up for working families," "It's time to take back OUR state," and "Plant more trees and less government," to quote just a few. Supporters and members don't fly yellow ribbons, but the group's symbol, #TimberUnity, in bold lettering and in front of a bright-green stand of trees, has become increasingly visible on stickers pasted to pickup trucks and on signs along rural highways. Like the Yellow Ribbon Coalition, Timber Unity is also evidence of the complicated and sometimes ambiguous class politics of twenty-first-century timber country. The group describes itself as a movement of "common working folks," and at the same time, it enjoys the support of company owners. "We have been incredibly impressed by this effort and are supportive," read a letter written by Todd Payne, chief executive officer of Eugene's Seneca Jones Lumber Company. Like the cross-class coalitions that emerged in the timber wars, Timber Unity is evidence of how environmental activism has pushed bosses and workers closer together.[42]

There's a good reason why Timber Unity's tactics resemble the tactics employed by rural communities thirty years ago: many of the group's members lived through the spotted-owl conflict and carried the experiences with them. One is Mike Pihl, who now serves as president of Timber Unity. Born in Oregon in the early 1960s, Pihl started logging at the age of seventeen while still in high school. By the early 1980s, he'd saved up enough money to start his own contract logging company. He did well for several years, until spotted-owl restrictions nearly put him out of business. The fear, anger, and frustration of those years are still fresh in his memory. "It destroyed our towns," he said, speaking of the spotted owl. "They're ghost towns now." Pihl explained that he's motivated by a desire to save recently recovered logging towns from that same fate: "The mainstream government hasn't always been friendly to rural Oregon. Cap-and-trade will just be another nail in our coffin. We don't matter to them. So, I plan on just hammering away at this cause."[43]

Although Pihl is president of Timber Unity, like many social movements organized online, the group has a fairly loose, undefined structure. In reality Pihl is more public face than leader. Still, he's a good candidate to be that public face. Tall and broad shouldered with a stubbly beard, he looks like a logger. When we met, he was wearing staged pants, bright-red suspenders, and a tattered flannel shirt, the same clothes he wears out in the woods. Pihl is also a good spokesperson because he's so passionate about logging. "I wouldn't do anything else," he said, "I love my job. I wake up in the morning and I say, 'I can't wait to get to work.'" Some readers may actually recognize Pihl. He and his crew were featured on the first two seasons of *Ax Men*, and they returned for the final tenth season. Pihl said he understands why many loggers have misgivings about the show, some of which he shares (he usually tries to keep his involvement in the show "on the down-low"). At the same time, he said that his involvement on the show brought him some notoriety, which he's been able to use to speak up for causes and organizations that he cares about, including (but not limited to) the timber industry.[44]

Pihl is also a good spokesperson for Timber Unity because he's as passionate about preserving the forests as he is about working in them. When we spoke, Pihl constantly used the term "steward" to describe his relationship to the landscape. He talked about how logging has the potential to improve the land, and he went on at length about the various animals he encounters in a typical day in the forests: "Being a steward of the land—to me, it's the right thing to do," he said, "and, it's fun. You get to see the trees grow." I asked him what Timber Unity hopes to accomplish in the long term. He said he was glad the group was able to defeat HB 2020 and explained that Timber Unity was gearing up to oppose a new version of the bill (which was subsequently introduced in February 2020). Despite the large rallies Pihl has helped organize and Timber Unity's political agenda, the group's goals are relatively modest. Pihl explained that he wants timber workers and people from rural communities to be included in conversations on climate policy and for politicians to see rural workers as partners in addressing climate change, rather than a source of the problem. "Don't shut us out," he said, "we keep carbon-eating machines [forests] healthy."[45]

This is not the image offered by journalists who've covered the group, which doesn't really surprise Pihl. "Normally the media is more-or-less against the working man and rural Oregon," he said. Indeed, journalists somehow always manage to find and interview someone at the group's rallies who dismisses climate change as a liberal hoax or subscribes to some far-flung right-wing conspiracy theory. Adding to the group's problems is that their Facebook page regularly attracts people who post racist, xenophobic, homophobic, and/or sexist comments. Pihl is frustrated by this and clearly stated that he did not and does not share those views, adding that such comments are particularly offensive because several women and people of color serve on Timber Unity's board. Pihl further explained that he and his group's staff have started to aggressively police their social-media pages, deleting hateful posts, though because the group has grown so large, monitoring its Facebook and Twitter accounts amounts to a full-time job, distracting members from organizing. All this still hasn't prevented many journalists from portraying Timber Unity as an extremist, far-right organization.[46]

It's certainly true that most of Timber Unity's activists reliably vote Republican, but the politics of the group's core members are more complicated and nuanced. Timber Unity has recently begun to be more proactive on climate-change discussions, proposing policies that would mitigate carbon emissions without adversely affecting rural producers. In February 2020 the group issued a new policy proposal suggesting ways that Oregon could fight carbon emissions while also maintaining healthy rural communities. Some of these seem so common sense it's a wonder why they're not already in place. The proposal, for instance, identifies many new areas throughout the state where afforestation (that is, planting forests where none have historically existed) could provide new ways of capturing carbon. The group further recommended that the state do more to contract with local companies and "implement a carbon metric into its public procurement process." It also called on the state to support local wood recycling (currently there are no timber recyclers in the Portland metro area) and provide tax breaks for timber operators who want to replace old machinery with new, more environmentally friendly machinery.[47]

These arguments are increasingly gaining traction throughout the rural Northwest and not just in logging communities. Pihl and his staff are actively working to include farmers, ranchers, and representatives from other resource-extraction industries in their movement. And, judging by some of the signs that have started appearing at the group's rallies, they're achieving some success on this front. One read, for example, "If you got it, a truck brought it! If you ate it, a farmer grew it! If you built it, a logger felled it! If you grilled it, a rancher raised it!" At the annual meeting of the Oregon Ryegrass Growers Association, after Pihl delivered a speech encouraging the state's grass and grass-seed farmers to get involved in the movement, we chatted in the lobby of the convention hall and were interrupted no fewer than a dozen times by audience members who wanted to shake his hand and thank him for the work he's doing.[48]

Payton Smith noticed support for Timber Unity growing throughout the rural Northwest, too. "I think that it is incredible the way all these people have been able to organize via social media and come together to make some change," she said. "When I am home in Coos Bay, I see 'Timber Unity' stickers and signs everywhere, and almost all of my Facebook friends from the area have the little 'Timber Unity' filter on their social-media profiles." Yet, Payton's enthusiasm is tempered by some of Timber Unity's activism, its large and disruptive rallies, and the divisive nature of some of its rhetoric: "You have to be willing to sit down and have a civil conversation with both parties in order to come to a solution that is going to be beneficial to both groups," she said. "Climate change already has and will continue to impact this industry, which is why we should be at the forefront of fighting it. Timber Unity should be working with legislators to come up with bills that will both benefit the environment and our industry."[49]

Payton's Trail

At this time, it's impossible to know how the debate over climate change and logging will play out. In February 2020 Oregon politicians introduced a new cap-and-trade bill that again appeared to overburden rural producers. In response, Timber Unity again filled Salem's streets with logging trucks and angry protesters. Then the COVID-19 pandemic brought an abrupt end to conversations about future forest management, just as it brought an abrupt end to just about everything throughout the world. The legislature sidelined the bill so they could focus on addressing the public-health crisis created by the spread of the coronavirus, and Timber Unity has been uncharacteristically quiet since quarantines and prohibitions on public gatherings began in March 2020. What will become of the movement is, at this time, unclear. Will Timber Unity ultimately bring rural Northwesterners together and help them push for legislation that simultaneously protects the climate and their communities, as Payton hopes? Or will the movement just heighten existing tensions, fuel anger on both sides of the debate, and make compromise and productive discussion impossible, as she fears?

There's no question that Timber Unity is evidence of just how much timber country has changed in the past century. From its politics to its ambiguous assertion of class identity—to say nothing of its use of social media—Timber Unity is a far cry from the industrial unions of an older era, which opposed employers rather than worked with them. Those changes have as much to do with the ways the character of the entire White working class has changed over the course of the twentieth century as they do the ways the industry has changed. Timber Unity's members are part of an industry that bears little resemblance to the timber industry of old. Few, if any of, Timber Unity's activists work for a large landholder or transnational timber company, as did their fathers and grandfathers employed in the woods. Instead, they're part of the industry that emerged out of the economic upheavals of the 1970s, one in which smaller producers and independent contractors working public lands and small private forests replaced those large companies and, in the process, blurred the boundaries that had once demarcated labor and capital in the Northwest woods. Timber Unity's members also exist in a very different cultural context than their predecessors who lived and worked in the woods, one shaped by the counterculture of the New Left of the 1960s and 1970s, which portrayed much of the working class and the rural working class, in particular, as behind the times and backward. And Timber Unity's members exist in a very different region, one in which resource extraction no longer dominates the economy, in which most people live in cities and think of the forests primarily as recreational spaces, and which, like many parts of the North American West, suffers from an urban-rural divide that can, at times, seem intractable. All these changes have shaped a movement like Timber Unity, as it has the life and labor of all those who continue to live and work in the Northwest woods.

Yet, in important ways, there are distinct echoes of timber country's past in a person like Payton Smith and a movement like Timber Unity. Chief among these is the ethic of forest stewardship that has so long been a part of timber country's culture. Timber Unity may be primarily driven by a desire to defeat current climate-change proposals but beneath that is a concern for the forests and communities that depend on them. That ethic was born in the company towns and logging camps of the eary twentieth century, shaped by work as much as by hunting, fishing, and outdoor recreation. That ethic found its political expression in the International Woodworkers of America and its assertion of labor environmentalism and New Deal conservationism. And though Timber Unity doesn't articulate its environmental politics in quite the same way, the core tenants of those environmental politics are still there. Many of Timber Unity's activists, like generations before, want a land-scape where wilderness exists alongside working forests, where the beauty of the woods is appreciated as much as the dignity of the people who work in and care for them, where human lives receive as much consideration as the lives of trees and owls, and where the people who live and work in the woods have a voice in managing those woods.

Because the forests of the Northwest can, indeed, be so beautiful and awe inspiring, it's often easy to forget that these are also working landscapes and must remain working landscapes. Not only do working forests provide society with much of the lumber it continues to rely on, despite the global economy's transition to a high-tech economy, logging continues to provide employment for long-struggling rural communities and when done properly helps ensure ecologically healthy forests. If nothing else, the history of timber country shows that the very people who live and work in the Northwest woods could and should play a role in helping manage those woods. Moreover, it's a history that should encourage us to see the forests in new ways, not exclusively as spaces of industrial accumulation, as early twentieth-century lumbermen often saw the forests, nor as exclusively wilderness, as the environmental movement of the late twentieth century too often saw them, but as places with multiple uses and values, as people from timber country have long seen them.

What we all need to do is see the forests a bit more like Payton Smith sees them. Like so many people from timber country, she would much rather be outdoors than in, fishing for salmon on the Millicoma River as it meanders near Coos Bay or struggling up the windswept dunes of Oregon's coast. But her favorite place of all to be is a narrow trail that cuts through a forest on a ridgeline on some industrial forestland not too far from her hometown that leads to a small waterfall. It's hardly the biggest waterfall in Oregon, nor for that matter the most spectacular, but it's special to her all the same.

I elk hunt near the falls that Payton describes, and one September eve-ning, in the waning hours of twilight, when the heat of the day has dissipated and the woods are starting to come alive, I go and have a look for myself. I find a trail up a steep, gravel logging road. For about two miles, the trail winds through industrial forest land in various stages of regeneration, across clearcuts, into what's known as "reprod," tightly packed forests yet to be thinned, and into stands that are probably thirty to forty years old and likely scheduled for harvest soon. From there, the trail cuts west and points toward the Pacific Ocean, just four or five ridgelines away. Also a few ridgelines away are two small wilderness areas. Those two wilderness areas are hardly Oregon's largest or most popular, but both do attract their share of visitors, mostly hikers and backpackers from Portland and California. Few of those visitors likely know of this neighboring industrial forest, and I suspect if they got lost and somehow found themselves here, they'd promptly turn around. From their perspective, the view from Payton's trail would probably appear unnatural and ugly. They might wonder why she would choose this path through the woods when there are other, more aesthetically pleasing trails so nearby.

But I think it's clear what Payton sees and why this is among her favorite places. In many ways, her trail traverses the very sort of landscape that timber workers have long wanted and long fought for: a working forest alongside a wilderness. Each of these is important in its own right. The industrial forests I walked through are actively providing jobs and economic stability to nearby Coos Bay. Had I been there on a weekday instead of a weekend, I'm certain I would have heard some of the sounds of that economic stability— the high-pitched bleat of signal whistles, the low rumble of diesel yarders, and the thunderous rumble of logging trucks speeding across gravel roads. This forest has provided just as much for people outside the rural Northwest. Its trees have been turned into homes, buildings, and paper. The wilderness, though, is no less extraordinary. It's dark and mysterious, as gorgeous as it is awe inspiring. The industrial forest I'm currently in and the wilderness areas a few ridgelines away are certainly meaningful and valuable independent of one another. But together, they're far more beautiful. There in that little slice of timber country is clear evidence that we don't have to choose between jobs and the environment, between healthy rural communities and healthy forests. There, on Payton's trail, is evidence that we can have both.

Eventually, after many miles and a few hours I finally arrive at the small falls, and it is, indeed, beautiful. But I don't stay long. Evening is approaching, and I think I hear some elk moving nearby.

Acknowledgments

This is a book about people who work in the Northwest woods. As forms of labor go, writing a book about people who work in the woods and actually working in the woods are nothing alike. Timber workers brave whirling saws, falling trees, and harsh weather over long, strenuous days. The only occupational hazards I worry about are sore backs from slumping over my desk and strained eyes from staring at my computer. There is, however, one—and by my count, only one—similarity between working in the woods and writing a book about working in the woods. Both are complicated activities that depend on entire crews of people, working in tandem. A big thanks to all my crewmates. You supported me, encouraged me, and like a logger's fellow workers, kept me safe when danger loomed (speaking metaphorically, of course).

Jim Gregory has been a steadfast supporter from the start and regularly dropped what he was doing to offer me encouragement, support, and advice. That advice was sometimes difficult to hear, and as Jim might be the first to explain, I sometimes resisted implementing his recommendations and resisted mightily. But that advice was always brilliant, and, in the end, I'm glad that, more times than not, I followed it. He always assured me I had something important to say, even when I didn't think so. Thanks, Jim. It wouldn't have happened without you.

Nor would it have happened without the advice and encouragement of Margaret O'Mara, who despite studying the history of cities and high tech, offered invaluable advice about the history of rural communities and the somewhat more low-tech timber industry.

Like everyone who knew her, I was deeply saddened by Linda Nash's sudden passing, just before this book was published. More than anyone else,

Linda encouraged me to see that stories about work are fundamentally stories about nature. This book wouldn't exist without her, and if nothing else, I hope it stands a testament to her passion for sharing and teaching environmental history.

Julie Greene deserves special mention and special thanks. In a way, she's been part of this project longer than anyone else. Julie sparked my interest in labor history when I was an undergraduate. Then, as a series editor of the University of Illinois Press's Working Class in American History series, she offered help and advice as I finished this book.

At the University of Oregon (UO), I've been lucky to have the support of truly great colleagues. Thank you to Lindsay Braun, Bob Bussel, Alex Dracobly, Julie Hessler, Ocean Howell, Ryan Jones, Vera Keller, David Luebke, Jeff Ostler, Brett Rushforth, Julie Weise, Marsha Weisiger, and Marcus Widenor. Lindsey Mazurek and Noah Eber-Schmid were unable to stay at UO, but I'll always consider them dear friends. Of course, we faculty would be utterly hopeless and lost without the support of great staff. Thank you to Fela McWhorter, Nick Mahlum, and Lauren Pinchin.

A wide range of scholars have also taken an interest in this project. For their feedback or all-around encouragement, thanks to Danny Besner, Jefferson Cowie, Ileen DeVault, Erik Loomis, Josh Reid, Ron Verzuh, everyone at the Pacific Northwest Labor History Association, and everyone at the DC Labor History Seminar.

As others have noted, the best way to learn something is to teach it. I owe a debt to all my students and especially students who've taken my Pacific Northwest history class. Your comments and questions—and sometimes your pushback—helped me refine my thinking. I consider myself especially grateful to have had the opportunity to work with amazing graduate students. Thank you to Marin Aurand, Collin Heatley, Tara Keegan, and Adam Quinn.

This project received the support of the Oregon Humanities Center and the Center for Environmental Futures. Their financial assistance was most welcomed but perhaps even more valuable was their work in creating an interdisciplinary and collaborative climate at UO.

Librarians and archivists at the British Columbia Archives and Royal BC Museum, Courtenay District and Museum, Oregon State Historical Society, University of Oregon Special Collections, University of Washington Special Collections, and Washington State Historical Society went out of their way to find sources and help with research.

While I spent considerable time in archives and libraries as I wrote this book, speaking with people working in the timber industry was my favorite form of research. Thanks to all who took the time, and especially Dick

Gilkison, Wilbur Heath, and Payton Smith. Lindsay Reaves and Tom Bauman deserve special thanks for making time in their insanely busy lives as small forestland owners to take my students and me around their property and show us all the marvelous beauty of a working forest.

At the University of Illinois Press, James Engelhardt took an immediate interest in this project and offered valuable feedback on early drafts. When James left the press, Alison Syring Bassford stepped in and helped me finish. She's been invaluable and along with Ellie Hinton, offered thoughtful advice and, more than once, responded calmly to panicked e-mails sent at 2:00 A.M..

For providing critical assessments of my analyses (often unsolicited), companionship at the bar (if not always covering the tab), and good-humored amusement (much of it juvenile and unbecoming of academics), a big thanks to some of my dearest friends, the fearsome fivesome (which has, over the years, grown in members): Johan Hurting, Wendi Lindquist, Devon McCurdy, Becca Mitchner, Brian Schefke, and Tim Wright.

Though I don't tell them enough (and, indeed, some might experience shock after reading it here), I'm extremely grateful to have a loving and supportive family. Jack and Linda Cronce welcomed me into their family as if I were their own son and shared with me their stories about living and working in the rural Northwest. Samantha, Abigail, Dolores, and Maeve comforted me at the end of the longest days of writing in the way only cats can. The rolling eyes of my sister, Amanda, kept my ego in check, and Bradley Castle shared with me his extensive knowledge of wildland fire. Being an uncle is the best thing ever. William and Josie: you're probably both a bit too young to make sense of this book right now, but I hope one day it will teach you something about your new home in Oregon. My mom, Joanne, has been my biggest supporter, and I can't think of anyone who's prouder of me. My father, Ron, passed away unexpectedly before this book was published, but I know he would've loved the parts about hunting and fishing.

The one person I have to thank the most, the one person I owe more to than anyone else, though, is Jessica Cronce. Jess read every chapter, multiple times, and offered thoughtful feedback. She then humored me when I complained that her often-modest suggestions for revisions were "subverting my artistic vision." But Jess has been so much more than a great editor. She's been a great friend and great partner. When I needed encouraging, she encouraged me. When I needed support, she supported me. And, when I needed to laugh, she laughed with me. Jess is the hardest-working, smartest, and most beautiful person I know. This book, and my life, are better because she's been a part of them.

Notes

Introduction

1. The story of Luoma, Zapp, and Morrison is based on Andrew Neufeld and Andrew Parnaby, *The IWA in Canada: The Life and Times of an Industrial Union* (Vancouver, BC: IWA Canada, 2000), 274; Tom Hawthorn, "Fallers' Risky Decision 20 Years Ago Continues to Pay Off for All," *Globe and Mail*, June 6, 2010, www.the globeandmail.com, accessed July 3, 2019.

2. Zapp, quoted in Neufeld and Parnaby, *IWA in Canada*, 274.

3. Zapp, quoted in Hawthorn, "Fallers' Risky Decision."

4. Trail sign, White River Provincial Park, British Columbia Parks Department, Canada.

5. Zapp, quoted in Hawthorn, "Fallers' Risky Decision."

6. For labor-environmental histories that explore working people's relationships and obligations to nature, see Lissa K. Wadewitz, *The Nature of Borders: Salmon, Boundaries, and Bandits on the Salish Sea* (Seattle: University of Washington Press, 2012); Thomas G. Andrews, *Killing for Coal: America's Deadliest Labor War* (Cambridge, MA: Harvard University Press, 2008); Chad Montrie, *Making a Living: Work and Environment in the United States* (Chapel Hill: University of North Carolina Press, 2008); Lawrence M. Lipin, *Workers and the Wild: Conservation, Consumerism, and Labor in Oregon, 1910–1930* (Urbana: University of Illinois Press, 2007); Andrew Hurley, *Environmental Inequalities: Class, Race, and Industrial Pollution in Gary, Indiana, 1945–1980* (Chapel Hill: University of North Carolina Press, 1995); Lisa M. Fine, "Workers and the Land in US History: Pointe Mouillee and the Downriver Detroit Working Class in the Twentieth Century," *Labor History* 53, no. 3 (2012): 409–34; Nichelle Frank, "Sanitizing History: Environmental Cleanup and Historic Preservation in U.S. West Mining Communities" (PhD diss., University of Oregon, 2020).

7. William Cronon, *Nature's Metropolis: Chicago and the Great West* (New York: Norton, 1991), 148–206. To give a few examples of science fiction and fantasy inspired by the Northwest: Frank Herbert was inspired to write *Dune* after visiting the dunes of Oregon's coast, Octavia Butler and Ursula Le Guin both lived in Portland and were inspired by the surrounding forests, and Stephenie Meyer set her *Twilight* series in Forks, Washington.

8. Donald Worster, *Rivers of Empire: Water, Aridity, and the Growth of the American West* (New York: Pantheon, 1985), 5.

For environmental histories of the Northwest's forests, see Nancy Langston, *Forest Dreams, Forest Nightmares: The Paradox of Old Growth in the Inland West* (Seattle: University of Washington Press, 1995); Robert Bunting, *The Pacific Raincoast: Environment and Culture in an American Eden, 1778–1900* (Lawrence: University of Kansas Press, 1997); Richard White, *Land Use, Environment, and Social Change: The Shaping of Island County, Washington* (Seattle: University of Washington Press, 1980).

For histories of the US Forest Service and state intervention in the Northwest's forests, see Emily K. Brock, *Money Trees: The Douglas Fir and American Forestry, 1900–1944* (Corvallis: Oregon State University Press, 2015); Kevin R. Marsh, *Drawing Lines in the Forest: Creating Wilderness Areas in the Pacific Northwest* (Seattle: University of Washington Press, 2009); Paul Hirt, *A Conspiracy of Optimism: Management of the National Forests since World War Two* (Lincoln: University of Nebraska Press, 1996); William G. Robbins, *Lumberjacks and Legislators: Political Economy of the U.S. Lumber Industry, 1890–1941* (College Station: Texas A&M University Press, 1982).

9. Erik Loomis, *Empire of Timber: Labor Unions and the Pacific Northwest Forests* (New York: Cambridge University Press, 2016), 235. One additional note on Loomis's study: readers familiar with Loomis's book may notice some overlap between my treatment of the International Woodworkers of America in chapters 4 and 5 and Loomis's treatment of the IWA in chapter 3 of his study. My analysis here of the IWA is based heavily, if not entirely, on my "Landscapes of Solidarity," completed two years before Loomis's book was published. See Steven C. Beda, "Landscapes of Solidarity: Timber Workers and the Making of Place in the Pacific Northwest, 1900–1964" (PhD diss., University of Washington, 2014).

For additional histories of timber workers, see Neufeld and Parnaby, *IWA in Canada*; Gordon H. Hak, *Capital and Labour in the British Columbia Forest Industry, 1934–74* (Vancouver: University of British Columbia Press, 2007); William G. Robbins, *Hard Times in Paradise: Coos Bay, Oregon, 1850–1986* (Seattle: University of Washington Press, 1998); Andrew Mason Prouty, *More Deadly Than War! Pacific Coast Logging, 1827–1981* (New York: Garland, 1985); Jerry Lembcke and William Tattam, *One Union in Wood: A Political History of the International Woodworkers of America* (Madeira Park, BC: Harbour, 1983); Vernon Jensen, *Lumber and Labor* (New York: Farrar and Rinehart, 1945).

For general histories of the Northwest timber industry that also pay attention to labor, see Thomas R. Cox, *The Lumbermen's Frontier: Three Centuries of Land Use, Society, and Change in American Forests* (Corvallis: Oregon State University Press,

2010); Richard A. Rajala, *Clearcutting the Pacific Rain Forest: Production, Science, and Regulation* (Vancouver: University of British Columbia Press, 1998); Robert Ficken, *The Forested Land: A History of Lumbering in Western Washington* (Seattle: University of Washington Press, 1987).

For histories of worker-environmentalist conflict in the Northwest, see Darren Frederick Speece, *Defending Giants: The Redwood Wars and the Transformation of American Environmental Politics* (Seattle: University of Washington Press, 2019); Richard Widick, *Trouble in the Forest: California's Redwood Timber Wars* (Minneapolis: University of Minnesota Press, 2009); William Dietrich, *The Final Forest: Big Trees, Forks, and the Pacific Northwest* (Seattle: University of Washington Press, 2011).

10. The classic work on place is Yi-Fu Tuan, *Space and Place: The Perspective of Experience* (Minneapolis: University of Minnesota Press, 1977).

Histories that center the concept of place and that have shaped my analysis here are Matthew Klingle, *The Emerald City: An Environmental History of Seattle* (New Haven: Yale University Press, 2007); Coll Thrush, *Native Seattle: Histories from the Crossing-Over Place* (Seattle: University of Washington Press, 2007); Kate Brown, *A Biography of No Place: From Ethnic Borderland to Soviet Heartland* (Cambridge, MA: Harvard University Press, 2004).

11. Two works stand as important exceptions in the trend of discounting community and family in the Northwest woods, and my study here builds off these. They are Robbins, *Hard Times in Paradise*, and Bob H. Reinhardt, *Struggle on the North Santiam: Power and Community on the Margins of the American West* (Corvallis: Oregon State University Press, 2020).

12. Timber workers' understanding of nature, work, and environmental change hews quite closely to what are arguably two of the most widely read articles in the field of environmental history: William Cronon, "The Trouble with Wilderness; or, Getting Back to the Wrong Nature," and Richard White, "'Are You an Environmentalist, or Do You Work for a Living?' Work and Nature," both in *Uncommon Ground: Rethinking the Human Place in Nature*, ed. William Cronon (New York: Norton, 1996), 69–90, 171–85, respectively. Perhaps not coincidentally, the title of White's article was taken from a bumper sticker popular in timber country during the height of the spotted-owl conflict.

13. Jefferson Cowie, *Stayin' Alive: The 1970s and the Last Days of the Working Class* (New York: New Press, 2010).

Chapter 1. "The New Empire"

1. On Roscoe Murrow and Polecat Creek, see A. M. Sperber, *Murrow: His Life and Times* (New York: Fordham University, 1998), 10–31; Joseph E. Persico, *Edward R. Murrow: An American Original* (New York: McGraw-Hill, 1988), 15–49.

2. Oregon Immigration Board, *The New Empire: Oregon, Washington, Idaho: Its Resources, Climate, Present Development, and Its Advantages as a Place of Residence and Field for Investment* (Portland: Oregon Immigration Board, 1888), 92, 93.

3. On Northwest forestland speculation, see Cox, *Lumbermen's Frontier*, 263–89; Robbins, *Hard Times in Paradise*, 26–39.

4. On Northwest logging's earlier, nineteenth-century history, see Thomas R. Cox, *Mills and Markets: A History of the Pacific Coast Lumber Industry to 1900* (Seattle: University of Washington Press, 1974).

5. Kenneth A. Erickson, "The Morphology of Lumber Settlements in Western Oregon and Washington" (PhD diss., University of California, Berkeley, 1965), 16.

6. Frederick Weyerhaeuser, "brewer" quote in Ficken, *Forested Land*, 91; Weyerhaeuser, "a great lot of it" comment, quoted in Ralph W. Hidy, Frank Ernest Hill, and Allan Nevins, *Timber and Men: The Weyerhaeuser Story* (New York: Macmillan, 1963), 213.

7. "Scalawag timber brokers" quote in Hidy, Hill, and Nevins, *Timber and Men*, 223; Oswald West, "Reminiscences and Anecdotes: Mostly about Politics," *Oregon Historical Quarterly* 50, no. 2 (1950): 108–9; "fierce rush to stake timber" quote in Donald MacKay, *Empire of Wood: The Macmillan Bloedel Story* (Vancouver, BC: Douglas and McIntyre, 1982), 20; land-ownership figures from US Bureau of Corporations, *The Lumber Industry, vol 2: Concentration of Timber Ownership in Selected Regions* (Washington, DC: Government Printing Office, 1913–14).

8. Everett G. Griggs, "The Lumber Industry in Its National Scope," *National Problems Affecting the Lumber Industry: Official Report, Ninth Annual Convention, National Lumber Manufacturers' Association* (Vancouver, WA: National Lumber Manufacturers Association, 1911), 125; on Weyerhaeuser's tax rates, see Ficken, *Forested Land*, 121–22.

9. Long, quoted in Charles E. Twining, *George S. Long: Timber Statesman* (Seattle: University of Washington, 1994), 42. On the collapse of the speculative market, see Cox, *Lumbermen's Frontier*, 306–7; Robbins, *Lumberjacks and Legislatures*, 24–32.

10. Census Office, *Report on Manufacturing Industries in the United States, Part I: Totals for States and Industries at the Eleventh Census: 1890* (Washington, DC: Government Printing Office, 1894), special statistics for Oregon and Washington; Bureau of the Census, *Census of Manufacturers for 1905, Part III: Special Reports on Selected Industries* (Washington, DC: Government Printing Office, 1908), special statistics for lumber and timber products; Bureau of the Census, *Census of Manufacturers for 1914, Vol. I: Reports by States* (Washington, DC: Government Printing Office, 1918), special statistics for Oregon and Washington; Herman M. Johnson, *Production of Lumber, Lath, and Shingles in Washington and Oregon, 1869–1939* (Portland, OR: Pacific Northwest Forest and Range Experiment Station, US Department of Agriculture, August 25, 1941). Board feet, or foot board measure (f.b.m.), has been the standard way to measure both standing timber and processed timber since the mid-nineteenth century. It is a measure of volume, with one f.b.m. being 144 in³, or the equivalent of a piece of lumber measuring 12 x 12 x 1 in.

11. Demographic overview of Blanchard based on US Department of Commerce, Bureau of the Census, *Fourteenth Census of the United States: 1920—Population*,

manuscript census forms on microfilm, Blanchard Precinct, Skagit County, Washington, enumerated January 2, 1920.

12. Alfred J. Van Tassel, *Mechanization in the Lumber Industry: A Study of Technology in Relation to Resources and Employment Opportunity*, report M-5 (Philadelphia: Works Projects Administration, 1940).

13. Steven Ruggles, J. Trent Alexander, Katie Genadek, Ronald Goeken, Matthew B. Schroeder, and Matthew Sobek, *Integrated Public Use Microdata Series: Version 5.0* (Minneapolis: University of Minnesota, 2010), 1900 sample, machine-readable database (database hereafter referred to as IPUMS).

14. IPUMS, 1920 sample.

15. Bureau of the Census, *Twelfth Census of the United States: 1900—Population*, manuscript census forms on microfilm, Cumberland Precinct, Barron County, Wisconsin, enumerated June 1900; Bureau of the Census, *Thirteenth Census of the United States: 1910—Population*, manuscript census forms on microfilm, Gig Harbor Precinct, Pierce County, Washington, enumerated May 1910; Murray Morgan, *The Mill on the Boot: The Story of the St. Paul & Tacoma Lumber Company* (Seattle: University of Washington, 1982), 3–54.

16. Axel H. Oxholm, *Swedish Forests, Lumber Industry, and Lumber Export Trade*, special agents series, no. 195 (Washington, DC: Department of Commerce, Bureau of Foreign and Domestic Commerce, 1921), 211; Forsamlingsbok, parish roll, "Sweden, Church Records, 1451–1943," database, Provo, Utah, Ancestry.com, accessed June 1, 2018.

17. IPUMS, 1920 sample; *Census of Manufacturers 1929—Vol. 1: Reports by States* (Washington, DC: Government Printing Office), 674–79.

18. R. W. Vinnedge, "President's Address of the 19th Annual Pacific Coast Logging Congress," special ed., *Timberman*, November 1928, 39. On the radicalism workers brought with them to the Northwest, see Aaron Goings, Brian Barnes, and Roger Snider, *The Red Coast: Radicalism and Anti-Radicalism in Southwest Washington* (Corvallis: Oregon State University Press, 2019).

19. For general histories of the IWW, see Philip S. Foner, *History of the Labor Movement in the United States, Vol. 4: The Industrial Workers of the World, 1905–1917* (New York: International, 1965) and Melvyn Dubofsky, *We Shall be All: A History of the Industrial Workers of the World* (New York: Quadrangle, 1969).

20. On IWW membership numbers, see Daniel A. Cornford, *Workers and Dissent in the Redwood Empire* (Philadelphia: Temple University Press, 1987), 191. The "new labor historians" of the 1960s were particularly taken with the Wobblies in the Northwest and often portrayed them as powerful, but rarely did these historians cite membership figures. Two of the most popular studies in this vein are Foner, *History of the Labor Movement*, 214–32, 518–48, and Dubofsky, *We Shall Be All*, 319–48. More recently, Loomis argues the IWW had a significant influence in the woods (*Empire of Timber*, 18–88), though he relies heavily on the IWW's paper, which, for reasons stated in the text, may not be the best of sources. For those interested in this debate,

worth looking at is Robert L. Tyler, *Rebels of the Woods: The I.W.W. in the Pacific Northwest* (Eugene: University of Oregon Books, 1967), one of the few books written in the 1960s to take a critical look at the IWW in the Northwest.

21. Everett Griggs to A. P. Le Doux, February 23, 1920, box 178, acc.# 0315–001, Records of the St. Paul & Tacoma Lumber Company, 1876–1958, Special Collections, University of Washington, Seattle; Charlotte Todes, *Labor and Lumber* (New York: International, 1931), 97–98.

22. Richard A. Rajala, "Bill and the Boss: Labor Protest, Technological Change, and the Transformation of the West Coast Logging Camp, 1890–1930," *Journal of Forest History* 33, no. 4 (1989): 174.

23. "Into the Jaws of Death," *Timberman* 19, no. 1, 1917, 1.

24. Constitution and oath, folder 4, box 1, Loyal Legion of Loggers and Lumbermen Records, 1918–1937, acc.# Bx 040, Special Collections and University Archives, University of Oregon Libraries, Eugene. On Brice P. Disque, see Joshua B. Freeman, "Militarism, Empire, and Labor Relations: The Case of Brice P. Disque," *International Labor and Working-Class History* 80 (Fall 2011): 103–20. On the Spruce Division, see Kathleen Crosman, "The Army in the Woods: Spruce Production Division Records at the National Archives," *Oregon Historical Quarterly* 112, no. 1 (2011): 100–106. On the 4L, see Loomis, *Empire of Timber*, 54–88.

25. Persico, *Edward R. Murrow*, 22. On Ethel Murrow, also see Sperber, *Murrow*, 10–14.

26. IPUMS, 1910, 1920, 1930, and 1940 samples.

27. For a discussion of the biases in progressive social investigation and IWW discourse, see Frank Tobias Higbie, *Indispensable Outcasts: Hobo Workers and Community in the American Midwest, 1880–1930* (Urbana: University of Illinois Press, 2003), 66–133.

28. Secretary's Report, *Proceedings of the Pacific Logging Congress* (Tacoma, Washington, Pacific Logging Congress, 1912), 5; Frank Lamb, "The Principles of Labor Maintenance," *Proceedings of the Pacific Coast Logging Congress* (Tacoma, WA: Pacific Coast Logging Congress, 1917), 30.

29. Rajala, "Bill and the Boss," 171.

30. Ibid., 174.

31. Margaret Crawford, *Building the Workingman's Paradise: The Design of American Company Towns* (London: Verso, 1995). For some recent works on the history of company towns, see also Marcelo J. Borges and Susana B. Torres, *Company Towns: Labor, Space, and Power Relations across Time and Continents* (New York: Palgrave Macmillan, 2012); Oliver J. Dinius and Angela Vergara, eds., *Company Towns in the Americas: Landscape, Power, and Working-Class Communities* (Athens: University of Georgia Press, 2011). For a classic on company towns in the American West, see James B. Allen, *The Company Town in the American West* (Norman: University of Oklahoma Press, 1968). For industry-specific histories of company towns, see Andrews, *Killing for Coal*, 197–232; William P. Jones, *The Tribe of Black Ulysses: African*

American Lumber Workers in the Jim Crow South (Champaign: University of Illinois Press, 2005), 15–88. On the makeover that some Appalachian coal towns received, see Hardy Green, *The Company Town: The Industrial Edens and Satanic Mills That Shaped the American Economy* (New York: Basic Books, 2010), 64. *Most* company towns in Appalachian coal country did *not* get the workingman's paradise treatment. Green estimates that only about 2 percent of coal towns were transformed into modern company towns.

32. Julia Ruuttila (née Bertram), quoted in Sandy Polishuk, *Sticking to the Union: An Oral History of the Life and Times of Julia Ruuttila* (New York: Palgrave Macmillan, 2003), 48. For more on the history of company towns in Northwest timber country, see Linda Carlson, *Company Towns of the Pacific Northwest* (Seattle: University of Washington Press, 2003).

33. While naming company towns after the industries they supported was a common practice both inside and outside the Northwest woods (several logging towns were named Timber, just as many coal towns were named Carbondale), the northern California logging town of Weed was, in fact, named for the late nineteenth-century lumberman Abner Weed, not what would become a major industry in northern California in the late twentieth century.

34. Richard Somerset Mackie, *Island Timber: A Social History of the Comox Logging Company, Vancouver Island* (Winlaw, BC: Sono Nis, 2000), 114–45.

35. See Ronald L. Gregory, *Life in Railroad Logging Camps of the Shevlin-Hixon Company, 1916–1950* (Corvallis: Oregon State University, 2001).

36. "Equipment for Camp Movies," *Timberman*, 24, December 1923, 160.

37. James Couack to A. H. Hilton, November 1913, box 1, CLR series 1, Comox Logging and Railway Company Records, Special Collections, Courtenay and District Museum, Courtenay, BC.

38. Ruth Manary, "Reminiscence: Ruth Manary on Life at a Lincoln County Logging Camp in the 1920s," *Oregon Historical Quarterly* 92, no. 1 (1991): 77–79.

39. Ibid., 78.

40. Office of the Census, *1900 Census: Volume IX, Manufactures, Part 3: Special Reports on Selected Industries* (Washington, DC: Government Printing Office, 1902), 434, 817; Office of the Census, *1920 Census: Volume 9, Manufactures, 1919, Reports for States, with Statistics for Principal Cities*, manuscript census forms on microfilm, 1554.

41. Edward R. Murrow, quoted in Persico, *Edward R. Murrow*, 34.

42. Sperber, *Murrow*, 24.

Chapter 2. "The Prodigal Yield of the Surrounding Hills"

1. Description of McCleary based on and McCleary quote from Ernest Teagle, *Out of the Woods: The Story of McCleary* (Montesano, WA: Simpson Logging, 1956), 9.

2. Angelo M. Pellegrini, *American Dream: An Immigrant's Quest* (San Francisco: North Point, 1986), 7; Angelo M. Pellegrini, *Lean Years, Happy Years* (Seattle: Madrona, 1983), 1; Pellegrini, *American Dream*, 8.

3. Pellegrini, *American Dream*, 7.

4. Angelo M. Pellegrini, *The Unprejudiced Palate: Classic Thoughts on Food and the Good Life* (1948; New York: Modern Library Paperback, 2005), 31.

5. On the Kinseys, see David A. James, *Grisdale, Last of the Logging Camps: A Photo Story of Simpson Camps from 1890 into 1986* (Belfair, WA: Mason County Historical Society, 1986), 21–22.

6. Ibid.

7. Sam Churchill, *Big Sam: The True Story of a Timberman and His Family in the Heyday of Northwest Logging* (Portland, OR: Binford and Mort, 1965), 92, 94.

8. Hahn Neimand, in-person interview by author, Eugene, Oregon, November 14, 2018.

9. Ibid.

10. Neimand interview. On company stores in logging camps and company towns, see Linda Carlson, *Company Towns of the Pacific Northwest* (Seattle: University of Washington, 2003), 101–14.

11. Manary, "Reminiscence," 81.

12. Churchill, *Big Sam*, 75.

13. Ted Goodwin, *Stories of Western Loggers* (Chehalis, WA: Loggers World, 1977), 39; Louise Wagenknecht, *White Poplar, Black Locust* (Lincoln: University of Nebraska Press, 2003), 21.

14. Darby and Buchanan, quoted in Mackie, *Island Timber*, 265.

15. "Bordeaux News," *Camp and Mill News* (Seattle, WA), October 1920, 15; Mackie, *Island Timber*, 271.

16. Chelsea Rose and Mark Axel Tveskov, "The Carolina Company: Identity and Isolation in a Southwestern Oregon Mountain Refuge," *Oregon Historical Quarterly* 118, no. 1 (2017): 95; Kayley Bass, "The Hidden History of Western Washington Logging Camps: St. Paul and Tacoma Lumber Company's Camp #5 ca. 1934–1947" (master's thesis, Central Washington University, 2017), 73.

17. Leo Lind, "Tales of a Logging Railroad Brakeman," *Journal of Forest History* 21, no. 4 (1977): 221.

18. Davidson to McGregor, February 23, 1928, folder 2, box 4, acc. # Bx 136, Oregon-American Lumber Company Records, Special Collections, University of Oregon.

19. Mackie, *Island Timber*, 271–72.

20. Teagle, *Out of the Woods*, 35. On people finding barrels of moonshine in the forests, see Ronald L. Gregory, *Shevlin-Hixon Oral History Project: Life in Railroad Logging Camps of Central Oregon, 1916–1950* (Bend: Central Oregon Community College, 1996), 34, 81. On the Rio Dell fire, see Cornford, *Workers and Dissent*, 209.

21. Lois Gumpert interview, in R. L. Gregory, *Shevlin-Hixon Oral History Project*, 31; on baseball in timber country, see Keith C. Petersen, *Company Town: Potlatch, Idaho, and the Potlatch Lumber Company* (Pullman: Washington State University Press, 1987), 129–30.

22. Gumpert, interview, 32; Anna Lind, "Women in Early Logging Camps: A Personal Reminiscence," *Journal of Forest History* 19, no. 3 (1975): 133.

23. Frederick Bracher, "Fishing in Untroubled Waters," *Oregon Historical Quarterly* 93, no. 3 (1992): 295, 293, 299, 302.

24. Wagenknecht, *White Poplar, Black Locust*, 3, 161.

25. Irma Lee Emmerson, *The Woods Were Full of Men* (New York: David McKay, 1963), 1, 18.

26. *Oregonian*, September 5, 1920. On the long history of critiques of logging, see Cox, *Lumbermen's Frontier*. On the importance of automobiles in shaping views of the Northwest woods, see Lipin, *Workers and the Wild*.

27. For descriptions of the environmental problems associated with early twentieth-century logging, see White, *Land Use, Environment, and Social Change*; Langston, *Forest Dreams, Forest Nightmares*; Rajala, *Clearcutting*.

28. On attempts to limit fire through controlled burns of slash, see C. T. Dyrness, C. T. Youngberg, and Robert H. Ruth, "Some Effects of Logging and Slash Burning on Physical Soil Properties in the Corvallis Watershed," PNW Old Series Research Paper 19, Pacific Northwest Research Station, Portland, OR, Forest Service, *US Department of Agriculture*, May 1957, usda.gov; W. F. McCulloch, "Slash Burning," *The Forestry Chronicle* 20, no. 2 (1944): 111–18.

29. On the ecological changes that a post–slash burned forest undergoes, see Matt D. Busse, Ken R. Hubbert, and Emily E. Y. Moghaddas, "Fuel Reduction Practices and Their Effects on Soil Quality," General Technical Report PSW-GTR-241, Pacific Southwest Research Station, Albany, California, Forest Service, *US Department of Agriculture*, 2014, usda.gov; Brittany G. Johnson, Dale W. Johnson, Watkins W. Miller, and Erin M. Carroll-Moore, "The Effects of Slash Pile Burning on Soil and Water Macronutrients," *Soil Science* 176, no. 8 (2011): 413–25.

30. For a summary of forest succession research, see Norman L. Christensen Jr., "An Historical Perspective on Forest Succession and Its Relevance to Ecosystem Restoration and Conservation Practice in North America," *Forest Ecology and Management* 330 (2014): 312–22. In the Northwest, Jerry Franklin has done some of the most extensive and important research on forest succession. See, for instance, Jerry F. Franklin and Miles A. Hemstrom, "Aspects of Succession in the Coniferous Forests of the Pacific Northwest," in *Forest Succession: Concepts and Application*, ed. Darrell C. West, Herman H. Shugart, and Daniel B. Botkin (New York: Springer-Verlag, 1981), 212–29. The classic paper on succession is Eugene P. Odum, "The Strategy of Ecosystem Development," *Science* 164, no. 3877 (1969): 262–70.

31. On Native burning in the Northwest, see Robert Boyd, "Strategies of Indian Burning in the Willamette Valley," and Nancy J. Turner, "Time to Burn: Use of Fire to Enhance Resource Production by Aboriginal Peoples in British Columbia," both in *Indians, Fire, and the Land in the Pacific Northwest* (Corvallis: Oregon State University, 1999), 94–138, 185–213, respectively.

32. Mackie, *Island Timber*, 265.

33. Ibid.

34. Pellegrini, *Unprejudiced Palate*, 42, 207.

35. On Pellegrini's influence, see Ruth Reichl, "Angelo Pellegrini, a Slow-Food Voice in a Fast-Food Nation," *Seattle (WA) Weekly*, April 14, 2001; Don Duncan, "Angelo Pellegrini Dies—UW Prof, Author, Gourmet," *Seattle (WA) Times*, November 2, 1991; Roger Downey, "In Babbo's Garden," *Seattle (WA) Weekly*, August 17, 2005.

Chapter 3. "A Goodly Degree of Risk"

1. Dorothy Marie Sherman, "A Brief History of the Lumber Industry in the Fir Belt Area" (master's thesis, University of Oregon, 1934), 22. For histories of technological and managerial change in the Northwest timber industry, see Hak, *Capital and Labour in the British Columbia Forest Industry*; Rajala, *Clearcutting*, and "The Forest as Factory: Technological Change and Worker Control in the West Coast Logging Industry, 1880–1930," *Labour/Le Travail* 32 (Fall 1993): 73–104; Ken Drushka, *Working in the Woods: A History of Logging on the West Coast* (Madeira Park, BC: Harbour, 1992).

2. Oiva Wirkkala, interview by David L. Myers, September 22, 1976, transcript on microfilm, PAC 76–32dm, general stacks, Washington State Oral/Aural History Project (hereafter WSOAHP), University of Washington Libraries, Seattle, 12.

3. Ibid.

4. Ibid.

5. Ibid., 12–13.

6. Ibid.

7. Oiva Wirkkala, interviewed by KCTS9, "Loggers and Their Lore: Becoming a Tree Topper," 1987, *YouTube*, www.youtube.com, accessed May 7, 2021.

8. Rajala, *Clearcutting*, 18. On animal logging, see White, *Land Use, Environment, and Social Change*, 77–93.

9. On John Dolbeer and the invention of Dolbeer's Donkey, see H. Brett Melendy, "Two Men and a Mill: John Dolbeer, William Carson, and the Redwood Lumber Industry in California," *California Historical Quarterly* 38, no. 1 (1959): 64; on developments to steam donkeys after Dolbeer, see Rajala, *Clearcutting*, 20–29.

10. George H. Emerson, "Logging on Grays Harbor," *Timberman* 8, September 1907, 20.

11. Clarence Ross Garvey, "Overhead Systems of Logging in the Northwest," *The University of Washington Forest Club Annual* 2 (1914): 1–13; Van Tassel, *Mechanization in the Lumber Industry*, 12–14.

12. Van Tassel, *Mechanization*, 23–24; Bureau of the Census, *Census of Manufactures for 1914, Vol. I: Reports by States* (Washington, DC: Government Printing Office, 1918), special statistics for Oregon and Washington.

13. Egbert S. Oliver, "Sawmilling on Grays Harbor in the Twenties: A Personal Reminiscence," folder 275, box 6, acc. # Bx 199, International Woodworkers of America Papers, Special Collections, University of Oregon Library, Eugene, 2, 4, 25.

14. For histories of the forestry profession in North America, see Brock, *Money Trees*, 25–99; Rajala, *Clearcutting*, 51–80; Langston, *Forest Dreams, Forest Nightmares*, 86–113.

15. George L. Drake, interview by Elwood R. Maunder, "A Forester's Log: Fifty Years in the Pacific Northwest," transcript, 1958, 1961, 1967, 1968, Forest History Society, Durham, North Carolina, 16, 32.

16. George Peavy and Henry Suzzallo, quoted in Rajala, *Clearcutting*, 56, 59, respectively; University of Washington, *Catalogue for 1915–1916* (Seattle: Frank M. Lamborn, 1916), 283; University of Washington, *Catalogue of the University of Washington: 1919–1920* (Seattle: University of Washington Press, 1920), 132–34, 211.

17. Rajala, *Clearcutting*, 62.

18. W. H. Corbett, "The Era of the Big Drum Yarder," *Timberman* 7, April 1906, 33; Geoffrey C. Brown, "The Bedaux System," *American Federationist* 45 (1930): 942.

19. Square mileage calculated from H. M. Johnson, *Production of Lumber*; James Kingston, "Statistical Record of the Lumber Industry in BC," Bureau of Economics and Statistics, 1908–1962, spreadsheet, bound, University of British Columbia Library; US Department of Agriculture, US Forest Service, "Douglas Fir: An American Wood," FS-235, October 1984. The numbers given are actually a conservative estimate of total area cut between 1909 and 1929. Two largely unknown variables make it difficult to definitively state how much forestland the industry cut: the average amount of board feet in a square mile and the waste ratio. I used the most conservative estimates in calculating the figures.

20. Joseph Morgan, "The Development of Logging Engineering at the University of Washington," *University of Washington Forest Club Annual* 4 (1925): 43–44.

21. Ellery Walter, *The World on One Leg* (New York, 1928), 92; *Seattle (WA) Star*, April 9, 1913, 8; "A Freak Shingle Weaver," *Shingle Weaver* (Seattle, WA), May 19, 1917, 1.

22. On danger in the timber industry, see Prouty, *More Deadly Than War*.

23. Washington Department of Labor and Industries, Division of Industrial Insurance, The Workmen's Compensation Act, "Annual Reports, 1925–1929," spreadsheet, bound, University of Washington Libraries, Seattle.

24. Prouty, *More Deadly Than War*, 112–14.

25. Todes, *Labor and Lumber*, 48; *Shingle Weaver* (Seattle, WA), February 17, 1917, 1.

26. On hillside stability, see Steven G. Archie, *Clearcutting in the Douglas-Fir Region of the Pacific Northwest* (Pullman: Cooperative Extension Services of Washington State University, 1974); Donald H. Gray, *Effects of Forest Clear-Cutting in the Stability of Natural Slopes: Results of Field Studies* (Ann Arbor: University of Michigan, College of Engineering, 1973).

27. C. V. Wilson, "Logging Engineering," *West Coast Lumberman* 31 (March 1917): 112.

28. Roderick Haig-Brown, *Timber* (1942, Morrow; repr., Corvallis: Oregon State University Press, 1993), x.

29. Rajala, *Clearcutting*, 5.

30. Bill Inud, "Let Me Tell You—," in Finley Hays, *Lies, Logs, and Loggers* (Chehalis, WA: Loggers World, 1961), 3; Andrews, *Killing for Coal*, 162–68.

31. John Liboky Sr., interview by Steve Addington, August 8, 1975, transcript, KIT 75–44sa, WSOAHP, 1.

32. Peter Boag, *Same-Sex Affairs: Constructing and Controlling Homosexuality in the Pacific Northwest* (Berkeley: University of California Press, 2003), 26.

33. Walter, *World on One Leg*, 92.

34. Hays, *Lies, Logs, and Loggers*, 49. Loggers didn't just have the physiques of marathoners. Some were actually marathoners. In 1927 Johnny Southard, a Karuk man from northern California, won the Redwood Marathon, a grueling 480-mile footrace that started in the San Francisco Bay area and ended in Grants Pass, Oregon. Southard would go on to work as a chocker setter in the woods. See Tara Keegan, "Running the Redwood Empire: Indigeneity, Modernity, and a 480-Mile Footrace" (PhD diss., University of Oregon, 2021).

35. Haig-Brown, *Timber*, 403.

36. Charles Ames, quoted in Mark A. Gullickson, "Work Pants Worn by Loggers in Western Oregon, 1920–1970" (master's thesis, Oregon State University, 2000), 57–58.

37. Elrick B. Davis, "Paul Bunyan Talk," *American Speech* 17, no. 4 (1942): 217. See also Guy Williams, *Logger-Talk: Some Notes on the Jargon of the Pacific Northwest Woods* (Seattle: University of Washington Bookstore, 1930).

38. Jasper Chase, interview by Steve Addington, July 16, 1975, transcript, KIT 75–40sa, WSOAHP, 5; Donnie Zapp, quoted in John Vaillant, *The Golden Spruce: A True Story of Myth, Madness, and Greed* (New York: Norton, 2005), 131; Elijah H. Meece, interview by Michael A. Runestrand, June 16, 1967, transcript, KIT 75–42sa, WSOAHP, 3.

39. See Joseph Stoneburt, interview by Steve Addington, August 1, 1975, transcript, KIT 75–42sa, WSOAHP, 26.

40. Rotschy, "Three Months with the Timber Buffaloes: Notes and Reflexions [*sic*] from a Logging Camp in 1929," unpublished ms., folder 2, box 3, acc. no. 3298–005, Edgar Rotschy Papers, Special Collections, University of Washington, Seattle.

41. Bob Whitmarsh, Otto Oja, and Walls, quoted in Robert E. Walls, "The High-climber's Performance: Private Labor, Public Spectacle, and Occupational Tradition in the Pacific Northwest Timber Industry," *Western Folklore* 65 (Winter–Spring 2006): 177.

42. Rajala, "Forest as Factory," 96, "caprices in day's logging" quote; on Bloedel, Stewart, and Welch's problems with hook tenders, see S. G. Smith, interview by C. D. Orchard, box 3, Orchard Collection, British Columbia Archives and Records Service, Royal BC Museum, Victoria; "human element," from R. D. Merrill to S. A. Stanm, June 26, 1933, box 12, acc. 736, Merrill and Ring Lumber Company Records, University of Washington Libraries, Seattle.

43. Keith Thor Carlson and Kristian Fagan, eds., *"Call me Hank": A Stó:lō Man's Reflections on Logging, Living, and Growing Old* (Toronto: University of Toronto Press, 2006), 36; T. Jerome to T. D. Merill, August 4, 1909, box 3, Merrill and Ring Lumber Company Records.

44. Carlson and Fagan, *Call Me Hank*, 58; Inud, "Let Me Tell You," 3; Hays, *Lies, Logs, and Loggers*, 50, 88; Andrew Larson, interview by Steve Addington, September 15, 1975, transcript, KIT 75-49aa, WSOAHP, 16.

Chapter 4. "Conservation . . . from the Guys Down Below"

1. Churchill, *Big Sam*, 142–68.
2. Ibid.
3. Ibid., 150, 154.
4. Dexter M. Keezer, "Production, Employment, Wages and Prices in Douglas-Fir Lumber Industry," *Monthly Labor Review* 53 (October 1941): 849–61; Lee Maker interview, transcript, in R. L. Gregory, *Shevlin-Hixon Oral History Project*, 81.
5. McKenna and West, quoted in Robbins, *Hard Times in Paradise*, 82, 83.
6. Curt Beckham, *Gyppo Logging Days* (Myrtle Point, OR: Hillside, 1978), 10; Goodwin, *Stories of Western Loggers*, 92; McClellan, *R. A. Long's Planned City*, 201; Ruuttila, quoted in Polishuk, *Sticking to the Union*, 165–66.
7. Robbins, *Hard Times in Paradise*, 91, 88.
8. For Greeley's background, see William B. Greeley, *Forests and Men* (Garden City, NY: Doubleday, 1951); for a discussion of Greeley's relationship with the industry, see Robbins, *Lumberjacks and Legislators*, 90, 73, 187; on Franklin Roosevelt's history of conservation, see Neil M. Maher, *Nature's New Deal: The Civilian Conservation Corps and the Roots of the American Environmental Movement* (Oxford: Oxford University Press, 2008), 17–41.
9. Robert Marshall, *The Social Management of American Forests* (New York: League for Industrial Democracy, 1930), 6.
10. *A National Plan for American Forestry*, S. Doc. 12, 73rd Cong., 1st sess. (March 13, 1933), at 1:vi.
11. Colin Cameron, *Forestry . . . B.C.'s Devastated Industry* (Vancouver, BC: CCF, 1941), 2.
12. David M. Kennedy, *Freedom from Fear: The American People in Depression and War, 1929-1945* (New York: Oxford University Press, 2000), 135. On New Deal agricultural policy, see Sarah T. Phillips, *This Land, This Nation: Conservation, Rural America, and the New Deal* (Cambridge: Cambridge University Press, 2007).
13. Greeley, *Forests and Men*, 134. On the NIRA production codes and the timber industry, see Robbins, *Lumberjacks and Legislatures*, 177–81; Rajala, *Clearcutting*, 123–53.
14. NIRA lumber code, Rajala, *Clearcutting*, 18.
15. Greeley, *Forests and Men*, 134.

16. Ellery Foster, "Woodworkers and World Forestry," *Unasylva: A Magazine of Forestry and Forest Products* 1, no. 3 (1947): 8.

17. On Depression-era forestry politics in British Columbia, see Rajala, *Clearcutting*, 154–66.

18. Lembcke and Tattam, *One Union in Wood*, 18–22.

19. Ernie Dalskog, interview by Clay Perry, October 29, 1979, transcript, folder 5, box 275, Records of the International Woodworkers of America, Special Collections, University of Oregon, Eugene, 21, 42, 48, 56, 60.

20. On women's role in organizing campaigns and wildcat strikes, see Myrtle Bergren, *Tough Timber: The Loggers of B.C.—Their Story* (Toronto: Progress Books, 1967), 82–89. Bergren was a union activist in timber country, and she'd later play a significant role in organizing the Women's Auxiliary of the International Woodworkers of America.

21. D.O. [District Organizing] District #12 to Organizing Commission, June 22, 1933, and District Organizing Bulleting, December 12, 1933, reel 254, delo 3288, Communist Party of the United States of America Papers, Tamiment Library and Robert F. Wagner Labor Archives, NYU Libraries, New York University, New York; J. M. Clarke, quoted in Neufeld and Parnaby, *IWA in Canada*, 43.

22. Lembcke and Tattam, *One Union in Wood*, 26–30.

23. "Lumber Workers for Strike Action May 6," *Voice of Action* (Seattle, WA), April 19, 1935, 1, 6; "Labor Leaders Hope for Peaceful Settlement as Timber Strike Nears," *Seattle (WA) Post-Intelligencer*, April 28, 1935, 3.

24. "Many Mills Close after 15,000 Strike," *Seattle (WA) Post-Intelligencer*, May 7, 1935, 1; "17,000 Idle in Mill Strike," *Seattle (WA) Post-Intelligencer*, May 8, 1935, 1; "30,000 Out as Lumber Strike Spreads!" *Voice of Action* (Seattle, WA), May 10, 1935, 1; "N.W. Lumber Cut Off 52 Per Cent," *Tacoma (WA) News Tribune*, May 17, 1935, 2.

25. "Lumber Strikers in Revolt over Sell-Out Plan," *Voice of Action* (Seattle, WA), May 31, 1935, 1; "Radicals Blamed in Lumber Strike," *Seattle (WA) Post-Intelligencer*, June 5, 1935, 1; "Delegates Meet in Aberdeen to Form N.W. Strike Committee; Longview Mills Down," *Voice of Action* (Seattle, WA), June 6, 1935, 1.

26. "Mill Men Voting on New Plan," *Tacoma (WA) News Tribune*, August 3, 1935, 1; "Back To Mills Again," *Tacoma (WA) News Tribune*, August 5, 1935, 1; "Union Wins 60 Cents per Hr. Minimum," *Voice of Action* (Seattle, WA), August 23, 1935, 3.

27. Jeanne Meyers Williams, "Ethnicity and Class Conflict at Maillardville / Fraser Mills: The Strike of 1931" (master's thesis, Simon Fraser University, 1982), 23–44; Fred Wilson, "A Woodworker's Story: Harold Pritchett Recalls IWA's Militant History," *Pacific Tribune* (British Columbia), April 29, 1977, 12–13.

28. On the CIO broadly, see Robert Zieger, *The CIO: 1935–1955* (Chapel Hill: University of North Carolina Press, 1995). For Pritchett on the importance of transborder unionism, see Harold Pritchett, "Our Bosses Are the Same on Both Sides of the International Border, So Why Not Our Unions?" *BC Lumber Worker*, August 8, 1940, 3.

29. Lembcke and Tattam, *One Union in Wood*, 26–30.

30. Federation of Woodworkers, *Proceedings of Special Convention of the Federation of Woodworkers* (Tacoma, WA, July 15–19, 1937), 72.

31. Frank Duffy, quoted in Margaret S. Glock, *Collective Bargaining in the Pacific Northwest Lumber Industry* (Berkeley, CA: Institute of Industrial Relations, 1955), 13. See also Lembcke and Tattam, *One Union in Wood*, 55; IWA executive board meeting minutes, November 2, 1937, folder 14, box 2, IWA Papers.

32. Ruuttila, quoted in Polishuk, *Sticking to the Union*, 46; "Portland I.W. of A. Women Don't Fear Goon Squads," *Timber Worker*, September 18, 1937, 1.

33. G. D. Meek, "Conservation—A Duty to Posterity," *Timber Worker*, April 9, 1938; "Forestry," *B.C. Lumber Worker*, November 24, 1937.

34. Don Hamerquist, "Timber Is a Crop?" *Timber Worker*, April 16, 1938; "Support Grows for Selective Logging," *Timber Worker*, October 22, 1938.

35. On early efforts to protect Olympic National Park, see David Louter, *Windshield Wilderness: Cars, Roads, and Nature in Washington's National Parks* (Seattle: University of Washington Press, 2006), 68–75; Carsten Lien, *Olympic Battleground: Creating and Defending Olympic National Park*, 2nd ed. (Seattle, WA: Mountaineers, 2000).

36. Lien, *Olympic Battleground*, 2–54.

37. Ibid.

38. Ibid.; Barry Mackintosh, "Harold L. Ickes and the National Park Service," *Forest & Conservation History* 29, no. 2 (1985): 78–84.

39. C. J. Buck, quoted in Ben W. Twight, *Organizational Values and Political Power: The Forest Service Versus the Olympic National Park* (University Park: Pennsylvania State University, 1983), 62; Mount Olympus National Park, Hearings before the Committee on The Public Lands House of Representatives, 74th Cong., 2nd sess. (1936), 253 (statement of Hon. Harold L. Ickes, secretary of the interior). On local opposition to the park, see "Hoh River News," *Forks (WA) Forum*, June 2, 1938.

40. Minutes of Executive Board Meeting of the IWA, October 31, 1937, folder 14, box 2, IWA Papers.

41. John Coffee, in IWA, *Proceedings of the Second Constitutional Convention of the International Woodworkers of America* (Seattle, Washington, September 12–16, 1938), 123. See also "Huge Throng on Hand to Meet President Here," *Everett (WA) Daily Herald*, June 10, 1938, 1, 7; "Everett in Readiness to Greet President," *Everett (WA) Daily Herald*, June 9, 1938, 1.

42. Harold Pritchett, in IWA, *Proceedings of the Third Constitutional Convention of the International Woodworkers of America* (Klamath Falls, Oregon, October 4–8, 1939), 25.

43. War Manpower Commission, *War Labor Reports* (Washington, DC: Bureau of National Affairs, 1943), 1:151, 2:1–19; "A New Spruce Division?" *International Woodworker*, March 10, 1943, 3; "Freeze Plan Seen as 'Escape' for Rich," *International Woodworker*, October 3, 1943, 7.

44. J. C. Hill and H. D. Bloch, "Report on Wage Stabilization Activities of the West Coast Lumber Commission" (Washington, DC: National War Labor Board, March

28, 1944); National War Labor Board, news releases: B-586, April 18, 1943, B-1123, November 19, 1943, B-1600, June 23, 1944, and Officers' Report, IWA, *Proceedings of the Eighth Constitutional Convention of the International Woodworkers of America* (Vancouver, British Columbia, October 24, 1944), 18.

45. Robert Cantwell, *Land of Plenty* (1934; Seattle, WA: Pharos, 2013), 5. For more cultural products depicting Northwest timber workers in the Depression era, see Louis H. Colman, "The Oiler," *New Masses*, March 1928, 12–26, and "The Marker," *New Masses*, April 1928, 14–32. For more on the Northwest proletarian literature of the Depression era, see Goings, Barnes, and Snider, *Red Coast*, 133–40; T. V. Reed, *Robert Cantwell and the Literary Left: A Northwest Writer Reworks American Fiction* (Seattle: University of Washington Press, 2014).

46. Haig-Brown, *Timber*, 16, 22, 340.

Chapter 5. "The Many Uses and Values of Forests"

1. For Foster's biography, see president's report, IWA, *Proceedings of the Ninth Constitutional Convention* (Eugene, OR: November 13, 1945), 180–81; executive board meeting minutes, August 2, 1945, folder 13, box 14, IWA Papers.

2. Ellery Foster, "The New Age of Wood," *International Woodworker*, June 27, 1946, 1, and "Woodworkers and World Forestry," 8.

3. Statistics on lumber production in US Department of Commerce, Bureau of the Census, *Census of Manufactures: 1947, Vol. 2, Statistics by Industries* (Washington, DC: Government Printing Office, 1948), 265. On IWA growth, bargaining, and carpenters in the postwar era, see John L. Dana, "Bargaining in the Western Lumber Industry: Negotiations Have Become Increasingly Industrywide as Contracts Approach Uniformity in Content," *Monthly Labor Review*, August 1965, 925–31.

4. On timber-industry changes in the postwar period, see Hak, *Capital and Labour in the British Columbia Forest Industry*, 147–54.

5. Carlson, *Company Towns*, 204.

6. On Goetz's influence and contributions to union newspapers broadly, see Gene Klare, "Let me say this about that," *Northwest Labor Press* (Seattle, WA), March 1, 2002, 6. Goetz's column in the IWA paper was called "About Open Spaces." For examples, see *International Woodworker*, December 26, 1956, May 22, 1957, and November 28, 1957.

7. James Falding, "President's Column," *International Woodworker*, August 26, 1945.

8. James Falding, "Rebuilding and Conserving Our Wood Crop—Another Must," *International Woodworker*, June 27, 1945, 7. On the forestry profession before and after the war, see Brock, *Money Trees*.

9. Ellery Foster, "On Working for a Labor Union," *Journal of Forestry* 44, no. 7 (1946): 475.

10. Ellery Foster, "The Development of Rural Land-Use Planning Committees: A Historical Sketch," *Journal of the American Institute of Planners* 8 (Spring 1942):

8, emphasis in original. On agrarian intellectualism, see Jess Gilbert, *Planning Democracy: Agrarian Intellectuals and the Intended New Deal* (New Haven, CT: Yale University Press, 2015).

11. International Woodworkers of America, *Proceedings of the Ninth Constitutional Convention* (Eugene, OR, November 13, 1945), 23, 227, 285–334.

12. "Resolution no. 29: Regional and Local Natural Resources Planning," ibid., 303. On the history of sustained-yield forestry, see Brock, *Money Trees*, 139–46; Robert O. Curtis, et al., "Silvicultural Research and the Evolution of Forest Practices in the Douglas-Fir Region," General Technical Report PNW-GTR-696 (USDA, Forest Service—Pacific Northwest Research Station, June 2007), 1–18; Langston, *Forest Dreams, Forest Nightmares*, 168–69. Some historians have credited USFS forester David Mason for introducing the modern concept of sustained-yield forestry to the profession in the 1920s. See Elmo Richardson, *David T. Mason, Forestry Advocate: His Role in the Application of Sustained Yield Management to Private and Public Forest Lands* (Durham, NC: Forest History Society, 1983).

13. Ellery Foster, "Lumber Snafu," *Journal of Forestry* 44, no. 6 (1946): 394, 395, 396.

14. Ibid., 399.

15. James Falding, "Statement of IWA Officers on the Problems of Forestry," *International Woodworker*, December 26, 1945, 4; reports of *Lumber Snafu*'s circulation in "Woodworkers Security Depend upon Success of Natl. Forestry Program," *International Woodworker*, February 6, 1946, 4; and "Senators Act on IWA Plea," *International Woodworker*, June 23, 1946, 2.

16. Mary Louise Hook Allen, *Fightin' Frank: The Biography of Upper Peninsula's 12th District Democratic Congressman* (Self-published, 2001), 39–66.

17. Ibid.

18. 92 Cong. Rec., part 10, appendix A2137 (1946) (extension of remarks of Hon. Frank E. Hook); explanation of bill based on Ellery Foster, "Forestry Department," *International Woodworker*, May 22, 1946, 2.

19. "Statement of IWA International Officers on the Problems of Forestry," *International Woodworker*, December 26, 1945, 4.

20. Independent Landowners Association, "Attention All Landowners: Important Facts You Need to Know about the Hook Forest Dictatorship Bill," *Escanaba (MI) Daily Press*, September 28, 1946, 3; Richard L. Neuberger, "The Woodmen and the Trees," *Nation*, October 5, 1946, 379.

21. "Congressman Defends His Forestry Bill at Labor Parley," *Escanaba (MI) Daily Press*, August 28, 1946, 7; CIO pro-forestry resolution quoted in Ellery Foster, "Hook Bill: For Sportsmen and Outdoor Enthusiasts, Too," *International Woodworker*, July 3, 1946, 2; on the CIO's stance on forestry prior to 1946, see "Forestry Program Resolution Adopted by CIO Convention," *International Woodworker*, February 28, 1945, 1; on the UAW's environmental politics, see Montrie, *Making a Living*, 91–112.

22. "Forestry 'Battle of the Century' Opens in Oregon-Skirmish Held in State Grange Hall," *International Woodworker*, July 17, 1946, 1; Neuberger, "Woodmen and

the Trees," 378; on environmentalist support for IWA and the Hook Bill, see Foster, "Hook Bill," 2, and Ellery Foster, "Hook and Thom Bills Add Up to a National Forestry Program," *International Woodworker*, May 29, 1946, 2.

23. Foster, "Hook and Thom Bills," 2.

24. On the CCF in postwar British Columbia, see Benjamin Isitt, *Militant Minority: British Columbia Workers and the Rise of a New Left, 1948–1972* (Toronto, ON: University of Toronto Press, 2011), 44–83; on Cameron, see ibid., 30, 98–99.

25. Cameron, *Forestry*, 13, 9.

26. Royal Commission on Forestry, GR 520, vol. 14, box 5, Royal Commission on Forestry, British Columbia Archives, Royal BC Museum, Victoria, British Columbia, 5336–51, 5348–49, 5365–66. On the Sloan Commission more broadly, see Scott Prudham, "Sustaining Sustained Yield: Class, Politics and Post-War Forest Regulation in British Columbia," *Environment and Planning D: Society and Space* 25 (2007): 258–83; Hak, *Capital and Labour in the British Columbia Forest Industry*, 50–51; Patricia Marchak, *Green Gold: The Forest Industry in British Columbia* (Vancouver: University of British Columbia Press, 1983), 35–39.

27. E. T. Kinney, quoted in Hak, *Capital and Labour in the British Columbia Forest Industry*, 51.

28. "Fire Blackened Stumps or Perpetual Forests?" *BC Lumber Worker*, March 12, 1947.

29. For the IWA's organizing efforts in the US South, see "International Officers' Report," International Woodworkers of America, *Proceedings of the Tenth Constitutional Convention* (Portland, Oregon, September 10, 1946), 201–7. For more on the IWA's role in Operation Dixie, see Jones, *Tribe of Black Ulysses*, 151–80.

30. Allen, *Fightin' Frank*, 15–35. After the defeat of the Hook Bill, the IWA passed a resolution at its 1946 constitutional convention calling on membership to continue fighting for the legislation. See "Resolution No. 17, Next Steps in IWA Wood Industries Program," IWA, *Proceedings of the Tenth Constitutional Convention*, 277.

31. Lembcke and Tattam, *One Union in Wood*, 117–34.

32. Hak, *Capital and Labour in the British Columbia Forest Industry*, 64–66. See also Isitt, *Militant Minority*, 3–18.

33. Ellery Foster to Denny Scott, April 9, 1977, folder 25, box 300, IWA Papers.

34. On increase in public lands harvest, see "FY 1905–2017 National Summary Cut and Sold Data and Graphs," *USDA Forestry Service*, https://www.fs.fed.us/, accessed December 4, 2019; on public lands harvest in Oregon, see Alicia Andrews and Kristin Kutara, *Oregon's Timber Harvest, 1849–2004* (Salem: Oregon Department of Forestry, 2005); on rise in employment, see Josh Lehner, "Historical Look at Oregon's Wood Product Industry," *Oregon Office of Economic Analysis*, January 23, 2012, oregoneconomicanalysis.com, accessed December 4, 2019; on the rise of "gyppo" logging, see Robert E. Walls, "Lady Loggers and Gyppo Wives: Women and Northwest Logging," *Oregon Historical Quarterly* 103, no. 3 (2002): 362–82.

35. Hirt, *Conspiracy of Optimism*, 44–170.

36. IWA, *Proceedings of the 14th Constitutional Convention of the International Woodworkers of America* (1951), 271.

37. Howard Zahniser, as quoted in Marsh, *Drawing Lines in the Forest*, 29. On the Wilderness Society's early members, see Paul S. Sutter, *Driven Wild: How the Fight against Automobiles Launched the Modern Wilderness Movement* (Seattle: University of Washington Press, 2002).

38. Al Hartung, "President's Column," *International Woodworker*, January 12, 1955, 6; "Minority Report, February 1954," *Hearing before the Subcommittee on Irrigation and Reclamation of the Committee on Interior and Insular Affairs*, 89th Cong., 1st sess. (1966), 312 (Olympic National Park Review Committee).

39. Marsh, *Drawing Lines in the Forest*, 19–37.

40. Hartung, "President's Column," 6; Onthank quoted in Michael Pebworth, "Evergreen Struggle: Federal Wilderness Preservation, Populism, and Liberalism in Washington State, 1935–1984," (PhD diss., University of Oregon, 2003), 138.

41. Onthank quoted in Marsh, *Drawing Lines in the Forest*, 34; *Redmond (OR) Spokesman* and *Eugene (OR) Register-Guard*, quoted in ibid., 36.

42. Senate Committee on Interior Affairs, *National Wilderness Preservation Act: Hearings*, 85th Cong., 2nd sess. (1958), 435–38.

43. Stewart Holbrook, "Daylight in the Swamp," in *Wobblies, Wildmen, and Whistle Punks: Stewart Holbrook's Lowbrow Northwest*, ed. Brian Booth (Corvallis: Oregon State University Press, 1992), 69. See also Stewart Holbrook, *Holy Old Mackinaw: A Natural History of the American Lumberjack* (New York: Macmillan, 1956). For a sample of Murray Morgan's writings, see Morgan, *Skid Road: An Informal Portrait of Seattle* (repr.; Seattle: University of Washington, 1983), and *Puget's Sound: A Narrative of Early Tacoma and the Southern Sound* (repr.; Seattle: University of Washington Press, 2003).

44. *Paul Bunyan* (Walt Disney Studios, Buena Vista, 1956), film reel. On Paul Bunyan mythology, see John Patrick Harty, "Legendary Landscapes: A Cultural Geography of the Paul Bunyan and Blue Ox Phenomenon of the Northwoods," (PhD diss., Kansas State University, 2007).

45. *International Woodworker*, July 16, 1949.

Chapter 6. "Strong Winds and Widow Makers"

1. Matt Love, *Sometimes a Great Movie: Paul Newman, Ken Kesey, and the Filming of the Great Oregon Novel* (South Beach, OR: Nestucca Spit, 2012).

2. Ibid., 23, 73–76, 96–109.

3. For a cultural analysis of how the image of the working class changed in the 1970s and beyond, see Cowie, *Stayin' Alive*.

4. Asian lumber demands and export figures from Jean M. Daniels, "The Rise and Fall of the Pacific Northwest Log Export Market," Gen. Tech. Report PNW-GTR-624, USDA, US Forest Service, Pacific Northwest Research Station (February 2005); IWA membership figures, see "Delegate Handbook, 1981–2," box 54, region 3, IWA Papers.

5. On the changing economy of the 1970s, see Judith Stein, *Pivotal Decade: How the United States Traded Factories for Finance in the Seventies* (New Haven, CT: Yale University Press, 2010); David Harvey, *A Brief History of Neoliberalism* (Oxford: Oxford University Press, 2005).

6. William White and Vincent Conway, "Futures Trading Can Lessen Risk in Plywood Market," *Forest Industries*, January 1970, 40.

7. William Davis, "Expanding Operations Result in New Logging Concept," *Forest Industries*, March 1971, 40. On the rise of real estate speculation on Northwest forestland, see Devon McCurdy, "Upstream Influence: The Economy, the State, and Oregon's Landscape, 1860–2000 (PhD diss., University of Washington, 2013), 246–48.

8. *Seattle (WA) Post-Intelligencer*, April 8, 1984; wage rates and information about Weyerhaeuser in "Southern Story Told to Region 3 Members," *International Woodworker*, April 21, 1976.

9. State of Oregon, Employment Department, "Workforce and Economic Research," 2008, spreadsheet; Robbins, *Hard Times*, 168.

10. Marcus R. Widenor, "Diverging Patterns: Labor in the Pacific Northwest Wood Products Industry," *Industrial Relations* 34, no. 3 (1995): 450–53. See also Marchak, *Green Gold*.

11. Fernie Valie, quoted in Widenor, "Diverging Patterns," 453.

12. Bill Prochnau, "Woodworkers Union Strikes Weyerhaeuser," *Washington Post*, June 17, 1986. See also Widenor, "Diverging Patterns," 450–55.

13. Keith Johnson, "Destroying Some Myths," *International Woodworker*, July 23, 1986, 1; "L-P to Tillamook: We Don't Owe You a Thing," *International Woodworker*, May 27, 1983, 8; Jim Lowery, phone interview with author, March 16, 2017.

14. On the IWA split, see Neufeld and Parnaby, *IWA in Canada*, 190–261.

15. Andrews and Kutara, *Oregon's Timber Harvests*, 4–5.

16. W. Scott Prudham, "Downsizing Nature: Managing Risk and Knowledge Economies through Production Subcontracting in the Oregon Logging Sector," *Environment and Planning* A34 (2002): 145–66. The origin of the term "gyppo" is debated. Some claim that the term stems from the fact that independent contractors were often "gypped" when it came time to collect their fees or that they often "gypped" their workers on payday. Others have suggested that independent contract loggers were constantly moving from job site to job site, like "gypsies." Given that nearly all explanations for the term's origins are deeply problematic, I've chosen to only refer to "gyppo loggers" as independent contractors. On the history of independent contract logging in the Northwest, see Walls, "Lady Loggers and Gyppo Wives."

17. Prudham, "Downsizing Nature," 149–50.

18. Dick Gilkison, in person interview with author, Cottage Grove, Oregon, December 30, 2019.

19. Ibid.

20. Ibid.

21. On the shift to smaller, family-owned mills, see J. Douglas Brodie, Robert O. McMahon, and William H. Gavelis, "Oregon's Forest Resources: Their Contribution in the State's Economy," research bulletin 23 (Corvallis: Oregon State University, 1978),

10–17; Charles E. Cline, "The Industrial Forester and the Changing Face of Timber Harvesting," *Journal of Forestry* 72, no. 11 (1974): 692–95. On Roseburg Lumber, see "Kenneth W. Ford," Roseburg, spec. ed., *Woodsman*, 1998, 2–15; Beverly A. Brown, *In Timber Country: Working People's Stories of Environmental Conflict and Urban Flight* (Philadelphia: Temple University Press, 1995), 99, 106.

22. On the changing demography of the rural Northwest, see B. A. Brown, *In Timber Country*, 3–35.

23. Tom McCall, quoted in Brent Walth, *Fire at Eden's Gate: Tom McCall and the Oregon Story* (Portland: Oregon Historical Society Press, 1994), 314. On California "equity migrants," see also B. A. Brown, *In Timber Country*, 12–13.

24. Victoria Sturtevant, "Impacts on Neighborhoods/Communities of the Bureau of Land Management Medford District Office's Resource Management Plan / Environmental Impact Statement Alternative," Medford District, Bureau of Land Management, December 1991, folder 9, box 51, acc. coll 317, Jefferson Center for Education and Research Records, 1935–2009, Special Collections, University of Oregon; B. A. Brown, *In Timber Country*, 101–2, 160.

25. B. A. Brown, *In Timber Country*, 160; "The Commune Comes to America," *Life*, July 18, 1969, 21. On communes in Oregon more broadly, see Kylie Young, "Mystical Science in a Matriarchal World: Oregon's Lesbian Separatist Communes and Female Nature, 1970–1990" (MA thesis, University of British Columbia, 2017); James Kopp, *Eden within Eden: Oregon's Utopian Heritage* (Corvallis: Oregon State University Press, 2009), 135–49.

26. "Many People of the World Are Sad, Mao Tse Tung Is Dead," *Together* 2, no. 4, 1976, 38; Gravy Rufkum, "Business as Usual," *Together* 1, no. 2, 1974, 1; Bodhiishvar, "Purification," *Together*. 2, no. 1, 1975, 1; Mike Bregsal to David Ellerman, October 11, 1979, folder 1, box 1, acc. coll 322, Hoedads Cooperative Inc., Records, Special Collections, University of Oregon, Eugene; Bob Zybach, in-person interview with author, Cottage Grove, Oregon, December 22, 2019.

27. Bodhiishvar, "Purification," *Together* 2, no. 1, 1975, 1; Wolfgang, "Please, Mr. Spaceman," *Together*, 1978–79, 2. On the IWA and the Hoedads, see Loomis, *Empire of Timber*, 180–91.

28. Theresa A. Satterfield, "Pawns, Victims, or Heroes: The Negotiation of Stigma and the Plight of Oregon's Loggers," *Journal of Social Issues* 52, no. 1 (1996): 73, 74, 77; Beverly Brown, quoted in Matthew S. Carroll, *Community and the Northwestern Logger: Continuities and Changes in the Era of the Spotted Owl* (Boulder, CO: Westview, 1995), 132.

29. For histories of the 1960s middle-class, urban environmental movement, see Adam Rome, *The Bulldozer in the Countryside: Suburban Sprawl and the Rise of American Environmentalism* (Cambridge: Cambridge University Press, 2001). On the relationships between the antiwar and civil rights movements and the environmental movement, see Keith Makoto Woodhouse, *The Ecocentrists: A History of Radical Environmentalism* (New York: Columbia University Press, 2018), 29–34.

30. Gary Snyder, *Myths and Texts* (1960; New York: New Directions, 1978), 4; David Shetzline, *Heckletooth 3* (New York: Random, 1969).

31. Ken Kesey, *Sometimes a Great Notion* (New York: Penguin, 1964).

32. Ibid., 529.

33. For Kesey's biography, including his history of drug use, see Rick Dodgson, *It's All a Kind of Magic: The Young Ken Kesey* (Madison: University of Wisconsin Press, 2013). For a discussion of Kesey's Okie roots, see James N. Gregory, *American Exodus: The Dust Bowl Migration and Okie Culture in California* (New York: Oxford University Press, 1989), 248.

34. On film and television portrayals of the rural working class, see Cowie, *Stayin' Alive*, 170–71.

35. Steve Prefontaine, quoted in Tom Jordan, *Pre: The Story of America's Greatest Running Legend Steve Prefontaine* (Emmaus, PA: Rodale, 1977), 72.

36. Ibid., 134.

37. Marty Liquori, "Prefontaine: What He Was Really Like," *New York Times*, June 8, 1975, 202; *Life* magazine, quoted in Robbins, *Hard Times*, 10; Steve Prefontaine, quoted in Jordan, *Pre*, 109.

38. Jerry Van Dyke, quoted in Liquori, "Prefontaine," 202.

39. On the cultural impact of southern migrants to timber country, see Robert Hunt Ferguson, "Tarheel Country in the Pacific Northwest," *Pacific Northwest Quarterly* 112, no. 2 (2021): 55–67; on Loretta Lynn, see James N. Gregory, *The Southern Diaspora: How the Great Migrations of Black and White Southerners Transformed America* (Chapel Hill: University of North Carolina Press, 2005), 175–78; on Willie Nelson, see Willie Nelson and David Ritz, *It's a Long Story: My Life* (New York: Little, Brown, 2015), 89–108; on country music and the White working class, see Cowie, *Stayin' Alive*, 167–209.

40. Curt Deatherage, "Buzz Martin, the 'Singing Logger,'" *Creswell's History* 24, October 2001, 1, 4; for Martin's biography, also see Leslie A. Johnson, "Logging Songs of the Pacific Northwest: A Study of Three Contemporary Artists," (MA thesis, Florida State University, 2007), 17–36.

41. Johnson, "Logging Songs of the Pacific Northwest," 21.

42. Buzz Martin, "There Walks a Man," *Where There Walks a Logger, There Walks a Man*, Ripcord Records, SLP-001, 1968.

43. Buzz Martin, "Strong Winds and Widow Makers," *Loggers Reward*, Ripcord Records, SLP-002, 1969.

44. On Merle Haggard and 1960s and 1970s country music, see Cowie, *Stayin' Alive*, 167–209; J. N. Gregory, *American Exodus*, 238–45.

45. Betty Dennison, "Learning Loggers Live—But What Does It Mean?" *Learning Loggers Live: Official Proceedings of the Oregon Logging Conference* (Eugene, Oregon, February 1980), 33.

46. Greg Nagle to Richard B. Rambo, March 28, 1980, folder 13, box 1, acc. coll 322, Hoedads Cooperative Inc., Records, Special Collections, University of Oregon, Eugene.

47. Ibid. See also Greg Nagle to Josephine County Board of Commissioners, March 28, 1980, ibid.

Chapter 7. "Tie a Yellow Ribbon for the Working Man"

1. Wilbur Heath, in-person interview by author, Cottage Grove, Oregon, December 20, 2019.

2. Ibid.

3. "Endangered Species," *Life*, January 1991; Heath interview.

4. Heath interview.

5. Ibid. The story of how Forsman became interested in the owl is told in Dietrich, *Final Forest*, 52–54.

6. Eric D. Forsman et al., *Population Demography of the Northern Spotted Owl* (Berkeley: University of California Press, 2011); Eric D. Forsman, E. Charles Meslow, and Howard M. Wight, "Distribution and Biology of the Spotted Owl in Oregon," *Wildlife Monographs* 87 (April 1984): 3–64; Eric D. Forsman, "Habitat Utilization by Spotted Owls in the West-Central Cascades of Oregon" (PhD diss., Oregon State University, 1980).

7. Discussion of Thomas's comments in Bob Zybach, *Historical Overview of Columbia Gorge Forestlands: Dynamics and Fragmentation, 1792–1996* (Corvallis, OR: NW Maps, 1996), 44; "Habitat Management for the Spotted Owl," planning report, Pacific Northwest Region, US Department of Agriculture, US Forest Service, April 1987, 23. On the difficulties of locating spotted owls and making overall habitat projections, see Andrew B. Carey, J. Reid, and S. Horton, "Spotted Owl Home Range and Habitat Use in Southern Oregon Coast Ranges," *Journal of Wildlife Management* 54, no. 1 (1990): 11–17.

8. Andy Kerr, in-person interview with author, Ashland, Oregon, August 1, 2018. For one account of Kerr being hung in effigy, see Timothy Egan, *Lasso the Wind: Away to the New West* (New York: Vintage, 1998), 194–211. Most environmental historians have almost certainly read of Kerr—they've just forgotten about it. Kerr is cited in Richard White's widely read and oft-quoted-from essay about work and nature as an example of an environmentalist who ignores work. See White, "Are You an Environmentalist," 172–73.

9. Heath interview; Kerr interview. On "crisis environmentalism," see Woodhouse, *Ecocentrists*, 54–94. See also Jacob Darwin Hamblin, *Arming Mother Nature: The Birth of Catastrophic Environmentalism* (New York: Oxford University Press, 2013); Frederick Buell, *From Apocalypse to Way of Life: Environmental Crisis in the American Century* (New York: Routledge, 2003).

10. Mississippi quote in Jeff Mapes, "Andy Kerr, the Lighting Rod of the Oregon Timber Wars, Now Plays Behind-the-Scenes Role in D.C.," *Oregonian*, August 21, 2015, https://www.oregonlive.com/, accessed June 3, 2019; Kerr interview.

11. Kerr interview. For a brief history of human thought on owls, see Dietrich, *Final Forest*, 53, 57. As Dietrich points out, though, a deep affinity for owls may be a purely Western phenomenon. Dietrich explains that in many parts of Africa, owls are considered a nuisance and routinely killed on sight.

12. On the history and definitions of "old growth," see Sabina Burrascano, "On the Terms Used to Refer to 'Natural' Forests: A Response to Veen et al.," *Biodiversity*

Conservation 19 (2010): 3301–5; Christian Wirth, Christian Messier, Yves Bergeron, Dorothea Frank, and Anja Kahl, "Old-Growth Forest Definitions: A Pragmatic View," in *Old-Growth Forests*, ed. C. Wirth, G. Gleixner, and M. Heimann, Ecological Studies 207 (New York: Springer-Verlag, 2009), 11–33, https://doi.org/10.1007/978-3-540-92706-8_2; Pacific Northwest Research Station, "New Findings about Old-Growth Forests," *Science Update* 4 (June 2003): 1–11; Jerry F. Franklin et al., "Ecological Characteristics of Old-Growth Douglas-Fir Forests," General Technical Report PNW-118, Pacific Northwest Forest and Range Experiment Station, Portland, Oregon, US Department of Agriculture, US Forest Service, 1981.

13. Kerr interview. See also Andy Kerr, "Starting the Fight and Finishing the Job," in *Old Growth in a New World: A Pacific Northwest Icon Reexamined*, ed. Thomas A. Spies and Sally L. Duncan (Washington, DC: Island, 2009), 134. Rather than "ancient forests," Kerr preferred the term "primeval forests," from a Henry Wadsworth Longfellow poem. Monteith countered that people might interpret "primeval" as "prime evil," so the ONRC went with "ancient forest."

14. "Jazz Artist Performs at Protest," *Democrat-Herald* (Albany, OR), May 27, 1986.

15. "Cutting Trees, Losing Forests," *Oregon Business*, May 1986; Christy Duncan, "Owl Politics," *Democrat Herald* (Albany, OR), October 3, 1986; "Habitat Management for the Spotted Owl."

16. "Rock Creek Wilderness," US Forest Service, *US Department of Agriculture*, https://www.fs.usda.gov/recarea/siuslaw/, accessed February. 28, 2021.

17. On FSEEE and some of the problems of USFS land management in the late twentieth century more broadly, see Hirt, *Conspiracy of Optimism*, 266–92; Heath interview.

18. Jim Standard, quoted in James D. Proctor, "Whose Nature? The Contested Moral Terrain of Ancient Forests," in *Uncommon Ground: Rethinking the Human Place in Nature*, ed. William Cronon (New York: Norton, 1996), 270–71; John Kuzman, "Local Groups React to Timber Summit Proposal Rejection," folder 52, box 2, Liz VanLeeuwen Spotted Owl Collection, Special Collections and Archives, Oregon State University, Corvallis.

19. David Keiser, quoted in Benjamin B. Stout, *The Northern Spotted Owl: An Oregon View, 1975–2002* (Victoria, BC: Trafford, 2003), 58. On the Northwest's pre-Columbian forests, see Bob Zybach, "The Great Fires: Indian Burning and Catastrophic Forest Fire Patterns of the Oregon Coast Range, 1461–1951" (PhD diss., Oregon State University, 2003); "Voices of the Forest: An Interview with Bob Zybach," *Evergreen* (March–April, 1994); Peter D. A. Teensma, John T. Rienstra, and Mark A. Yeiter, "Preliminary Reconstruction and Analysis of Change in Forest Stand Age Classes of the Oregon Coast Range from 1850 to 1940," technical note T/N OR-9, filing code 9217, Bureau of Land Management, US Department of Interior, October 1991; Russell G. Congalton, Kass Green, and John Teply, "Mapping Old Growth Forests on National Forest and Park Lands in the Pacific Northwest from Remotely Sensed Data," *Photogrammetric Engineering and Remote Sensing* 59, no. 4 (1993): 529–35.

20. "Cutting Trees, Losing Forests," *Oregon Business*, May 1986; Carroll, *Community and the Northwestern Logger*, 132; Heath interview.

21. Troy Reinhart, "The Truth about Our Ancient Forests," *Evergreen* 9, no. 3 (1989). On the Ancient Forest Alliance, see Stout, *Northern Spotted Owl*, 56–57; Native Forest Society, "End the Chainsaw Massacre," in Proctor, "Whose Nature," 272, emphasis in original.

22. Shannon Peterson, "Congress and Charismatic Megafauna: A Legislative History of the Endangered Species Act," *Environmental Law* 29, no. 2 (1999): 467.

23. On the history of Earth First! and its political and cultural influences and its early activism in both the Southwest and Northwest, see Woodhouse, *Ecocentrists*; Speece, *Defending Giants*.

24. Dave Foreman and Bill Haywood, eds., *Ecodefense: A Field Guide to Monkey-wrenching*, 2nd ed. (Tucson, AZ: Ned Ludd, 1987), 27; song titles and lyrics from Steve Ongerth, *Redwood Uprising: From One Big Union to Earth First! and the Bombing of Judi Bari*, May 24, 2020, IWW Environmental Unionism Caucus, https://ecology.iww.org/texts/SteveOngerth/RedwoodUprising, 127; on Earth First! activism in the Northwest, see Woodhouse, *Ecocentrists*, 139.

25. "Bonnie Abbzug," in person interview by author, Sandy, Oregon, April 19, 2018; "Mark Keiser: A Timber Faller Talks about Tree Spikes," *Evergreen*, July 1988; William Turnage, quoted in Woodhouse, *Ecocentrists*, 140.

26. Kerr interview; David Brower, quoted in Philip Brick, "Taking Back the Rural West," in *Let the People Judge: Wise Use and the Private Property Rights Movement*, ed. John D. Echeverria and Raymond Booth Eby (Washington, DC: Island, 1995), 62.

27. Steven Lewis Yaffee, *The Wisdom of the Spotted Owl: Policy Lessons for a New Century* (Washington, DC: Island, 1994), 83–114.

28. Jeffrey T. Olson, "Pacific Northwest Lumber and Wood Products: An Industry in Transition," in Wilderness Society, *National Forests: Policies for the Future* (Washington, DC: Wilderness Society, 1988); David S. Wilcove, "Protecting Biological Diversity," *National Forests*; Brian J. Greber, "Technological Change in the Timber Industries in the Pacific Northwest: Historic Background and Future Implications," unpublished briefing paper, stapled manuscript, October 1991, Department Forest Resources, College of Forestry, Oregon State University, Corvallis; Joseph L. Conrad IV, W. Dale Greene, and Patrick Hiesl, "A Review of Changes in US Logging Businesses 1980s–Present," *Journal of Forestry* 116, no. 3 (2018): 291–303.

29. Bruce Harris, editorial, *Salem (OR) Statesman Journal*, January 11, 1989.

30. Ellen Tigart, quoted in B. A. Brown, *In Timber Country*, 247. On timber-sharing payments, see Michelle W. Anderson, "The Western, Rural Rustbelt: Learning from Local Fiscal Crisis in Oregon," *Willamette Law Review* 50, no. 4 (2014): 471–75.

31. Cherie Girod, quoted in Alton Chase, *In a Dark Wood: The Fight Over Forests and the Myths of Nature* (New Brunswick, NJ: Transaction, 2001), 284.

32. McCurdy, "Upstream Influences," 341.

33. Jim Petersen, editorial, *Evergreen*, March–April 1989.

34. Yaffee, *Wisdom of the Spotted Owl*, 180; Committee on Resources, House of Representatives, "Joint Hearing on the Sierra Club's Proposal to Drain Lake Powell or Reduce Its Water Storage Capability," 105th Cong. (September 24, 1997) (1998), 59 (David Brower, quoted in statement of John Shadegg).

35. Robert G. Lee, "Moral Exclusion and Rural Poverty: Myth Management and Wood Products Workers," *Conservation of the Northern Spotted Owl*, hearing before the Subcommittee of Environmental Protection, 102nd Cong. (1992), attachment D; Cowie, *Stayin' Alive*; Robert Heilman, *Oregonian*, May 3, 1988, editorial.

36. On the ancient-forest campaign, Neufeld and Parnaby, *IWA in Canada*, 274–80; Norm Rivard, quoted in ibid., 277.

37. Ibid., 284, 285. See also Karena Shaw, "Encountering Clayoquot, Reading the Political," in *A Political Space: Reading the Global through Clayoquot Sound*, ed. Warren Magnusson and Karena Shaw (Montreal: McGill-Queen's University Press, 2002), 25–65.

38. Neufeld and Parnaby, *IWA in Canada*, 280; Jeremy Wilson, *Talk and Log: Wilderness Politics in British Columbia* (Vancouver: University of British Columbia Press, 1998), 301–32.

39. Yaffee, *Wisdom of the Spotted Owl*, 115–51; Chase, *In a Dark Wood*, 274–89; Catherine Caufield, "The Ancient Forest," *New Yorker*, May 14, 1990, 46–7.

40. Cherie Girod and Doug Hirons, quoted in Chase, *In a Dark Wood*, 286, 287, respectively; Bruce Thiel, letter to the editor, *Oregonian*, June 4, 1989, 12.

41. Heath interview.

42. *Mill City (OR) Enterprise*, September 1, 1988; on the yellow-ribbon coalition, Elizabeth Medford, "Lumber, Community, and the Anti-Environmentalist Movement: Environmentalists Cannot See the Wood for the Trees" (master's thesis, University of Oregon, 2005).

43. Todd A. Bryan and Julia M. Wondolleck, "When Irresolvable Becomes Resolvable: The Quincy Library Group Conflict," in *Making Sense of Intractable Environmental Conflicts: Frames and Cases*, ed. Roy J. Lewicki, Barbara Gray, and Michael Elliott (Washington, DC: Island, 2003), 68; Heath interview; Gilkison interview.

44. *Mill City (OR) Enterprise*, April 19, 1989; "Legislators Chide Lyons Mill for Paying Employees at Rally," *Statesman Journal* (Salem, OR), February 25, 1989. See also Reinhardt, *Struggle on the North Santiam*, 147; Tarso Ramos, "Wise Use in the West: The Case of the Northwest Timber Industry," in *Let the People Judge: A Reader on the Wise Use Movement*, ed. John Echeverria and Ray Eby (Washington, DC: Island, 1995), 82–118.

45. Yellow Ribbon Coalition newsletter and Tisdale, quoted in Allan S. Galper, "The Killing Fields," *Harvard Crimson* (Cambridge, MA), September 18, 1992; on the coalition's more divisive actions see Yaffee, *Wisdom of the Spotted Owl*, 97–114.

46. Steven Rood, quoted in Mark Stein, "Loggers See Owl as Harbinger of Doom," *Los Angeles Times*, July 14, 1989; Girod, quoted in Chase, *In a Dark Wood*, 287; GCO

newsletter, quoted in Reinhardt, *Struggle on the North Santiam*, 148. For more on the CGO, see Reinhardt, *Struggle on the North Santiam*, 147–49.

47. "Loggers Stage Their Own Protests," *Register Guard* (Eugene, OR), May 6, 1989, 6.

48. Yaffee, *Wisdom of the Spotted Owl*, 115–51.

49. Don Brown, "Timber Still Needs to Be Cut," *World* (Coos Bay, OR), July 24, 1991, 12.

50. Yaffee, *Wisdom of the Spotted Owl*, 115–51.

51. Ibid.; Hugh Dellios, "Concern at Timber Summit," *Chicago Tribune*, April 2, 1993.

52. Heath interview.

Chapter 8. "We Keep Carbon-Eating Machines Healthy"

1. Payton Smith, in-person interview with author, Eugene, Oregon, February 15, 2019.

2. Jason Wilson, "The Job No One Wants: Why Won't Young People Work in Logging?" *Guardian*, August 23, 2017, www.theguardian.com, accessed March 24, 2020.

3. P. Smith, interview, February 15, 2019.

4. Federal Ecomanagement Assessment Team, *Forest Ecosystem Management: An Ecological, Economic, and Social Assessment* (Portland, OR: FEMAT, July 1993), 3; on FEMAT, Chase, *In a Dark Wood*, 385–92; Yaffee, *Wisdom of the Spotted Owl*, 143–51.

5. Daniel Nelson, *Nature's Burdens: Conservation and American Politics, the Reagan Era to the Present* (Logan: Utah State University Press, 2017), 150; Amanda M. A. Minter, Robert W. Malmsheimer, and Denise M. Kelle, "Twenty Years of Forest Service Land Management Litigation," *Journal of Forestry* 112, no. 1 (2014): 32–40. For a more thorough listing of species that are endangered, threatened, or under review, see "Oregon's Endangered Species" and "Washington's Endangered Species," both on *U.S. Fish and Wildlife Service*, www.fws.gov, accessed March 2, 2020.

6. Woodhouse, *Ecocentrists*, 262–69.

7. US Forest Service, and Department of Interior, Bureau of Land Management, *Final Supplemental Environmental Impact Statement on Management of Habitat for Late-Successional and Old-Growth Forest Related Species within the Range of the Northern Spotted Owl*, appendices, February 1994, 2:F-14.

8. Sonja N. Oswalt, Patrick D. Miles, Scott A. Pugh, and W. Brad Smith, "Forest Resources of the United States, 2017: A Technical Document Supporting the Forest Service Update of the 2010 RPA Assessment," RPA review draft (Washington, DC: US Department of Agriculture, Forest Service, 2017).

9. Max Bennett, Stephen A. Fitzgerald, Daniel Leavell, and Carrie Berger, *Fire FAQs: Have the Size and Severity of Forest Wildfires Increased in Oregon and across the West?* (Corvallis: Oregon State University, Extension Service, October 2018), 1.

10. On the relationship between increased forest fires and climate change, see Jessica E. Halofsky, David L. Peterson, and Brian J. Harvey, "Changing Wildfire, Changing Forests: The Effects of Climate Change on Fire Regimes and Vegetation in the Pacific Northwest, USA," *Fire Ecology* 16, no. 4 (2020): 1–26. On the ways in which fire is exacerbating climate change, see US Department of Agriculture, Forest Service, "There's Carbon in Them Thar Hills: But How Much? Could Pacific Northwest Forests Store More Carbon?" *Science Findings* 195 (April 2017): 1–5. See also Bureau of Land Management and US Department of Agriculture, Forest Service, Region 6, "2018 Pacific Northwest Wildland Fire Season: Summary of Key Events and Issues," 2019.

11. On deer, elk, bear, and cougar populations, see US Fish and Wildlife Service, *Elk Management Plan Environmental Assessment for the Willamette Valley National Wildlife Refuge Complex* (Corvallis, OR: USFWS, February 2014); Oregon Department of Fish and Wildlife, *Oregon Black-Tailed Deer Management Plan* (Salem: Oregon Dept. of Fish and Wildlife, November 14, 2008), 34.

12. Catherine M. Dugger et al., "The Effects of Habitat, Climate, and Barred Owls on Long-Term Demography of Northern Spotted Owls," *Condor* 118, no. 1 (2016): 57–116, https://doi.org/10.1650/CONDOR-15-24.1; Stan G. Sovern et al., "Barred Owls and Landscape Attributes Influence Territory Occupancy of Northern Spotted Owls," *Journal of Wildlife Management* 78, no. 8 (2014): 1436–43; Elizabeth G. Kelly, Eric D. Forsman, and Robert G. Anthony, "Are Barred Owls Displacing Spotted Owls?" *Condor* 106, no. 1 (2003): 45–53.

13. For a sense of that debate, see William R. Freudenburg, Lisa J. Wilson, and Daniel J. O'Leary, "Forty Years of Spotted Owls? A Longitudinal Analysis of Logging Industry Job Losses," *Sociological Perspectives* 41, no. 1 (1998): 1–26; and Matthew S. Carroll, Charles W. McKetta, Keith A. Blatner, and Con Schallau, "A Response to 'Forty Years of Spotted Owls? A Longitudinal Analysis of Logging Industry Job Losses,'" *Sociological Perspectives* 42, no. 2 (1999): 325–33.

14. FEMAT, *Forest Ecosystem Management*, 114; US Department of Agriculture, US Forest Service, "Northwest Forest Plan: Outcomes and Lessons Learned from the Northwest Economic Adjustment Initiative," Pacific Northwest Research Station, General Technical Report, PNW-GTR-484, November 1999.

15. Robert Lee, quoted in FEMAT, *Forest Ecosystem Management*, 18; Ted Sickinger, "Financial Crisis Hits Hard at the County Level, Too," *Oregonian*, December 3, 2010. For more on the Secure Rural Schools and Community Self-Determination Act of 2000 and the collapse of social services, see Anderson, "Western, Rural Rustbelt," 465–513.

16. On the history of Cobain and Nirvana, see Michael Azerrad, *Come as You Are: The Story of Nirvana* (New York: Doubleday, 1993); Christopher Sandford, *Kurt Cobain* (New York: Carroll and Graf, 1995); Charles R. Cross, *Heavier Than Heaven: A Biography of Kurt Cobain* (New York: Hyperion, 2001).

17. Michael Azerrad, "Nirvana: Inside the Heart and Mind of Kurt Cobain," *Rolling Stone*, April 16, 1992, www.rollingstone.com, accessed June 1, 2014.

18. Ibid.; Cross, *Heavier Than Heaven*, 330–42.

19. Azerrad, "Nirvana," emphasis in original.

20. Greg Latta, Tim Nadreu, Olli-Pekka Kuusela, and David Rossi, "Oregon's Forest Economy—2019 Forest Report," *Oregon Forest Resources Institute*, 2019, theforestreport.org. On tourism in the Northwest, see Jason Pierce, "The Winds of Change: The Decline of Extractive Industries and the Rise of Tourism in Hood River County, Oregon," *Oregon Historical Quarterly* 108, no. 3 (2007): 410–31.

21. P. Smith interview, February 15, 2019.

22. There's considerable literature on technological changes in the Northwest's timber industry since the 1990s. For a good overview, see Conrad, Greene, and Hiesl, "Review of Changes in US Logging Businesses."

23. Jason Smith, interview with author, North Bend, Oregon, December 14, 2018.

24. Ibid.

25. Ibid.

26. On timber country's relationship to the state in the post–timber wars era and for a more thorough explanation of county payment programs, see Anderson, "Western, Rural Rustbelt."

27. J. Smith interview; P. Smith, interview, February 15, 2019.

28. SCS Global Services, *Chain of Custody: FSC Controlled Wood Public Summary, Roseburg Forest Products, Version 4-0*, SCS Global Services, FSC-A00521, September 2020.

29. P. Smith, interview, February 15, 2019.

30. Indroneil Ganguly, "Global Warming Mitigating Role of Working Forests in Washington State," Center for International Trade in Forest Products, School of Environmental and Forest Services, University of Washington, February 2019.

31. Jonathan Watts, "Concrete: The Most Destructive Material on Earth," and John Vidal, "Concrete Is Tipping Us into Climate Catastrophe. It's Payback Time," both in *Guardian*, February 25, 2019, www.theguardian.com, accessed February 26, 2019.

32. Payton Smith, interview with author, Springfield, Oregon, December 4, 2020.

33. Benton Johnson, quoted in Henry Fountain, "Towers of Steel? Look Again," *New York Times*, September 23, 2013, www.nytimes.com, accessed February 5, 2020. See also Stephen Wallis, "The Trees and the Forest of New Towers," *New York Times*, November 20, 2019, www.nytimes.com, accessed November 20, 2019.

34. P. Smith, interview, February 15, 2019; on 2006 poll, see Andy Kerr, "Logjam: Nine Oregon Logging Mills Stuck in the Past," *Oregon Wild*, 2010. For 2016 poll, see "Northwest Forest Plan Poll, Executive Summary," *Wilderness Society*, 2016, www.wilderness.org, accessed January 12, 2017. For more on public opinion of logging, see Jean Mater, "Perceptions of the Forest Products Industry," in *Studies in Management and Accounting for the Forest Products Industry*, monograph 44 (Corvallis: College of Business, College of Forestry, Oregon State University, June 1997).

35. P. Smith, interview, December 4, 2020.

36. Anna Lowenhaupt Tsing, *The Mushroom at the End of the World: On the Possibility of Life in Capitalist Ruins* (Princeton, NJ: Princeton University Press, 2015), 76.

37. Scott Van Doviak, "How 'Redneck Reality' Became the New Rural Working-Class Sitcom," *Onion A.V. Club*, April 11, 2013, www.avclub.com, accessed June 1, 2014.

38. Dass and Geisinger, quoted in John Foyston, "Oregon Loggers See Tall Tales in 'Ax Men,'" *Oregonian*, March 27, 2009, www.oregonlive.com, accessed June 1, 2014; Browning, quoted in Chelsea Gorrow, "Ax Men Spill Secrets," *Daily Astorian* (Astoria, OR), June 29, 2012, www.dailyastorian.com, accessed June 1, 2014.

39. Joint Committee on Carbon Reduction, "HB 2020 a Staff Measure Summary," May 17, 2019, and Legislative Revenue Office, "Revenue Impact of Proposed Legislation: HB 2020 A," May 20, 2019, both 80th Ore. Legislative Assembly, 2019 Regular Sess. For a description of HB 2020 as well as opposition, see Alex Hasenstab, "Some Fear That House Bill 2020 Would Cost People Jobs in Rural Oregon," *KVAL News* (Eugene, OR), June 21, 2019, www.kval.com, accessed March 18, 2020; David Brock Smith, "HB 2020 Will Devastate Oregon Families, Communities, and Businesses," *Salem (OR) Statesman-Journal*, February 15, 2019, www.statesmanjournal.com, accessed March 18, 2020.

40. The walkout of Republican senators received considerable regional and national press coverage. A timeline and a good summary of the issues are in Ted Sickinger, "Oregon Senate Republican Walkout: What Do They Want?" *Oregonian*, June 21, 2019, www.oregonlive.com, accessed March 18, 2020.

41. Again, Timber Unity's rallies received considerable media attention. For a good example of some of that coverage, see Nigel Jaquiss, "Loggers Rallied against Climate Bill in Salem Today," *Willamette Week* (Portland, OR), June 27, 2019, www.wweek.com, accessed March 18, 2020.

42. For signs, ibid.; "common working folks" quote from "Shared Values, One Voice," *Timber Unity*, www.timberunity.com, accessed March 18, 2020; Todd Payne to All Seneca Contractors, June 25, 2019, *Seneca Companies*, www.senecasawmill.com, accessed March 18, 2020.

43. Mike Pihl, interview by author, Albany, Oregon, January 15, 2020.

44. Ibid. In addition to serving as Timber Unity's president, Pihl is also active in several conservation organizations and the local historical society.

45. Ibid.

46. Ibid.

47. Megan Allison, "Timber Unity Proposes Alternative to Cap-and-Trade," *KATU* (Portland, OR), February 10, 2020, www.katu.com, accessed March 18, 2020.

48. Ted Sickinger, "Timber Unity Members Protest Cap-and-Trade Climate Bill with Convoy, Rally in Salem," *Oregonian*, February 6, 2020, www.oregon.live.com, accessed April 4, 2020.

49. P. Smith to author, e-mail, February 2, 2020.

Index

Page numbers in italics refer to illustrations

Abbey, Edward, 198
Abbzug, Bonnie (pseudonym), 199
Aberdeen, WA, 122, 223–25
Adams, Archie, 62
afforestation, 238
AFL (American Federation of Labor), 86,
    112, 114, 116, 117, 118, 119
African American workers, 117, 141
agrarian intellectualism, 132, 134, 139
Albany (OR) Democrat-Herald (newspa-
    per), 193
American Federation of Labor (AFL), 86,
    112, 114, 116, 117, 118, 119
American Forest Resources Council, 201
Ames, Charles, 93–94
anarchism, 31–32, 198
Ancient Forest Alliance, 197
"ancient forests," 13, 158, 192–98, 202, 205–7,
    270n13
Anderson, Charles, 30, 31
Anderson, John, 33–34
Andrews, Thomas, 91
angling. *See* fishing
Antone, Bob, 181
Asian immigrants, 31
Association of Oregon Loggers, 234
Audubon Society, 197, 218
automation, 201, 217, 222, 226

automobiles, 67, 137
Ax Men, 233–34, 237
Azerrad, Michael, 224–25

back-to-the-landers, 170–71
Bailey, Eva, 72
Baltic immigrants, 32
B&B Complex Fire, 221
bark harvesting, 61–62, 72
barred owls, 222
baseball, 42, 64
Beard, James, 73
beaver, 63
Beckham, Curt, 106
Beckham, Dow, 106
Bedaux system, 86
beekeeping, 62–63, 62
Bennet, John, 142
Bergren, Myrtle, 260n20
berrying, 49, 58, 59, 66, 72, 103
Bertram (Ruuttila), Julia, 39, 106, 118–19
Beverly Hillbillies, The, 175
blacklists, 33, 35, 36
Black workers, 117, 141
Blanchard, WA, 27–28, 46
BLM (Bureau of Land Management), 200,
    222
Bloedel, Stewart, and Welch, 98
Bloedel Donovan Lumber Company, 4, 5, 38
Blue River, OR, 221

Boag, Peter, 92
board feet, definition of, 250n10
bonus systems, 38
Boorman, John, 175, 176
bootlegging, 63
Bordeaux, WA, 60
Bowerman, Bill, 177
Bracher, Frederick, 65
British Columbia, 25, 28, 108–9, 111, 125,
    142–43, 161; national park in, 205–7; 1980s
    timber industry in, 162–63, 205–7; post-
    war forestry in, 139–41, 143
British merchants, 3
Brooks-Scanlon, 161
Brower, David, 200, 204
Brown, Beverly, 172
Brown, Don, 212
Brown, Ivan, 137–38
Brown, Jack, 113
Brown, Kate, 236
Browning, Jay, 234
Buchanan, Melda, 59
Buck, C. J., 122
buckers, 86, 95
Bureau of Land Management (BLM), 200,
    222
Bush, George H. W., 212
busheling, 86
"bush sense," 95–96
Butler, Octavia, 248n7

California, 8, 32, 155, 232, 235. See also spe-
    cific cities and towns
Californication, 168–71
camas, 58–59, 72
Cameron, Colin, 109, 139–41
Camp and Mill News (newsletter), 33, 60
Canada: in Great Depression, 107–9, 112–14,
    117; in 1970s, 162; in World War II, 124,
    125. See also British Columbia
canning, 60–61
Canning, Bruce, 88
Cantwell, Robert, 125, 149, 151, 172, 233
cap-and-trade proposals, 235–38, 239
carbon capture, 230, 238
Carrol, Matthew, 196–200
cars, 67, 137
Carson, Rachel, 172
cascara, 61–62
Cash, Johnny, 180
Cathedral Forest, 192

Caulfield, Catherine, 207
caulks, 2, 93, 94
CCC (Civilian Conservation Corps), 109,
    111
CCF (Co-operative Commonwealth Federa-
    tion), 109, 139, 140
Chase, Jasper, 95
chasers (chocker setters), 92–93, 96
Chicago Mercantile, 160
children, 54, 55–57; forest recreation of,
    64–65. See also schools
Chinook jargon, 95
chittem, 61–62
chocker setters (chasers), 92–93, 96
Church, Frank, 148
Churchill, Sam, 54, 58, 103–5, 107, 108, 111
CIO (Congress of Industrial Organizations),
    12, 117–18, 137–38, 141. See also Interna-
    tional Woodworkers of America
city-country divide, 181, 182, 187, 240; cli-
    mate change and, 235
Civilian Conservation Corps (CCC), 109,
    111
Clarke, J. M., 114
Clayoquot Sound, BC, 206
Clearing House, 33
Clear Lake Lumber Company, 77
Clemons Logging Company, 52
Cliffe, Joe, 71
climate change, 216, 221, 229–31, 232, 235–39,
    240
Clinton, Bill, 212–13, 217, 218, 222–23
Coast Salish, 3
Cobain, Kurt, 223–25
Coffee, John, 122–23, 126
commodities markets, 160–61
Communists, 74, 140, 142, 172; in Canada,
    112, 114, 116
Comox Logging and Railway Company,
    40–41
company towns and camps, 38–43, 181–82;
    animals in, 54; in Appalachia, 39, 253n31;
    cooking in, 54; families and children in,
    54, 55–57; fire in, 63; human and nonhu-
    man interwoven in, 52, 54, 66–67; mobility
    of, 41; naming of, 40, 253n33; photography
    of, 50–56, 51–53, 55–57, 67; remoteness of,
    50–52; shuttering of, 129–30
Congress of Industrial Organizations (CIO),
    12, 117–18, 137–38, 141. See also Interna-
    tional Woodworkers of America

Co-operative Commonwealth Federation (CCF), 109, 139, 140
Cooperative Land Use Program, 127
Coos Bay, OR, 66, 106, 162, 215–16, 217, 228, 232, 239, 242
Copeland, Royal S., 108, 109, 111
Cornwall, George, 85
Corvallis, OR, 200
Cosmopolis, WA, 83
Cottage Grove, OR, 214
Couack, James, 42, 43
cougars, 63, 221
country music, 158, 178–81
COVID-19, 239–40
Cowie, Jefferson, 204–5
Craig & Terry, 181
Crawford, Margaret, 39
Creswell, OR, 201
crisis environmentalism, 190, 191, 193, 198
Cronon, William, 8, 249n12
Cumberland, WI, 29
cut-and-run logging, 27, 105, 108, 110, 122, 124, 133, 141, 208, 232

Dalskog, Ernie, 112–15
dangers, 2, 75–100, 180–81; in topping trees, 76–79; vocabulary of, 94; workers' acceptance of, 79
Daniels, Charlie, 178
Darby, Ralph, 59
Dass, Archie, 234
Davis, Elrick B., 95
deer, 59–60, 71, 72, 106, 221
Deliverance, 175
Democrats, 141–42, 212, 236
Dennison, Betty, 182
Department of Labor and Industries, Washington, 88
Dethlefs, Dwayne, 234
Dies, Martin, 135
Dietrich, William, 269n11
Dillard, OR, 231
Disney, 150–51
Disque, Brice, 34
Dixiecrats, 141
Dokter, Ted, 122
Dolbeer, John, 81
domestic abuse, 203
donkey punchers, 80–81, 91, 92, 97
donkeys, steam, 80–82, 80
Donovan-Corkery Logging Company, 53

Drake, George, 84–85
Duffy, Frank, 118
Duncan, Christy, 193
Dune (Herbert), 248n7
Dwyer, William, 200, 203, 207
Dylan, Bob, vii
dynamite, 76–78

Earth Day, 172
Earth First!, 197–200, 206, 207, 209, 218
Eastern European immigrants, 22
Easy Rider, 175
Eches, Arnold, 88
Ecodefense: A Field Guide to Monkeywrenching (Foreman), 198
ecofeminism, 170, 198
ecosystem management, 219
ecotage (monkeywrenching), 198–200, 206
education. See schools
Edwards, William, 88
Ehrlich, Paul, 172
elk, 60, 120, 221, 241–42
Emergency Conservation Committee, 121
Emerson, George H., 82
Emmerson, Irma Lee, 66–67, 69, 72
employment agencies, 28–29, 37
Endangered Species Act (ESA) (1973), 189, 197, 207, 211–12, 218
engineered lumber, 231
engineering, 82, 85, 86, 87, 89–90, 97
English immigrants, 96, 116
environmental history, 72, 148, 219
environmentalism, crisis, 190, 191, 193, 198
environmentalists: "ancient forests" and, 13, 158, 192–98, 202, 205–7, 270n13; in Canada, 205–7; economic woes attributed to automation by, 201, 222, 226; mainstream national groups of, 191, 196–200, 212, 218; music of, 192–93, 198–99; NWFP implementation and, 218–19; radical, 197–200, 206, 218; social background of, 3, 138, 171, 172, 187, 193, 212; views of forests shaped by, 50, 69; workers' divide with, 3, 14, 149–51, 155–58, 170–77, 182, 183. See also labor environmentalism; spotted-owl conflict; wilderness movement; specific groups and topics
equity migrants, 169–70
ESA (Endangered Species Act) (1973), 189, 197, 207, 211–12, 218
Escanaba (MI) Daily Press (newspaper), 137

Eugene, OR, 200–201, 211
Eugene (OR) Register-Guard (newspaper), 147, 196, 210
Evergreen (trade journal), 203, 208

Facebook, 238, 239
Falding, James, 131, 135
families, 35–38, 54, 55, 57
fantasy, 8, 248n7
farmers markets, 73–74
fast-food restaurants, 73
Federal Bureau of Corporations, 25
Federal Ecomanagement Assessment Team (FEMAT), 217–18, 222
fellers, 86, 88, 95–96, 96
Finnish immigrants, 32, 76, 99, 112
fires, 26, 70–71, 173, 196; in camps and towns, 41, 63; NWFP and, 219–21; set by Indigenous peoples, 13, 69, 71, 191, 195, 220
First Nations, 206
fishing, 67, 90, 106; by author, 10–11; clearcuts' effect on, 67; elite vs. pot, 65; Haig-Brown on, 90, 126, 140; IWA's focus on, 130–31, 136, 137; near logging camps, 58, 61; Pellegrini on, 73; as recreation and subsistence, 65, 66, 74; workers' views shaped by, 6–7, 9, 17–18, 241
Fish and Wildlife Service, US (FWS), 189, 197, 207, 211–12, 218
Fonda, Henry, 175
foraging: by author, 16; bark gathering, 61–62, 72; berrying, 49, 58, 59, 66, 72, 103; near logging camps, 58, 59, 61; mushroom gathering, 16, 58, 73, 233; Pellegrini on, 73, 74; as recreation and subsistence, 66, 74; workers' views shaped by, 6–7, 9
Ford, Kenneth, 168
Ford, Tennessee Ernie, 57
Foreman, Dave, 198
Forest Practices Act (British Columbia) (1947), 140–41, 143
forestry: democratization of, 133–34, 139–40, 144, 145, 148–51; education in, 84–87; expert vs. worker knowledge in, 132; farm policy compared with, 134; in Great Depression, 107–12; Hook Bill on, 135–39, 141–42, 145, 264n30; industrial, criticism of, 128; IWA proposals in, 132–35, 141–42; multiuse, 123, 136, 145, 149; 1930s schism in, 131; in postwar British Columbia,

139–41, 143; sustainable, sustained-yield, 119–20, 121, 131, 133–34, 136, 145–46, 229–30, 263n12; technocratic, 131, 139
Forestry.B.C.'s Devastated Industry (Cameron), 139
forests. *See* Northwest forests; old-growth forests
Forest Service, British Columbia, 143
Forest Service, US (USFS), 85, 107, 111, 121, 122, 127, 138, 144, 146, 147, 194, 195, 218, 222; spotted-owl conflict and, 188, 189, 192, 193, 200, 210
Forest Service Employees for Environmental Ethics (FSEEE), 194
Forest Stewardship Council (FSC), 229
Forsman, Eric D., 188–89, 217
Fort Victoria, 3
Foster, Ellery, 127–28, 132–35, 137, 138–39, 229; resignation of, 143–44
4L (Loyal Legion of Loggers and Lumbermen), 34–35, 112
Freres Lumber Company, 210
FSC (Forest Stewardship Council), 229
FSEEE (Forest Service Employees for Environmental Ethics), 194
FWS (US Fish and Wildlife Service), 189, 197, 207, 211–12, 218

Gakin, Fred, 88
gardening, 59, 61, 73–74, 170
gathering. *See* foraging
GCO (Greater Communities of Oregon), 211
Geisinger, Jim, 234
Georgia-Pacific, 161
Gilbert, Jess, 132
Gilkison, Dick, 166–67, 181
Girod, Cherie, 202–3, 207, 211
Goodwin, Ted, 59, 106
Goodyear Logging Company, 57
Graves, Henry S., 107, 108
Grays Harbor, WA, 53
Great Depression, 103–23, 131; forestry policy in, 107–12; shifting views of nature in, 103–5
Greater Communities of Oregon (GCO), 211
Greber, Brian, 217
Greek immigrants, 32. *See also* Mediterranean immigrants
Greeley, William, 107–12, 116, 134
Green, Hardy, 253n31
Greenpeace, 206

Grey, Zane, 65, 150
Griggs, Edward, 26, 29–30, 38
grouse, 72
grunge music, 223–25
Guardian (newspaper), 184, 216, 231
Gumpert, Lois, 64
"gyppos" (independent contractors), 144, 165–67, 181, 240, 266n16

Haggard, Dave, 206
Haggard, Merle, 178, 180, 181
Haida Gwaii (Queen Charlotte Islands), 6, 205
Haig-Brown, Roderick, 90, 93, 125–26, 140, 149, 151, 172, 233
Hall, J. Alfred, 133
Hamerquist, Don, 119
Harris, Michael, 201–2
Hartung, Al, 146, 147
Hays, Finley, 93, 100
health services, 42
Heath, Wilbur, 184–88, 190, 194, 195, 200–201, 203, 205, 208, 214
Heckletooth 3 (Shetzline), 173
Heinlein, Robert, 205
Herbert, Frank, 248n7
Hermach, Tim, 218
high climbers (riggers), 76–79, 77, 97, 99
high-lead systems, 82, 98
Hill, James J., 25
Hilt, CA, 59
Hilton, A. H., 42
Hirons, Doug, 207
History Channel, 233–34
Hoedads, 171, 182–83
Hoedown, 179–80
Holbrook, Stewart H., 149–50, 175
Homestead, PA, 39
honey, 62–63, 66
Hook, "Fightin'" Frank, 135–39, 141
Hook Bill, 135–39, 141–42, 145, 264n30
hook tenders, 91, 92, 97, 98, 99, 105–6
Hopper, Dennis, 175, 176
Hoquiam, WA, 122
House Committee on Public Lands, US, 121–22
Hudson's Bay Company, 3
hunting, 67, 106, 126; by author, 241–42; of cougars, 63; industrial forests conducive to, 71–72; IWA's focus on, 130–31, 136, 137; near logging camps, 59–60, 61; Pellegrini

on, 73, 74; as recreation and subsistence, 65–66, 74; workers' views shaped by, 6–7, 9, 11, 17–18, 241

IAM (International Association of Machinists), 164
IAM Woodworker Division, 164
Ickes, Harold, 121, 122, 123, 126
IFAWA (International Fishermen and Allied Workers of America), 137
immigrants: Asian, 31; Baltic, 32; Eastern European, 22; English, 90, 116; Finnish, 32, 76, 99, 112; Greek, 32; Italian, 32, 48–49, 63; Mediterranean, 22, 28, 32; Scandinavian, 22, 28, 29, 30, 31–32, 99
independent contractors ("gyppos"), 144, 165–67, 181, 240, 266n16
Indigenous peoples, 3; forest management by, 13, 69, 71, 191, 195, 220
Industrial Workers of the World (IWW; Wobblies), 32–33, 36, 37, 38, 43, 112, 251–52n20
influenza, 88
Inman-Poulsen mill, 27
International Association of Machinists (IAM), 164
International Fishermen and Allied Workers of America (IFAWA), 137
International Slow Food Movement, 73
International Woodworker, 135, 136
International Woodworkers of America (IWA), 141–48, 168, 174, 248n9, 260n20; communism and, 142–43; decline of, 157, 164, 171; Foster's forestry proposals and, 127–28, 132–35; Gilkison's disillusionment with, 166; Hoedads' rejection of, 171; Hook forestry bill and, 135–39, 141–42, 145, 264n30; labor environmentalism of, 12, 15–16, 116–26, 128, 131–35, 144–48, 241; membership numbers for, 125, 144, 159, 171; 1945 convention of, 133, 134; 1980s setbacks of, 163–64; outdoor columns written for, 130–31; wilderness and, 12–15, 123, 128, 144–51, 174, 194; in World War II, 124; younger vs. older workers in, 164
International Woodworkers of America—Canada, 5, 139–43, 162–66, 205–7
Inud, Bill, 91, 100
Isle Royal National Park, 136
Italian immigrants, 32, 48–49, 63. *See also* Mediterranean immigrants

IWA. *See* International Woodworkers of America
IWW (Industrial Workers of the World; Wobblies), 32–33, 36, 37, 38, 43, 112, 251–52n20

Jackson, Henry "Scoop," 135
Jenkins, Craig, 181
Johnson, Arne, 113
Johnson, Benton, 231
Johnson, Lyndon B., 148
Johnson, Norm, 207
Jones, George, 180
Josephine County, OR, 169, 183, 223
Journal of Forestry, 132, 135

Keiser, David, 196, 199
Kerr, Andy, 190–91, 196–97, 200, 269n8, 270n13
Kesey, Ken, 156–57, 173–76, 178, 180
Kinney, E. T., 140
Kinsey, Clark, 50–56, 67
Kinsey, Mary, 50–56, 67
Knight, Phil, 177
Kwakwaka'wakw, 3

labor environmentalism, 105, 208; Hook Bill and, 135–39, 141–42, 145, 264n30; of IWA, 12, 15–16, 116–26, 128, 131–35, 144–48, 241; Olympic National Park and, 120–23
labor unions, 12, 31–35, 43, 112–16, 159–60, 172, 174; Marxist ideology ineffective in, 114; no-strike pledge and, 124; Reagan and, 163, 164; strikes by, 32–33, 39, 114–17, 119, 124–25, 142, 162–63, 173; Taft-Hartley and, 142. *See also* labor environmentalism; *specific unions*
Lamb, Frank, 37
Land of Plenty (Cantwell), 125
landslides, 67, 89, 126
Langlie, Arthur B., 145–46
Larson, A. J., 100
Lavender Records, 179–80
Lee, Robert, 204, 222
Le Guin, Ursula, 248n7
Leopold, Aldo, 145
Lewis, John L., 117, 138
Liboky, John, 91
Life magazine, 177, 184–88, *186*, 194–95, 214
Lind, Anna, 65

Lind, Leo, 62
Linnton, OR, 118
literature, 156–57, 173–76, 198–99, 233, 248n7; historical, 8–10, 36, 251–52n20
logging. *See* Northwest timber industry; Northwest timber workers
logging engineering, 82, 85, 86, 87, 89–90, 97
logging roads, 129
Long, George S., 26
Long-Bell Lumber, 28, 39
Longview, WA, 39, 106
Lorax, The (Dr. Seuss), 210
Los Angeles Times (newspaper), 211
Louisiana-Pacific, 161, 163
Love, Matt, 156–57
Lowery, Jim, 163–64
Loyal Legion of Loggers and Lumbermen (4L), 34–35, 112
LSD (lysergic acid diethylamide), 175, 176
Lumber Snafu (Foster), 132–35, 136
Lumber Workers International Union (LWIU), 112, 114
Luoma, Dave, 1–7
Lynch, David, 233
Lynn, Loretta, 178–79
lysergic acid diethylamide (LSD), 175, 176

Ma and Pa Kettle, 175
MacKaye, Benton, 145
Malheur National Wildlife Refuge, 236
Manary, Ruth, 43, 58
Manley-Moore Lumber Company, *55*
marathons, 258n34
marbled murrelet, 218
Marshall, Robert, 108, 109, 111, 131, 145, 146, 172
Martin, Clarence D., 115
Martin, Lloyd Earl "Buzz," 15, 179–80, 181, 203–4
Mason, David, 263n12
Mather, Stephen, 67
McCall, Thomas Lawson, 169
McCleary, Henry, 48, 129
McCleary, WA, 47–49, 74, 129–30
McCormick Lumber Company, *68*
McKenna, Bill, 106
McKinnis, Terry, 181
McMoen, M., 88
Mediterranean immigrants, 22, 28, 32; Greek, 32; Italian, 32, 48–49, 63

Meek, G. D., 119
Merrill, Dwight, 33
Merrill and Ring Lumber Company, 99
Meyer, Stephenie, 248n7
Michigan, 31, 127, 135–36
Mill City, OR, 202–3
Miller, Gregg, 209
Ministry of Forests, British Columbia, 111
Minnesota, 25, 29
Monkeywrench Gang (Abbey), 198
monkeywrenching, 198–200; ecotage, 206
Monteith, James, 192, 270n13
Montgomery Ward, 57
moonshining, 63
moral exclusion, 204
Morgan, Joseph, 87
Morgan, Murray, 149–50, 175
Morrison, Dave, 1–7
Morse, Wayne, 124–25, 135
Mountaineers, 138
Mount Olympus National Monument, 120–21
Muir, Abe, 115, 116
multiuse forestry, 123, 136, 145, 149
Munich Olympics, 176, 177
Munro, Jack, 163
murrelet, marbled, 218
Murrow, Edward R. (Egbert), 44–46, *45*, 72
Murrow, Ethel Lamb, 35, *45*
Murrow, Roscoe, 21–23, 27–28, 35–36, *45*
mushroom gathering, 16, 58, 73, 233
music: country, 15, 158, 178–81; of environmentalists, 192–93, 198–99; punk, 223–25

Nagle, Greg, 183
National, WA, *51*
National Industrial Recovery Act (NIRA) (1933), 109–10
National Labor Relations (Wagner) Act (NLRA) (1935), 117, 142
National Labor Relations Board, 163
National Lumber Workers Union (NLWU), 112, 114
National Park Service, 67; Olympic National Park, 120–23, 128, 136, 144, 145, 147
National War Labor Board, 124
National Wildlife Federation, 197, 218
Native Americans. *See* Indigenous peoples
Native Forest Council, 218
Neimand, Hahn, 54, 55, 57

Nelson, Daniel, 218
Nelson, Hank, 181
Nelson, Willie, 179, 180
Neuberger, Richard, 135
New Deal, 107, 124, 128, 138, 140, 145, 148, 172, 241; agrarian intellectualism and, 132, 134, 139; forestry self-regulation in, 109–11, 119, 121, 123; Hook Bill and, 135–36, 141–42; Olympic National Park and, 122
New Democratic Party, 143
new labor historians, 251n20
New Left, 149, 158, 175, 176, 205, 240
Newman, Paul, 156–57, 175, 176, 178
New Yorker magazine, 207
New York Times (newspaper), 135, 177, 231
Nike, 177
NIRA (National Industrial Recovery Act) (1933), 109–10
Nirvana, 223–25
Nixon, Richard M., 197
NLRA (National Labor Relations Act; Wagner Act) (1935), 117, 142
NLWU (National Lumber Workers Union), 112, 114
Nomad, Don, 234
North Bend, OR, *130*
Northern Pacific Railroad, 25
northern spotted owl. *See* spotted-owl conflict
Northwest Forest Plan (NWFP), 212–14; active management limited by, 219–21; ecosystem management and, 219; human impact of, 222–23; implementation of, 217–22, 227; timber country after, 215–42
Northwest forests: abundance in, 49–50, 57–61; as agricultural goods vs. industrial commodities, 109, 134; annual subsistence cycle in, 57–61; descriptions of, 7–8, 24, 43, 47–48, 103, 219–20; dichotomous narratives about, 6, 13; economic risks in, 24; excess timber mortality in, 220; fluidity of, 13–14, 69, 89, 195; Great Depression in shifting views on, 103–5; height of trees in, 1–2; industrialization of, 26, 27, 28, 47–48, 79–84; logging's effect on, 67–72; overdense understory in, 219–20; rainfall in, 47; regeneration in, 69–72; succession in, 70–72; surveying of, 84; taxes on, 26; topographic maps of, 85–86, 87. *See also* fires; forestry; old-growth forests

Northwest timber country: labor itinerancy overemphasized in, 12, 36; in 1970s and 1980s, 155–83; after Northwest Forest Plan, 215–42; and outsiders' views of nature, 169–70; peopling of, 27–31; in postwar era, 128–32; as site of family, home, and community, 11–12, 106

Northwest timber industry: Asia in 1960s success of, 159; blacklists in, 33, 35, 36; as bringing "new Empire," 23, 47; climate change and, 216, 221, 229–31, 232, 235–39, 240; commodities markets and, 160–61; controlling radicalism in, 31–43, 44; cut-and-run logging in, 27, 105, 108, 110, 122, 124, 133, 141, 208, 232; dominance of, 22, 44; in early twentieth century, 21–46; employer-employee closeness in, 168–69, 178, 208, 209, 228–29; employment agencies in, 28–29, 37; export boom in, 159, 160, 161; family men favored in, 35–38; 1935 strike in, 114–15; in 1970s and 1980s, 158–65; 1980s housing construction and, 192; 1986 BC strike and, 163; NIRA lumber code of, 109–11; origins of, 23–24; postwar boom in, 128–29, 144; public lands' increasing role in, 165, 192; scale of, 27, 44, 86–87, 129, 144, 159, 257n19; scientific management in, 84–87; small-diameter logs in, 227–29; sounds of, 80, 83, 92, 104; southern companies in, 161; speculators' role in, 23–27, 161; strikes rare in, 98; technological change in, 26–27, 28, 79–84, 129; truck logging introduced into, 129, 130; whistling code in, 92. See also company towns and camps; Great Depression; spotted-owl conflict; specific topics

Northwest timber workers: autonomy of, 79, 90, 97, 100; changing identity of, 167–68, 178; clothing of, 2, 93–94, 94; as craftsmen, 90–91; cultural portrayals of, 156–57, 173–76, 198–99, 233–34; dangers to, 2, 75–100, 180–81; death and accident rates of, 88, 89; demographics of, 29–30; disparaging views of, 5, 6, 9, 14–15, 17, 171–72, 204, 213, 232–34, 235, 238; environmentalists' divide with, 3, 14, 149–51, 155–58, 170–77, 182, 183; families of, 35–38, 54, 55, 57; forest stewardship ethic of, 5, 7, 15–16, 17, 167, 187, 196, 208, 210, 216, 230, 237–38, 241; historical literature on, 8–10, 36, 251–52n20; humor of, 87–88; job roles of, 86; knowledge of, 31, 79, 90, 91, 95–96, 97, 98, 100, 128; language of, 94–95; in large vs. small firms, 165–66; mislabeled "unskilled," 31, 32, 90–91, 115, 117; occupational diseases of, 89; occupational ladder of, 91–97; pace set by, 98–99; performance valued by, 97–98; physiques of, 93; Prefontaine and image of, 176–77; protests by, 98–99; recreation of, 38, 41–42, 64–67; retraining of, 222; unemployment of, 105, 121, 122, 155, 157, 161, 162, 216, 223, 224, 226. See also International Woodworkers of America; labor environmentalism; labor unions; and specific topics

Norwegians, 32. See also Scandinavian immigrants

Novoselic, Krist, 225

NWFP (Northwest Forest Plan), 212–14

"Okie from Muskogee" (Haggard), 181

old-growth forests, 195–96; as "ancient forests," 13, 158, 192–98, 202, 205–7, 270n13; varying definitions of, 189, 191–92

Old Left, 158, 172. See also labor unions; specific unions

Oliver, Egbert S., 83

Olympic National Park, 120–23, 128, 136, 144, 145, 147

ONCR (Oregon Natural Resources Council), 190–91, 192, 193, 197, 199, 201–2, 270n13

Onthank, Karl, 147

Opal Creek Wilderness, 210

Oregon, 25, 26, 28, 32, 232; cap-and-trade proposal in, 235–38, 239; population of, 30. See also specific cities and towns

Oregon, University of, 147, 175, 176, 177, 190, 215, 216–17

Oregon-American Lumber Company, 62–63, 105–6

Oregon Business (magazine), 193, 196

Oregon Grange, 138

Oregonian (newspaper), 67, 169, 234

Oregon Logging Conference, 182

Oregon Natural Resources Council (ONRC), 190–91, 192, 193, 197, 199, 201–2, 270n13

Oregon Ryegrass Growers Association, 239

Oregon State University, 85, 200, 220, 227

Oregon Wilderness Coalition. See Oregon Natural Resources Council

Oregon Women in Timber, 182

Oregon Women's Land Trust, 170

organic food, 73–74
owls: barred, 222. *See also* spotted-owl conflict

Pacific Coast Loggers Association, 37
Pacific Coast Logging Congress, 85
Pacific National Lumber Company, *51*
Panama Canal, 29
Parton, Dolly, 178–79
Paul Bunyan, 150–51
Payne, Todd, 237
Peavey, George, 85
Pellegrini, Angelo, 47–49, 72–74, 129
Petersen, James, 203–4, 208, 209
Petrini, Carlo, 73
Petticoat Junction, 175
Phoenix, OR, 221
photography, of company towns, 50–56,
    51–53, 55–57, 67
picnics, 64
Pihl, Mike, 237–38, 276n44
Pihl Logging, 234
Pinchot, Gifford, 107, 108
place, 11–12, 136
pneumonia, 89
Polecat Creek, NC, 21–22, 27, 28
Pollak, Kim, 206
Pollan, Michael, 73
Popular Front, 114
Population Bomb (Ehrlich), 172
Portland, OR, 106, 117, 118, 130, 150, 193, 203,
    204, 210, 223, 235
Portland (OR) Reporter (newspaper), 130
Port Moody, BC, 116
Powers, OR, 106
Prefontaine, Steve, 176–77, 224
Principles of Scientific Management (Taylor), 86
Pritchett, Harold, 116–18, 123, 124, 140
Progressives, 26, 36, 84, 86, 125
Pullman, IL, 39
punk music, 223–25

Queen Charlotte Islands (Haida Gwaii), 6,
    205

radical environmentalists, 197–200, 206, 218
radicalism, worker, 31–43, 44; company
    towns in effort against, 38–43; families as
    strategy against, 35–38
radios, 43
railroads, 24, 25, 29, 43, 82–83, 84, 120

Rajala, Richard A., 90
Rankin, John, 135
recycling, wood, 239
Reagan, Ronald, 163, 164
real estate prices, 168–69
recreation, 64–67; company-sponsored, 38,
    41–42, 64; subsistence mixed with, 65–66,
    74. *See also* fishing; foraging; hunting
Redmond (OR) Spokesman (newspaper), 147
Redwood Marathon, 258n33
reforestation, 227, 229, 233
Reinhardt, Bob H., 249n11
religion, 38, 42
Remick, Lee, 175–76
Republicans, 142, 236
Rhodes, Brad, 163
riggers (high climbers), 76–79, *77*, 97, 99
Rio Dell, CA, 63
Rivard, Norm, 205–6
Robbins, William, 162, 249n11
Roberts, John, 29–30, 31
Rock Creek Wilderness, 194
Rocky, 177
Rolling Stone magazine, 224–25
Rood, Steve, 211
Roosevelt, Franklin D., 107–11, 121, 123, 134
Roosevelt, Theodore, 120
Roseburg Forest Products, 215, 229–30, 231,
    232–33
Roseburg Lumber, 168
Rose Festival Parade, 210
Ruuttila (Bertram), Julia, 39, 106, 118–19
Ryderwood, WA, 106

Saginaw Timber Company, *96*
Sagle, Bob, 208, 209
Salish, Coast, 3
salmon, 8, 10, 58, 66, 67, 106, 131, 140, 241
Samish Bay Logging Company, 27
San Francisco, CA, 29
Santiam Canyon, OR, 211
Santiam Valley, OR, 207
Satterfield, Theresa, 172
Saturday Evening Post (newspaper), 33
Saturday Night Live, 225
Sawmill and Timber Workers Union
    (STWU), 112, 114–16, 117
Scandinavian immigrants, 22, 28, 29, 30,
    31–32, 99
schools, 38, 42, 48, 54, 56; budgets of, 168,
    202, 222, 223; of forestry, 85–86
science fiction, 8, 248n7

scientific management, 84–87
Sears, Roebuck, and Company, 57
Seattle, WA, 31, 34, 117, 150, 155, 197, 203, 223, 225
Seattle (WA) Post-Intelligencer (newspaper), 161
Seattle (WA) Star (newspaper), 87
Seattle (WA) Times (newspaper), 225
Secure Rural Schools and Community Self-Determination Act (2000), 223
Seneca Jones Lumber Company, 237
Seuss, Dr. (Theodor Geisel), 210
Sherman, Dorothy Marie, 75
Shetzline, David, 173
Shevlin, OR, 64, 105
Shevlin-Hixon Logging Company, 41
Shey, Joseph, 88
shingle weavers, 89
Sierra Club, 138, 172, 200, 210, 218
Sierra Club Legal Defense, 197
signalmen, 91–92
Silcox, Ferdinand A., 127, 146
Silent Spring (Carson), 172
Silver Fire Roundup, 208
Simmons, Buddy, 179
Simpson Logging Company, 28, 53, 62, 85, 129–30
Siuslaw National Forest, 194
skiing, 64
slash burns, 70–71
Sloan, Gordon McGregor, 140
Smith, Cecil "Cougar," 63
Smith, Jason, 227–29
Smith, Payton, 215–17, 225–26, 229–31, 232, 234, 239, 240–42
Snyder, Dave, 211
Snyder, Gary, 173
socialism, 31–32, 38; in Canada, 108–9
Sometimes a Great Notion (Kesey), 156–57, 173–76
Southard, Johnny, 258n34
Southport Lumber, 215, 226–29
Soviet Union, 142
spar trees, 82, *83*
speculators, 23–27, 161, 169–70
spotted-owl conflict, 5–6, 14, 18, 158, 184–205, 237; assessments of economic impact of, 201; county budgets affected by, 202, 222–23; Dwyer decision in, 200, 203, 207; Earth First! in, 197–200, 207, 209, 218; ESA listing in, 189, 197, 207, 211–12, 218; Forest Service and, 188, 189, 192, 193,

200, 210; Jason Smith and, 227; jobs-or-environment narrative in, 185–87; moral exclusion in, 204; Northwest Forest Plan and, 212–14, 217, 221–22; as not about owl, 188; origins of, 193; owl biology and, 189; owl charisma in, 191, 269n11; scientific papers in, 188–91; social crisis after, 215, 222–23, 225–26; social crisis during, 202–3; timber country after, 215–42
springboards, 96
spruce, Sitka, 120–21
Stallone, Sylvester, 177
Standard, Jim, 195
steam donkeys, 80–82, *80*
St. Paul & Tacoma Lumber Company, 29–30, 38, *56*, 60, *68*, 88
Strand, Cheryl, 233
"Strong Winds and Widow Makers" (Martin), 180
Sturtevant, Victoria, 169
STWU (Sawmill and Timber Workers Union), 112, 114–16, 117
subsistence, 6–7, 57–61; annual cycle of, 57–61; canning, 60–61; gardening, 59, 61, 73–74, 170; recreation mixed with, 65–66, 74. *See also* fishing; foraging; hunting
suspenders, 93–94, *94*
sustainability, 119–20, 121, 131, 133–34, 136, 145–46, 229–30, 263n12
Suzzallo, Henry, 85
Sweden, 30
Swedes, 32. *See also* Scandinavian immigrants
Sweet Home, OR, 192

Taft-Hartley Act (1947), 142
Talent, OR, 221
Taylor, Frederick Winslow, 86
Tennessee Valley Authority (TVA), 139–40
Thomas, Jack Ward, 189, 217
Thompkins, Morton, 138
Thorwald, Cliff, 106
Three Percenters, 236
Three Sisters Primitive Area, 146–47
Tigart, Ellen, 202
Timber (Haig-Brown), 125–26
timber industry. *See* Northwest timber industry
Timbers Restaurant and Lounge, 155–56, 175
Timber Unity, 235–39, 240–41, 276n44
timber wars. *See* spotted-owl conflict
Timber Worker (newspaper), 119

Time magazine, 184, 210
Tisdale, Sallie, 210
Todes, Charlotte, 33
Toledo, OR, 155–57
topographic maps, 85–86, 87
trapping, 63
tree-sitting, 198
tree-spiking, 6, 198–99, 206–7
Tsing, Anna Lowenhaupt, 233
tuberculosis, 89
Turnage, William, 199
Turner, Frederick Jackson, 150–51
TVA (Tennessee Valley Authority), 139–40
Twilight (Meyer), 248n7
Twin Peaks, 233
Twitter, 238

Union of Soviet Socialist Republics (USSR),
 142
United Auto Workers (UAW), 137
United Brotherhood of Carpenters and
 Joiners (UBCJ), 115, 118, 129, 130
United Mine Workers of America, 117, 138
Unprejudiced Palate, The (Pellegrini), 73
urban-rural divide. *See* city-country divide
USFS. *See* Forest Service, US
USSR (Union of Soviet Socialist Repub-
 lics), 142

Vail, WA, 39
Vancouver, BC, 31, 155
Van Dyke, Jerry, 177
Van Orsdel, J. P., 38
Vidal, John, 231

Wagenknecht, Louise, 59, 65–66
Wagner Act (National Labor Relations Act)
 (1935), 117, 142
Wallgren, Monrad, 121, 122
Walther, Ellery, 87, 92
War Manpower Commission, 124
War Production Board, 127
Washington, University of, 73, 85–86, 87, 230
Washington state, 25, 26, 28, 32, 232; popu-
 lation of, 30. *See also specific cities and
 towns*
Waters, Alice, 73
weather, 89
Weed, Abner, 253n33
Weed, CA, 253n33

West, Oswald, 25
West Coast Lumbermen's Association, 107,
 134
Western Lumber Company, 42
Western Operators' Association, 33
Western Public Lands Coalition, 210
Weyerhaeuser, 25–26, 28, 29, 37, 39, 161, 163,
 166, 227
Weyerhaeuser, Frederick, 25
White, Richard, 249n12, 269n8
White River grove, 1–7
widow makers, definition of, 2
Wild (Strand), 233
Wilderness Act (1964), 148, 149
Wilderness Act (1984), 194
wilderness movement, 13, 131, 132, 138, 172,
 187, 190–91, 194, 195, 196, 207, 210, 241,
 242; IWA and, 12–15, 123, 128, 144–51, 174,
 194; on Olympic Peninsula, 120, 123; on
 White River, 5–7
Wilderness Society, 145–46, 147, 172, 197, 199,
 201, 232
Willamette Industries, 192, 193, 194, 196
Willamette National Forest, 146
Winter, Paul, 192–93
Wirkkala, Oiva, 76–79, 97
Wisconsin, 25, 29, 31
Wishkah River Valley, WA, 53
witches, 183
Wobblies (Industrial Workers of the World),
 32–33, 36, 37, 38, 43, 112, 251–52n20
women, 35, 37, 54, 106, 113, 118–19, 260n20
wood recycling, 239
working class. *See* Northwest timber work-
 ers
working men's paradises, 39, 253n31
World (Coos Bay, OR), 212
World War I, 34
World War II, 124–26
Worster, Donald, 8

Yaffee, Steven, 204
yarding, 81, 84, 86, 88, 89, 92
Yellow Ribbon Coalition, 208–11, 236
yellow ribbons, 185, 208–13; divisive nature
 of, 210–11

Zahniser, Howard, 145, 147–48, 172
Zapp, Don, 1–7
"zero cut" policy, 218

STEVEN C. BEDA is an assistant professor of history at the University of Oregon.

THE WORKING CLASS IN AMERICAN HISTORY

Worker City, Company Town: Iron and Cotton-Worker Protest in Troy and Cohoes, New York, 1855–84 *Daniel J. Walkowitz*

Life, Work, and Rebellion in the Coal Fields: The Southern West Virginia Miners, 1880–1922 *David Alan Corbin*

Women and American Socialism, 1870–1920 *Mari Jo Buhle*

Lives of Their Own: Blacks, Italians, and Poles in Pittsburgh, 1900–1960 *John Bodnar, Roger Simon, and Michael P. Weber*

Working-Class America: Essays on Labor, Community, and American Society *Edited by Michael H. Frisch and Daniel J. Walkowitz*

Eugene V. Debs: Citizen and Socialist *Nick Salvatore*

American Labor and Immigration History, 1877–1920s: Recent European Research *Edited by Dirk Hoerder*

Workingmen's Democracy: The Knights of Labor and American Politics *Leon Fink*

The Electrical Workers: A History of Labor at General Electric and Westinghouse, 1923–60 *Ronald W. Schatz*

The Mechanics of Baltimore: Workers and Politics in the Age of Revolution, 1763–1812 *Charles G. Steffen*

The Practice of Solidarity: American Hat Finishers in the Nineteenth Century *David Bensman*

The Labor History Reader *Edited by Daniel J. Leab*

Solidarity and Fragmentation: Working People and Class Consciousness in Detroit, 1875–1900 *Richard Oestreicher*

Counter Cultures: Saleswomen, Managers, and Customers in American Department Stores, 1890–1940 *Susan Porter Benson*

The New England Working Class and the New Labor History *Edited by Herbert G. Gutman and Donald H. Bell*

Labor Leaders in America *Edited by Melvyn Dubofsky and Warren Van Tine*

Barons of Labor: The San Francisco Building Trades and Union Power in the Progressive Era *Michael Kazin*

Gender at Work: The Dynamics of Job Segregation by Sex during World War II *Ruth Milkman*

Once a Cigar Maker: Men, Women, and Work Culture in American Cigar Factories, 1900–1919 *Patricia A. Cooper*

A Generation of Boomers: The Pattern of Railroad Labor Conflict in Nineteenth-Century America *Shelton Stromquist*

Work and Community in the Jungle: Chicago's Packinghouse Workers, 1894–1922 *James R. Barrett*

Workers, Managers, and Welfare Capitalism: The Shoeworkers and Tanners of Endicott Johnson, 1890–1950 *Gerald Zahavi*

Men, Women, and Work: Class, Gender, and Protest in the New England Shoe Industry, 1780–1910 *Mary Blewett*

Workers on the Waterfront: Seamen, Longshoremen, and Unionism in the 1930s
    Bruce Nelson

German Workers in Chicago: A Documentary History of Working-Class Culture from
    1850 to World War I   *Edited by Hartmut Keil and John B. Jentz*

On the Line: Essays in the History of Auto Work   *Edited by Nelson Lichtenstein
    and Stephen Meyer III*

Labor's Flaming Youth: Telephone Operators and Worker Militancy, 1878–1923
    Stephen H. Norwood

Another Civil War: Labor, Capital, and the State in the Anthracite Regions
    of Pennsylvania, 1840–68   *Grace Palladino*

Coal, Class, and Color: Blacks in Southern West Virginia, 1915–32
    Joe William Trotter Jr.

For Democracy, Workers, and God: Labor Song-Poems and Labor Protest, 1865–95
    Clark D. Halker

Dishing It Out: Waitresses and Their Unions in the Twentieth Century
    Dorothy Sue Cobble

The Spirit of 1848: German Immigrants, Labor Conflict, and the Coming of the Civil
    War   *Bruce Levine*

Working Women of Collar City: Gender, Class, and Community in Troy, New York,
    1864–86   *Carole Turbin*

Southern Labor and Black Civil Rights: Organizing Memphis Workers
    Michael K. Honey

Radicals of the Worst Sort: Laboring Women in Lawrence, Massachusetts, 1860–1912
    Ardis Cameron

Producers, Proletarians, and Politicians: Workers and Party Politics in Evansville and
    New Albany, Indiana, 1850–87   *Lawrence M. Lipin*

The New Left and Labor in the 1960s   *Peter B. Levy*

The Making of Western Labor Radicalism: Denver's Organized Workers, 1878–1905
    David Brundage

In Search of the Working Class: Essays in American Labor History and Political
    Culture   *Leon Fink*

Lawyers against Labor: From Individual Rights to Corporate Liberalism
    Daniel R. Ernst

"We Are All Leaders": The Alternative Unionism of the Early 1930s
    Edited by Staughton Lynd

The Female Economy: The Millinery and Dressmaking Trades, 1860–1930
    Wendy Gamber

"Negro and White, Unite and Fight!": A Social History of Industrial Unionism
    in Meatpacking, 1930–90   *Roger Horowitz*

Power at Odds: The 1922 National Railroad Shopmen's Strike   *Colin J. Davis*

The Common Ground of Womanhood: Class, Gender, and Working Girls' Clubs,
    1884–1928   *Priscilla Murolo*

Marching Together: Women of the Brotherhood of Sleeping Car Porters
    Melinda Chateauvert

Down on the Killing Floor: Black and White Workers in Chicago's Packinghouses,
    1904–54   *Rick Halpern*
Labor and Urban Politics: Class Conflict and the Origins of Modern Liberalism in
    Chicago, 1864–97   *Richard Schneirov*
All That Glitters: Class, Conflict, and Community in Cripple Creek
    Elizabeth Jameson
Waterfront Workers: New Perspectives on Race and Class   *Edited by Calvin Winslow*
Labor Histories: Class, Politics, and the Working-Class Experience
    Edited by Eric Arnesen, Julie Greene, and Bruce Laurie
The Pullman Strike and the Crisis of the 1890s: Essays on Labor and Politics   *E
    dited by Richard Schneirov, Shelton Stromquist, and Nick Salvatore*
AlabamaNorth: African-American Migrants, Community, and Working-Class
    Activism in Cleveland, 1914–45   *Kimberley L. Phillips*
Imagining Internationalism in American and British Labor, 1939–49   *Victor Silverman*
William Z. Foster and the Tragedy of American Radicalism   *James R. Barrett*
Colliers across the Sea: A Comparative Study of Class Formation in Scotland and the
    American Midwest, 1830–1924   *John H. M. Laslett*
"Rights, Not Roses": Unions and the Rise of Working-Class Feminism, 1945–80
    Dennis A. Deslippe
Testing the New Deal: The General Textile Strike of 1934 in the American South
    Janet Irons
Hard Work: The Making of Labor History   *Melvyn Dubofsky*
Southern Workers and the Search for Community: Spartanburg County, South
    Carolina   *G. C. Waldrep III*
We Shall Be All: A History of the Industrial Workers of the World (abridged
    edition)   *Melvyn Dubofsky, ed. Joseph A. McCartin*
Race, Class, and Power in the Alabama Coalfields, 1908–21   *Brian Kelly*
Duquesne and the Rise of Steel Unionism   *James D. Rose*
Anaconda: Labor, Community, and Culture in Montana's Smelter City   *Laurie Mercier*
Bridgeport's Socialist New Deal, 1915–36   *Cecelia Bucki*
Indispensable Outcasts: Hobo Workers and Community in the American Midwest,
    1880–1930   *Frank Tobias Higbie*
After the Strike: A Century of Labor Struggle at Pullman   *Susan Eleanor Hirsch*
Corruption and Reform in the Teamsters Union   *David Witwer*
Waterfront Revolts: New York and London Dockworkers, 1946–61   *Colin J. Davis*
Black Workers' Struggle for Equality in Birmingham   *Horace Huntley*
    and David Montgomery
The Tribe of Black Ulysses: African American Men in the Industrial South
    William P. Jones
City of Clerks: Office and Sales Workers in Philadelphia, 1870–1920
    Jerome P. Bjelopera
Reinventing "The People": The Progressive Movement, the Class Problem, and the
    Origins of Modern Liberalism   *Shelton Stromquist*
Radical Unionism in the Midwest, 1900–1950   *Rosemary Feurer*

Gendering Labor History   *Alice Kessler-Harris*

James P. Cannon and the Origins of the American Revolutionary Left, 1890–1928
  Bryan D. Palmer

Glass Towns: Industry, Labor, and Political Economy in Appalachia, 1890–1930s
  Ken Fones-Wolf

Workers and the Wild: Conservation, Consumerism, and Labor in Oregon, 1910–30
  Lawrence M. Lipin

Wobblies on the Waterfront: Interracial Unionism in Progressive-Era Philadelphia
  Peter Cole

Red Chicago: American Communism at Its Grassroots, 1928–35   *Randi Storch*

Labor's Cold War: Local Politics in a Global Context   *Edited by Shelton Stromquist*

Bessie Abramowitz Hillman and the Making of the Amalgamated Clothing Workers
  of America   *Karen Pastorello*

The Great Strikes of 1877   *Edited by David O. Stowell*

Union-Free America: Workers and Antiunion Culture   *Lawrence Richards*

Race against Liberalism: Black Workers and the UAW in Detroit   *David M. Lewis-
  Colman*

Teachers and Reform: Chicago Public Education, 1929–70   *John F. Lyons*

Upheaval in the Quiet Zone: 1199/SEIU and the Politics of Healthcare Unionism
  Leon Fink and Brian Greenberg

Shadow of the Racketeer: Scandal in Organized Labor   *David Witwer*

Sweet Tyranny: Migrant Labor, Industrial Agriculture, and Imperial Politics
  Kathleen Mapes

Staley: The Fight for a New American Labor Movement   *Steven K. Ashby
  and C. J. Hawking*

On the Ground: Labor Struggles in the American Airline Industry   *Liesl Miller Orenic*

NAFTA and Labor in North America   *Norman Caulfield*

Making Capitalism Safe: Work Safety and Health Regulation in America, 1880–1940
  Donald W. Rogers

Good, Reliable, White Men: Railroad Brotherhoods, 1877–1917   *Paul Michel Taillon*

Spirit of Rebellion: Labor and Religion in the New Cotton South   *Jarod Roll*

The Labor Question in America: Economic Democracy in the Gilded Age
  Rosanne Currarino

Banded Together: Economic Democratization in the Brass Valley   *Jeremy Brecher*

The Gospel of the Working Class: Labor's Southern Prophets in New Deal America
  Erik Gellman and Jarod Roll

Guest Workers and Resistance to U.S. Corporate Despotism   *Immanuel Ness*

Gleanings of Freedom: Free and Slave Labor along the Mason-Dixon Line, 1790–1860
  Max Grivno

Chicago in the Age of Capital: Class, Politics, and Democracy during the Civil War
  and Reconstruction   *John B. Jentz and Richard Schneirov*

Child Care in Black and White: Working Parents and the History of
  Orphanages   *Jessie B. Ramey*

The Haymarket Conspiracy: Transatlantic Anarchist Networks   *Timothy Messer-Kruse*

Detroit's Cold War: The Origins of Postwar Conservatism   *Colleen Doody*

A Renegade Union: Interracial Organizing and Labor Radicalism   *Lisa Phillips*

Palomino: Clinton Jencks and Mexican-American Unionism in the American
     Southwest   *James J. Lorence*

Latin American Migrations to the U.S. Heartland: Changing Cultural Landscapes in
     Middle America   *Edited by Linda Allegro and Andrew Grant Wood*

Man of Fire: Selected Writings   *Ernesto Galarza, ed. Armando Ibarra
     and Rodolfo D. Torres*

A Contest of Ideas: Capital, Politics, and Labor   *Nelson Lichtenstein*

Making the World Safe for Workers: Labor, the Left, and Wilsonian
     Internationalism   *Elizabeth McKillen*

The Rise of the Chicago Police Department: Class and Conflict, 1850–1894
     Sam Mitrani

Workers in Hard Times: A Long View of Economic Crises
     Edited by Leon Fink, Joseph A. McCartin, and Joan Sangster

Redeeming Time: Protestantism and Chicago's Eight-Hour Movement, 1866–1912
     William A. Mirola

Struggle for the Soul of the Postwar South: White Evangelical Protestants and
     Operation Dixie   *Elizabeth Fones-Wolf and Ken Fones-Wolf*

Free Labor: The Civil War and the Making of an American Working Class
     Mark A. Lause

Death and Dying in the Working Class, 1865–1920   *Michael K. Rosenow*

Immigrants against the State: Yiddish and Italian Anarchism in America
     Kenyon Zimmer

Fighting for Total Person Unionism: Harold Gibbons, Ernest Calloway, and Working-
     Class Citizenship ˙ *Robert Bussel*

Smokestacks in the Hills: Rural-Industrial Workers in West Virginia   *Louis Martin*

Disaster Citizenship: Survivors, Solidarity, and Power in the Progressive Era
     Jacob A. C. Remes

The Pew and the Picket Line: Christianity and the American Working Class
     Edited by Christopher D. Cantwell, Heath W. Carter, and Janine Giordano Drake

Conservative Counterrevolution: Challenging Liberalism in 1950s Milwaukee
     Tula A. Connell

Manhood on the Line: Working-Class Masculinities in the American Heartland   *S
     teve Meyer*

On Gender, Labor, and Inequality   *Ruth Milkman*

The Making of Working-Class Religion   *Matthew Pehl*

Civic Labors: Scholar Activism and Working-Class Studies   *Edited by Dennis
     Deslippe, Eric Fure-Slocum, and John W. McKerley*

Victor Arnautoff and the Politics of Art   *Robert W. Cherny*

Against Labor: How U.S. Employers Organized to Defeat Union Activism
     Edited by Rosemary Feurer and Chad Pearson

Teacher Strike! Public Education and the Making of a New American Political Order
     Jon Shelton

Hillbilly Hellraisers: Federal Power and Populist Defiance in the Ozarks
     J. Blake Perkins

Sewing the Fabric of Statehood: Garment Unions, American Labor, and the
    Establishment of the State of Israel   *Adam Howard*
Labor and Justice across the America   *Edited by Leon Fink and Juan Manuel Palacio*
Frontiers of Labor: Comparative Histories of the United States and Australia
    Edited by Greg Patmore and Shelton Stromquist
Women Have Always Worked: A Concise History, Second Edition
    Alice Kessler-Harris
Remembering Lattimer: Labor, Migration, and Race in Pennsylvania Anthracite
    Country   *Paul A. Shackel*
Disruption in Detroit: Autoworkers and the Elusive Postwar Boom   *Daniel J. Clark*
To Live Here, You Have to Fight: How Women Led Appalachian Movements for Social
    Justice   *Jessica Wilkerson*
Dockworker Power: Race and Activism in Durban and the San Francisco Bay Area
    Peter Cole
Labor's Mind: A History of Working-Class Intellectual Life   *Tobias Higbie*
The World in a City: Multiethnic Radicalism in Early Twentieth-Century Los Angeles
    David M. Struthers
Death to Fascism: Louis Adamic's Fight for Democracy   *John P. Enyeart*
Upon the Altar of Work: Child Labor and the Rise of a New American Sectionalism
    Betsy Wood
Workers against the City: The Fight for Free Speech in *Hague v. CIO*
    Donald W. Rogers
Union Renegades: Miners, Capitalism, and Organizing in the Gilded Age
    Dana M. Caldemeyer
The Labor Board Crew: Remaking Worker-Employer Relations from Pearl Harbor to
    the Reagan Era   *Ronald W. Schatz*
Grand Army of Labor: Workers, Veterans, and the Meaning of the Civil War
    Matthew E. Stanley
A Matter of Moral Justice: Black Women Laundry Workers and the Fight for Justice
    Jenny Carson
Labor's End: How the Promise of Automation Degraded Work   *Jason Resnikoff*
Toward a Cooperative Commonwealth: The Transplanted Roots of Farmer-Labor
    Radicalism in Texas   *Thomas Alter II*
Working in the Magic City: Moral Economy in Early Twentieth-Century Miami
    Thomas A. Castillo
Where Are the Workers? Labor's Stories at Museums and Historic Sites
    Edited by Robert Forrant and Mary Anne Trasciatti
Labor's Outcasts: Migrant Farmworkers and Unions in North America, 1934–1966
    Andrew J. Hazelton
Fraying Fabric: How Trade Policy and Industrial Decline Transformed America
    James C. Benton
Harry Bridges: Labor Radical, Labor Legend   *Robert W. Cherny*
Strong Winds and Widow Makers: Workers, Nature, and Environmental Conflict in
    Pacific Northwest Timber Country   *Steven C. Beda*

The University of Illinois Press
is a founding member of the
Association of University Presses.

Composed in 10.5/13 Minion Pro
with Frutiger LT Std display
by Lisa Connery
at the University of Illinois Press
Manufactured by Versa Press, Inc.

University of Illinois Press
1325 South Oak Street
Champaign, IL 61820-6903
www.press.uillinois.edu